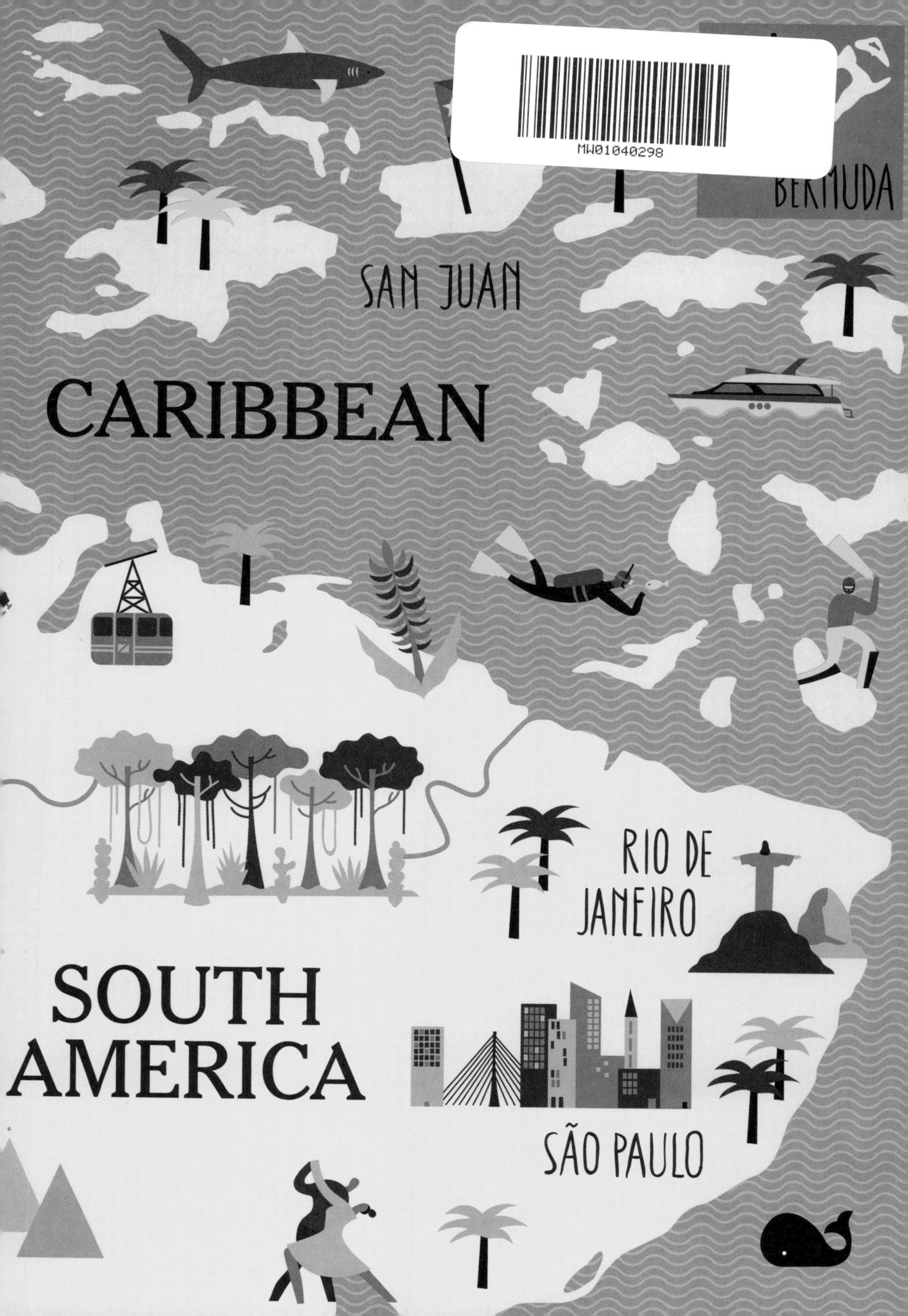
MW01040298
BERMUDA
SAN JUAN
CARIBBEAN
RIO DE
JANEIRO
SOUTH
AMERICA
SÃO PAULO

The New York Times

36 HOURS

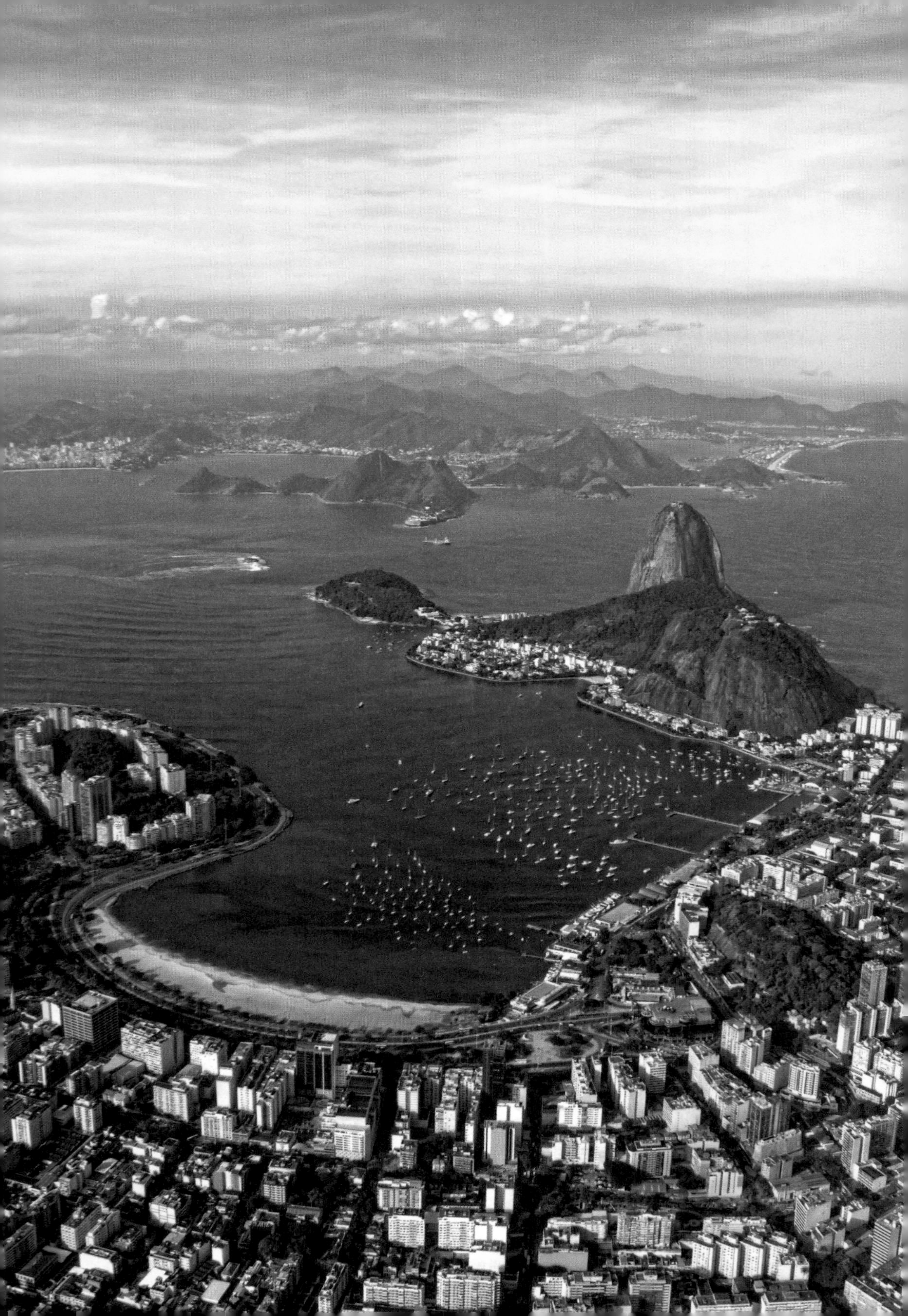

EDITED BY BARBARA IRELAND

The New York Times

HOURS
LATIN AMERICA & THE CARIBBEAN

TASCHEN

Contents

MEXICO & CENTRAL AMERICA

SOUTH AMERICA

THE CARIBBEAN

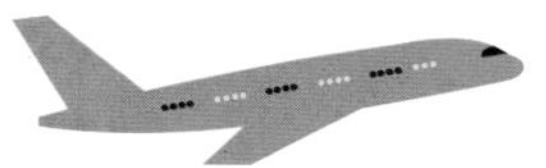

Foreword

Paddle above the coral in the clear, caressing waters of the Caribbean. Greet the sunrise from a Mayan pyramid. Gyrate to techno with the beautiful people in Brazil, or try the tango in Buenos Aires. Follow Mark Twain's route across the Nicaraguan isthmus toward a volcanic island. Tour a winery, a conquistador's fort, and a cloud forest. From Mexico south to Chile and Argentina, and east into the Atlantic to Bermuda, experiences both celebrated and undiscovered are ready to be enjoyed, one well-plotted weekend at a time.

36 Hours, *the peripatetic weekly feature in* The New York Times *that roams the world in the span of a weekend trip, has made dozens of stops in the sun-blessed countries south of the United States border. In this volume, the series of* Times *and TASCHEN travel books based on* 36 Hours *follows its own southern route, gathering together 60 new and updated articles into a weekend adventurer's guide — or an armchair traveler's dream book — for Latin America and the islands of the Caribbean Sea.*

As 36 Hours *has done every week now for a dozen years, each article in this book lays out a carefully researched itinerary for a weekend trip to an interesting and embraceable place. Mexico City, the hemisphere's largest metropolis, in just a two-night stay? You won't cover it all, but with the right selection and time line, you can catch its spirit and see its essentials, and — not incidentally — eat well and rest well along the way. A weekend excursion high in the Andes? Once you're there, knowing where to venture and what to look for can allow you to pile up rich memories in just a couple of days.*

Overwhelmingly, these are regions of warmth and blue skies, bridging the Equator, stretching north and south from there into the tropics and subtropics, and finally nudging into the temperate zones. All that sunshine nourishes a long-acknowledged tendency to liveliness and ease that's perfect for the traveler to tap into: the Latin exuberance that struts forth in the samba and Carnaval, the laid-back serenity of an afternoon on a sugary Caribbean beach. The rum punches and caipirinhas are there for the sipping, there's a kick in the red-chile salsa, and somebody will be happy to rent you a kayak or teach you to surf. Even the stingrays are friendly.

There's plenty here, too, to engage the intellect and keep the body toned. This is the oldest part of the New World, where cathedrals date to the height of the Baroque and cities claim ownership of Christopher Columbus's bones. You can clamber over Spanish city walls in Cartagena or gaze out to sea from the lookout point in St. Thomas where Francis Drake once scanned the horizon for ships under sail. Check out Frida Kahlo's blue house in Mexico City or the secret passageway behind Pablo Neruda's dinner table in Santiago. Hike up the Gros Piton in St. Lucia; kayak in the Solentiname Islands; bicycle around Bogotá.

Your guides, the authors of 36 Hours, *include many whose names will be familiar to readers of* The New York Times. *Michelle Higgins leads you through the highland colonial cities of Ecuador, and Seth Kugel ushers you around Brazil. David Carr invites you to brush away the butterflies in Colombia. Penelope Green coaches you through a clay mud treatment in Tulum.*

Their work is incorporated into this book along with the efforts of hundreds of others: writers and photographers; editors and photo editors; art directors, designers, and mapmakers; fact checkers and administrators. The result is here to invite you to Latin America and the Caribbean for your own weekends in the sun. — BARBARA IRELAND, EDITOR

PAGE 2 Sugar Loaf Mountain and Rio de Janeiro.

PAGE 4 Snorkeling in the clear waters of the Bahamas.

OPPOSITE The long-abandoned Mayan temples of Tikal emerge from dense Guatemalan jungle — and from a hazy past.

Tips for Using This Book

Plotting the Course: Travelers do not make their way through the world alphabetically, and neither does this book. Each of its three sections is based on a region — Mexico and Central America, South America, and the Caribbean. Each is introduced with a regional illustrated map, begins in a prominent city or destination, and winds from place to place as a touring adventurer might. Alphabetical indexes appear at the end of the book.

On the Ground: Every *36 Hours* follows a workable numbered itinerary that is both outlined in the text and shown with corresponding numbers on a detailed destination map. The itinerary is practical: it is possible to get from one place to the next easily and in the allotted time. Travelers should keep in mind that in the Caribbean many businesses shut down from September through mid-November.

The Not So Obvious: The itineraries do not all follow exactly the same pattern. A restaurant for Saturday breakfast may or may not be recommended; after-dinner nightlife may or may not be included. The destination dictates, and so, to some extent, does the personality of the author who researched and wrote the article. Some information well known to most travelers is not covered, but should be kept in mind; for example, it is always wise to make a reservation at a restaurant before going there for dinner.

Travel Documents: Although most countries in Latin America share the Spanish language (with the notable exception of Portuguese-speaking Brazil), they are sovereign nations with their own laws about passports, visas, and border crossings, as well as import and export rules. Many exercise vigilance because of concerns about the drug trade and money laundering. The islands of the Caribbean, many of which are English-speaking, are often easily approachable, but the wise traveler will make sure of the rules there, too, before booking a trip. For United States citizens, there are strict rules about travel to Cuba.

Safety: The destinations itemized in this book are generally safe for travelers, especially in the hours recommended in the itineraries, but many of these countries do battle poverty and crime. Cities always present possible hazards at night, and some neighborhoods should be avoided at any hour. In general, taxis recommended by hotels will be a safer choice than public transportation, and women traveling alone must, of course, always be careful. If you are uncertain about safety, stick close to the recommended itinerary and seek the advice of the staff at your hotel.

Updates: While all of the articles in this volume were updated and fact-checked in 2013, it is inevitable that some of the featured businesses and destinations will change in time. If you spot any errors in your travels, please feel free to send your corrections via email to 36hours@taschen.com. Please include "36 Hours Correction" in the subject line of your email to assure that it gets to the right person for future updates.

OPPOSITE Traditional hoop-skirted costumes endure, especially at Carnaval time, in Salvador, Brazil.

THE BASICS

A brief informational box for the destination, called "The Basics," appears with each *36 Hours* article in this book. The box provides some orientation on transportation for that location and recommends two or three reliable hotels or other lodgings, with contact information and a price range in U.S. dollars.

PRICES

Hotel room, standard double:
Budget, under $125 per night: $
Moderate, $126 to $250: $$
Expensive, $251 to $375: $$$
Luxury, $376 and above: $$$$

Restaurants, dinner without wine:
Budget, under $15: $
Moderate, $15 to $29: $$
Expensive, $30 to $44: $$$
Very Expensive: $45 and up: $$$$

Restaurants, full breakfast, or lunch entree:
Budget, under $10: $
Moderate, $10 to $19: $$
Expensive, $20 to $29: $$$
Very expensive, $30 and up: $$$$

San Miguel de Allende 18

40 Mérida

MEXICO CITY 12

TIKAL 52

Puebla 22

San Cristóbal 36

Oaxaca 28

COSTA CHICA 32

Southwes
Nicarag

MEXICO & CENTRAL AMERICA

CANCÚN 44

Tulum 48

Managua 56

Granada 60

Solentiname Islands 64

68

MONTEVERDE 72

Puerto Viejo 78

PANAMA CITY 82

San Blas Islands 86

Mexico City

The largest Spanish-speaking city in the world, Mexico City is always re-creating itself as a cultural leader for hundreds of millions of people in Latin America and beyond. Despite Mexico's highly publicized drug violence (which is mostly concentrated up north near the United States border), the time to visit this ancient capital — a megacity with about 20 million people living in its metropolitan area — has rarely been better. Cool new hotels have opened, the contemporary art scene is thriving, and the notorious air pollution is down to a semi-endurable level. More restaurants and galleries have sprung up in chic neighborhoods like Condesa and Roma, where a local moneyed crowd hangs out and jet-setters drop in. And Mexico City has probably never been this clean. Even the street vendors now cart around big bottles of hand sanitizer.
— BY BROOKS BARNES

FRIDAY

1 *Aztec Assimilation* 4 p.m.

A stroll through **Condesa**, the lush neighborhood where Paris Hilton frolicked when she visited (don't hold that against it), will quickly vanquish the stereotype of Mexico City as nothing but an unsafe eyesore. Start at **Parque Mexico** (intersection of Avenida Sonora and Avenida Mexico), where locals and their dogs mix with hipsters en route to sidewalk espresso bars. A Macarena dance contest (irony included) was in full swing in the band shell one warm weekend. Atlixco, a side street nearby, is becoming a hub for boutiques.

2 *Restaurant Row* 9 p.m.

The posh district of **Polanco**, with its leafy streets named after famous writers, is the center of the city's foodie scene. There are newer restaurants, like **Astrid & Gastón** (Tennyson 117; 52-55-5282-2666; astridygaston.com; $$$$), from the Peruvian restaurateur Gastón Acurio. But the young, moneyed crowd still flocks to an older favorite: **Ivoire** (Emilio Castelar 95; 52-55-5280-7912; ivoire.com.mx; $$). The menu is French-Mexican, and the buzzy rooftop bar has candlelit views.

3 *No Worm, Just Chicken* 11 p.m.

Mezcal, once spurned as the poor man's tequila in Mexico and historically sold in the United States with a gimmicky worm floating inside, was embraced by trendsetters here a few years ago, and the craze has endured. **La Botica** (Campeche 396, Condesa; 52-55-5211-6045; labotica.com.mx) serves up over 30 varieties, including one steeped with chicken breasts during distillation. Locals insist that the chicken softens the alcohol's smoky flavor, and they are right. Sip, don't slam.

SATURDAY

4 *Art Injection* 11 a.m.

Two stars of the contemporary art world — Gabriel Orozco and Miguel Calderón — have been nurtured by the quirky **Kurimanzutto Gallery** (Rafael Rebollar 94; 52-55-5256-2408; kurimanzutto.com), in a renovated lumberyard in San Miguel. Older galleries are clustered in the adjacent Roma district, including **OMR** (Plaza Rio de Janeiro 54; 52-55-5207-1080; galeriaomr.com), which handles artists like Rafael Lozano-Hemmer, known for working with electronics and sound.

OPPOSITE Mexico City, home to 20 million people, spreads its modern veneer over the ancient city-state of the Aztecs.

RIGHT A monument to the muralist Diego Rivera.

5 *Taco Tradition* 1 p.m.

Foreigners who think they know all about tacos may be in for a surprise at **Beatricita (**Londres 190-D, Zona Rosa; 52-55-5511-4213; beatricita.com; $), a century-old operation known for tacos de guisado. In this taco version, a Mexico city favorite, tortillas straight from the griddle are rolled around fillings that are basically slow-cooked stews. Chicken versions come with a variety of sauces from mole poblano to tinga. Look for the filling flavored with pumpkin seeds.

6 *Bizarre Bazaar* 2 p.m.

You've done high art, now go low. **Bazar del Sábado** (Plaza de San Jacinto, San Ángel) is a Saturday flea market where locals and tourists alike go to haggle for deals on handicrafts (blankets, baskets, jewelry) and chat with street artists. Pick up a glittery, kitschy Our Lady of Guadalupe box shrine, and don't miss the adjacent flower market, a dank but fascinating rabbit warren of cement stalls displaying over-the-top arrangements like a lion's head made out of yellow spider mums.

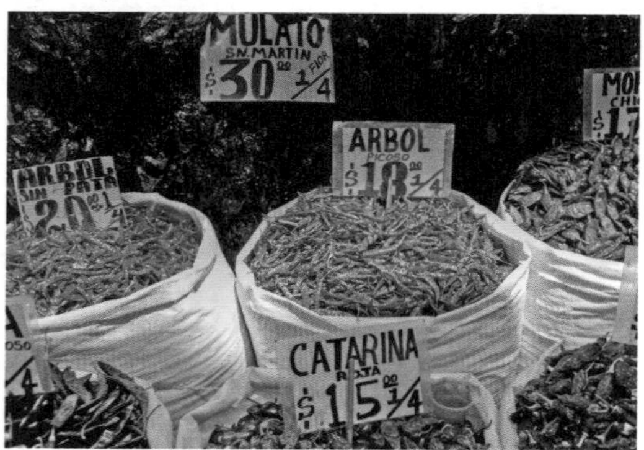

7 *Our Lady Frida* 4 p.m.

Homage must be paid to Frida Kahlo, the seemingly ubiquitous unibrowed painter and wife of the muralist Diego Rivera. Most visitors head to her former home, now **Museo Frida Kahlo** (Londres 247, Coyoacan; 52-55-5554-5999; museofridakahlo.org.mx). Known as the Casa Azul, or Blue House, it brims with possessions that reflect her love of color and Mexican folklore. In the former home of a socialite art collector, the **Museo Dolores Olmedo** is a less touristy gem (Avenida Mexico 5843, Xochimilco; 52-55-5555-1221; museodoloresolmedo.org.mx) where some of Kahlo's famous canvases hang. Look for the self-portrait depicting her spine as a broken stone column. To see some of her husband's famous

ABOVE The National Museum of Anthropology, a treasure trove of pre-Columbian artifacts.

LEFT Chilies grown in many regions of Mexico for sale at one of the city's markets.

work, join the sightseers at the 17th-century **Palacio Nacional** (Avenida Pino Suárez facing the Zócalo, the main square).

8 *Floating Party* 6 p.m.

Get in touch with your inner Aztec with a visit to the nearby "floating gardens" of **Xochimilco** (www.xochimilco.df.gob.mx). In the days when Mexico City was the Aztec capital named Tenochtitlan, this network of shallow canals connected artificial islands where farmers grew food for the city. Now locals arrive on weekends for raucous fiestas on trajineras, wooden boats painted in wild colors that can seat as many as 20 people. Hire your own boat for a small fee. Other boats sell food (tacos, circles of jicama on a stick) and beer. Feel like joining the party? Hire a mariachi band (prices vary) to sail with you.

9 *Gastronomic Glitz* 9 p.m.

Rejoin the 21st century at **Distrito Capital** (Juan Salvador Agraz 37; 52-55-5257-1300; hoteldistritocapital.com/restaurante; $$), a sleek restaurant in a skyscraper in the ritzy Santa Fe business district. One night's menu here included surf (sea bass marinated with guajillo peppers and garlic in a pineapple sauce) and turf (New York steak with guacamole and prickly pears). If it's a clear night, the building offers spectacular views of the volcanoes beyond the city.

SUNDAY

10 *Free Ride* 9 a.m.

After a busy Saturday, unwind on a bicycle: the government lends them free (with helmets) from kiosks along the **Paseo de la Reforma**. To skip the line, rent a bike from one of the vendors set up in front of the **National Museum of Anthropology**, although

TOP Boats called trajineras line up to take customers out for floating parties on the canals of Xochimilco, which once connected Aztec farmers' island plots.

ABOVE Prickly pear cactus in a food market.

if you haven't seen its collection, you may want to forget the biking and go inside (Paseo de la Reforma at Gandhi; 52-55-4040-5300; mna.inah.gob.mx). The Paseo de la Reforma, modeled in part on the Champs-Élysées, is closed to cars on Sundays until early afternoon to accommodate bicyclists. It's liberating to zoom through the circular plaza marking the Mexican War of Independence—and not only because it is usually choked with traffic. A good pit stop is the entrance to the Bosque de Chapultepec, the city's largest park, where vendors sell freshly peeled, spice-covered oranges for a few pesos.

11 *Cacao Mexican Style* 11 a.m.

Reward yourself with Mexican chocolates from **Princesse Cacao** (Fernando Montes de Oca 81, Condesa; 52-55-5211-0276), a chocolatier specializing in artisanal candy from Tabasco and Chiapas, the two southern Mexican states where some historians say chocolate was invented, or at least refined. Fabuloso!

ABOVE Frida Kahlo lived most of her life, with and without her husband, Diego Rivera, in this house, now a museum.

OPPOSITE Diego Rivera's murals in the Palacio Nacional.

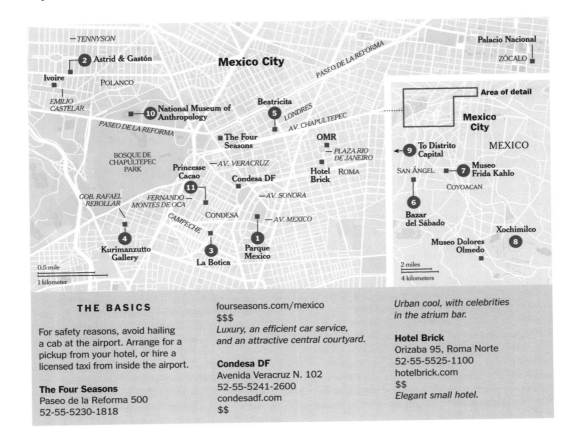

Mexico City
TENNYSON
2 Astrid & Gastón
Ivoire
POLANCO
EMILIO CASTELAR
10 National Museum of Anthropology
PASEO DE LA REFORMA
BOSQUE DE CHAPULTEPEC PARK
Beatricita 5
LONDRES
AV. CHAPULTEPEC
The Four Seasons
OMR
PLAZA RIO DE JANEIRO
Hotel Brick
ROMA
AV. VERACRUZ
Princesse Cacao 11
Condesa DF
AV. SONORA
GOB. RAFAEL REBOLLAR
FERNANDO MONTES DE OCA
CONDESA
AV. MEXICO
CAMPECHE
4 Kurimanzutto Gallery
3 La Botica
1 Parque Mexico
0.5 mile
1 kilometer
Palacio Nacional
ZÓCALO
Area of detail
Mexico City
MEXICO
9 To Distrito Capital
SAN ÁNGEL
7 Museo Frida Kahlo
COYOACAN
6 Bazar del Sábado
Xochimilco
Museo Dolores Olmedo 8
2 miles
4 kilometers

THE BASICS

For safety reasons, avoid hailing a cab at the airport. Arrange for a pickup from your hotel, or hire a licensed taxi from inside the airport.

The Four Seasons
Paseo de la Reforma 500
52-55-5230-1818
fourseasons.com/mexico
$$$
Luxury, an efficient car service, and an attractive central courtyard.

Condesa DF
Avenida Veracruz N. 102
52-55-5241-2600
condesadf.com
$$
Urban cool, with celebrities in the atrium bar.

Hotel Brick
Orizaba 95, Roma Norte
52-55-5525-1100
hotelbrick.com
$$
Elegant small hotel.

San Miguel de Allende

San Miguel de Allende easily embodies a string of contradictory adjectives. Rustic and sophisticated. Historic and trendy. Tranquil and energetic. It is the frisson between the extremes that makes this 500-year-old city in the mountains of Central Mexico a perennially beloved tourist destination. Here you can see burros delivering wood outside a glitzy, internationally acclaimed restaurant. Sometimes the only sounds among snaking cobblestone alleys are the bells from the crown-shaped church that stands guard over the central square; at other times (during the many festivals), the thin high-altitude air is overloaded with fireworks and mariachi music. American retirees have long been a familiar presence, but lately a younger, more urbane set from around the world is putting its mark on this city of colonial buildings in delectable fruit-bowl-meets-spice-rack colors (think mango and avocado next to paprika and turmeric). This is Mexico at its loveliest and liveliest. — BY JEANNIE RALSTON

FRIDAY

1 *In the Sister 'Hood* 4 p.m.

The most famous building in town is the multi-spired pink **Parroquia de San Miguel Arcángel**, the Gothic-style parish church standing guard over the town's heart, the tree-shaded square known as El Jardín. But the most beautiful building is the 250-year-old Centro Cultural Ignacio Ramírez "El Nigromante," aka **Bellas Artes** (Hernandez Macias 75; 52-415-152-0289; elnigromante.bellasartes.gob.mx). Originally a convent, then an art college, it is now a community center and art gallery. It's easy to imagine nuns scurrying off to mass under soaring boveda ceilings and through the large interior courtyard surrounded by high arched colonnades. Though exhibitions rotate through five gallery spaces, the permanent art is the most impressive: frescoes by one of Mexico's finest muralists, David Siqueiros.

OPPOSITE A traditional dancer's mask at The Other Face of Mexico, a museum and folk-art gallery.

RIGHT The brightly colored buildings lining San Miguel's cobblestoned alleyways shelter the attractively decorated homes, sophisticated restaurants, and intriguing shops that serve an increasingly urbane population.

2 *Choose Your View* 5:30 p.m.

San Miguel has many memorable views, and from **Azotea** (Calle Umaran 6; 52-415-152-8275; azoteasanmiguel.com) you can see two of the best. Located on a rooftop off the Jardín, this sleek bar offers on one side a crane-your-neck close-up of the Parroquia. The ideal perch at sunset, however, is the outside patio, where you can sip your margarita while watching the light disappear over a panorama of the Guanajuato Mountains in the distance.

3 *Piece of Peru* 7:30 p.m.

Leche de tigre figures prominently in the delights of the beautiful, airy **La Parada** (Recreo 94; 52-415-152-0473; laparadasma.weebly.com; $). That's the name for the citrus concoction that "cooks" the unusual ceviches (fish, corn, and sweet potatoes, for instance) at this popular bistro. Also memorable are dishes like pork ribs and gnocchi with shrimp and pecans — and don't leave without having a pisco mojito.

4 *The Fat Mermaid Awaits* 9:30 p.m.

Traditionally, military men, police officers, and women aren't allowed in a cantina, a down-and-dirty version of a gentlemen's club. But everyone's welcome at **La Sirena Gorda** (Calle Barranca 78; 52-415-110-0007), which retains the hole-in-the-wall

look of a cantina—swinging doors, dim light, faded paint on the walls—but with a more refined bar (and fewer chances of a fight). It's also known by its original name, El Manantial, which is still painted on the front. Nestle in for the late evening hours, drinking the signature ginger or tamarind margaritas.

SATURDAY

5 *Start in the Middle* 9 a.m.

Situated right in the Jardín, **El Rincon de Don Tomas** (Portal de Guadalupe 2; 52-415-152-3780; $) provides front-and-center seats as the city wakes up. Sit outside under the arched portico and dig into wonderful traditional breakfasts such as huevos otomi (scrambled eggs in a bean stew) and huevos divorciados (one fried egg with green salsa, the other with red).

6 *On the Hunt* 10 a.m.

Treasures can be found on every San Miguel street, but with limited time for exploration, you can zero in on two locations. In the **Mercado de Artesanías**, which runs along a narrow alley from Hidalgo Street up to the fruit-and-vegetable marketplace known as Mercado Ignacio Ramirez, you'll find stalls selling pewter bowls, mesquite cutting boards, handmade paper books, beaded Huichol Indian figurines, and pressed-tin lights and frames. For higher-end treasures, stop at **Fabrica La Aurora** (Calzada de la Aurora, 52-415-152-1312; fabricalaaurora.com), an old muslin factory that has been transformed into shops and art galleries. Browse through antiques, textiles, accessories, and home furnishings, as well as paintings and sculptures created by members of San Miguel's accomplished artist community.

7 *Shack Chic* 1 p.m.

De Temporada (Camino a San Miguel el Viejo 8; 52-415-114-8914; de-temporada.com; $) offers the reverse of the farm-to-table concept. The table is literally at the farm, 10 minutes from the city center, overlooking fields of organic produce. The restaurant is in a humble, colorful shed, built by its young owners from wood pallets, and dining there has the feeling of a picnic. But this is not your ordinary picnic food. Dishes like the spicy papaya and octopus salad, quail eggs on mustard butter with arugula purée, and a divine lemon panna cotta indicate a mature but playful hand in the kitchen.

8 *Costume Party* 4 p.m.

Some resemble deranged Wile E. Coyotes; others look like dentally challenged Gandalfs. But all 500 of the masks at **The Other Face of Mexico**, a museum in the Casa de la Cuesta hotel (Cuesta de San Jose 32; 52-415-154-4324; casadelacuesta.com; call to make an appointment for a visit), are fascinating. The owners, Bill and Heidi LeVasseur, have spent years traveling through rural Mexico, collecting masks that have been used in traditional dance ceremonies. Buy a mask of your own at the adjoining folk-art gallery.

9 *On the Foodie Map* 8 p.m.

Enrique Olvera, a culinary star who won numerous accolades at his Mexico City restaurant, Pujol, has brought his revamp of Mexican cuisine to **Moxi**, part of the stylish Hotel Matilda (Aldama 53; 52-415-152-1015; moxi.com.mx; $$$$). Standout dishes have included pescado al pastor (fish of the day with pineapple puree and serranos) and cactus salad. Equally striking is the décor: velvet banquettes under low-hanging pleated lampshades and mirrored walls. After a stop in the Jardín to listen to the mariachis croon under the tightly trimmed laurel trees, head to the bar at **El Mesón** hotel (El Mesón hotel, Mesones 80; 52-415-152-4343; hotelelmeson.com/93/patio3/), where you can sip wine or martinis and may catch a guest D.J. or live music.

SUNDAY

10 *God's Graphic Novel* 10 a.m.

Baroque Mexican churches are not unusual, but the 250-year-old **Santuario de Atotonilco** (santuariodeatotonilco.org), in the main plaza of the

ABOVE Bellas Artes, a convent turned art gallery.

nearby town of Atotonilco, stands alone. Its exterior is deceptively simple, but inside, it is over-the-top ornate, a dizzying visual cacophony. Nearly every inch of wall and ceiling space is filled with detailed Biblical scenes and passages, which is why the church is known as Mexico's Sistine Chapel. The sanctuary is also a pilgrimage site for penitents who self-flagellate to atone for sins. Note the rope flails sold by vendors outside the church.

11 *Steam Scene* 11 a.m.

Atotonilco is surrounded by thermal springs. On your way back toward San Miguel, stop for a soak at **Escondido Place** (Caraterra Dolores Hidalgo, Kilometer 10; 52-415-185-2022; escondidoplace.com). There are several outdoor pools, but the showpiece is the series of brick and stone bathing houses. The 100-degree water is piped from the ground into one, then flows down to fill a second and then a third, cooling off slightly as it travels. For the steamiest, dreamiest end to the weekend, loll a while in the hot house.

ABOVE The popular bar at the El Mesón hotel.

THE BASICS

The nearest commercial airports are Querétaro, about 45 miles away, and León-Guanajuato, about 70 miles away.

Rosewood San Miguel
Nemesio Diez 11
52-415-152-9700
rosewoodhotels.com
$$$$
On the edge of Parque Juarez, with good views of the Parroquia.

Dos Casas Boutique Hotel
Quebrada 101
52-415-154-4958
doscasas.com.mx
$$$
Seven elegant rooms in a former private home two blocks from the Jardín.

Casa de Sierra Nevada
Hospicio 42
52-415-152-7040
casadesierranevada.com
$$$
Six renovated mansions, dating from the 16th century, converted into 37 rooms and suites.

5 miles
10 kilometers
Atotonilco
Sanctuario de Atotonilco 10
11 Escondido Place
GUANAJUATO MOUNTAINS
MEXICO
San Miguel de Allende
CAMINO A SAN MIGUEL EL VIEJO
Area of detail
De Temporada 7
To León-Guanajuato
To Querétaro
U.S.
MEXICO
Gulf of Mexico
San Miguel de Allende
Mexico City
Pacific Ocean
Fabrica La Aurora
Mercado de Artesanías 6
The Other Face of Mexico 8
Martinez/ El Mesón
1 Parroquia de San Miguel Arcángel
Bellas Artes
5 El Rincon de Don Tomas
San Miguel de Allende
Dos Casas Boutique Hotel
2 Azotea
Casa de Sierra Nevada
RECREO
4 La Sirena Gorda
Moxi 9
3 La Parada
0.25 mile
0.5 kilometer
Rosewood San Miguel
PARQUE JUAREZ

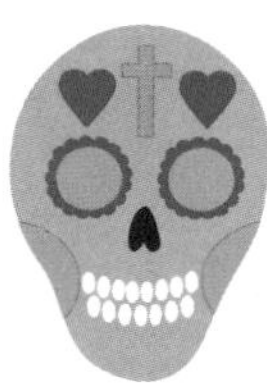

Puebla

Puebla is best known as the gastronomic capital of Mexico, home to classic Mexican dishes — most notably its namesake mole poblano. Between meals, there's much more to enjoy. A two-hour drive from Mexico City, past snow-capped peaks and volcanoes, Puebla is a wealthy city of 1.3 million people, a university town chock-full of colonial treasures, cafe-lined squares, and the visual riches of a vibrant arts-and-crafts culture. Just a few miles away, a massive 2,000-year-old pyramid juts skyward in the tiny town of Cholula.
— BY DAVID KAUFMAN AND FREDA MOON

FRIDAY

1 *When in Puebla* 3 p.m.

Like every Mexican town, Puebla has its soul in the zócalo, the central square of the old city. In this case, the zócalo is the **Plaza de la Constitución**, a rectangular slice of colonial Mexican cosmopolitanism bordered by arcaded walkways and anchored by the sprawling **Catedral de Puebla**, which dates from 1575. The cathedral is dominated by a pair of towers rising nearly 230 feet. Inside, its crypt signifies Puebla's status as one of colonial Mexico's wealthiest towns, with statues of saints and angels intricately carved from onyx, one of the city's numerous natural resources. A few blocks away, walk among the sculptures and gardens of a former textile factory at **Parque San Francisco** (Callejón de la 10 Norte, Barrio del Alto), where just-married couples and girls in colorful quinceañera dresses pose for photos.

2 *Poblano Típico* 8:30 p.m.

Puebla is famous for its regional comida típica (typical foods), like chiles en nogada (a poblano chile stuffed with meat, fruits, and nuts and topped with a walnut cream sauce and pomegranate seeds) and camotes de Santa Clara (a sweet-potato candy). For tacos árabes, marinated pork on flatbread that originated in the city's Lebanese community, and spicy, meaty frijoles charros (cowboy beans), wait your turn at **Las Ranas** (Avenida 2 Poniente 102; 52-222-242-4734; $). For a newer, and much more expensive, take on Mexican food, try the nuevo-Mexicano restaurant at the **Purificadora** hotel (Callejón de la 10 Norte 802; 52-222-309-1920; www.lapurificadora.com; $$$$). Menus there have included corn risotto spiked with poblano peppers; chipotle peppers stuffed with cheese in a black bean broth; and corn cakes with lime and cream cheese gelato.

3 *The Sidewalk Scene* 10 p.m.

Pull up a stool at an outdoor table beneath the jacarandas in **Barrio del Artista**, where the arched portals of a former market have been converted into closet-size studios. More often than not, the paintings — pastel landscapes, lusty nudes — are mediocre, but the blocklong arcade is beautiful. At night, cafes on the small plaza are crowded with students who come for live music and drinks specials.

SATURDAY

4 *Classic Breakfast* 8 a.m.

In a terra-cotta-colored courtyard, **Casona de la China Poblana** (Calle 4 Norte 2; 52-222-242-5621; casonadelachinapoblana.com; $) serves vibrant preparations of classic Mexican breakfasts. Choose chilaquiles (fried tortilla chips, in red or green sauce, with fresh cheese) or scrambled eggs with huitlacoche (corn fungus), nopal (cactus), and corn.

OPPOSITE Past, present, and prehistory meet in Cholulua, a few miles outside of Puebla. A 16th-century church, still in use for events like this young woman's quinceañera, sits atop a pyramid built in the second century B.C.

RIGHT The Catedral de Puebla, which dates from 1575, borders Puebla's zócalo, or central square.

5 *Pyramid Town* 10 a.m.

Watch as artisans turn black clay into elaborately painted pottery at the workshop of **Talavera de la Reyna** (Camino a la Carcaña 2413, Recta a Cholula; 52-222-225-4132; talaveradelareyna.com.mx), in the neighboring town of Cholula. The Talavera pottery, distinctive for its beauty and craftsmanship, has been made in this area for centuries. Across the highway, in a yellow cube, the **Museo Alarca** (Lateral Sur Recta a Cholula 3510, Cholula; 52-222-225-4058) shows the work of contemporary artists who have been paired with traditional artisans to create gorgeous sculptures. Cholula is best known for the **Cholula Pyramid** (Zona Arqueológica del Gran Pirámide de Cholula, Puebla State; inah.gob.mx/index.php/zonas-arqueologicas), built in the second century B.C. You can climb the exterior staircase or tunnel through endless antechambers and barren tombs. At the pyramid's top are both the Iglesia de los Remedios, a 16th-century church, and great views of the snow-covered Popocatépetl volcano.

6 *Lunch Like a Local* 1 p.m.

The **Mercado de Cholula**, the town's covered food market (Camino Real a Cholula and 20 Norte), is an action-packed nexus of butchers, fishmongers, vegetable farmers, and spice sellers. Arrive hungry and skip the taquerías. Instead, grab a seat at one of the quesadillerias near the rear of the market. The corn tortillas are thick, oblong, and purple and are filled with stringy white cheese, colorful zucchini blossoms, dark huitlacoche, or flecks of chicharon (fried pork skin). Stands nearby sell just-made pico de gallo and fruity juices for an easy lunch. Before leaving, pick up a packet of spicy mole paste for back home.

7 *Maya to Modern* 3 p.m.

Although Puebla may lack the grand museums of Mexico City, its **Museo Amparo** (2 Sur 708, Centro Histórico; 52-222-229-3850; museoamparo.com) has one of Latin America's finest collections of Mexican art. Amparo's holdings date from 2500 B.C. through the present, with work by pre-Hispanic, colonial, modern, and contemporary artists. The city is also home to the first public library in the New World, the **Biblioteca Palafoxiana** (Casa de la Cultura, 5 Avenida Oriente No. 5), founded in 1646. The nonprofit **Profética** (Calle 3 Sur 701; 52-222-246-9101; profetica.com.mx), in a sprawling 16th-century house, has another public library and an excellent bookstore.

8 *Like Dinner for Chocolate* 8:30 p.m.

The highlight of any visit to Puebla is its namesake dish: mole poblano, the sauce made with 30-odd ingredients including chilies, cinnamon, and

ABOVE Puebla's Palacio Municipal, on the zócalo.

chocolate. And one of the best places to taste it is at **Mesón Sacristía de la Compañía** (6 Sur 304, Callejón de los Sapos, Centro Histórico; 52-222-232-4513; mesones-sacristia.com; $$$$), an 18th-century mansion. In one preparation, the mole poblano smothers slices of chicken breast — rich, spicy, and with just enough chocolate to remind you why Montezuma was so smitten with the cacao bean.

9 *Qué Pasa?* 10:30 pm.

Drink like a local and try a pasita, a liqueur made from the local pasa fruit. There's no better place to order it than **La Pasita** (5 Oriente 605; 52-222-232-4422), a tiny bar hidden near the Callejón de los Sapos, a popular flea-market street. Crammed with bric-a-brac, the bar serves the liqueur in a shot glass, with either goat or panela cheese. La Pasita also serves rompope — a type of eggnog sometimes made by local nuns — along with a clutch of other fiery brews.

SUNDAY

10 *Souvenir Stop* 10 a.m.

The silversmith at **Manos de la Tierra** (Calle 6 Sur 4, Centro Histórico; manosdelatierrapuebla.com.mx) creates jewelry using antique Talavera ceramics and onyx. The shop also sells tooled leather bags in deep

ABOVE Try a shot of pasita, a raisin-like liqueur that is a local specialty, at La Pasita, a tiny, hidden bar crammed with bottles and bric-a-brac.

BELOW The Biblioteca Palafoxiana, in operation since 1646, is the oldest public library in the New World and has been designated as a Unesco World Heritage Site.

vibrant colors. For Pop Art a la Mexicana (lucha libre photo frames, papier-mâché Catrina figurines), try **Tierra Verde** (Avenida 5 Oriente 601, Plazuela de los Sapos, Centro Histórico; 52-222-232-0722; tierraverde.com.mx), just down the street. And for traditional textiles, made with natural dyes and woven on backstrap looms, drop into **Siuamej Puebla Crafts Cooperative** (Avenida Juan de Palafox y Mendoza 206; 52-222-232-3694).

ABOVE A taquería at a local food market. While you're shopping, pick up the mole paste that is the base for Puebla's famous culinary namesake, mole poblano.

OPPOSITE Talavera pottery at the artisan market.

11 *Fancy Food Court* Noon

For lunch, try the **Mercado de Sabores Poblanos** (4 Poniente between Calles 11 and 13 Norte), a sprawling version of the traditional Mexican market, where stalls sell cemitas (a local sandwich), sweets, and other regional dishes. Then, walk over to the **Museo Nacional de los Ferrocarriles Mexicanos** (Calle 11 Norte, 1005, Centro Histórico; 52-222-774-0105; museoferrocarriles.org.mx), an outdoor train museum. Retired rail cars and steam engines rest on a lawn beside a former terminal, and an impressive collection of photographs documents train lines and the lives of railway workers.

THE BASICS

Arrive by air at Puebla's airport, or take a two-hour bus ride from Mexico City International Airport. The city center is compact and easily traversed on foot.

Hotel Puebla de Antaño
Calle 3 Oriente 206, Centro
52-222-246-2403
hotelpuebladeantano.com
$
Housed in the former Italian Consulate, with 19 opulent suites.

La Purificadora
Callejón de la 10 Norte 802
52-222-309-1920
lapurificadora.com
$$
Cool and stylish boutique hotel in an old ice factory.

Real del Cristo Hotel
2 Oriente 1007
52-222-246-1575
$
In a charming 15th-century house with an airy central courtyard.

MEXICO
Gulf of Mexico
Mexico City
Puebla
Pacific Ocean
Mercado de Cholula
Talavera de la Reyna
Cholula
Museo Alarca
Cholula Pyramid/ Iglesia de los Remedios
Area of Detail
Puebla
MEXICO
2 miles
4 kilometers
Museo Nacional de los Ferrocarriles Mexicanos
CALLE 11 NORTE
Mercado de Sabores Poblanos
CALLE 7 NORTE
REFORMA
AVE. 2 PTE
Puebla
CALLE 3 SUR
Hotel Puebla de Antaño
Las Ranas
Siuamej Puebla Crafts Cooperative
Barrio del Artista
La Purificadora
BARRIO DEL ALTO
Casona de la China Poblana
Plaza de la Constitución
Profética
CENTRO HISTÓRICO
Catedral de Puebla
Manos de la Tierra
Parque San Francisco
Real del Cristo Hotel
CALLE 7 SUR
Biblioteca Palafoxiana/ Casa de la Cultura
Tierra Verde
AV. JUAN DE PALAFOX Y MENDOZA
Museo Amparo
Mesón Sacristía de la Compañía
DOS SUR
CALLE 4 SUR
La Pasita
0.25 mile
0.5 kilometer

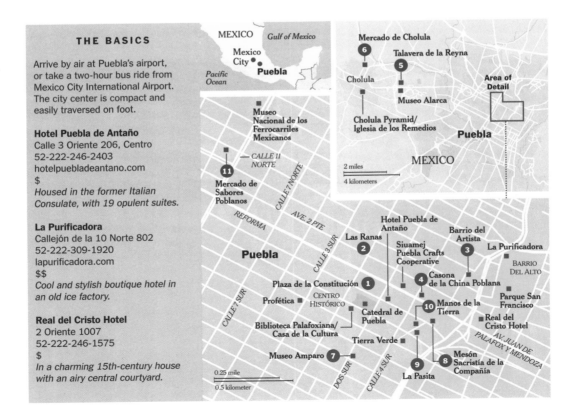

Puebla
Puebla
Puebla
Puebla
Puebla
Puebla
MI CASA
ES TU CASA

Recuerdo de mi Visita
CUENTO
BENDIGO

Oaxaca

With Oaxaca's imposing Baroque churches, plant-filled courtyards, and shady plazas perfect for people-watching, it's tempting to see the city as a photogenic relic of Mexico's colonial past. But Oaxaca, a college town teeming with students and the capital of one of the country's poorest states, is a dynamic city. Politically inspired stencil art has turned adobe walls and concrete sidewalks into a public gallery, a counterpoint to a long-established studio art scene. Add a vibrant cafe culture, a mezcal-fueled night life, and one of Mexico's most exciting regional cuisines, and Oaxaca quickly proves itself as cosmopolitan as it is architecturally stunning. — BY FREDA MOON

FRIDAY

1 *Smoke and Meats* 3 p.m.

Start at the culinary heart of the city, the **Mercado 20 de Noviembre**, which occupies an entire city block south of Aldama (between 20 de Noviembre and Cabrera). Family-run fondas — food stalls with colorful signs, long counters, and short stools — sell Oaxacan staples like chicken with mole to campesinos, office workers, and backpackers. Alongside the main building, a smoke-filled covered alley is lined with carne asada (grilled meat) vendors, each selling a selection of fresh cuts — thin-sliced beef or links of spicy chorizo. Your choice is tossed on the grill with accompaniments from the nearby vegetable stalls, where you'll find onions and chilies to add to the fire, as well as prepared sides like sliced radishes, guacamole, strips of nopal (cactus), and homemade corn tortillas.

2 *Culture Hour* 5 p.m.

Named for Mexico's revolutionary hero, **Espacio Zapata** (Porfirio Díaz 509; espaciozapata.blogspot.com) brings Oaxaca's radical street art indoors with prints of stencil designs and graffiti on canvas. It also hosts workshops, readings, and music. Around the corner, in a series of high-ceilinged rooms set around a courtyard pool, the **Centro Fotográfico Manuel Álvarez Bravo** (M. Bravo 116; 52-951-516-9800; cfmab.blogspot.com) hosts photo exhibitions and screenings. The **Instituto de Artes Gráficas de Oaxaca** (Alcalá 507; institutodeartesgraficasdeoaxaca.blogspot.com; 52-951-516-6980), founded by the painter Francisco Toledo, exhibits the work of influential designers like the artist and activist Rini Templeton.

3 *Slow Food* 7 p.m.

In a country where leisurely meals are the rule, **La Biznaga** (García Vigil 512; 52-951-516-1800; labiznaga.com.mx; $) goes further, billing itself a "very slow food" establishment and issuing a warning that dishes take time. But with Biznaga's relaxed, multicolored courtyard, eclectic background music, and extensive list of wines by the glass, the wait is a pleasure. The menu, scrawled on large green chalkboards, includes a selection of unusual soups, like the one called La Silvestre, with mushrooms, bacon, and cambray onions (served with fixings like chopped onion, cilantro, avocado, jalapeño, and lime); fried squash blossoms in poblano chili sauce; and shrimp with garlic, chilies, and tamarind mole.

4 *Boho Night Life* 10 p.m.

Next door, **La Zandunga** (512 García Vigil; 52-951-516-2265) serves food that's best suited to soaking up mezcal, the Mexican agave liquor, and sharing among friends — doughy deep-fried empanadas or fried plantain and cheese croquettes. Zandunga's tables are perfect for lingering over a bottle before hitting a dance floor. For that, head to **Café Central** (Hidalgo 302; cafecentraloaxaca.blogspot.com), a

OPPOSITE Icons on display in Oaxaca.

RIGHT Vibrant yarns, the staple material for local weavers.

late-night spot with a stylized old Havana aesthetic — a stuffed marlin above the door, black-and-white tiled bar, red stage curtains — and live music or D.J.'d dance parties on weekends.

SATURDAY

5 *Wholesome Day Trip* 8 a.m.

For a quick breakfast, return to the market for pan de yema, a sweet egg bread, and Oaxaca's famous hot chocolate. Then, get a glimpse of the countryside with **Fundación En Vía** (Instituto Cultural Oaxaca; Avenida Juarez 909; 52-951-515-2424; envia.org/upcoming-tours), a local nonprofit micro-finance organization that helps rural women develop small-scale businesses. Its tour functions as a cultural exchange between travelers and borrowers — often indigenous Zapotec craftspeople. For another kind of cultural immersion, try a four-hour cooking class at **Casa Crespo** (Allende 107; 52-951-516-0918; casacrespo.com), in a converted colonial home, where you'll learn to construct such local specialties as 17-ingredient mole de fiesta, incorporating chilies, spices, and chocolate.

6 *Cafe con Arte* 3:30 p.m.

For a house-roasted coffee and surprisingly authentic bagels, visit **Café Brújula** (García Vigil 409-D; 52-951-516-7255; cafebrujula.com). First, drop by **Amate Books** (Alcalá 507A; 52-951-516-6960; amatebooks.com), an excellent English-language bookstore, for your requisite coffeehouse reading material. For some shopping, walk uphill to the city's defunct aqueduct and the **Instituto Oaxaqueño de las Artesanías**, known as Aripo (García Vigil 809; 52-951-514-1354; artesaniasaripo.com), an emporium of crafts, including filigreed silver jewelry, etched leather bags, wood carvings, and black pottery.

7 *Colorful Crafts* 5 p.m.

The brilliant weavings of Teotitlán del Valle, a small nearby village, are among the most celebrated of Mexican folk arts. The **Museo Textil de Oaxaca** (Hidalgo 917; 52-951-501-1104; museotextildeoaxaca.org.mx) is devoted entirely to textiles and has an excellent museum store and an in-house preservation workshop. The family-run shop **Galeria Fe y Lola** (5 de Mayo 408, No. 1; 52-951-524-4078) sells a gorgeous selection of wool rugs made with organic dyes. For those with a deep interest in the subject, the Oaxaca Cultural Navigator Web site (oaxacaculture.com) is a wonderful resource.

8 *Updated Tradition* 7 p.m.

It has crisp white walls and waiters who are a bit too aloof, but unlike many restaurants of its kind, **Pitiona** (5 de Mayo 311; 52-951-514-4707; pitiona.com; $$$) avoids culinary flamboyance. Instead, it serves well-made regionally inspired dishes — like an amuse-bouche of beef tongue and bulgur meatballs with chintextle sauce (garlic, vinegar, and guajillo chili), venison with yellow mole, and mango tacos with pear mousse — that hew surprisingly close to tradition. For the full experience, go with the ever-changing six-course tasting menu.

9 *Mas Mezcal* 9 p.m.

La Mezcaloteca (Reforma 506; 52-951-514-0082; mezcaloteca.com) is a dark, signless, speakeasy-style mezcal bar that feels like a library devoted to the study of Oaxaca's prized beverage. Try uncommon varieties like the rare wild agave tobala as part of a three-tasting flight. Across town, **Cuish** (Diaz Ordaz 712; 52-951-516-8791) is less studious but equally passionate about mezcal.

SUNDAY

10 *Breakfast of Champions* 10 a.m.

On an out-of-the-way stretch of residential street in the Reforma neighborhood, **Casa Oaxaca Café** (Jazmines 518; 52-951-502-6017; casaoaxacacafe.com; $), a luxurious outpost of the downtown restaurant of the same name, is a go-to brunch spot. This courtyard restaurant has wooden furniture, trees strung with vines, and a bamboo canopy. Guayabera-wearing

ABOVE Oaxaca's mariachis are still popular, but now the musical spectrum in town also extends to D.J.'s.

waiters float between the tables and the open kitchen delivering chilaquiles with guajillo, omelets with huitlacoche corn fungus, and mole empanadas. The fresh fruit juices and coffee are excellent.

11 *Return to Sender* Noon

The city's stamp museum, **Museo de Filatelia de Oaxaca** (Reforma 504; 52-951-514-2366; mufi.org.mx), is a fitting sendoff. One exhibition featured bicycle-centric stamps from around the world, using bike rims as makeshift frames for international postal art. For a final stop, grab a nieve (snow), a generic word for frozen desserts, at another museum of sorts, the **Museo de las Nieves Manolo** (Alcalá 706; 52-951-143-9253; museodelasnieves.com). Flavors include pistachio, cheese with basil, and mezcal. Enjoy your cone next to one of the twin fountains at **Paseo Juárez**, a leafy square with orange-flowered flame trees and a white oak donated by Oaxaca's sister city, Palo Alto, California.

ABOVE Woven belts ready for buyers at a Oaxaca market. Weaving, a refined Mexican folk art, is celebrated at the Museo Textil de Oaxaca, and many of the country's finest textiles come from the nearby village of Teotitlán del Valle.

THE BASICS

Several airlines serve Oaxaca. The compact Centro Histórico is pedestrian friendly; taxis and buses connect to nearby towns.

El Diablo y La Sandia
Libres 205
52-951-514-4095
eldiabloylasandia.com
$
Five-room hotel with a blue-tiled kitchen in the courtyard and a roof deck rimmed by potted plants.

Hotel Azul
Abasolo 313
52-951-501-0016
hotelazuloaxaca.com
$$
Elegant modern rooms surround a stone-and-cactus courtyard with a fountain designed by one of Oaxaca's best-known artists, Francisco Toledo.

Hotel Camino Real Oaxaca
Calle 5 de Mayo 300
52-951- 501-6100
camino-real-oaxaca.com
$$
Aristocratic serenity amid courtyards of archways, gardens, and fountains.

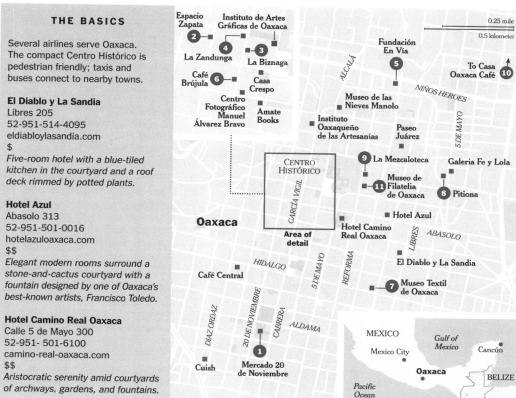

Espacio Zapata 2
Instituto de Artes Gráficas de Oaxaca
4 La Zandunga
3 La Biznaga
Café Brújula 6
Casa Crespo
Centro Fotográfico Manuel Álvarez Bravo
Amate Books
Fundación En Vía 5
To Casa Oaxaca Café 10
Museo de las Nieves Manolo
Instituto Oaxaqueño de las Artesanías
Paseo Juárez
9 La Mezcaloteca
Galeria Fe y Lola
11 Museo de Filatelia de Oaxaca
8 Pitiona
Hotel Azul
Hotel Camino Real Oaxaca
El Diablo y La Sandia
7 Museo Textil de Oaxaca
Café Central
Cuish
1 Mercado 20 de Noviembre
Centro Histórico
Oaxaca
Area of detail
Alcalá
Niños Heroes
5 de Mayo
García Vigil
Abasolo
Libres
Reforma
Hidalgo
20 de Noviembre
Cabrera
Diaz Ordaz
Aldama
0.25 mile
0.5 kilometer
MEXICO
Mexico City
Gulf of Mexico
Cancún
Oaxaca
BELIZE
Pacific Ocean
GUATEMALA

Costa Chica

The four small neighboring towns of the Costa Chica, on southern Mexico's Pacific coast — San Agustinillo, Mazunte, Zipolite, and Ventanilla — used to be nearly empty except for fishermen hunting sea turtles or harvesting their eggs. That all began to change in the 1980s, as the turtle population dwindled and the first mass of Italian tourists arrived, undaunted by the area's monstrous waves and dangerous undertows. Then the Mexican government banned turtle hunting in 1990, and the Costa Chica became a test case for shifting from an industry that degraded the natural environment to others that are eco-friendly. Now, the area has mostly found its sustainable groove. Much new construction is built to blend in with the surroundings, walkers outnumber drivers, and several business owners are raving about plans for solar-powered streetlights. — BY DAMIEN CAVE

FRIDAY

1 *Sea Monsters* 3 p.m.

Loud and large, the waves define this coast, so head down to the sand and have a look. The **Costa Chica beaches** demand respect, but you will find that the threat of the breakers cannot be separated from the area's appeal. The tubes of green surf rolling along the empty beach at Ventanilla and the undertow at San Agustinillo that pulls heavy rocks out to sea with ease are a perfect match for the cactus plants and palm trees, and even the fishermen hunting sharks (illegally). They all reflect a Mexico still rough and raw in form, dominated by nature and the struggle for identity.

2 *Dip Your Toes* 5 p.m.

Yes, you can get into the water, especially at low tide. The waves simply require caution — and choosing your spot. Surfers dominate at Zipolite, but even families can venture out in the small coves near a series of large rocks in **San Agustinillo**, starting shallow and then slowly moving out a little deeper. It is a great way to show children who are sharpening their swimming skills why the ocean needs to be respected.

3 *Dinner and Music* 7 p.m.

The little village of San Agustinillo has more charm than the other three towns on this coast, with its smaller beach, its preference for cafes, and its handful of newer, upscale hotels. Have a casual dinner at **La Termita** (Principal Mazunte Puerto Angel; 52-958-589-3046; posadalatermita.com; $), a restaurant attached to a small inn. Tables are arranged to help you watch the sun sink into the ocean over your brick-oven pizza. Afterward, if the night feels young, no need to turn in yet. San Agustinillo falls dark and quiet before midnight, but Mazunte, an easy walk away, is busier. Live music blares until a loosely enforced closing time — some say it is midnight; others guess 2 a.m.

SATURDAY

4 *Backpacker Breakfast* 9 a.m.

At sunrise, on the main road between the towns, women in baggy pants appear with yoga mats in their arms. Find a class and join them, or settle for the rigors of a beach walk and a search for sustenance. Breakfast seems to extend into the afternoon at the restaurants on **Mazunte**'s main drag, where young backpackers finish their eggs and hitch rides to Puerto

OPPOSITE Sea turtles, once hunted nearly to extinction here and now ardently protected and nurtured, are many tourists' reason for visiting the Costa Chica. These babies are making their first trip to the sea.

RIGHT Riding the waves near Mazunte, one of the four towns of the Costa Chica. Some of the area's powerful surf is deadly, but quieter spots are safe to enjoy.

Escondido or to Huatulco National Park — each about an hour's drive away.

5 *Body Shoppers* 11 a.m.

Costa Chica's shift from turtle hunting to earth-friendly ways of earning a living seems complete, accomplished with the help of investment from government, nonprofits, and green-minded businesses. One successful venture that's also a tourist magnet is **Cosméticos Naturales de Mazunte** (Mazunte; 52-958-583-9656; cosmeticosmazunte.com), which has been aided by the Body Shop and its ecology-minded founder, Anita Roddick. Its hair and skin products are made with oils from avocados, soybeans, sesame, corn, and coconut, as well as ingredients like beeswax and Vitamin E. On one business day, the small factory's shop was filled with day-trippers from the cities nearby — some Mexican, many from colder places like Canada — stocking up on shampoo, sun-screen, and even mosquito repellent.

6 *Turtle Alternatives* 1 p.m.

Traditionally, sea turtles were viewed in Mexico as food. Now, with the turtle trade banned, that attitude is dying out. You certainly won't see any turtles on menus in this ecologically conscious area. But you will eat almost as well as anywhere else in Mexico, for less money. At **Olas Altas** (San Agustinillo; $), the dorado steamed with cheese and Sacred Herb (no, not that herb) was fresh, simple, and heavenly, and four people had lunch for the price that one person would expect to pay in an American resort town.

7 *Giants of the Sea* 2 p.m.

The Costa Chica's totem of green conversion, the **Mexican Turtle Center** (Mazunte; 52-555-449-7000; centromexicanodelatortuga.org), operates near what used to be a turtle slaughterhouse. In those days, the giant sea turtles that come ashore here by the thousands to nest on the beach were killed for their meat, eggs, and shells. Now armed guards protect them when they parade onto the sand. At the Turtle Center, an aquarium and research center, five of the seven turtle species found on the Mexican coast are on display, and the aim is to encourage conservation. Visitors on one spring day watched giant turtles, called golfinas in Spanish and olive ridleys in English, race around an aboveground pool just a few yards from crashing waves. The staff interacted warmly with the crowd.

8 *Thank You, Italy* 7 p.m.

For tonight's dinner with a sunset view, try the restaurant at **Punta Placer** (San Agustinillo; puntaplacer.com; $), a small, upscale hotel. The fantastic risotto at one visit offered a reminder that wherever Italians show up, good food, wine, and coffee usually follow.

SUNDAY

9 *Life in the Mangroves* 10 a.m.

Beaches aren't the whole story of this coast. At Ventanilla, mangrove swamps fringe a quiet lagoon, furnishing habitat for animals and birds, including some that are endangered. To see them, take a boat tour with **Servicios Ecoturisticos de La Ventanilla** (Playa Ventanilla; 52-958-584-0549; laventanilla.com.mx), a cooperative operated by about 20 local families who embraced this strategy after the end of the turtle trade. The boats are set up to take small groups, but even if no one else shows up, the obliging and friendly staff will probably accommodate you at a price that will keep you smiling. On the 90-minute trip, expect to float through mangroves teeming with water birds, lazy crocodiles, and neon-green iguanas as your guide identifies them while quietly paddling the boat.

OPPOSITE Fishermen off to sea at dawn from the San Agustinillo beach.

ABOVE A crocodile at Ventanilla, where wildlife thrives in the mangrove swamps surrounding a quiet lagoon.

MEXICO
OAXACA
Puerto Escondido
200
Costa Chica beaches
1
HUATULCO INTERNATIONAL AIRPORT
Huatulco National Park
10 miles
20 kilometers
Pacific Ocean
Area of detail
Costa Chica
Servicios Ecoturisticos de La Ventanilla
9
Ventanilla
San Agustinillo
2
Mazunte
4
La Termita
3
Un Sueño
Zipolite
Puerto Angel
Cosméticos Naturales de Mazunte
5
Casa Pan de Miel
6
Olas Altas
Mexican Turtle Center
7
8
Punta Placer/ Cabañas Punta Placer
1 mile
2 kilometers
UNITED STATES
Gulf of Mexico
MEXICO
Cancún
Mérida
Mexico City
OAXACA
BELIZE
Area of detail
Pacific Ocean
GUATEMALA

THE BASICS

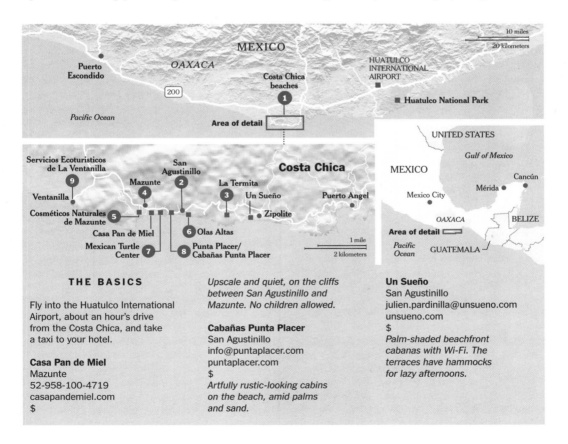

Fly into the Huatulco International Airport, about an hour's drive from the Costa Chica, and take a taxi to your hotel.

Casa Pan de Miel
Mazunte
52-958-100-4719
casapandemiel.com
$
Upscale and quiet, on the cliffs between San Agustinillo and Mazunte. No children allowed.

Cabañas Punta Placer
San Agustinillo
info@puntaplacer.com
puntaplacer.com
$
Artfully rustic-looking cabins on the beach, amid palms and sand.

Un Sueño
San Agustinillo
julien.pardinilla@unsueno.com
unsueno.com
$
Palm-shaded beachfront cabanas with Wi-Fi. The terraces have hammocks for lazy afternoons.

San Cristóbal

The state of Chiapas, bordered by the Pacific Ocean to the west and Guatemala to the south, is home to one of Mexico's largest Mayan populations—one million strong and fiercely sovereign. Despite its quirky independent streak (many of the Maya still dress in village-specific tribal wear), Chiapas has its worldly element. The cultural and commercial heart is the lively, bohemian town of San Cristóbal de las Casas. The town made global news in 1994 during a 12-day Zapatista rebellion. Though there's still evidence of the uprising in political graffiti and kitschy memorabilia, more striking are brilliant blue skies, colonial architecture, dark-roasted coffee, and finely made textiles and handicrafts. —BY ANN SCHLOTT HILLERS

FRIDAY

1 *The Doctor Will See You* 4 p.m.

Part magician, part humanitarian, Sergio Castro, who runs the **Museo de Trajes Regionales Guadalupe** (Victoria 38; 52-967-678-4289; sergiocastrosc.blogspot.mx) found his calling as patron saint of the area's indigenous population 45 years ago. Self-taught in medicine and seven languages, he treats burn victims in his home, relying on donations for medical supplies. His museum holds a fascinating array of native costumes—ceremonial and wedding attire as well as everyday wear—grouped by village. Make an appointment before visiting.

2 *Savor Some Mexican Wines* 6 p.m.

Real de Guadalupe, a pedestrian corridor running east to west through the center of town, is ultra-alive in the evenings as the bar crowd takes over the sidewalk cafes, the waft of garlic from Italian restaurants perfumes the air, and swallows fly over the main plaza, with its brilliant yellow church. Evening light here is nonpareil; take your camera and grab a seat at one of the wooden tables at **La Viña de Bacco** (Real de Guadalupe 7b; lavinadebacco.com), which offers multiple wines by the glass, many of them Mexican and surprisingly good. Sample several; most are inexpensive. Every drink arrives with a tapa of smoked fish, chorizo, or some other small delight.

3 *Mayan Theatrics* 8 p.m.

A little back story will go a long way in the enjoyment of **Palenque Rojo** (palenquerojo.com) at the Teatro Daniel Zebadúa (1 de Marzo and 20 de Noviembre; 52-967-678-1357), a nightly festival of live music, dance, and acrobatics put on by 20 actors in wild costumes. Set in the year 711, the play was inspired by the real-life discovery of a 1,000-year-old statue depicting a bound king. As the multisensory theater recreates a battle between the rulers of the Mayan fortress cities Toniná and Palenque—just north of San Cristóbal—the culture of the Indians and their pre-Hispanic history unfolds.

SATURDAY

4 *Horseback to Chamula* 9 a.m.

Arrange through your hotel for a guided horseback ride into the countryside. An especially nice route, weaving through lush hills and valleys, is to the indigenous village of **San Juan Chamula**, seven miles away. Catholicism is overshadowed in this small town by pre-conquest Mayan customs. The main church, where pine needles cover the floor and the air is thick with hundreds of burning candles, allows visitors to witness its rituals. Live chickens are sacrificed to the saints, Coca-Cola is used as an agent to rid the body of evil spirits, and eggs are rolled across a woman's skull to increase fertility.

OPPOSITE San Cristóbal, with a large indigenous population, retains strains of Mayan culture beneath a Spanish overlay.

RIGHT Figures in traditional costume for sale at Sna Jolobil, a cooperative of local weavers.

5 *Eat Your Greens* 1 p.m.

Have lunch at **El Punto** (Comitan 13a; 52-967-678-0047; $$). Intimate and off the beaten track, this Italian spot behind the Santo Domingo Church supplies your daily serving of green vegetables — as well as brick-oven pizza and pastas. Try one of 12 zodiac-named salads, perhaps the Taurus, which has Bibb lettuce, apples, raisins, and blue cheese.

6 *Co-op Hopping* 2 p.m.

The textiles made by San Cristóbal's women are the lifeblood of this city, and female village elders have formed co-ops to display the talents of hundreds of the highland weavers. Still woven on back-strap looms, pieces can take between a week and a year to create, and prices reflect this. **Balamil**, a shop inside the **Madre Tierra** restaurant (Insurgentes 19; 52-967-678-4297), represents two groups: El Camino de Los Altos (whose members handcrafted all the weavings and spreads at Hotel Bo) and Maddalena Forcella. Here and at **El Encuentro** (Real de Guadalupe 63a; 52-967-678-3698) you'll see table linens and pillowcases in strong stripes or small geometrics on white backgrounds. **Sna Jolobil**, a co-op of 800 weavers (Calzada Lázaro Cárdenas 42; 52-967-678-2626; snajolobil.com) sells exquisite, more expensive pieces from several villages.

7 *Craft Paper* 4 p.m.

Taller de Leñateros (Flavio Paniagua 54; 52-967-678-5174; tallerlenateros.com), a printing press and literary salon run by contemporary Mayan artists, has created what are thought to be the first books to be written, illustrated, printed, and bound by indigenous Mexicans in more than 400 years. In a humble backyard studio, fiber is obtained from palm fronds, cornhusks, and cardboard boxes using a bicycle-driven mill; the paper is dyed with flowers and wild plants. A few years ago the workshop published the first-ever collection of Mayan women's poetry, *Incantations*, and its hefty, handmade collector's edition is for sale here.

LEFT A little night music on San Cristóbal's zócalo, or central city square.

8 *Mole and Squash Blossoms* 7 p.m.

Traditional Mexican ingredients and dishes are a prominent part of the fare at **La Paloma** (Miguel Hidalgo 3; 52-967-678-1547; lapaloma-rest.com; $$): moles, the corn fungus called huitlacoche, chiles rellenos. Look for squash blossoms, which make their appearance in soup and stuffed with cheese.

9 *Revolution Time* 8 p.m.

The youngish, international crowd — which neatly defines the tourist demographic of San Cristóbal — flocks to **Café Bar Revolución** (20 de noviembre and 31 de marzo; 52-967-678-6664; facebook.com/CafeBarRevolucion), where live bands perform every evening. On one typical night, there were two sets back to back: a dynamite kumbia-klezmer fusion group and a funky combo of rockabilly banjo, tiny ukulele, eight-string guitar, and a beautiful girl tap-dancing on a wooden box. It's like your favorite college dive, but the clientele is much more interesting, and there's a sophisticated cheese plate on the menu.

SUNDAY

10 *Sunday Market* 8 a.m.

The nearby villages of San Juan Chamula and Zinacantán offer a stunning church and distinctive textiles, so most travelers venturing out of San Cristóbal make one of those villages their destination. But it's worth venturing farther to experience the Sunday market at **Tenejapa**, a 45-minute taxi ride

away. It's a strictly local affair where foreigners are so few you'll find folks staring at you, especially if you're more than five feet tall. As you stroll the narrow outdoor aisles lined with Tenejapans selling what Tenejapans need, suss out fabulous finds of handwoven felts, pom-pom-adorned wool purses, and white embroidered sashes (worn by men only) that can double as table runners.

11 *Breakfast at Bo* 11 a.m.

Show off your finds over breakfast at **Hotel Bo** (Cinco de Mayo 38; 52-967-678-1515; hotelbo.mx), the liveliest spot in town for your fix of sopa de gato (no, there's no cat in it), a heavenly mash of tortillas, chorizo, and black beans. Buzzing with joyful diners, the patio next to the reflecting pools is the spot frequented by affluent travelers, yet prices are surprisingly affordable. Join the owner, Fernando Gutiérrez, for a Bloody Mary. As a native who grew up on the hotel grounds he knows the region inside and out.

ABOVE Cured ham hanging at a shop in San Cristóbal. For a picnic, buy it by the kilo and add locally baked bread.

THE BASICS

Fly to Ángel Albino Corzo International Airport near the Chiapas city of Tuxtla Gutiérrez. The taxi or shuttle ride to San Cristóbal takes about an hour and 15 minutes.

Hotel Bo
Cinco de Mayo 38
52-967-678-1515
hotelbo.mx
$$-$$$$
Stylishly decorated boutique-style hotel; works of the area's master weavers are incorporated into bedcovers, accessories, and staff uniforms.

Villas Kukurutz
Real de Mexicanos 21/25
kukurutz.com.
$
Apartment hotel two blocks west of the Santo Domingo church and its daily handicrafts market.

Casa del Alma Hotel Boutique & Spa
16 de Septiembre 24
52-967-674-7784
casadelalma.mx
$$
In the heart of the city; decorated with regional touches.

4 miles
8 kilometers
El Punto 5
Tenejapa 10
San Juan Chamula 4
Tuxtla Gutiérrez
Café Bar Revolución 9
San Cristóbal de las Casas
Area of detail
Zinacantán
CHIAPAS
MEXICO
1 Museo de Trajes Regionales Guadalupe
ÁNGEL ALBINO CORZO INTERNATIONAL AIRPORT
CALZADA LÁZARO CÁRDENAS
Sna Jolobil
San Cristóbal de las Casas
Villas Kukurutz
Hotel Bo 11
REAL DE MEXICANOS
20 DE NOVIEMBRE
Taller de Leñateros
7
FLAVIO PANIAGUA
CINCO DE MAYO
Casa del Alma Hotel Boutique & Spa
Palenque Rojo/ Teatro Daniel Zebadúa 3
1 DE MARZO
El Encuentro
REAL DE GUADALUPE
16 DE SEPTIEMBRE
La Paloma 8
MIGUEL HIDALGO
2 La Viña de Bacco
Balamil/ Madre Tierra 6
Gulf of Mexico
Mexico City
MEXICO
CHIAPAS
San Cristóbal de las Casas
Pacific Ocean
GUATEMALA
0.25 mile
0.5 kilometer

Mérida

Yucatecans are fiercely proud of their culture, sprinkling their Spanish with Mayan words and quick to recount the stories of resistance and revolution that set this region apart from the rest of Mexico for centuries. Somehow, those tales seem a little distant now in Yucatán's capital, Mérida, a languid city of pastel mansions and evening promenades. The city, now one of the safest in Mexico, is an architectural jewel, and has one of the country's largest historic centers outside Mexico City. Block after block of houses dating to the mid-19th century and earlier are in the midst of a restoration boom, and the city's cultural and restaurant scenes are flourishing. — BY ELISABETH MALKIN

FRIDAY

1 *Yucatecan Feast* 3 p.m.

Sample Yucatecan cuisine at the **Hacienda Teya** (Mérida-Cancún Highway, Kilometer 12.5; 52-999-988-0800; haciendateya.com; $), a 17th-century plantation that switched from cattle to henequen, a fibrous plant used for making rope, at the end of the 19th century, and is just a 15-minute drive from downtown. From the colonial dining room, with walls that are filled with photographs of Mérida in the early 1900s, the view stretches to the brilliant flamboyant trees that fringe the expansive grounds. Try the classics: sopa de lima, a fragrant chicken and tortilla soup flavored with lime juice; cochinita pibil, tangy slow-roasted pork marinated in citrus and a paste made from achiote seeds; or poc chuc, grilled pork marinated in sour orange juice.

2 *Promenade in the Plaza* 5 p.m.

In the late afternoon, the whole city, it seems, congregates in the leafy **Plaza Grande** under the towers of Mérida's austere 16th-century Cathedral of San Ildefonso. Have a sorbet at **Sorbetería Colón** on the north side (along 61st Street), and then wander into the **Governor's Palace** next door and take in the giant paintings, depicting Yucatán's violent history, by the 20th-century Mérida-born artist Fernando Castro Pacheco. The **Casa Montejo** (506 63rd Street; 52-999-923-0633; museocasamontejo.com) on the south side, now a cultural center and museum, is the city's oldest building, erected by Don Francisco Montejo, Yucatán's conquistador, in the 1540s. Look on the facade for the carving of two Spanish conquistadors standing atop the heads of Indians. The four front rooms have been sumptuously restored to late-19th-century splendor. The gift shop sells excellent handicrafts. As night falls, walk north a few blocks to the small church of **La Tercera Orden** on the corner of 59th and 60th Streets; it was built by the Jesuits in 1618. You may catch a wedding or a quinceañera Mass.

3 *Mojitos by Starlight* 9 p.m.

The outdoor bar at the **Piedra de Agua** hotel (498 60th Street, 52-999-924-2300; piedradeagua.com; $) has a spectacular view of the brilliantly lighted cathedral towers. Local groups play jazz and blues on Fridays. The specialties are mojitos and lemon daiquiris accented with basil leaves. Try a pizza topped with huitlacoche, Mexico's signature corn fungus. Another night life option is **Hennessy's Irish Pub** (486A Paseo de Montejo; 52-999-923-8993; hennessysirishpub.com), a hip Mérida spot. The photos of the Irish countryside and '80s classics on the soundtrack seem a little off, but the outdoor terrace on the Paseo de Montejo fills up.

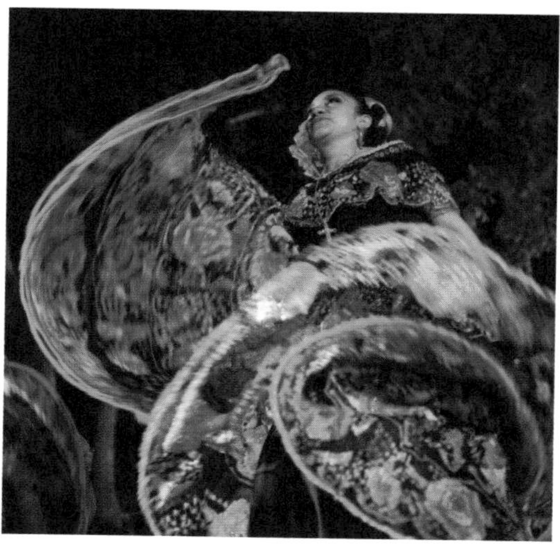

OPPOSITE Sunday cycling in the mansion district.

RIGHT Folk dancing in traditional costume, part of a regular Saturday night show on an outdoor stage in Mérida.

SATURDAY

4 *Curbside Breakfast* 9 a.m.

The Loría family have run the **Wayan'e** street stand for more than two decades (92E 20th Street at 15th Street, Colonia Itzimná; 52-999-927-4160; $). They serve savory tacos and tortas throughout the morning, scooping fragrant fillings like smoky chicken fajitas and scrambled eggs with acelgas (Swiss chard) out of clay pots for customers seated at a stainless steel counter.

5 *Frozen in Time* 11 a.m.

During the henequen boom, when the agave plant was turned into rope for the world, Yucatán's aristocratic landowners built magnificent houses, many of them now luxury hotels. But **Hacienda Yaxcopoil** (Federal Highway 261, Kilometer 186; 52-999-900-1193; yaxcopoil.com), about 20 miles south of Mérida, has been preserved as though in amber, a noble near-ruin where yellowing photos of the family that has owned it for five generations hang askew on the frescoed walls. Wander through silent rooms offering a glimpse into the past, from the chapel's figurine of St. Geronimo wearing a Yucatán straw hat to French porcelain bathroom fixtures coated in dust.

6 *A Mayan Diner* 2 p.m.

At **Chaya Maya** (481 62nd Street at 57th Street; 52-999-928-4780; $), a woman in traditional Mayan dress makes corn tortillas in the window as families pile in. Try the house specialty, Los Tres Mosqueteros, which combines three classic Yucatecan dishes: relleno negro (a black sauce made from burnt chilies and spices) over pork; papadzul (an egg dish); and pipián (a sauce with a pumpkin-seed base) over turkey.

7 *Take Home a Hammock* 3 p.m.

El Aguacate (604 58th Street; 52-999-289-5789; hamacaselaguacate.com.mx) sells hammocks for every budget. A finely woven cotton or nylon hammock, which takes about two months to weave, will cost about $175, but the cheapest one is about $20. (The store is in Mérida's tiny red-light district, which is safe by day.) Back near the city center, shop for a guayabera, the Cuban shirt that is worn untucked. It was a favorite with early 20th-century Yucatecan grandees, who would go to Cuba to stock up. After the Cuban Revolution, Yucatecans began making their own. A polyester-cotton blend at **Guayaberas Jack** (507A 59th Street, 52-999-928-5999; guayaberasjack.com.mx) costs about $30, and an embroidered linen model popular with Mexican presidents sells for about $170.

8 *Fine Folk* 7 p.m.

Every Saturday, the city stages a free show for tourists and locals alike, featuring folk dancing, comedy, mariachi, marimba, and romantic trova music (1 Paseo de Montejo at 49th Street; 52-999-928-1800; hotelcasasanangel.com). You can watch from the street or have a drink on the terrace of the **Hotel Casa San Angel**. For more information on cultural events, check *Yucatán Today*, the city's free bilingual monthly tourist guide (yucatantoday.com).

9 *Chocolate Delight* 9 p.m.

At the restaurant inside a boutique hotel, **Rosas & Xocolate** (480 Paseo de Montejo at 41st Street; 52-999-924-2992; rosasandxocolate.com; $$), try dishes like the catch of the day prepared on a fried tortilla accompanied by prickly-pear salad, or duck served with singed corn, local sausage, melon compote, and a chili and raisin sauce.

LEFT Get into the Latin American spirit with a guayabera shirt. You can have it made to order at Guayaberas Jack.

SUNDAY

10 *Riding Down the Avenue* 9 a.m.

Grab coffee at **Café la Habana** (corner of 59th and 62nd Streets; 52-999-928-6502), and then explore the **Paseo de Montejo**, lined with Beaux Arts–style mansions, most of them built with henequen money. The most stunning is the **Palacio Cantón**, which houses the **Regional Anthropology Museum** (485 Paseo de Montejo, 52-999-923-0507). The street is closed to traffic to make way for cyclists between 8 a.m. and 12:30 p.m. every Sunday. Bikes are available for 15 pesos an hour from municipal offices at the corner of 62nd and 63rd Streets or along the avenue. For a map, go to merida.gob.mx/biciruta/.

11 *Two-Step Back in Time* Noon

Mérida's old-time dancers go to the **Santa Lucía Park**, at 60th and 55th Streets, where they dance Mexican danzón and cha-cha-cha to live music under a canopy. The dancers' moves recall a bygone time of smoky dance halls, and they dress the part.

ABOVE Rosas & Xocolate, where the catch of the day is on the bill of fare and chocolate treatments are on the spa menu.

THE BASICS

Walk and take taxis, or hire a car service with a bilingual driver.

Rosas & Xocolate
480 Paseo de Montejo at 41st Street
52-999-924-2992
rosasandxocolate.com
$$
A 17-room luxury boutique hotel in two 1930s renovated mansions, decorated with the bright colors of the tropics.

Los Arcos
448B 66th Street
52-999-928-0214
losarcosmerida.com
$
Three-room bed-and-breakfast in a renovated 1890s house crammed with bric-a-brac. Breakfast in a luscious garden.

Hotel Eclipse
491 57th Street, between 58th and 60th Streets
52-999-923-1600
eclipsehotel.com.mx
$
Each of the 14 rooms is designed around a theme (lava, disco, Zen).

Mérida
Area of detail
MÉRIDA INTERNATIONAL AIRPORT
1 Hacienda Teya
MÉRIDA-CANCÚN HWY.
MEXICO
FEDERAL HIGHWAY 261
5 Hacienda Yaxcopoil
4 miles
10 kilometers
4 Wayan'e street stand
20TH ST.
COLONIA ITZIMNÁ
Mérida
ALEMÁN ST.
PASEO DE MONTEJO
9 Rosas & Xocolate
41ST ST.
Palacio Cantón/ Regional Anthropology Museum
Hennessy's Irish Pub
47TH ST.
60TH ST.
72ND ST.
Los Arcos
49TH ST.
8 Hotel Casa San Angel
Guayaberas Jack
59TH ST.
Chaya Maya 6
11 Santa Lucía Park
Café la Habana 10
Hotel Eclipse
61ST ST.
La Tercera Orden
Sorbetería Colón/ Governor's Palace
3 Piedra de Agua
65TH ST.
Plaza Grande 2
63RD ST.
Casa Montejo
66TH ST.
62ND ST.
58TH ST.
0.25 mile
0.5 kilometer
El Aguacate 7
U.S.
Gulf of Mexico
MEXICO
YUCATÁN PENINSULA
Mexico City
Mérida
Pacific Ocean

Cancún

Built from the sand up less than 50 years ago to become what is now Mexico's No. 1 travel destination, Cancún may always conjure images of spring break debauchery. But the city's 17-mile-long hotel-zone peninsula, home to most of its 150 hotels, draws everyone from middle-class families to jet-setters. The best place to feel the city's true pulse, though, is in the other Cancún: downtown, in the mostly tourist-free tangle of squares, market stalls, and shiny new developments offering their own destination-worthy nightspots, shops, and restaurants. —BY BETH GREENFIELD

FRIDAY

1 *Everybody's Promenade* 4:30 p.m.

Get a sense of perspective by strolling downtown's **Malecón Américas** (Avenida Bonampak), a three-quarter-mile paved, palm-lined promenade that hugs the shore of the Nichupte Lagoon, which separates this part of town from the hotel zone. It's part of a development that includes **Las Américas Cancún Mall**, where locals converge in Mexican chains like the Liverpool department store, and in surprisingly lovely outdoor atriums outfitted with kiddie diversions including a festive carousel. Pop in for a true taste of Cancún living.

2 *Gone the Sun* 6 p.m.

Sunset watching takes some planning here, as the magic happens lagoonside in the hotel zone, not at the beach. Snag a coveted table at **La Habichuela Sunset** (Kukulcán Boulevard, kilometer 12.6; 52-998-840-6280; lahabichuela.com), an outpost of the family-owned downtown favorite La Habichuela. Whether indoors in the sweeping, high-ceilinged, Mayan-themed dining room with its west-facing wall of glass, or outside on a stone patio leading right up to the lapping waters, you'll have a perfect view. Draw out the afterglow with a mixed seafood ceviche and a Golden Margarita, made with 1800 gold tequila and Grand Marnier.

3 *Pasta and After* 8:30 p.m.

Join in-the-know locals at the festive, quirky **Cheester** ($) for creative and reasonably priced pizzas and pastas; options include the thin-crusted salmon-topped pie and the Mama Mia, a pan of linguine, big enough for two, tossed in a cilantro cream sauce. A branch location (Las Plazas Outlet; 52-998-880-8080) has sunny yellow walls and tables topped with red-and-white-checked oilcloths, while the original spot (Calle Mazatlàn; 52-998-887-8786) has outdoor seating and graffiti-covered walls. After carb loading, walk around the **Parque de las Palapas**, the social square of downtown that jumps to life nightly. Go for the live music, arts-and-crafts tables for little ones, food vendors (don't miss the marquesitas, crispy crepes filled with sweetened Edam cheese then rolled up tight), and an infectious happy mood.

4 *Night Life, Miami-Style* 11:30 p.m.

With shimmering new condos, hotels, and shopping centers rising along its edges, **Avenida Bonampak** strives to become the Miami-style Ocean Drive of downtown, with nightspots providing a mellower grown-up answer to Cancún's party-hearty shenanigans. At the shopping center **Plaza Peninsula** (Avenida Bonampak 9; plazapeninsula.com), you can find a fresh option on a rooftop: **Barezzito Live** (52-998-889-9966, barezzitocancun.com), a popular nightclub with pop and rock shows and a breezy alfresco deck that looks toward the hotel zone twinkling in the distance.

OPPOSITE A paddleboarder on the beach at Isla Mujeres, an alternative to the congested hotel zone. Cancún is Mexico's leading travel destination.

BELOW Late night at Barezzito Live, a club with live music and a breezy outdoor deck.

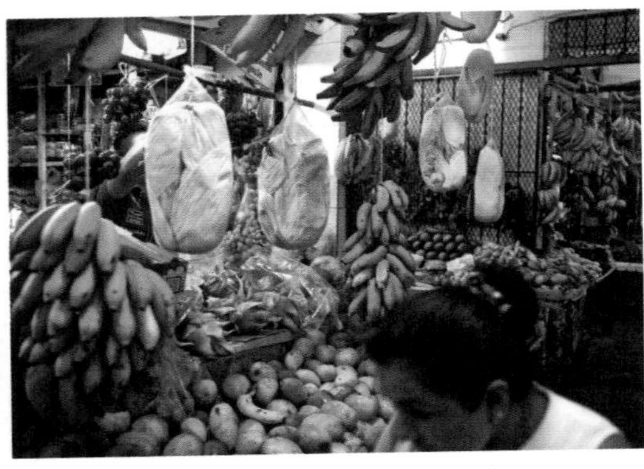

SATURDAY

5 *Take It With You* 9:30 a.m.

Hit the main downtown markets: **Mercado 23** (SM 23 west of Avenida Tulum) with staples from Oaxacan cheese and fresh papayas to plastic sandals and piñatas, and the side-by-side **Mercado 28** and **Plaza Bonita** (enter Calle Xel-ha, at Sunyaxchen, for both), where mazes of stalls are packed with a dizzying array of souvenirs — embroidered shoulder bags, hand-sewn dolls, tooled leather sandals, Mayan blouses, silver jewelry, woven sun hats. At **Pewter Mexicano** (Plaza Bonita Local del 4 al 9 "H" Planta Baja), you're spoiled for choice when it comes to sturdy yet elegant plates, bowls, picture frames, and ornate serving trays made by hand from shiny pewter.

6 *Isla Bonita* Noon

Pack a beach bag and take a day trip to **Isla Mujeres**, so named for the many images of goddesses found here by the Spanish, left by Mayans who worshiped the fertility goddess Ixchel. To get to the four-mile-long island from downtown Cancún, take a cab to Puerto Juárez or a bus marked Puerto Juárez to the Gran Puerto Cancún ferry terminal (granpuerto.com.mx), where you'll take a 15-minute fast-ferry ride on the *UltraMar*.

7 *Ceramics and Yuca Fries* 12:30 p.m.

Make a beeline to the center of town, where the main pedestrian street, Avenida Hidalgo, is packed with shops and eateries, including a wave of businesses opened by global expats. For lunch, try **Qubano** (Avenida Hidalgo, Plaza los Almendros; 52-998-214-2118) for Cuban sandwiches, fresh yuca fries, and terrific salads, or **Barlito** (Avenida Hidalgo at Abasolo; 52-998-105-2883), which has an impressive array of panini and baked goods. Then shop, hitting snappy boutiques for casual clothing or brightly colored crafts from various areas of Mexico. **Galeria L'Mento Arte** (Avenida Hidalgo, Plaza los Almendros; 52-998-158-4277) sells jewelry, wood sculptures, and ceramics from Spain, Switzerland, and beyond.

8 *Sand, Sun, Tequila* 2 p.m.

Grab a chaise and umbrella at the hip **Fenix Lounge** (52-998-274-0073; fenixisla.com) on North Beach. You can wade into the warm thigh-high water — or skim across it with a stand-up paddleboard, available by the day from the on-site **SUPIM: Stand Up Paddle Boarding Isla Mujeres** (998-108-5064, supim.com). To say adios to the sinking sun, belly up to the palapa-topped bar for a nibble from the tapas menu; try the patatas bravas, flecked with slivers of smoky guajillo peppers, and a sweet and spicy ginger margarita.

9 *Beyond Rice and Beans* 9 p.m.

Back on the mainland, treat yourself to a feast at **Chef Cristian Morales** (Avenida Xpuhil; 52-998-251-9145; chefcristianmorales.com; $$-$$$$), named for its owner, who is from Argentina. He presents his Mexican food within the chandeliered and red-drapery-bedecked dining room of his elegant home. "It's my concept to always take care of my customers," Morales says of his tableside presence. It's a noteworthy touch, especially since his food — artfully plated creations like lobster carpaccio with black tomatoes, microgreens tangled with watermelon and goat cheese, cream of corn soup dusted with

ABOVE A fruit stall at Mercado 23, a city market.

BELOW Adventurous snorkelers at Isla Mujeres.

truffled tortilla ashes, house-made huitlacoche ravioli, blue-cheese-filled chocolate fondant—takes good care of you all on its own. Try the seven-course tasting menu.

SUNDAY

10 *Barracuda!* 11:30 a.m.

As you shop around for snorkeling excursions, you'll be tempted to investigate the much touted **MUSA: Museo Subacuático de Arte** (the Underwater Museum; musacancun.com). But this sunken sculpture garden of more than 400 permanent creations by the English artist Jason deCaires Taylor is better in concept than reality because of an unfortunate thick algae bloom covering the pieces. Still, if you're curious, there's a tour that includes other stops (preferably around Manchones reef and the lighthouse in Bahía de Mujeres), where you are likely to see a worth-the-hype riot of stingrays, barracudas, sea turtles, angelfish, and Technicolor blue tangs.

11 *Last Meal* 3 p.m.

Before heading to the airport, grab some antojitos, tasty snacklike savories that make a quick meal, at **El Rincón de los Antojos** (Calle Luciernaga 356; 52-998-849-2678) in the quiet Santa Fe neighborhood (Avenida Santa Fe y Rio Amazonas, Plaza Amazonas). Gorditas (fat tortillas stuffed with cheese), pressed sandwiches called pambazo, and quesadillas en comal (grilled cheese quesadillas) make ideal send-offs.

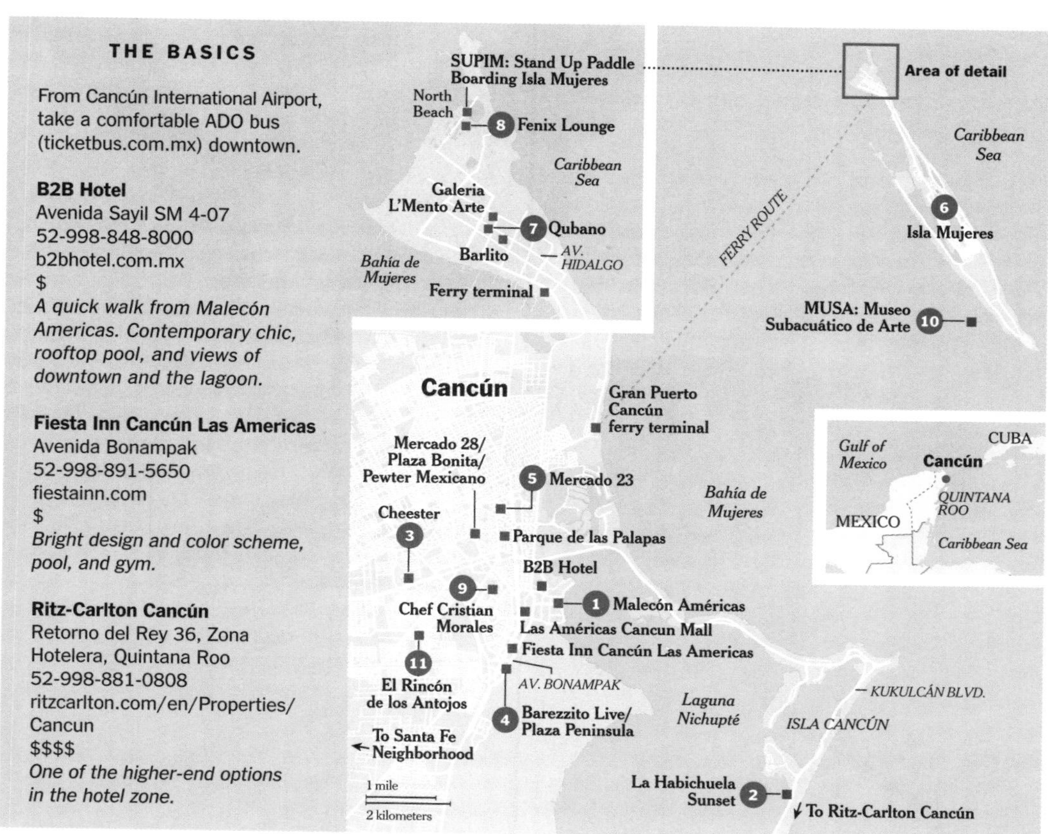

THE BASICS

From Cancún International Airport, take a comfortable ADO bus (ticketbus.com.mx) downtown.

B2B Hotel
Avenida Sayil SM 4-07
52-998-848-8000
b2bhotel.com.mx
$
A quick walk from Malecón Americas. Contemporary chic, rooftop pool, and views of downtown and the lagoon.

Fiesta Inn Cancún Las Americas
Avenida Bonampak
52-998-891-5650
fiestainn.com
$
Bright design and color scheme, pool, and gym.

Ritz-Carlton Cancún
Retorno del Rey 36, Zona Hotelera, Quintana Roo
52-998-881-0808
ritzcarlton.com/en/Properties/Cancun
$$$$
One of the higher-end options in the hotel zone.

Tulum

It is hard to know who recited the first Om or unfurled the first yoga mat upon Tulum's epic beach. But it is true that Tulum, on the southern edge of Mexico's Riviera Maya (and a healthy distance from the bunkerlike developments there) is a hot spot for yoga tourists. Don't be afraid if you don't know your downward dog from your dolphin: it's more of a yoga aesthetic that prevails here, a mood and a look. Tulum draws misty-eyed boomer professionals (heavy on the fashion and publishing industries) with fond memories of youthful forays to Thailand for Ko Phangan's full-moon festival—or maybe just those who wish they'd hit that Lonely Planet *trail when their knees could still take it. Tulum is a strip of beach and jungle peppered with stylish haute-bohemian huts. And instead of hallucinogens to bend your mind, there is stunning (and pricey) cuisine that reflects the eclectic tastes of the expats—from Italy, France, Germany, and the two coasts of the United States—who have settled here.*
— BY PENELOPE GREEN

FRIDAY

1 *Dial It Down* 4 p.m.

Be an exhibitionist and have a massage on the beach. Many hotels will offer you a spot in a palapa just above the high-tide line for Swedish or deep-tissue massage, reflexology, or another choice from the usual spa menu. (Ask when you check in.) The breeze is redress for any lingering travel fug. Afterward, you can stagger to one of the beachfront bars and have a margarita with a view.

2 *Bohemian Grove* 8 p.m.

Casa Violeta (52-1-984-879-0294; casavioletatulum.com; $$$), a thatch-roofed, palm-boughed, comely one-room restaurant, is a fine example of Tulum's architectural vernacular—think Gilligan's Island as decorated by Stevie Nicks. One evening's menu included zucchini carpaccio (shaved zucchini with olive oil, pine nuts, and Parmesan) and aqua pazzo, white fish (which unfortunately was frozen, not fresh, but was still delicious) cooked with tomatoes, capers, and olives.

SATURDAY

3 *Make Mine Mexican* 11 a.m.

You're in Mexico, so have a Mexican brunch at **Don Cafeto** (Avenida Tulum between Centauro and Orion; 52-984-871-2207; $), where the huevos rancheros and chilaquiles are homestyle and portions are big enough for a hungry conquistador. If that seems daunting, you can always concentrate on the yogurt and fruit. Take a seat on the patio.

4 *Into the Blue* 12:30 p.m.

Cool down at the **Gran Cenote**, 20 minutes from Tulum (drive through the lights on the way to Cobá; you'll see the Gran Cenote sign on your right after about 2.5 miles). Cenotes—the word evolved from the Mayan "dzonot," which means "well"—are freshwater caves and underground rivers you can snorkel or dive in. This one is rather small and sweet, featuring all the usual suspects: stalagmites, stalactites, and lots of tourists just like you.

5 *An Ancient Port* 3:30 p.m.

The **Tulum Ruins** are small compared with those at Chichén Itzá (three hours away), but you can experience them in an hour, thus scratching a cultural itch without expending too much effort. They are the haunting stone remains of an ancient Mayan port city, perched on a cliff overlooking the Caribbean.

OPPOSITE Yoga for two on the beach at Tulum.

RIGHT A swim in the Gran Cenote, a freshwater cave formed by a collapsing sinkhole and perfect for exploring.

6 *Shopping Strip* 5 p.m.

Perambulate the Tulum strip — **Avenida Tulum** (make a left on 307 from the ruins and head through the traffic lights) — with its identical concrete tchotchke stalls all selling pretty much the same things: knotted friendship bracelets, coconut pendant lights, dream catchers, painted pottery, hammocks, and those naif parchment paintings of Mexican weddings and other quotidian affairs. You know you'll be taking home at least one of these items.

7 *Lounge Culture* 6:30 p.m.

Close to souvenirland, find liquid refreshment at **Ginger** (Avenida Tulum between Jupiter and Acuario; 52-1-984-116-4033; gingertulum.com; $), a restaurant and bar that's improbably groovy-looking, like the lounge of a boutique hotel. The menu is Mexican modern. Have an appetizer along with your drink, perhaps classic guacamole or a goat-cheese tart.

8 *Strictly Italian* 8 p.m.

"It's a good story, and I have a method," Alessandro Carozzino, charmingly dictatorial, and with more body art than a Maori warrior, will tell you as he directs you on what and how to eat in his glamorous beachfront restaurant, **Posada Margherita** (52-1-984-801-8493; posadamargherita.com; $$$). Locals call him the Pasta Nazi, but you will enjoy submitting to his rules (God help you if you try to customize your order) and his extraordinary Italian meals, which begin with an earthenware platter brimming with starters like focaccia, raw cauliflower, Parmesan, and spiced olives. The menu — Alessandro's oratory — is three or four fresh pastas, fresh fish ("best fish," in Alessandro's parlance, usually cooked in seawater and tomatoes, and he's right); and dessert.

ABOVE The Tulum Ruins, remnants of a fortified port city built by the ancient Maya.

LEFT Meditating while smeared with mud and honey at one of Tulum's yoga resorts. Next step: a rinse in the sea.

SUNDAY

9 *Salutations* 10 a.m.

Just as the spring breakers must gorge on body Jello shots in nearby Cancún, it wouldn't be right to buck custom and not perform a sun salutation or two while in Tulum. **Maya Tulum** (888-515-4580; mayatulum.com), right on the beach, has a full and varied schedule, and hosts programs and retreats headed by coastal stars (your favorite New York City or Los Angeles studio's guru might be on deck). Namaste, man.

10 *Mayan Schmear* Noon

Amansala (amansalaresort.com), with its bright orange cushions and hippie-chic ethos, draws a crowd that self-identifies by its Indian caftans and decorous tattoos. Get mummified in Mayan clay here, and you'll look and feel like a participant at Burning Man (that is to say, dust-covered and vaguely renegade). You will be covered from head to toe with yellow clay and honey, and then led to the water's edge for a guided meditation. When you're dry and crumbly, hit the water: dunk, rinse, repeat.

ABOVE Shops like this open-air boutique serve a hip and affluent crowd that has discovered the laid-back, bohemian flavor of Tulum.

THE BASICS

Cancún is just a few hours by plane from New York or Los Angeles, and Tulum is about 75 miles to the south via Route 307. If you rent a car rather than relying on taxis, be extremely aware of the speed limits: they drop precipitously at each town. Tulum itself is a walking town.

Las Ranitas
Boca Paila Road, Kilometer 9
52-984-871-1090
lasranitashotel.com
$$$$
Architecturally organic, Gaudíesque cement rooms and pods that sprout from each other and are tiled and painted in fetching tropical colors.

Hotel Nueva Vida de Ramiro
Boca Paila Road, Kilometer 8.5
52-984-877-8512
tulumnv.com
$$$
Wooden beachfront bungalows on stilts, with grass-thatched roofs.

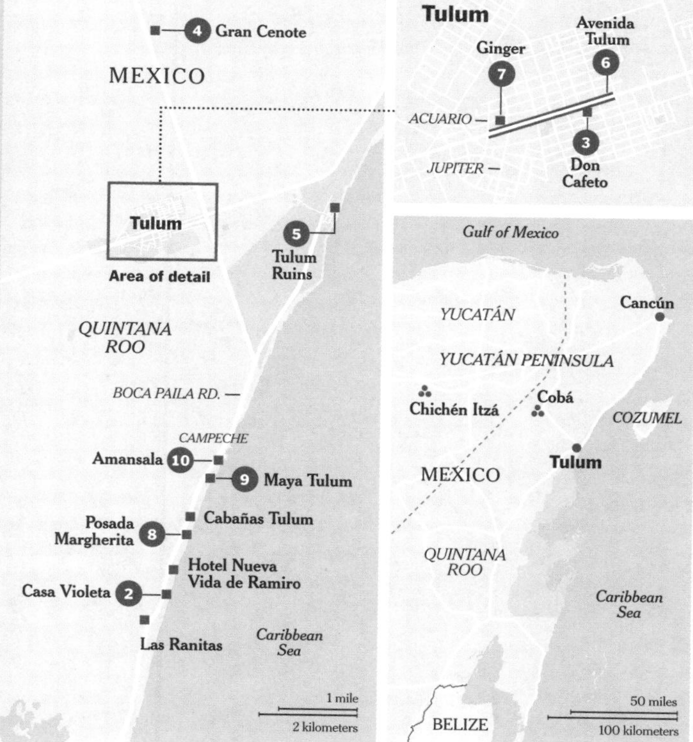

Tikal

The very word "ruin" suggests a fallen city or temple, a one-time New York or Jerusalem whose inhabitants died out, taking the life of the place with them. But Tikal, the ancient Mayan city in northern Guatemala, has the paradoxical feeling of a living ruin. Surrounded by ever-creeping vegetation and screeching wildlife, and since 1996 once again used for rituals by the Mayan people, it feels organic and strangely vivid. It is as if when the inhabitants of the city left, the jungle moved in, keeping it alive until the Mayans could return. Some parts of the city date back to 800 B.C., and at its apex it was a dominant city-state, the home of about 70,000 people spread over 25 square miles. Only six of those square miles can be visited now, all on foot. — BY ETHAN TODRAS-WHITEHILL

FRIDAY

1 *Island City* 3 p.m.

The gateway city to Tikal National Park (visitguatemala.com) is **Flores**, 40 miles away. Built on a tiny island in Lake Petén Itzá, it has its own attractions: sunsets over the water, cobblestone streets, colonial red-roofed houses, a Spanish-style church and central plaza. Take the time to stroll around and browse in the shops selling souvenirs and local handicrafts. Buy tickets through your hotel for your tour of Tikal or a minivan ride to get you there tomorrow morning.

2 *Lakeside Mojitos* 5 p.m.

For happy hour at lakeside, complete with colors of the sunset rippling over the placid water, find a seat at **Il Terrazzo** (Calle Union, Flores; 502-7867-5479; $). A tourist-heavy crowd on the open-air terrace stays convivial with pitchers of mojitos, and the appetizers include tempting bruschetta.

3 *Pepper Sauce* 7:30 p.m.

The best meal you are likely to have on a sojourn to the ancient Mayan heartland around Tikal will be at **La Luna** (Calle 30 de Junio, Flores; 502-7867-5443; $), an attractively decorated restaurant in a brightly painted blue and yellow building. Make a reservation, and try the steak in pepper sauce, or the vegetarian calabacitas (stuffed pumpkins). Relax and eat heartily. The food will not be this good tomorrow in the national park restaurants.

SATURDAY

4 *Pyramids in the Jungle* 9 a.m.

Begin your tour of Tikal in the central Great Plaza, and get oriented for wandering amid these ruins, which feel both monumental and recognizably urban. Temple I draws the eye first. A symmetrical, nine-level step pyramid on the plaza's east end, with a base of 10,000 square feet and reaching 150 feet high, it is Tikal's iconic image, the photograph on every postcard. In A.D. 784, it became the burial place of the ruler Jasaw Chan K'awiil I. To the south is the Central Acropolis, a five-story palace where the nobles might have sat to watch ceremonies or the famous Quidditch-like Mayan ball games. To the west rises Temple II, three levels and 125 feet, the burial place of Jasaw's queen, Lady Twelve Macaw. The acropolis spreads out in a complex of altars and tombs and giant stone faces constructed over millenniums, like a one-stop-shop religion superstore.

OPPOSITE A Mayan ceremony at Tikal, the city of many Guatemalan people's ancient ancestors.

RIGHT A scene in Flores, the lovely lake city that is a gateway to Tikal for travelers.

5 *Mayan World* 11 a.m.

The plaza itself is about the size of a baseball diamond, large enough to give scope but small enough so the weight of the buildings presses in. This was the center of life in the city's heyday, from the third century A.D. through the ninth. In the 1996 accords that ended the Guatemalan civil war, the Mayan people were given the right to worship in their ancient sites. Fire pits were built in the Great Plaza, and if you're lucky enough to visit on a festival day, you may see shamans igniting ritual flames and people dancing in the smoke. Pilgrims come at other times, too, more casually and often on Sunday. Look up and you'll see that each pyramid temple has a tiny room at the very top that was once used for rituals, the only indoor space on these massive structures, covered by a "roof comb" decorated with stone carvings.

6 *Sustenance* 1 p.m.

The quality of food around Tikal is generally lower than most tourists expect. In the park, unreliable refrigeration keeps food in the hotels inconsistent at best. But lunchtime must be observed. **El Comedor Tikal**, one of the very few restaurants at the park, just across from the entrance, serves no-frills grilled chicken for a modest price.

7 *The Buried City* 2 p.m.

Walking on the old Mayan footpaths outside the Great Plaza feels right, even though, between the humidity and the frequent jungle rain, you're pretty much guaranteed to be dripping at day's end. Tikal was opened to the public in 1955. Although excavation continues to this day, some buildings have been left partly or fully covered by jungle to give visitors a sense of how the site looked when it was found: scores of unnaturally symmetrical mounds, blanketed by grass and dirt. Leaving the soil in place also protects against erosion from wind and rains. A recently unearthed area is the Plaza of the Seven Temples, just southwest of the Great Plaza, with seven small but identical buildings on a right angle and three ball courts. Temple V is the most recently excavated major temple, a 150-foot behemoth that gives you no warning when you come upon it in the jungle.

8 *Under the Mosquito Net* 8 p.m.

Prices are high, by Guatemalan standards, in the hotels within the park, and the amenities are minimal. This jungle is impossibly humid and filled with mosquitoes (the driest, most comfortable weather is from December through February), and the power is likely to go off at night. But unless you stay in the park, you will not be able to see sunset and sunrise in Tikal. So book a room, and take a battery-powered fan.

SUNDAY

9 *The Din of Dawn* 8 a.m.

Dawn is not seen—it is heard. First, a roar. Then a responding roar, then another and another—not

ABOVE The view from the top of Temple V. Much of the ancient city is still buried under dirt and vegetation.

RIGHT Rickety steps to the top of Temple IV, climbed each morning by tourists who want an up-close experience of the jungle gradually coming awake at dawn.

from jaguars, but from howler monkeys, proclaiming their presence. A squeaking counterpoint begins: the raccoonlike coatimundi greeting one another as they forage for food. Finally the birds join in, toucans clicking their long bills and parrots shrieking. For your seat at this jungle symphony, join the other tourists climbing seemingly endless flights of rickety wooden steps to the top of Temple IV. In the dim light of early morning, a green sea of leaves stretches out before you, fog banks float about like dinghies, and only the resident leviathans, Temples I and III, dare to lift their stony heads above the horizon. Slowly, the city below the canopy begins to take shape.

10 *Treetop Zip* 10 a.m.

Before leaving Tikal, sample a much newer activity. **Canopy Tours Tikal** (502-5615-4988; canopytikal.com) opened a few years ago in the park and offers zip-line and suspended-bridge tours of the jungle canopy. Advertised with breathless enthusiasm ("Tarzan-style. More jungle, longer, faster!"), the zip line nonetheless lives up to its billing. The suspended bridges are less exciting, unless you encounter angry spider monkeys, unhappy with the intrusion into their treetops, that might greet you with a fusillade of nuts and twigs.

ABOVE Offerings gathered for burning at a Mayan festival on the Great Plaza. The 1996 accords ending the Guatemalan civil war gave the Maya the right to hold traditional ceremonies in their ancient sites, and many come to join in.

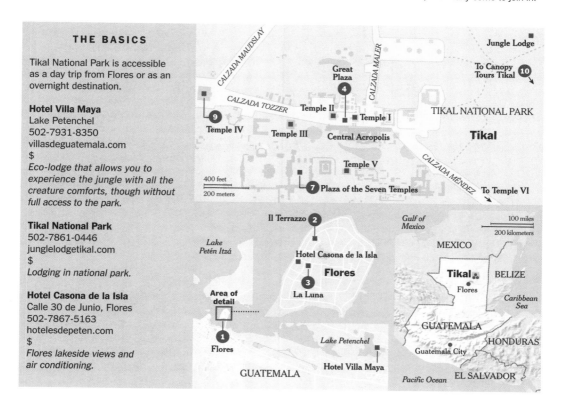

THE BASICS

Tikal National Park is accessible as a day trip from Flores or as an overnight destination.

Hotel Villa Maya
Lake Petenchel
502-7931-8350
villasdeguatemala.com
$
Eco-lodge that allows you to experience the jungle with all the creature comforts, though without full access to the park.

Tikal National Park
502-7861-0446
junglelodgetikal.com
$
Lodging in national park.

Hotel Casona de la Isla
Calle 30 de Junio, Flores
502-7867-5163
hotelesdepeten.com
$
Flores lakeside views and air conditioning.

Calzada Maudslay
Calzada Maler
Jungle Lodge
Great Plaza 4
To Canopy Tours Tikal 10
Calzada Tozzer
Temple II
Temple I
9 Temple IV
Temple III
Central Acropolis
Tikal National Park
Tikal
Calzada Méndez
Temple V
7 Plaza of the Seven Temples
To Temple VI
400 feet
200 meters
Il Terrazzo 2
Lake Petén Itzá
Hotel Casona de la Isla
Flores
3 La Luna
Area of detail
1 Flores
Lake Petenchel
Hotel Villa Maya
GUATEMALA
Gulf of Mexico
100 miles
200 kilometers
MEXICO
Tikal
Flores
BELIZE
Caribbean Sea
GUATEMALA
Guatemala City
HONDURAS
Pacific Ocean
EL SALVADOR

INRI

Managua

Founded just before the Spanish left Nicaragua in the early 19th century, Managua, the capital, is a city without a center and, bizarrely, without conventional addresses; instead there are locations, many referring to Lake Managua, which the city otherwise doesn't much celebrate. A devastating earthquake in 1972 shattered Managua's once glorious boulevards, and today architectural styles vary wildly: squat residential buildings that popped up soon after the quake, majestic neo-Classical structures that survived it, and modern styles added more recently. But despite an initial impression of chaos, you will find smooth roads and a full range of hotels and restaurants serving hearty local fare. Travelers who rush through Managua on their way to the coasts or quaint colonial towns are missing a blossoming of culture in this city that is the key to understanding modern Nicaragua.
— BY SARAH WILDMAN

FRIDAY

1 *Up, Down, Over* 3 p.m.

In what is now the **Parque Histórico Nacional Loma de Tiscapa**, set high on a hill above the Crowne Plaza Hotel, the Somoza family dictators looked down for 40 years upon the sprawling city from an enormous Moorish-style palace. The palace no longer stands (the earthquake all but destroyed it, and the revolution of 1979 finished the job) but the exquisite view remains. A massive sculptural silhouette of the guerrilla fighter Augusto Sandino, inspiration of the modern Sandinistas, stands guard over the city. Below ground, a concrete basement once used as a prison now holds a photo exhibit tracking the history of Sandino, who fought the occupation of Nicaragua by the United States military, only to be assassinated by Anastasio Somoza's men in 1934. For the adventurous, a zip-line tour begins in the park and hurtles through a cloud canopy.

OPPOSITE Inside the Nueva Catedral, a structure with multiple domes. The more conventionally designed old cathedral is an earthquake-ravaged shell.

RIGHT Clouds of sulfur obscure the low, ridge-like peaks at Parque Nacional Volcán Masaya, just outside Managua. It is Nicaragua's largest national park.

2 *Cathedrals Old and New* 4 p.m.

Venture down to old Managua to the neo-Classical **Vieja Catedral de Managua**. Rocked by 20th-century earthquakes, it is now a gorgeous shell, a paper doll of a church, with the walls standing but the ceiling almost entirely gone. Then check out the bizarre **Nueva Catedral** (Carr Masaya Zona Rosa; 505-278-4232), about a 10-minute drive away. Built by the Mexican architect Ricardo Legorreta in 1993, it looks like a place where Mad Max might worship (or, as the locals say, like 63 enormous breasts).

3 *Homestyle Cooking* 8 p.m.

For decades Nicaragua's dealmakers have dined at **Los Ranchos** (Bo Altagracia, Montoya, 3 cuadras al oeste; 505-266-0526; $) on grilled steak, pork, and guapote ("the big handsome"), a white fish pulled from Lake Nicaragua and thrown in the deep fryer. Best of all may be the appetizer of cazuela de frijoles, a thick stew of refried beans accompanied by sliced plantains and fried fresh cheese. More traditional Nicaraguan fare, like the beef stew Indio Viejo ("old Indian"), vigorón (a sort of pickled cabbage salad with boiled yuca and pork cracklings), and homey gallo pinto (fried rice and beans), is found at **La Cocina de Doña Haydée** (505-270-6100; lacocina.com.ni). Finish the evening at **Bar Cultural El Caramanchel**, "the shack" (Bolonia, Del Hospital Militar, 3 cuadras al norte, 1/2 cuadra al oeste; 505-8931-4199). Once a metal music bar, it's now a hangout for hippie do-gooders and cool Managuan 20- and 30-somethings. The music ranges from salsa to electronica to new house.

SATURDAY

4 *Snack Like a Local* 10 a.m.

Quesillos are a national treasure: a yogurtlike fresh cheese, boiled and salted, with diced vinegar-fermented onions, wrapped in a tortilla, drenched in cream, and served in a plastic bag. Managuans swear the best are at **Quesillos el-Pipe** (Kilometer 12 1/2 Carretera a Masaya; 505-8823-3556), a roadside restaurant with a shiny-clean kitchen and ingredients made on site.

5 *Market Day* 11 a.m.

The village of **Masaya** boasts markets known for bright woven hammocks, carvings, ceramics, and other crafts. Start at the **Mercado Nacional de Artesanías**, enclosed by 19th-century walls. Then head up to the **Mercado Municipal de Ernesto Fernández** at the central bus station, where locals shop. It's grittier and more crowded, with dozens of food hawkers and a row of men who patch shoes.

6 *Lava Walk* 1 p.m.

You can't go far without running into a volcano. Just outside Managua, close to Masaya village, is the 21-square-mile **Parque Nacional Volcán Masaya**. Twelve miles of flower-studded rocky hiking trails meander past petrified lava fields and an enormous crater spewing sulfur (hard hats required) perched atop a volcanic cone. Just up the highway are the white walls of the eerily beautiful **Coyotepe Fortress** on a dormant volcano. Now a park with a glorious vista, it once held political prisoners in dank, horrific cells, which can be toured.

7 *French Style* 6 p.m.

The **Alliance Française** (505-2267-2811; alianzafrancesa.org.ni) is known for its concerts, talks, and art exhibitions. **Le Bistro**, on site, offers French wines and light French fare. But if it's just cocktails you crave, the favorite watering hole of nearby Granada, **El Tercer Ojo** (the Third Eye), now has a Managua outpost in the center of town (505-2277-4487; eltercerojo.com.ni), graced by an enormous carved Buddha.

8 *Spanish Spoken* 8 p.m.

Grab a seat under the thatched roof at **Taska Kiko** (Funeria Monte de los Olives, 1 cuadra al este, Casa No. 6; 505-2270-1569; $$) where expat Spaniards serve pulpo (octopus) and excellent pargo (red snapper) grilled with garlic, olive oil, and bits of chile. After dinner, move on to **Zona Viva** outdoors at the Galerías Santo Domingo mall. It may look a bit Potemkin-like, but it's packed. There's a taquería, a steakhouse, a sushi joint, and the **Reef** (505-2276-9289), a popular surf-themed bar with D.J.'s, live music, and an outdoor deck.

SUNDAY

9 *Sunny Side Up* 10 a.m.

Claudia Chamorro's bright small eatery, **Zacate Limón** (El Tiangue, Módulo 2 del Club Terraza, 300 meters Arriba; 505-2255-0504; $), is known for breakfastlike huevos norteños, a sunny-side-up egg

ABOVE A viewpoint at the Masaya Volcano park. Twelve miles of trails meander through the park's 21-square-mile landscape of lava rock, cones, and craters. In some parts of the park, visitors are required to wear hard hats.

BELOW A plateful of tradition at La Cocina de Doña Haydée. Managua's classic foods include beef and pork, fish from Lake Managua, plantains, yuca, and beans.

over refried beans on a crispy tortilla, topped with salsa ranchera, cream, and Parmesan cheese.

10 *Trace the Revolution* Noon

The **Museo de la Victoria Sandinista** (Frente al Estadio Nacional) is an open-air museum of artifacts in the midst of city traffic. Its small but evocative collection documents the heady months that followed the Sandinista victory on July 19, 1979, and includes a downed statue of Anastasio Somoza. Take a look around and then head to the **Teatro Nacional Rubén Darío** (www.tnrubendario.gob.ni), named for the country's most famous poet. It's a 1960s-era theater showcasing classical music and traditional dance. Even if there's no event, the halls, filled with rotating exhibitions of modern Nicaraguan art, are worth a meander.

11 *Snare a Souvenir* 1 p.m.

Wind up where everyone else does: at the **Mercado Roberto Huembes**, which wraps around Managua's central bus station and is full of crafts, from crocodile and python skin bags to piñatas, as well as fruit and vegetables.

ABOVE Relaxing after dark in the pool at the InterContinental hotel. The hotel's sushi bar is a good place to glimpse Managua's upper class at play.

THE BASICS

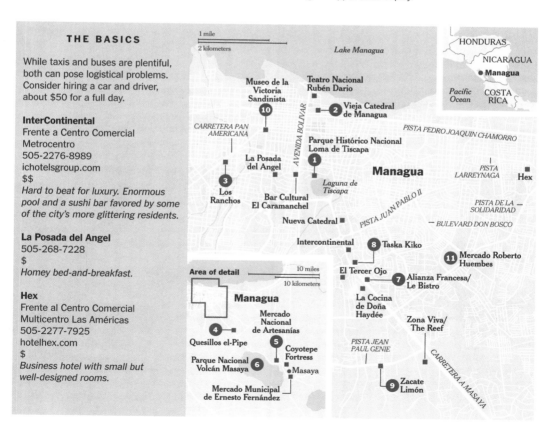

While taxis and buses are plentiful, both can pose logistical problems. Consider hiring a car and driver, about $50 for a full day.

InterContinental
Frente a Centro Comercial Metrocentro
505-2276-8989
ichotelsgroup.com
$$
Hard to beat for luxury. Enormous pool and a sushi bar favored by some of the city's more glittering residents.

La Posada del Angel
505-268-7228
$
Homey bed-and-breakfast.

Hex
Frente al Centro Comercial Multicentro Las Américas
505-2277-7925
hotelhex.com
$
Business hotel with small but well-designed rooms.

1 mile
2 kilometers
Lake Managua
Museo de la Victoria Sandinista 10
Teatro Nacional Rubén Dario
2 Vieja Catedral de Managua
CARRETERA PAN AMERICANA
AVENIDA BOLIVAR
PISTA PEDRO JOAQUIN CHAMORRO
Parque Histórico Nacional Loma de Tiscapa 1
La Posada del Angel
3 Los Ranchos
Bar Cultural El Caramanchel
Laguna de Tiscapa
Managua
PISTA LARREYNAGA
Hex
PISTA JUAN PABLO II
PISTA DE LA SOLIDARIDAD
BULEVARD DON BOSCO
Nueva Catedral
Intercontinental
8 Taska Kiko
11 Mercado Roberto Huembes
El Tercer Ojo
7 Alianza Francesa/ Le Bistro
La Cocina de Doña Haydée
Zona Viva/ The Reef
PISTA JEAN PAUL GENIE
CARRETERA A MASAYA
9 Zacate Limón
HONDURAS
NICARAGUA
Managua
Pacific Ocean
COSTA RICA
Area of detail
10 miles
10 kilometers
Managua
4 Quesillos el-Pipe
Mercado Nacional de Artesanías 5
Coyotepe Fortress
Parque Nacional Volcán Masaya 6
Masaya
Mercado Municipal de Ernesto Fernández

RASPADOS

Granada

For the tourist in search of Nicaraguan culture, new and old, Granada is a must stop. Founded in 1524 by the conquistador Francisco Hernández de Córdoba, Granada is one of the oldest colonial cities in the Americas. It was also one of the most frequently sacked, thanks to its location on Lake Nicaragua, which can be reached from the Caribbean by way of the San Juan River. But despite frequent sieges by pirates and would-be imperialists, a good portion of the city's colonial architecture remains miraculously intact. Add the narrow cobblestone streets and courtyard cafes, and it's one of Central America's loveliest spots. — BY JEFF KOYEN AND GREGORY DICUM

FRIDAY

1 *High Point* 3:30 p.m.

Like every other city in Nicaragua, Granada is in a spectacular location. A richly forested volcano, Mombacho, overlooks the city, which is perched at Lake Nicaragua's edge. A cityscape of restored colonial buildings with tile roofs comes together in the **Parque Central**, lorded over by the massive, mustard-yellow Cathedral of Granada, which shines bright in the afternoon sun. For a view that takes it all in, climb to the top of the bell tower of another landmark church, **La Merced** (Calle 14 de Septiembre). The tower's staircase is tiny and winding, but the panorama at the top is worth it.

2 *Central Park* 5 p.m.

Back at ground level, blend into the scene in the Parque Central. Horse-drawn carriages, which serve as taxis — and not just for tourists — line up here to wait for fares, and townspeople come to while away the hours. On one bright afternoon on a festival day, hot dog vendors sought refuge under the palm trees' slowly shifting shadows, their carts painted with slap-dash cartoon characters like a Mickeyesque mouse and a clumsily drawn Pokémon. Vendors had set up small folding tables to sell bracelets, rings, and other jewelry from local artisans, and families sat under spreading flame trees drinking pitaya, a cool and tangy juice of cactus fruit and lime with a stunning fuchsia color.

3 *Fish and Folk Songs* 7 p.m.

After dark, it's time to join the crowds of tourists and locals who fill the half dozen restaurants along Calle La Calzada, a bustling street filled with live guitar music and outdoor cafes that runs east from the Parque Central. At **El Tranvia** (Calle La Calzada; 505-2552-3400; hoteldario.com; $$), an elegant, colonial-style restaurant downstairs at the Hotel Dario, a button-down crowd feasts on a Latin-Caribbean menu that includes grilled fish straight from the lake and Creole-spiced steaks from local farmers. The crowd is a blend of young Nicaraguan couples enjoying the romantic atmosphere and American baby boomers poring over the list of Central and South American wines. Friday is Folk Night, when musicians play Nicaraguan music.

SATURDAY

4 *Fresh-Air Breakfast* 10 a.m.

Find your Nicaraguan morning coffee at **Lilly's** (505-2552-7226; hotelplazacolon.com/dining; $), an open-air cafe on the Parque Central next to the Hotel Plaza Colón, a restored colonial-style building with a veranda and balconies. Make it brunch with pastries or a breakfast burrito, and sit back to observe the morning activity in the plaza.

OPPOSITE The Cathedral of Granada, part of the city's rich heritage of historic architecture.

RIGHT A few of the islands of Las Isletas, an enchanting archipelago of tiny, close-set islands in Lake Nicaragua. Companies in town offer boat tours.

5 *Colonial Stroll* 11 a.m.

Take a walk around town, along streets lined with tiny clothing shops, scruffy coffee shops, and cantinas. In the open market a few blocks south of Parque Central, you can shop for fresh fruit, household goods, or live chickens. Stop in at **Mi Museo** (505 Calle Atravesada; 505-2552-7614; granadacollection.org) a small museum housing a private collection of Nicaraguan ceramics dating from 2000 B.C. to the time of the Spanish conquest.

6 *Islets in the Sun* 2 p.m.

At the foot of the city, an enchanting archipelago of tiny, close-set islands beckons. **Las Isletas** are heaps of rock that were spewed out of the volcano and are now covered in big, leafy tropical vegetation. Some are private estates, opulent getaways for captains of Nicaraguan industry. Others are modest, primordial knobs concealing rustic cottages. Take a boat trip through the islands, enjoying the beauty of the setting and the scenes that glide by: white egrets wolfing down sardines, fishermen in brightly painted rowboats. Several tour companies in town offer the boat trips; one to try is Nicaragua Adventures (Calle El Consulado in front of the Hotel Kekoldi; 505-2552-8461; nica-adventures.com).

7 *Churrasco Grill* 7 p.m.

For steak or lake fish grilled churrasco-style, take a table in the pretty courtyard at **El Zaguán** (Calle El Arsenal; 505-2552-2522; $), generally considered the city's best spot for this traditional open-fire cooking. In an old house tucked on a side street behind the cathedral, the restaurant fills up in the evenings with tourists and locals primed for an enjoyable night out.

ABOVE Horse-drawn taxis lined up for fares at the Parque Central, the main square in downtown Granada. Tourists can hire the taxis to explore a cityscape of restored colonial buildings topped by tile roofs.

LEFT Fried ripe plaintains and fried cheese, a favorite Nicaraguan snack.

8 *An Eye for Atmosphere* 10 p.m.

Stop in for a drink or dessert at **El Tercer Ojo** (Calle El Arsenal; 505-2552-6451; eltercerojo.com.ni). The name means the Third Eye, a reference to the Buddhist leanings of Glenda Castro Navarro, who runs the cafe with her husband, the French painter Jean Marc Calvet. Buddhist and Hindu icons decorate the converted colonial building, and the place is popular with bohemian expats who are increasingly drawn to Granada's low cost of living and easygoing tropical charm.

SUNDAY

9 *Rain Forest Waters* 11 a.m.

Take a taxi a few miles out of the city to **Laguna de Apoyo**, a high freshwater lake inside a volcanic crater that's surrounded by a rain forest populated by howler monkeys and toucans. Although several guesthouses have opened near its shores, the lake remains relatively undeveloped, free of unsightly hotels and resorts. The crater's rim is lightly forested: green in some spots, brown in others. And thanks to restrictions on motorized watercraft, the water is clean, clear, dark blue. Cool off with a swim at the public beach before proceeding to **Mirador Catarina**, an overlook above the lake where rustic restaurants serve empanadas and snack food like fried cheese, beans, and tostones (crispy fried plantains).

ABOVE A rain forest view above Laguna Apoyo.

THE BASICS

Fly to Managua and make an easy one-hour drive to Granada by hired car or, if you are especially adventurous, in a rental car.

Hotel Plaza Colón
Parque Central
505-2552-8489
hotelplazacolon.com
$
In Parque Central. One of the city's finest hotels, with courtyard pool, air-conditioning, and high-speed, in-room Internet access.

La Gran Francia
Esquina Sureste del Parque Central
505-2552-6000
lagranfrancia.com
$
In a carefully restored building next to the cathedral. High ceilings and imposing dark wood furniture on cool floors of old tile.

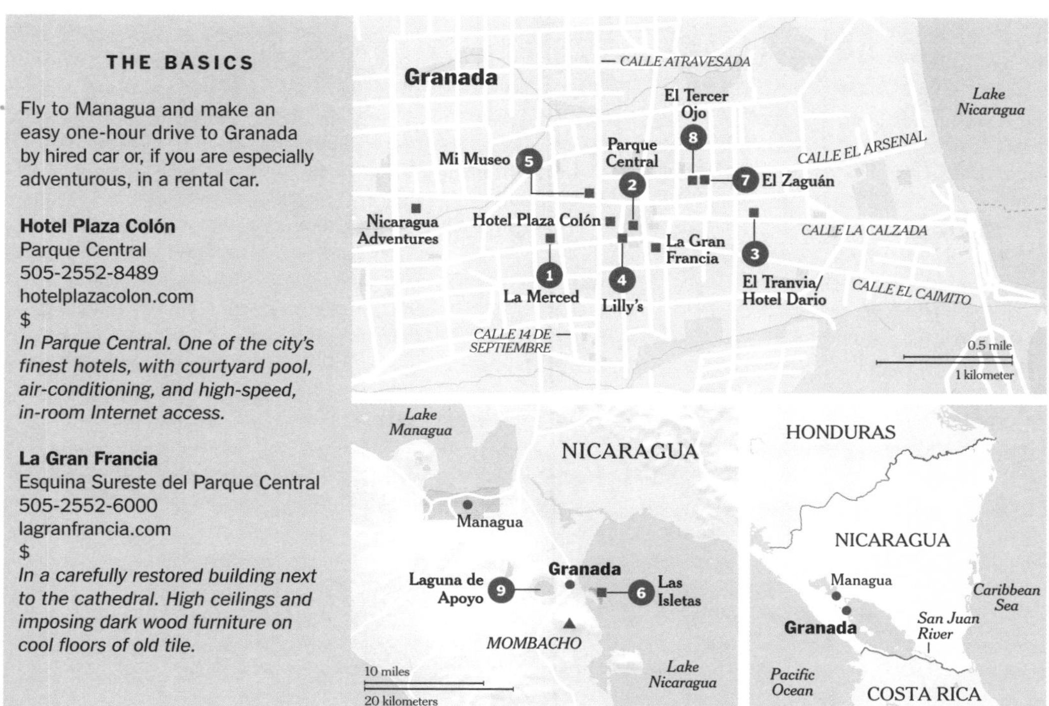

Solentiname Islands

The Solentiname Islands in Lake Nicaragua are known for two things: primitivist art and liberation theology, both thanks to the work in the 1960s of an unusual priest, poet, and political activist, Ernesto Cardenal. His landmark book The Gospel in Solentiname *is a record of his discussions with islanders about the Bible, discussions that led some islanders to insurrection against Nicaragua's infamous Somoza dictatorship. He also provided art supplies and encouraged people to paint. For half a century, Solentiname (so-LEN-te-NAH-me) artists have depicted their islands as a paradise of impossibly lush flora, exotic birds, distinctive hanging birds' nests, and people happily going about their daily lives. To visit the Solentinames is to walk into one of these paintings.* — BY STEVE BAILEY

FRIDAY

1 *In Time for the Ferry* 1 p.m.

The 36 volcanic islands of the Solentiname archipelago emerge from an isolated southeastern corner of Lake Nicaragua. Only four have full-time inhabitants, and the total population is about 750. The islands are close enough to each other for kayakers to paddle between them, but they're well out into the lake, and from the mainland most people reach them by ferry from the small city of San Carlos. Have your hotel send a local Solentinames guide to meet you in San Carlos; the ferries (505-8828-2243) run only twice a week, and you don't want to miss yours. (Arrange for a private boat to take you back to San Carlos on Sunday.) The scale of the lake, one of the world's largest, impresses itself as you make the crossing and the islands come into view. Debark at **San Fernando Island**, also known as Elvis Chavarría Island.

2 *Artists' Corridor* 3 p.m.

The Solentinames have no roads and no cars. On San Fernando, the only thoroughfare is a paved, half-mile-long lakefront walkway, the **Corredor de los Pintores**, where many island artists are based. Visitors are welcome to watch the painters at work in their homes and, of course, to buy paintings. It was in 1967 that Cardenal, a sculptor as well as a serious poet, first encouraged the islanders, mostly subsistence farmers, to express themselves through art. He gave them materials and told them to create whatever they wanted. The result was Solentiname's distinctive art style: highly detailed oil and acrylic paintings of idealized rain forests and watery scenes populated by white egrets, blue herons, and oropendolas, the black birds whose nests hang from trees like Christmas ornaments. Collectors discovered the paintings, and now vivid Solentiname Islands art can be found all over Nicaragua and has been exhibited far beyond.

3 *Paintings and Pangas* 4 p.m.

Along the walkway are the island's two inns, its one small shop, the community dock, and steps leading up to a small cooperative art gallery, the **Gallery of the Union of Painters and Artisans**, where you can see and purchase the island's signature paintings. At the eastern end is a short but steep path to **Musas** (solentiname.org/welcome/muse-musas), a small museum focusing on the cultural and natural history of the islands. As you walk along the lakeshore, you

OPPOSITE AND BELOW A Solentiname Islands painting by Rodolfo Arellano and the simple church of Father Ernesto Cardenal. When Cardenal gave art materials to the islanders in the 1960s, they responded by creating a unique and magical primitivist style.

may see fishermen paddling dugout canoes or rowing the small boats called pangas.

4 *Veranda Sunset* 6 p.m.

Even if you're not staying at **Albergue Celentiname**, the inn at the walkway's western end, you'll be welcome to enjoy the sunset on its large porch, especially if you buy a Toña beer or a bottle of wine. Ask to meet the innkeeper, Maria Guevara Silva. Back in the 1960s and '70s, she was known by the nickname Mariíta, and she is among the parishioners who relate the Beatitudes to modern life in *The Gospel in Solentiname*. She was also one of the first island painters, and her art is displayed for sale on the porch. This inn was the first in the Solentinames, built at Father Cardenal's suggestion to house international visitors who came to see his ministry.

5 *Inn for Dinner* 7 p.m.

There are no restaurants in the Solentinames, so dinner is at your hotel. There's sure to be a pot of black beans, kept warm atop a candle in a terracotta bean warmer. You may be offered a choice of grilled chicken or grilled freshwater fish, both served with white rice. A salad—eat at your own risk if the greens have been washed in unfiltered water—may complete the main course. Dessert is likely to be fresh local fruit, often bananas and mangoes.

SATURDAY

6 *Real Howlers* 9 a.m.

You could get to Mancarrón Island, the largest of the Solentinames, by paying for a ride on an islander's boat, but a better plan is to rent a kayak and go under your own power. The paddle from San Fernando takes about half an hour. En route you'll pass **Padre Island**, the only Solentiname island that has howler monkeys. Look for them in the treetops.

ABOVE San Fernando Island, one of the chain's largest.

7 *The Peasant Gospel* 9:30 a.m.

Near the dock on Mancarrón is Cardenal's **church**, an open-air stone building with window screens painted to resemble stained glass, multicolored backless benches, a simple blocklike altar, and white interior walls decorated with paintings. When he conducted services here during the dictatorship of Anastasio Somoza, Cardenal invited the islanders to interpret Biblical passages. He began taping the discussions, and they were assembled into *The Gospel in Solentiname,* which is now a touchstone text of liberation theology. "As the peasants of Solentiname got deeper and deeper into the Gospel," Cardenal wrote in the book's epilogue, "they could not help but feel united to their brother and sister peasants who were suffering persecution and terror." After the Nicaraguan revolution in 1979, Cardenal became minister of culture under the Sandinistas, a position that allowed him to help the Solentiname Islands rebuild. Eventually he became disenchanted and left the party, while remaining in Managua. Near the church is a tiny museum with some interesting pre-Columbian carvings.

8 *Island Panoramas* 10 a.m.

Two hikes attract visitors—especially the young and adventurous types—on Mancarrón. The easier one, about 90 minutes round-trip, takes you to a mirador, or scenic overlook, with broad views over the lake to the other islands. For a more strenuous adventure, take the longer hike, four hours round trip, to Piñón, the highest point in the Solentinames, with views of the entire archipelago and even a bit of Costa Rica.

9 *Balsa Birds* 2 p.m.

Mancarrón is home to an artisans' community called **El Refugio**. In homes strung along a circular paved walkway, residents carve and paint balsa wood to create inexpensive colorful fish, birds, frogs, and turtles. You can buy directly from the artists or at **Casa Taller**, a small co-op gallery. Between

El Refugio and the community dock are the tiny **Mancarrón archaeological museum** — which has pre-Columbian carvings — and a black and red memorial erected by the Sandinista government. It is dedicated to the islanders who in 1977 attacked a national guard base in San Carlos in a daring raid. They expected to be part of a nationwide revolt against the Somoza regime, but it was called off and word did not reach them. The Somoza forces took revenge by destroying most of the farms and homes on the islands.

SUNDAY

10 *Magical Forest* 10 a.m.

El Trogón trail on San Fernando Island begins at Albergue Celentiname and leads to a pre-Columbian petroglyph, a volcanic boulder carved with what appear to be intertwining snakes. The trail wends its way through a rain forest where fantastical trees drip with bromeliads and orchids and where the sound of footsteps prompts large colorful birds to take flight. After about 45 minutes you will reach the petroglyph, which is protected by a shed-like roof. You can return the way you came or ramble downhill through farms and banana trees until you reach the Corredor de los Pintores.

ABOVE The waterfront walkway on San Fernando Island.

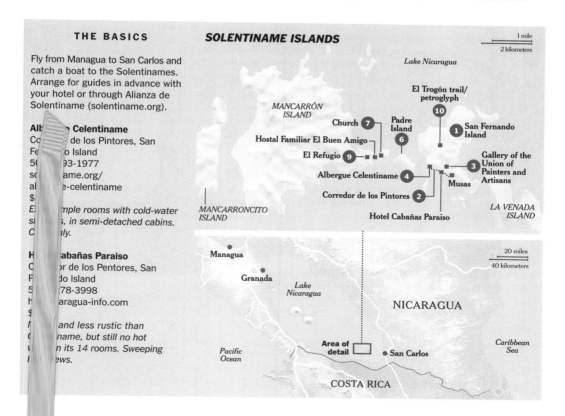

THE BASICS

Fly from Managua to San Carlos and catch a boat to the Solentinames. Arrange for guides in advance with your hotel or through Alianza de Solentiname (solentiname.org).

Alb[illegible] Celentiname
Co[illegible] de los Pintores, San
Fe[illegible]o Island
5[illegible]93-1977
s[illegible]ame.org/
al[illegible]e-celentiname
$
E[illegible]mple rooms with cold-water s[illegible], in semi-detached cabins. C[illegible]ly.

H[illegible]abañas Paraiso
C[illegible]r de los Pentores, San
F[illegible]do Island
5[illegible]78-3998
h[illegible]aragua-info.com
$
[illegible] and less rustic than [illegible]name, but still no hot [illegible]n its 14 rooms. Sweeping [illegible]ews.

SOLENTINAME ISLANDS

1 mile
2 kilometers
Lake Nicaragua
El Trogón trail/ petroglyph 10
MANCARRÓN ISLAND
Church 7
Padre Island 6
San Fernando Island 1
Hostal Familiar El Buen Amigo
El Refugio 9
Gallery of the Union of Painters and Artisans 3
Albergue Celentiname 4
Musas
Corredor de los Pintores 2
MANCARRONCITO ISLAND
Hotel Cabañas Paraiso
LA VENADA ISLAND
Managua
Granada
Lake Nicaragua
20 miles
40 kilometers
NICARAGUA
Pacific Ocean
Area of detail
San Carlos
Caribbean Sea
COSTA RICA

Southwest Nicaragua

Nicaragua is gifted with an abundance of coast, not only on the Pacific Ocean and the Caribbean Sea, but on gleaming blue lakes, including Lake Nicaragua, the 10th-largest body of fresh water in the world. In the Nicaraguan southwest, a 20-minute drive across a narrow strip of land takes a traveler from some of the best surf breaks in the world, on the Pacific Ocean, to the western shore of Lake Nicaragua. From there, a ferry cruises quickly to Ometepe, a volcanic lake island with its own gifts of tropical beauty and adventure. If anyone doubted that Nicaragua packs an amazing variety of alluring experiences into handily manageable spaces, this itinerary makes the point. —BY FREDA MOON AND GREGORY DICUM

FRIDAY

1 *Mark Twain's Gateway* Noon

In the surf-and-sand boomtown of **San Juan del Sur**, wrapped around a small Pacific Ocean bay in southwestern Nicaragua, structures line the beach in Jolly Rancher shades: apple green, lemon yellow, watermelon pink. At the northern edge of the bay, large houses climb a steep hillside toward a towering statue of Jesus. It didn't look quite this way in December 1866, when Mark Twain arrived in town by ship from San Francisco, on his way to New York. At the time—before the opening of the transcontinental railroad in 1869 and the Panama Canal in 1914—this town was the Pacific outlet for a major interoceanic route through the Americas that included a steamboat ride across Lake Nicaragua. You will probably be arriving by land, over the 80 or so miles of road from Managua, but make your way to the beach for a look around and a sense of Twain's perspective on San Juan del Sur, which he described as "a few tumble-down frame shanties—they call them hotels—nestling among green verdure and overshadowed by picturesque little hills."

2 *Surfer Heaven* 1 p.m.

The wind in southern Nicaragua almost always blows offshore, so even in the blustery season, the warm, massive waves retain good shape. As the world has learned about this gift of nature, the coast near San Juan del Sur has grown famous for surfing. Outfitters around town will happily take you out to the best beaches nearby for an afternoon of challenging the waves; water taxis leave in the morning for the closest ones, **Playa Maderas** and **Playa Majagual**. Nicaragua's best-known wave is a reef break at Popoyo, a rocky beach at the end of a dirt road about 20 miles up the coast from San Juan del Sur, but a much longer trek by road.

3 *Slacker Heaven* 2 p.m.

Not interested in grabbing a board to join the surfer dudes? Spend a lazy afternoon in town. Stroll on narrow streets, past tiled churches and Sandinista murals, and on the palm-lined promenade. At the open-air cafes on the beach, you can relax with a setup that includes a bottle of fine, clean Flor de Caña rum, a bucket of ice, a few bottles of Coke, and a dish of limes. Walk out for a dip in the warm, shallow water from time to time, and then return to the restaurant and snack on salty fried cheese and sweet maduros (fried ripe bananas) as you watch kids play soccer on the beach. Boats bob just behind the soft, curling surf. From some angles, you can catch a glimpse of the palatial beach retreats of rich Nicaraguan families who have long made San Juan a favorite getaway.

OPPOSITE A street in San Juan del Sur.

RIGHT Surfers heading home after a day on the waves of Nicaragua's southwestern coast.

4 *Dinner in a Banana Leaf* 8 p.m.

As tourism has increased here, so has the number of places to find a meal at the water's edge. At the **Bambu Beach Club** (505-2568-2101; thebambubeachclub.com; $), seasonal menus include dishes like fish filet wrapped in banana leaf and shrimp with oregano pasta, as well as sandwiches, salads, and desserts. Diners while away the evening over drinks, and D.J.'s spin. Out on the beach, couples in rainbow-hued T-shirts, arms linked at the hips, cuddle in the shadows of swaying palm trees.

SATURDAY

5 *Ocean to Lake* 9 a.m.

Take a taxi for the 12-mile ride east over the **Rivas Isthmus** through cattle country to the shore of Lake Nicaragua, over hills and past wood-frame houses with laundry hanging over the branch-and-barbed-wire fences. Twain and his fellow passengers made this leg of their trip on horse-drawn wagons, on their way to meet the steamer that would ferry them across the 40-mile-wide lake to a stern-wheeler plying a river route to the Caribbean. Twain, then 31, documented this journey in a series of letters to the *Alta California* newspaper in San Francisco that were posthumously published in 1940 as *Travels With Mr. Brown*. Your destination is San Jorge, where you can catch a ferry (ometepenicaragua.com/ferryboat.php) for Ometepe Island, several miles out into the lake.

6 *Shore to Shore* 10 a.m.

Lake Nicaragua seems majestic, especially when seen from the ferry. It's a near-mythical tropical lake, ringed by volcanoes and forest. Its waters are home to strange beasts, including freshwater sharks and sawfish, both sadly in decline; and according to legend it was an Eden that was drowned after a Romeo and Juliet tragedy. It is shallow, and turbid from volcanic ash, but it is warm and clean, and lends a freshness to the air along its shores. **Ometepe** is composed of twin volcanoes rising from the lake, and you should stake out a good place on deck to watch as they come into view. Twain described them as "two magnificent pyramids, clad in the softest and richest green, all flecked with shadow and sunshine, whose summits pierce the billowy clouds."

7 *Onto the Volcano* 11 a.m.

Ometepe feels like a magical little Hawaii—one that remains barely discovered. For an adventurous afternoon, climb up the lower slopes of **Volcán Maderas**, the more southerly of the twin peaks. The trail winds up past fields of rice and corn accessible only on foot or horseback. Then it passes pasture and enters a cloud forest where howler monkeys roar, green parrots squawk, and parakeets chirp.

8 *Chronicles in Stone* 4 p.m.

For a less arduous but still eye-opening outing, concentrate on the island's ancient past, starting with the archaeological displays at the **Museos El Ceibo** (El Sacramento; 505-8874-8076 elceibomuseos.com), and then touring to some of the fascinating stone statues and petroglyphs (ometepenicaragua.com/petroglyphs) that dot the island.

9 *Lake Fish and Lager* 7 p.m.

Nicaraguan food has a hearty simplicity: often you will be offered a local fish with tostones (medallions of fried plantains) and gallo pinto, or red beans

BELOW Volcán Maderas, the more southerly of the twin volcanic peaks of Ometepe Island in Lake Nicaragua.

and rice, washed down with a Toña, a classic tropical lager. If sauces seem sweet, it is perhaps a symptom of Nicaragua's being a sugar-producing country. Regardless, in such a small country with so much agriculture and so many climate zones, virtually everything is fresh and holds up well to simple preparation. On Ometepe, the dinner specialty is fish hauled in a few hours earlier from the lake. Try yours at the restaurant of the **Hotel Charco Verde** (505-8887-9302; charcoverde.com.ni; $).

SUNDAY

10 *Freshwater Beach* 10 a.m.

Don't leave Ometepe without putting in some beach time. One good spot is in front of the modest Hotel Villa Paraíso (if you're not staying there, ask at your hotel about alternatives). The water is warm, and wind-blown waves roll gently onto long stretches of sand. Swim or sit in a beach chair and listen to the clatter of coconut fronds. And feel sorry for Mark Twain, whose journey took him right past Ometepe, on toward the Caribbean coast and the long trip north.

OPPOSITE ABOVE The Victoriano Hotel, once a home of the widow of the dictator Antonio Somoza.

ABOVE The sheltered bay at San Juan del Sur.

HONDURAS
NICARAGUA
Managua
Area of detail
Pacific Ocean
Caribbean Sea
COSTA RICA

San Juan del Sur
Bambu Beach Club 4
Pelican Eyes Hotel & Resort
Victoriano Hotel

Lake Nicaragua
Southwest Nicaragua
Ometepe 6
Museos El Ceibo/ El Sacramento 8
10 Hotel Villa Paraíso
San Jorge
9 Hotel Charco Verde
RIVAS ISTHMUS
7 Volcán Maderas
Playa Majagual
Pacific Ocean
2 Playa Maderas
1 San Juan del Sur
Area of detail
10 miles
20 kilometers

THE BASICS

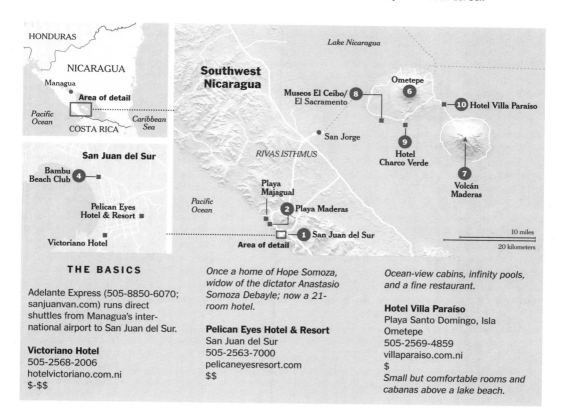

Adelante Express (505-8850-6070; sanjuanvan.com) runs direct shuttles from Managua's international airport to San Juan del Sur.

Victoriano Hotel
505-2568-2006
hotelvictoriano.com.ni
$-$$
Once a home of Hope Somoza, widow of the dictator Anastasio Somoza Debayle; now a 21-room hotel.

Pelican Eyes Hotel & Resort
San Juan del Sur
505-2563-7000
pelicaneyesresort.com
$$
Ocean-view cabins, infinity pools, and a fine restaurant.

Hotel Villa Paraíso
Playa Santo Domingo, Isla Ometepe
505-2569-4859
villaparaiso.com.ni
$
Small but comfortable rooms and cabanas above a lake beach.

Monteverde

Costa Rica is small in area and huge in variety, with beaches, volcanoes, and rain forests filled with exotic animals and plants. Twenty-seven percent of the country's land is devoted to national parks and reserves, one of the highest percentages for any country. The Monteverde Cloud Forest Reserve, in the Tilarán Mountains northwest of the capital city, San José, is a Disneyland for eco-tourists, with exotic animals and 1,000 endemic plant species — the pilgrimage to nature that many seek in the tropics. The Monteverde area is well prepared for tourism, with hotels, restaurants, shops, and art galleries. And it is close enough to the coast so that after sampling the rich primordial forest, the traveler can take a side trip to the Pacific for a visit to the beaches of Manuel Antonio National Park and a taste of what legions of visitors come to find in Costa Rica: sun, sand, and sybaritic relaxation.
— BY ETHAN TODRAS-WHITEHILL

FRIDAY

1 *The Overview* 11:30 a.m.

For a sense of perspective and a glimpse of what's around you in the cloud forest of Monteverde, start your weekend with a zip-line canopy tour. Skimming across the tops of trees several hundred feet above the lush tropical flora and fauna not only will make you feel exhilarated, but will also let you see some of the topography of this country of hillsides and ravines. Two companies that offer the tours are **Original Canopy Tour** (canopytour.com) and **Selvatura Park** (selvatura.com).

2 *Cheese Amid the Trees* 2 p.m.

It may seem odd to mix a trip to a cloud forest with a tour of a cheese factory, but then, who would have expected that the town of Monteverde was settled by Quakers from Alabama? They arrived in the 1950s, bringing their cheesemaking skills with them, and you can hear their story and tour their factory at the **Monteverde Cheese Factory** (506-2645-7090; monteverdecheesefactory.com). They will also be happy to sell you a little Gouda, some Swiss, or a milkshake. There are more opportunities for agricultural tourism at nearby coffee plantations.

3 *Jungle Night* 5:30 p.m.

You stare into the dark jungle, hoping to see something staring back. You have a flashlight, a tour guide, and high hopes of seeing big mammals like jaguars, ocelots, or tapirs. What you are more likely to find in a night tour at the **Monteverde Cloud Forest Reserve** is proof that the plants and insects can be just as captivating — and as deadly. Consider the alligator tree, whose broad, conical spikes evolved to repel the elephant-size sloths that roamed the Americas as recently as 10,000 years ago. Or the strangler fig, which begins life as an innocent epiphyte delivered into an unsuspecting tree's branches by a bird, then grows vines up to the sunlight and down to the ground, eventually enveloping the host tree and strangling it. Animals are visible in your flashlight's beam, too: orange-kneed tarantulas, raccoon-like coatis, tree frogs, porcupines — and some of them are just waking up.

4 *A Little of This and That* 9 p.m.

Refuel after your walk with drinks and tapas at **Chimera** (506-2645-6081; $$), a restaurant in the

OPPOSITE The Monteverde Cloud Forest Reserve, a Disneyland for eco-tourists. The reserve provides habitat for exotic animals and 1,000 endemic plant species.

RIGHT A resident at the Monteverde Butterfly Garden.

adjacent town of Santa Elena. Sample the small plates with a variety of well-prepared choices: salads, steak, calamari, shrimp coconut curry, plantains and other vegetarian bites, chocolate mousse. Don't linger too long. Tomorrow starts early.

SATURDAY

5 *Howlers and Hummers* 7:30 a.m.

Daytime tours in the Monteverde Reserve start soon after dawn, and you should have reservations — your hotel will make the bookings. Your guide will point out huge, leafy elephant-ear plants and miniature orchids no more than a millimeter or two across, as monkeys howl and birds twitter overhead. Sloths sleep 20 feet above ground in cradles of branches. The real joy bringers are the hummingbirds, sporadic companions within the reserve but constant ones just outside it, where sugar-water feeders are set up. The names by themselves are enough to bring smiles: green-crowned brilliants, purple-throated mountain-gems, coppery-headed emeralds, violet sabrewings. Around the feeders, the hummingbirds buzz close to tourists' ears like a squadron of tiny propeller planes.

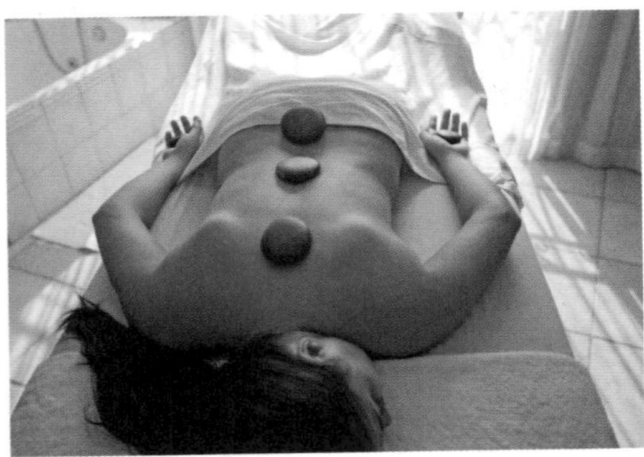

6 *Out of the Forest* 2 p.m.

Board a shuttle bus for the four- to five-hour trip from Monteverde to **Manuel Antonio** on the Pacific coast. As you leave the highlands and come down toward the water, you will find yourself in the midst of a strip of tourist restaurants, spas, and hotels — fruits of the wider world's discovery of this coast. It's a contrast from the country's quieter interior, but compared with Mexican resort towns like Cancún or Cabo San Lucas, the area still doesn't feel overdeveloped, despite the growth of a luxury

ABOVE The pool at the Hotel Parador in Manuel Antonio, a coastal town that draws travelers whose focus is sybaritic relaxation in a tropical setting.

LEFT Spas are plentiful in the beachside strip at Manuel Antonio. This one is at the Hotel Parador.

infrastructure where three decades ago there were no more than a few cheap cabanas. The most inviting lodges are on a high bluff overlooking the ocean, close to where some of the country's best beaches are preserved as parkland.

7 *Mahi-Mahi and Lime Pie* 8 p.m.

It's been a big day, so take your time over dinner at **Kapi Kapi** (Kilometer 5 on the main road; 506-2777-5049; restaurantekapikapi.com; $$), an attractive restaurant that serves dishes with both Costa Rican and Thai influences. One evening's offerings included a brilliant macadamia-crusted mahi-mahi, sugar cane–skewered prawns, and magnificently tart mandarin-lime pie.

ABOVE The beach at Manuel Antonio National Park, a welcome sight for hikers emerging from the steamy jungle.

BELOW A slide into the pool at the Si Como No Hotel.

SUNDAY

8 *Beach Sampler* 9 a.m.

Manuel Antonio National Park itself is Costa Rica's smallest and most popular national park, with about 4,000 acres and 150,000 annual visitors. Take a walk over trails upraised on concrete blocks under cotton-silk, almond, and coconut-palm trees. Then step out of the steaming jungle onto breezy

beaches—an experience that feels almost *Robinson Crusoe*-like despite the inevitable discovery that other people are already sunbathing on the sand. Sample the beaches fronting the turquoise water: Biesanz, a tiny cove where igneous boulders the size of small dogs or small trucks break up the waterline; Puerto Escondido, comfortably accessible only at low tide; Espadilla, with more wave action than the others.

9 *No Stress Allowed* 1 p.m.

This is a part of Costa Rica where luxury is part of the experience, so soothe away the rigors of the morning with a massage. If there's no spa at your hotel, book one nearby. Under the capable hands of the masseur or masseuse, let any lingering tension that you brought with you to Costa Rica seep quietly away.

ABOVE Tours of Monteverde coffee plantations like this one, part of a local cooperative, are a break from the forest.

OPPOSITE A quiet moment in the cloud forest. The placid surroundings conceal abundant and busy wildlife.

THE BASICS

From Juan Santamaría International Airport in San Jose, take a local flight to Monteverde. Shuttle Bus (shuttlebuscr.com) runs afternoon shuttles from Monteverde to Manuel Antonio. Reserve in advance.

Hotel Belmar
Monteverde
506-2645-5201
hotelbelmar.net
$$
Near jungle and gardens. Off the main road near Monteverde Reserve.

Parador Resort & Spa
Manuel Antonio
506-2777-1414
hotelparador.com
$$$
Sprawls over the tip of a bluff.

Si Como No Hotel
Manuel Antonio
506-2777-0777
sicomono.com
$$-$$$
Environmentally conscious hotel that blends with its tropical surroundings.

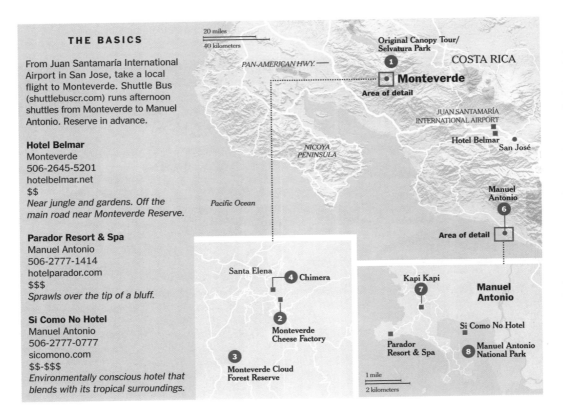

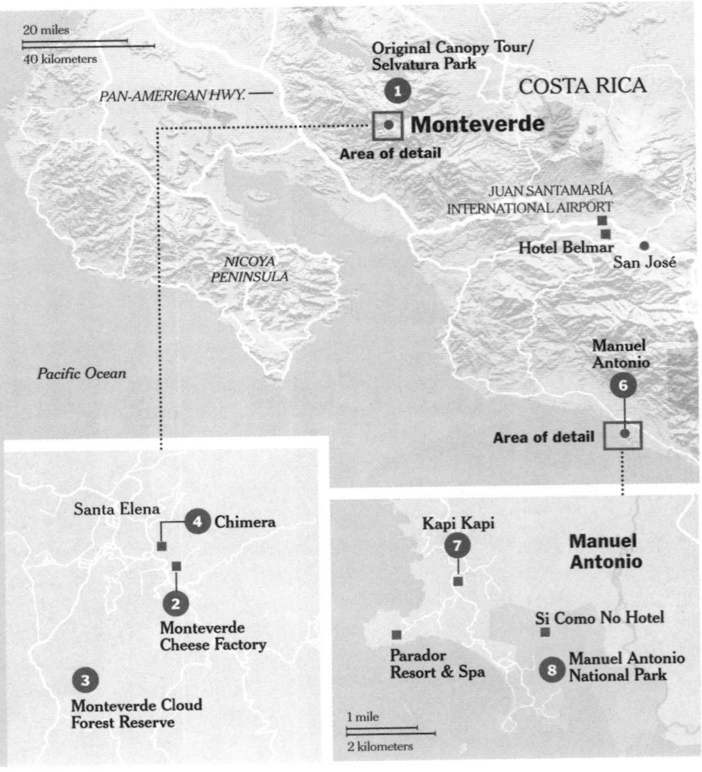

20 miles
40 kilometers
PAN-AMERICAN HWY.
1 Original Canopy Tour/ Selvatura Park
COSTA RICA
Monteverde
Area of detail
JUAN SANTAMARÍA INTERNATIONAL AIRPORT
Hotel Belmar
San José
NICOYA PENINSULA
Pacific Ocean
6 Manuel Antonio
Area of detail
Santa Elena
4 Chimera
2 Monteverde Cheese Factory
3 Monteverde Cloud Forest Reserve
7 Kapi Kapi
Manuel Antonio
Si Como No Hotel
Parador Resort & Spa
8 Manuel Antonio National Park
1 mile
2 kilometers

Puerto Viejo

From the small surfer town of Puerto Viejo de Talamanca southeast to the equally tiny Manzanillo, a wild, often overlooked eight-mile-long necklace of small sandy coves stretches out along the Caribbean coast of Costa Rica. Drive along the rutted, mostly dirt main road, and you'll find pristine beaches where palm trees bend and sway over the water's edge. Reggae music emanates from cheerful pastel-painted shacks, and an old-growth forest, often just yards from the shore, is alive with sloths, toucans, and monkeys. The area's human population is a diverse blend of Costa Ricans, English-speaking Afro-Caribbeans, indigenous Cabécar and Bribrí Indians, and plenty of expatriates, from French fashion designers to old German hippies. The laid-back, untamed vibe and a growing presence of small hotels and restaurants make this peaceful strip an attractive alternative to Cost Rica's more touristy Pacific coast.

— BY GISELA WILLIAMS

FRIDAY

1 *Wave Power* 3 p.m.

The famous wave known as **Salsa Brava** (Wild Sauce) breaks a few hundred yards from Puerto Viejo's shore, luring surfers in the know. When this Hawaiian-style barrel swells, it's considered the most powerful wave in Costa Rica. It's also an appropriate metaphor for the surrounding area: beautiful and wild. Stroll down to watch the surfers who ride the Salsa Brava, a group dominated by hardcore adrenaline addicts.

2 *Jungle Tuna* 7 p.m.

Drive a few miles down the coast to **Jungle Love** (506-2750-0162; junglelovecafe.com; $$), an intimate open-air restaurant owned by two American expatriates, Yamu Myles and Poppy Williams. Situated behind some thick foliage across the road from Playa Chiquita, at night it gives off a cozy glow. The soundtrack tends toward soul and funk tunes, while the menu offers healthy comfort food like tuna in a tamarindo sauce with wasabi and brown rice, along with wine and drinks. Myles, the chef, is a former D.J. who hails from Oakland, California.

3 *Armani Architecture* 9 p.m.

Just south of Puerto Viejo, stop in for cocktails at the **Numu Restaurant and Lounge** in the Le Caméléon boutique hotel (between Puerto Viejo and Cocles Beach; 506-2750-0501; lecameleonhotel.com), an example of the luxury trade just beginning to creep into this historically poor area. The hotel was such a departure that the president of Costa Rica came to celebrate its opening in 2009. The guest rooms are in small buildings of glass and wood, and behind the lobby, another low-lying building houses this trendy bar and restaurant. Although the complex is meant to blend into the landscape, its Miami-style design sticks out like an Armani-clad banker among barefoot bohemians.

SATURDAY

4 *Howl to the Monkeys* 9 a.m.

Drive south to Manzanillo, the gateway town to the **Gandoca-Manzanillo Wildlife Refuge**, more than 12,000 acres of jungle, beaches, and coral reefs. Make

OPPOSITE Surfing along the pristine and undeveloped coast at Puerto Viejo, on Costa Rica's Caribbean side.

RIGHT A baby sloth, part of the ecosystem that thrives in old-growth forest just off the coastal road.

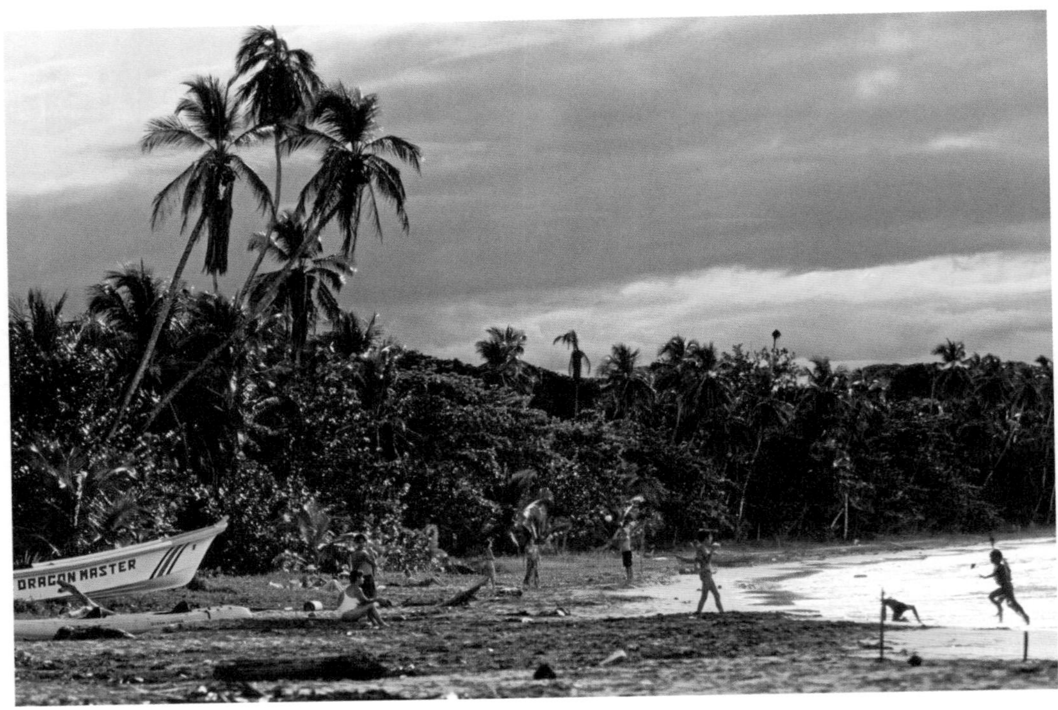

an advance reservation to explore some of this green expanse with Florentino Grenald (506-8841-2732), a charismatic local guide better known as Tino, who offers a four-hour hike into the refuge. Keeping up a lively and informative dialogue, he points out so-called Velcro plants (after their ability to stick to passers-by) and bullet ants, tracks red-eyed tree frogs, and calls out to the howler monkeys that scramble in the trees overhead. On one tour, he stopped in front of a slender gray tree covered with multiple small growths. He touched the tree and suddenly the bumps came alive. Small gray cicada-like insects flew into the air and hovered; they all had long, feathery white tails, like tiny boas.

5 *Town Center* 2 p.m.

In the town of **Manzanillo**, the tree trunks are painted with Rasta colors and many of the residents still fish for a living. The undeniable heart of Manzanillo is **Maxi's Bar and Restaurant** (506-2759-9073; $$), a slapped-together, locally owned two-story place that looks over the waves and serves as a meeting place for locals and tourists. The ceviche may be a little rubbery, but the Maxi's vibe is always authentic and sea-breeze fresh. On Saturday night the place is hopping, but it has an active daytime life, too.

ABOVE Playa Negra, a good spot for a quiet swim away from this coast's monster waves.

OPPOSITE An ocean view near the town of Manzanillo. The Gandoca-Manzanillo Wildlife Refuge protects jungle habitat, beaches, and coral reefs.

6 *Playa to Playa* 3 p.m.

Wind your way back up the coast, past a series of beaches: Playa Manzanillo (a good spot for snorkeling), Playa Grande, Playa Punta Uva, Playa Chiquita, Playa Cocles. Meander at your own speed, stopping where you can to enjoy the sand, the sea breeze, and the views. (If you'd like more beach time, you could rent a bicycle and pedal your way.)

7 *The Black Sheep* 7 p.m.

Make a reservation for dinner at **La Pecora Nera** (506-2750-0490; $$), near Playa Cocles. The name means "The Black Sheep," but the chef's family need not be ashamed of this elegant Italian restaurant. Relax over your pizza or pasta, drink a glass of wine, and chill away the rigors of the day.

SUNDAY

8 *Organic, Two Creams* 9 a.m.

Costa Rica is a coffee country, and you can get your morning wake-up close to the source at **Caribeans** (Cocles; 506-8341-2034; caribeanscr.com),

a fair-trade organic-coffee roasting business with an on-site cafe selling coffee, chocolate, and pastries. The owners, Paul Johnson and his wife, Jeanne, who are originally from Minnesota, have expanded into making chocolate and growing some of their own cacao trees. Call in advance if you'd like a chocolate factory tour. If you prefer breakfast in town, try **DreadNut Coffee** (downtown Puerto Viejo; 506-8995-6103), one of several local spots that serve Caribeans coffee.

9 *Back to the Beach* 10 a.m.

There's an exclusive beach club, with curtained day beds and bar service, at Le Caméléon, but if you're staying elsewhere, try out the more egalitarian **Playa Negra**, adjacent to Salsa Brava but with much less intimidating waves. Rent a board and take a surfing lesson, or wade in for a swim. Watch the currents.

10 *Eat Like a Costa Rican* 1 p.m.

For authentic and very inexpensive Costa Rican fare, have lunch at a soda, one of the small and unpretentious family-run restaurants that often share space with convenience stores. In Puerto Vieja, **Soda Lidia** (Avenia 67 and Calle 215; $) is a popular example of the type, serving casados (plates of meat or fish, rice and beans, and salad) and juice shakes called batidos.

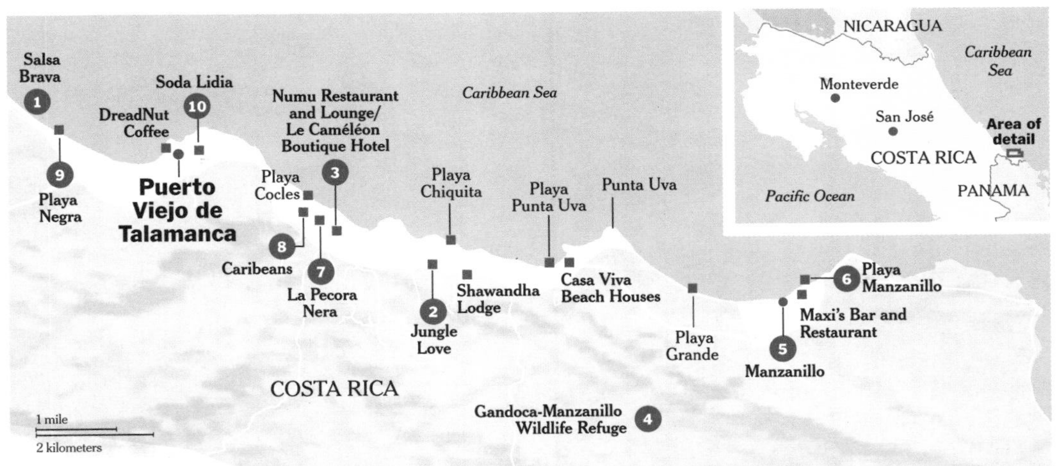

THE BASICS

Rent a four-wheel-drive vehicle at Juan Santamaría International Airport in San José for the four-hour drive to Puerto Viejo.

Le Caméléon
Between Puerto Viejo and Cocles Beach
506-2750-0501
lecameleonhotel.com
$$$$
Boutique hotel with all-white rooms and a foliage-lined pool.

Shawandha Lodge
Playa Chiquita
506-2750-0018
shawandhalodge.com
$$
Individually decorated bungalows in appealing Mayan-inspired design.

Casa Viva Beach Houses
Punta Uva
506-2750-0089
puntauva.net
$$
Private one- or two-bedroom bungalows on the beach.

Panama City

At the crossroads of two oceans and two continents, Panama City is a dynamic metropolis. That's never been truer than it is today. Everywhere in this steamy tropical town are foreign investors talking shop in upscale cafes, expat fortune-seekers toasting their fates in wine bars, cranes stalking the rooftops of a skyline that seems to grow before your eyes, and — on the downside — traffic that puts even the most congested North American city to shame. All of the building and hype has local residents calling Panama City the "Dubai of the Americas." They're only half-joking.
— BY FREDA MOON

FRIDAY

1 *Start With Ceviche* 3 p.m.

The Peruvian chef Gastón Acurio's ceviche restaurant **La Mar** (507-209-3323; lamarcebicheria.com) serves an eclectic selection of citrus-marinated fish, from the classic to the Asian-inspired perú tai. For Panamanian-style ceviche, walk the Cinta Costera — a boardwalk park that follows the waterfront — to the **Fish Market** (Panamerican Highway and Calle 15 Este), where paper cups of shrimp, octopus, corvina, or black conch ceviche are priced for snacking. Or buy fresh fish or lobster and head upstairs to the restaurant, which will cook your catch for a modest fee.

2 *The Old Neighborhood* 6 p.m.

On the cusp of revival for years, Casco Viejo, the city's formerly dilapidated colonial quarter, has turned the corner. The area still buzzes with a creative energy. But, for good or ill, the old town seems comfortable in its newly painted, nouveau riche skin. Watch the sun set with a glass of wine or a cold Panamanian cerveza while neighborhood kids play among the mangroves in front of **La Rosa de los Vientos** (Calle Octava, Casco Viejo; 507-211-2065), an Italian restaurant with waterfront seating. After sunset, explore the avant-garde scene at the neighborhood's shops and galleries.

3 *Caribbean Style* 8:30 p.m.

Manolo Caracol (Avenida Central and Calle 3, Casco Viejo; 507-228-4640; manolocaracol.net; $$) holds a mirror to the place it calls home, reflecting the country's Caribbean-infused culinary traditions with a swaggering self-confidence. Stashed away on a side street across from a ruined church, the restaurant takes its name from a famous Spanish flamenco singer. But the real star here is the restaurant's Spanish owner, Manuel Madueño, whose 10-course chef's menu offers simple preparations of seasonal ingredients, like essence-of-seafood soup or a salad of bitter lettuce and green mango.

4 *Moonlit Promenade* 10 p.m.

Walk off dinner on the promenade, where lovers canoodle in the moonlight. Then kill an hour at **DiVino Enoteca** (Avenida A and Calle 4, Casco Viejo; 507-202-6867; enotecadivino.com), an upscale wine bar with low light, Iberian ham hanging behind the counter, and black-and-white movies playing silently on a far wall. Peruse the lounge's art, food, and design books, or schmooze with the crowd of urbane expats, artists, and intellectuals.

OPPOSITE Panama City, dynamic and forthrightly international, thrusts its hotels and office towers skyward and seaward at the Pacific entrance of the Panama Canal.

RIGHT Photographs of Cuban music stars set the tone at Habana Panama, a retro dance hall and nighttime hot spot in Casco Viejo, the city's old quarter.

5 *Shake a Tail Feather* 11:30 p.m.

In keeping with its old Cuba vibe, **Habana Panama** (Calle Eloy Alfaro and Calle 12 Este, Casco Viejo; 507-212-0152; habanapanama.com) blends in with the crumbling edifices at the edge of Casco Viejo's refurbished core. Inside this retro dance hall, there's a plush red interior featuring photographs of Cuban musical greats and hours of steamy salsa dancing. With live bands, a modest cover charge, and a clientele of limited inhibitions, this is one of the hottest dance spots in town.

SATURDAY

6 *Euro-Panamanian Mix* 10 a.m.

Set up in the home of the French designer Hélène Breebaart, a former Christian Dior representative who has lived in Panama for more than 40 years, **Breebaart Boutique** (Calle Abel Bravo, Casa No. 5; Obarrio; 507-264-5937; breebaartpanama.com) produces custom clothing that puts a contemporary spin on the elaborate textile art of the country's indigenous Guna people. Embroidered napkins are easily affordable; clothing is varied in price and the production time is about a week.

7 *Gehry Tours* 1 p.m.

The new **BioMuseo** (Amador Causeway; www.biomuseopanama.org), devoted to exhibitions on natural history and science, was expected to be a multiyear building project from the start of construction in 2004, and delays stretched it out farther and farther, with opening day postponed more than once. But even unfinished, this eye-popping Frank Gehry-designed structure, combining Gehry's signature clash of angles and shapes with vivid exterior colors, quickly became an attraction just for its mind-bending appearance. You won't miss it on the skyline, but for a closer view, sign up for a tour.

8 *Fast Boat, Slow Boat* 3 p.m.

See the Panama Canal from the vantage of the ships that use it. From the Balboa Yacht Club (Amador Causeway; 507-228-5196) take the "rapida" (fast boat) to **Taboga Island**, the day trip of choice for beach-obsessed Panamanians. The 30-minute, 12-mile trip departs from the Amador Causeway, a palm-tree-lined peninsula built from canal construction debris, and makes its way through the maze of freighters lined up at the waterway's mouth. Taboga, nicknamed the Island of Flowers, is famous for its varied flora, its tan beaches, and its fish shacks. Splash in the warm Pacific before returning on the 5 p.m. slow boat, the *Calypso Queen* ferry (Isla Naos, Amador Causeway; 507-314-1730).

9 *Into the Night* 7 p.m.

La Posta (Calle Uruguay and Calle 49; 507-269-1076; lapostapanama.com; $$) is the flagship restaurant in the David Henesy–Carolina Rodriguez mini-empire. The place has an unpretentious air — fans whirring overhead, joshing guayabera-wearing servers. The fare is Caribbean-Italian, and reservations are a must on weekend nights. Try house-made pasta or seafood dishes like jumbo prawns with passion fruit. Have an after-dinner beer at **La Rana Dorada** (Via Argentina and Calle Arturo Motta, El Cangrejo; 507-269-2989), an

ABOVE The locals go to Taboga Island to enjoy its beaches. But the bonus on the boat ride over is a close-up view of ships lined up for the Panama Canal.

RIGHT Make a Sunday morning stop at Las Clementinas, in the Casco Viejo, for its fixed-price brunch.

Irish pub–style bar named for Panama's most famous endangered species, the golden frog. Later, move on to the poolside lounge on the roof of the **Manrey Hotel** (Calle Uruguay and Avenida 5a Sur, Bella Vista; 507-203-0000; manreypanama.com), where D.J.'s play on weekends.

SUNDAY

10 *Prix Fixe Brunch* 10 a.m.

For a leisurely meal, **Las Clementinas** (Avenida B and Calle 11, Casco Viejo; 507-228-7613; lasclementinas.com) has a fixed-price brunch that includes a selection of omelets, empanadas, risottos, and parfaits. There are English-language magazines to skim and a collection of New York–centric sketches and memorabilia on the bathroom walls.

11 *Green Zone* Noon

Succumb to the weekend's lazy pace with a stroll through **Parque Recreativo Omar** (Avenida Belisario Porras), a 140-acre expanse of green at the city's center. Omar is a respite from urban life and home to an impressive sculpture garden, the National Library, and a prominent statue of the Virgin Mary. There are also soccer and baseball fields, tennis courts, and a flower-lined swimming pool. Pick up a fresh fruit juice near the park's entrance. Then savor your tropical elixir beneath a towering tree on a picnic-perfect lawn.

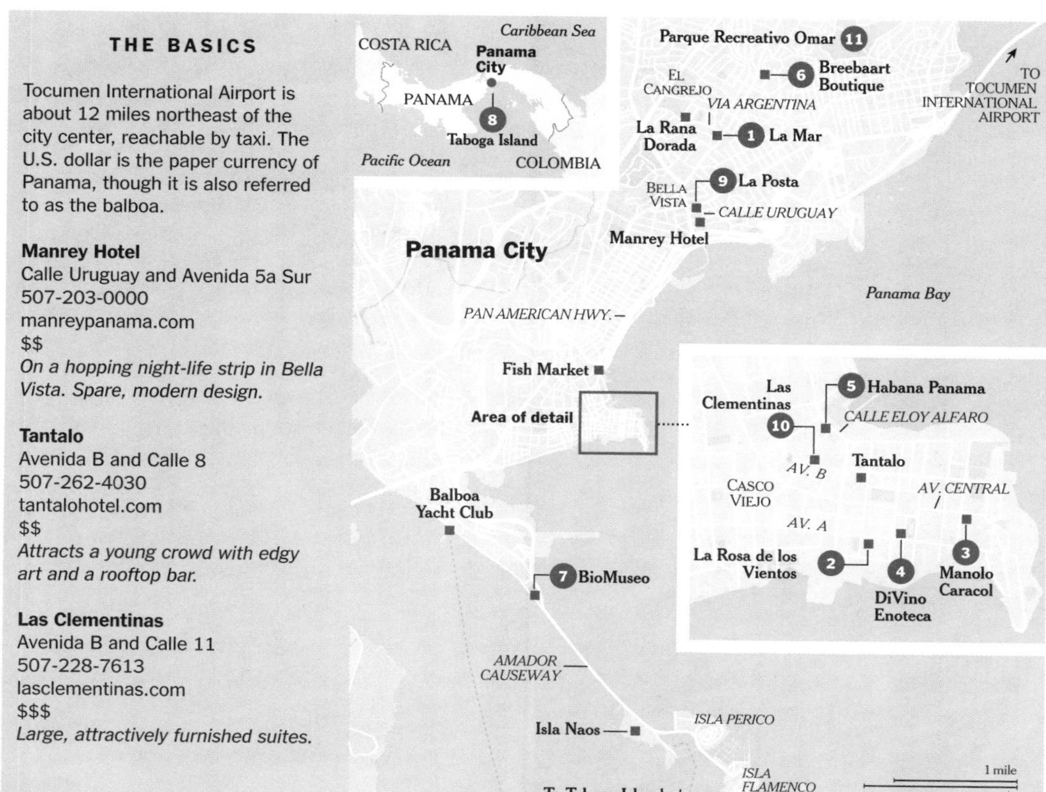

THE BASICS

Tocumen International Airport is about 12 miles northeast of the city center, reachable by taxi. The U.S. dollar is the paper currency of Panama, though it is also referred to as the balboa.

Manrey Hotel
Calle Uruguay and Avenida 5a Sur
507-203-0000
manreypanama.com
$$
On a hopping night-life strip in Bella Vista. Spare, modern design.

Tantalo
Avenida B and Calle 8
507-262-4030
tantalohotel.com
$$
Attracts a young crowd with edgy art and a rooftop bar.

Las Clementinas
Avenida B and Calle 11
507-228-7613
lasclementinas.com
$$$
Large, attractively furnished suites.

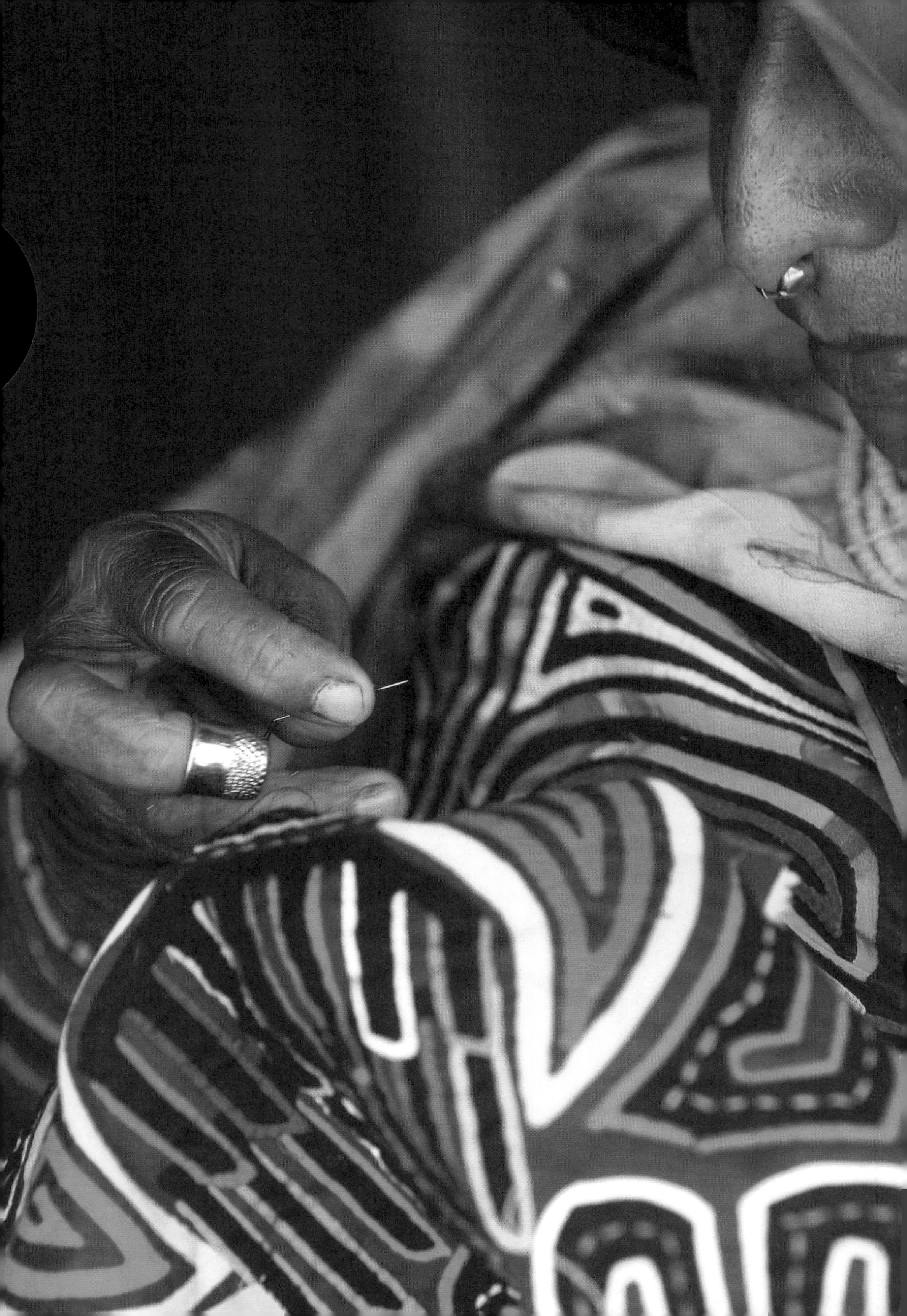

San Blas Islands

The San Blas Islands, or the Guna Yala Reserve, are a rare confluence of two types of paradise: tropical and cultural. They are a rare vacation spot that an anthropologist and a beach bum can agree on. A few ethnic groups like the Guna (formerly spelled Kuna) still exist—groups that have stuck to many of their ancient ways despite the pressures of modernity. To see most of them means traveling to remote and sometimes unsafe corners of the world like the mountains of Burma or the Congolese jungle. The home of the Guna, however, is beautiful, tranquil, and accessible—an archipelago of coral islands on Panama's Caribbean coast.

— BY ETHAN TODRAS-WHITEHILL

FRIDAY

1 *Private Island in Paradise* Noon

There are nearly 400 San Blas islands, all of them small and some of them tiny. One of the most visited is El Porvenir, and you could make that your base, but for a more relaxing experience, head for a quieter spot. In the small community of Playón Chico (which includes several islands), you might even be the only guest at your hotel. If this happens, savor it, because it means you will have a private island to yourself. **Sapibenega The Kuna Lodge**, for instance, which claimed fame in a brief television appearance as a reward vacation for cast members on the television series *Survivor*, is little more than a few cabanas on stilts over the water, bamboo-walled oases of luxury with large beds, mosquito nets, and hammocks on the porches for relaxing while you drink in the ocean view. The islands of the Guna Yala are ringed with coral reefs and are themselves made of coral, with topsoil that is shallow and low on nutrients. A small, stubbly grass covers Sapibenega's island, interrupted every so often by palm trees and protruding chunks of brain coral; it looks something like a tropical miniature-golf course.

2 *Robinson Crusoe Afternoon* 1 p.m.

San Blas hotels typically offer to take their guests island hopping. From Sapibenega, a small boat will take you to one of countless nearby islands, most of which are small, uninhabited, and perfect. One popular option is **Isla Iguana**, where for a couple of American dollars a local will scurry up a tree for a coconut, hack it open with a machete, and throw a shot of rum in it for you. Spend several hours exploring palm-overhung coves, hunting for shells on the beach, and lounging on the water's edge with hands and feet sinking into the chunky coral sands. Each island is a new castaway fantasy, the first few minutes of *The Swiss Family Robinson* or *Robinson Crusoe* before the plot thickens.

3 *The Freshest Catch* 6 p.m.

Meals in San Blas are whatever your hotel staff catches that day. Expect fish served on the bone, octopus, and langostino, a sort of crab-shrimp-lobster hybrid with soft, flavorful meat. Panama is close enough to the Equator so that the sun sets at about 6 p.m. all year, and as darkness falls, you may be dining by the light of the expected (but still pleasant) tiki torches.

SATURDAY

4 *Gossiping With Ghosts* 9 a.m.

On the sun-drenched mornings in **Playón Chico**, the graveyard is the liveliest place to be. The Guna believe that each person has a good and a bad spirit, and that after death the good spirit needs help to get to heaven. So every morning, the women of the town march up the slippery jungle slope to the hilltop graveyard to keep their deceased relatives company

OPPOSITE Needlework on one of the bright, layered molas made by the Guna people, owners of the San Blas Islands.

BELOW A thatch-roofed house on Playon Chico.

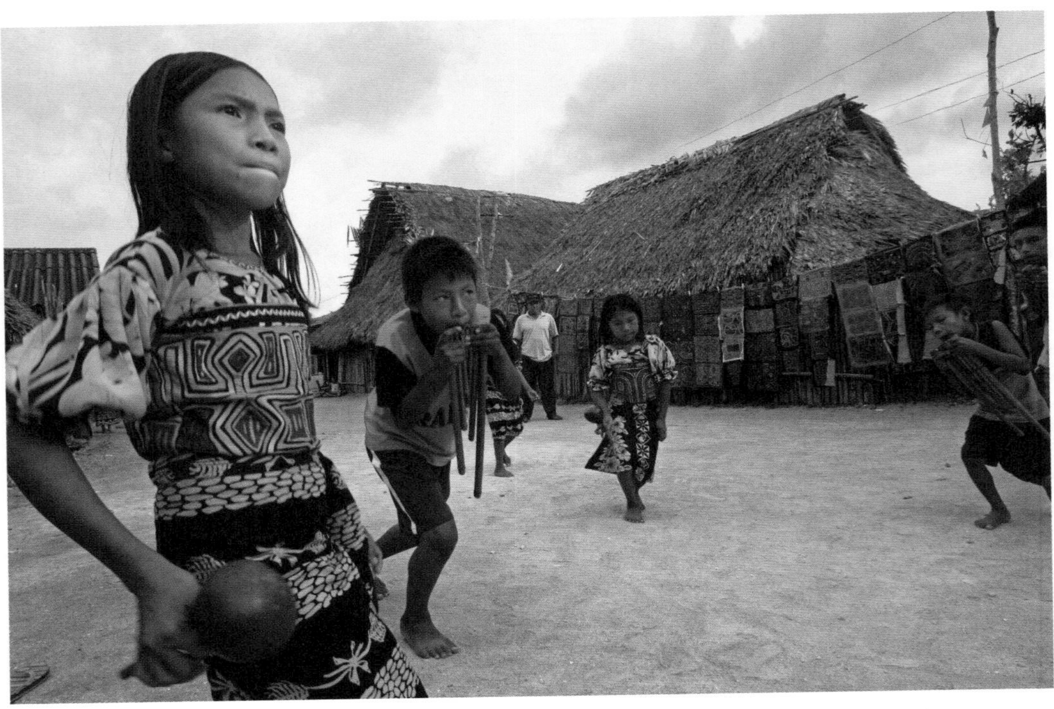

and provide a little celestial boost. Join them for the sweaty, slippery hike, and observe quietly from nearby as the women chat and laugh in their hammocks, their calves wrapped in loops of bright yellow and red beads, the family fortune adorning the older women's noses and ears in the form of thick gold loops.

5 *The Big (Small) Island* 2 p.m.

Playón Chico starts to wake up around mid-afternoon. Most islands in San Blas are in sight of the mainland, but Playón Chico is close enough to be connected by a footbridge. The town strains against its sea boundary, the outer ring of houses ending well beyond the water's edge, listing on their stilts. Playón Chico is a Pied Piper's dream, 80 percent children, because young adults generally seek their fortune elsewhere in Panama, many never to return. After returning from school across the footbridge, the children run and play in the street, some practicing their traditional dances, hopping from one foot to the other to the music of panpipes and maracas, while others fly makeshift kites constructed of garbage bags, twigs, and cassette-tape reels. Walk the streets and discover that you are the real attraction, as you gather a stream of admirers who will hold your hands, dance around you and—most remarkably for anyone who has visited poor corners of the world—rarely ask for anything but your attention.

6 *Interactions, Only $1* 3 p.m.

Guna Yala is a semi-autonomous region of Panama, and its communities are ruled by sahilas, regional chiefs who serve four-year terms and set the laws. On the issue of tourism, the sahilas try to strike a balance between benefiting and becoming dependent. So when you take photographs of some of the locals—and given their vividly patterned blouses, leathery skin, and intricate jewelry, you will want to—don't be taken aback when you are asked for a dollar per subject (not per photo). It's the official policy of the sahilas.

7 *Mad for Molas* 4 p.m.

By now you will have undoubtedly noticed the Guna molas, placemat-sized cloths made from several layers of bright fabrics and used in a variety of decorative ways, most notably as the centerpieces of the women's blouses. You will probably leave San Blas with at least one mola, if not 10 of them. The quality of a mola depends on the evenness of its stitching and the number of cloths used to make it. Those with simple geometric patterns are traditional, while the ones showing parrots and other recognizable shapes

ABOVE Practicing a traditional Guna dance.

OPPOSITE A fisherman near Playon Chico. At your hotel, expect dinner to be whatever was caught that day.

are made for tourists. One of the great pleasures of San Blas can be moving through the stretches of molas, hung like vividly colored quilts out to dry in the street, hunting for the best designs and haggling with the locals, many of whom do not even speak Spanish.

SUNDAY

8 *Swim With the Fishes* 9:30 a.m.

For a little extra money, your hotel staff will probably take you pretty much anywhere you want to go around the nearby islands, so ask for clear water and healthy coral. Borrow snorkeling equipment and have your boat drop you on one of the smaller islands, from which you can paddle languidly through an underwater garden that specializes in the pointy: staghorn corals, forbidding black sea urchins, and the slightly friendlier starfish. You may even see one of the langostinos that have been making your evenings so pleasant, but stay away from its spiky claws.

9 *Sail Away* Noon

If by now you can't bear the thought of leaving and want a different angle on the archipelago, consider signing up for a kayaking trip or even chartering a yacht. Multi-day sailing trips are one of the most popular ways to explore the Guna Yala Reserve, allowing travelers to visit even the remote, uninhabited cays like Cayos Holandéses and Coco Bandero, pristine spots with stellar reefs for snorkeling. There are no accommodations there—just waves, sand, and tropical breezes. But that's pretty much the point.

EL PORVENIR
SAN BLAS ISLANDS
2 Isla Iguana
PANAMA
1 Playón Chico/ Sapibenega The Kuna Lodge/ Yandup Island Lodge
Dolphin Lodge Panama
Caribbean Sea
10 miles
20 kilometers

COSTA RICA
Caribbean Sea
Area of detail
PANAMA
Panama City
Gulf of Panama
Pacific Ocean
COLOMBIA

THE BASICS

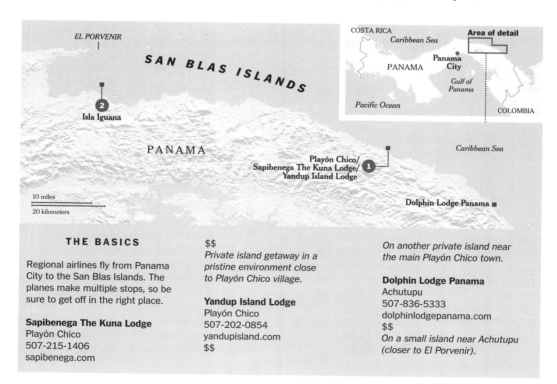

Regional airlines fly from Panama City to the San Blas Islands. The planes make multiple stops, so be sure to get off in the right place.

Sapibenega The Kuna Lodge
Playón Chico
507-215-1406
sapibenega.com
$$
Private island getaway in a pristine environment close to Playón Chico village.

Yandup Island Lodge
Playón Chico
507-202-0854
yandupisland.com
$$
On another private island near the main Playón Chico town.

Dolphin Lodge Panama
Achutupu
507-836-5333
dolphinlodgepanama.com
$$
On a small island near Achutupu (closer to El Porvenir).

Cartagena
98
Villa de Leyva
102
BOGOTÁ
92
Quito 110
116
Cuenca
LIMA
120
Salta 170
Viña del Mar
178
Mendoza
164
SANTIAGO
174

SOUTH AMERICA

SURINAME
106

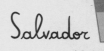

Salvador
136

Bahia
142

Brasília
146

RIO DE JANEIRO
124

SÃO PAULO 130

BUENOS AIRES
158

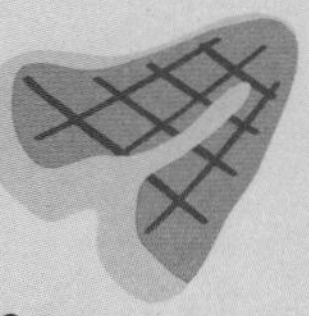

Montevideo

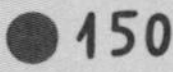

150

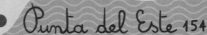

Punta del Este 154

eguros
equendama

Bogotá

There seems to be a fine line between a drug-war battlefield and a hip bohemian city, and Bogotá has crossed it. In just a few years, this subtropical metropolis has clamped down on violence, cleaned up its act, and emerged as the trendy capital of Colombian cool. With its stretches of drab urban jungle, Bogotá is not conventionally pretty and its pleasures not immediately clear. But it rewards intrepid travelers who hop across its archipelago of neighborhoods to unearth artistic and cultural gems.
— BY ANAND GIRIDHARADAS

FRIDAY

1 *Do the Macarena* 5 p.m.

Don't be embarrassed by this Macarena. It's a hilly neighborhood, lined with turquoise, pink, and orange buildings, and its air of downtown obscurity attracts a fashionable, in-the-know crowd. The trendsetters can be spotted at **Valenzuela Klenner Galería** (Carrera 5 No. 26B-26; 57-1-243-7752; vkgaleria.com), a contemporary art gallery once visited by wealthy drug lords looking for trophy paintings of lions but disappointed by its avant-garde offerings. Nearby is a local artisanal leather workshop, **Giraldo Taller Manual del Cuero** (Carrera 5 No. 26A-18; 57-1-342-8964; tallermanualdelcuero.blogspot.com), which stitches sumptuous handbags, briefcases, belts, and backpacks in every color imaginable. And next door is **Luvina** (Carrera 5 No. 26A-06; 57-1-284-4157), a bookstore where local writers hold forth with admirers.

2 *Slow-Fire Fusion* 8 p.m.

At **Matiz** (Calle 95 No. 11-17; 57-1-520-2003; matizrestaurante.com; $$), a little restaurant that continues to reinvent itself, a young Chilean chef trained in Peru and attuned to Mediterranean influences, Nicolas Quintano, applies his methods to Colombian ingredients and low-fire cooking. The tables, draped in white, are spaced far apart and illuminated by candles; the terrace is warmed by gas lamps; jazz wafts gently through the place. One day's menu included pork belly cooked for 40 hours, served with a sauce made from lulo, a tangy Colombian fruit, and hummus purée.

3 *Chicha in Candelaria* 10 p.m.

Bogotá's night life is thriving, and it can be dizzying to watch local residents argue over the coolest new spot. Things are liveliest in the fashionable Zona Rosa district, but the newer scene in **Candelaria,** a district of one- and two-story pastel-painted houses and cobblestone streets, attracts people from across Bogotá. University students toss down glasses of a potent alcoholic chicha, distilled from maize, in lively bars that spill off a graffiti-splattered square called the Chorro **de Quevado**. Once scorned as the drink of the "Indians," chicha has become increasingly popular in Colombia. Stroll until you find your spot, and give chicha a try.

SATURDAY

4 *Colombian Culture* 10 a.m.

Return to Candelaria by daylight to check out three of Bogotá's premier cultural institutions banrepcultural.org). The **Botero Museum** (Calle

OPPOSITE La Macarena, a hilly Bogotá neighborhood favored by a fashionable, in-the-know crowd.

RIGHT Giraldo Taller Manual del Cuero, an artisanal leather workshop in the Macarena, turns out well-crafted handbags, briefcases, belts, and backpacks.

11 No. 4-21; 57-1-343-1212) holds the personal art collection of the Colombian artist Fernando Botero, which includes works by Renoir, Monet, and Picasso, not to mention full-figured works by Botero himself. In a city whose colonial influences are apparent, the **Biblioteca Luis Ángel Arango** (Calle 11 No. 4-14; 57-1-343-1202; lablaa.org), just across the street, emphasizes the precolonial past and includes a collection of musical instruments indigenous to the region. Nearby, the eye-opening collection at the **Gold Museum** (Calle 16, No. 5-41; 57-1-343-2222; banrep.gov.co/museo), includes pre-Columbian gold masks and sculptures that help explain why the Spanish conquerors were so fixated on New World treasure.

5 *Octopus and Olives* 1 p.m.

Tucked inside one of Macarena's steep streets is a fashionably dim tapas restaurant called **Donostia** (Calle 29 No. 5-84; 57-1-287-3943; $$$). Install yourself in one of its multicolored leather booths and start off with soft, delicious bread and a dipping sauce of olive oil, tomato pulp, and spices. Try the chorizo santarrosano made in-house; the lemony octopus ceviche; the lamb meatballs with salsa; or the shrimp with garbanzo beans.

6 *Boutiquey Bogotá* 3 p.m.

A resurgent Bogotá is bursting with boutiques, and some of the best are in the trendy districts of Zona Rosa and Zona T. Wander and drop in at will. One to look for is **Amelia Toro** (Calle 82 No. 12-10 (57-1-610-9296; ameliatoro.com), where the Bogotá designer of the same name sells her youthful, urbane designs for women.

7 *Take It From the Top* 6 p.m.

Bogotá is a vast urban frenzy—that is, until it runs into the Andes mountains, where it quietly ends. Take the funicular up to the top of **Monserrate** (Carrera 2 este No. 21-48; 57-1-284-5700; cerromonserrate.com), and find yourself with the throbbing city on one side and the green, virtually deserted mountains on the other. Then settle in for a glass of wine at **Casa San Isidro** (Cerro de Monserrate; 57-1-281-9309; restaurantecasasanisidro.com), a mountaintop restaurant with a wide selection.

8 *Club Steak* 8:30 p.m.

Colombians love to "rumbear," a word that captures the country's culture of music and dance and late-night revelry. **Andrés D.C.** (Calle 82 No. 12-21; 57-1-863-7880; andrescarnederes.com; $$$$) is the downtown location of a beloved restaurant that offers a hard-to-explain combination of

ABOVE The pastel-painted, cobblestoned Candelaria district attracts university students and night-life seekers.

steakhouse and all-night dance party. Come early, install yourself at a table, and feast on its famous steak (the peppery lomo sellado is excellent), washed down with a customary bottle of rum. Then, as the music grows louder and the night grows older, watch the place morph into a nightclub. If you leave six hours after you came, you're leaving too early.

SUNDAY

9 *Bicycle Power* 9 a.m.

Bogotá's flirtation with a post-automobile city is being studied — and copied — by urban planners worldwide. Under a program called Ciclovia, more than 70 miles of streets in the city center are open only to bicycles on Sundays from 7 a.m. to 2 p.m. The car-free thoroughfares are spiced up with vendors selling fresh juices and snacks, as well as active offerings like aerobics and rumba lessons. Rent a beach cruiser or mountain bike from **Bogotá Bike Tours** (Carrera 3 No. 12-72; 57-312-502-0554; bogotabiketours.com) and pedal into the action.

ABOVE An alley in La Candelaria, the oldest part of Bogotá and one of its liveliest districts.

BELOW Andrés D.C. starts the evening as a steakhouse and ends the night in the wee hours as a nightclub.

10 *Fashionable Brunch* 11 a.m.

A traditional Bogotá breakfast would include steaming chicken tamales, a spiced egg soup, and hot chocolate. But as the city looks outward, brunches have gained a foothold. A fashionable

favorite is **La Bagatelle** (Carrera 11A No. 94-45 Esquina; 57-1-256-1619; bagatelle.com.co; $$), which serves fusion fare to young Colombians hiding hangovers behind sunglasses. The fried egg and chorizo comes in an iron skillet, with corn arepas.

11 *Orchids and Butterflies* 1 p.m.

Despite its congestion, Bogotá has plenty of green, with tree-lined avenues and, on its edge, the hulking Andes that always seem just around the corner. Make your way to the **Jardín Botánico José Celestino Mutis** (Calle 63 No. 68-95; 57-1-437-7060; jbb.gov.co), a 50-acre oasis of palm trees and lush tropical gardens. There is an orchid gallery and butterfly tent, a trove of cactuses, and floating lotuses the size of dinner tables. It is a quiet refuge in a city working feverishly to become part of the global bustle.

ABOVE At La Bagatelle, morning eggs and chorizo arrive at the table in an iron skillet.

OPPOSITE Amazonian plants at the Botanical Garden. Although Colombia is on the Equator and has a share of Amazon jungle, Bogotá, high in the Andes, stays cool.

5 Donostia
Giraldo Taller Manual del Cuero
Luvina
1 Valenzuela Klenner Galería
MACARENA
CALLE 19
CARRERA 7
AV. CIRCUNVALAR
CARRERA 3
CALLE 16
Gold Museum
Biblioteca Luis Ángel Árango
Hotel Ambalá
9 Bogotá Bike Tours
Hotel de la Opera
Chorro de Quevado
CANDELARIA
3
4 Botero Museum
11 Jardín Botánico José Celestino Mutis
PARQUE METROPOLITANO SIMÓN BOLÍVAR
Bogota Marriott Hotel
Area of detail
AV. CIRCUNVALAR
Bogotá
PAN-AMERICAN HWY.
Area of detail
7 Monserrate
Casa San Isidro
1 mile
2 kilometers
La Bagatelle 10
CARRERA 9
CALLE 94
CALLE 95
CALLE 93
CALLE 92
Matiz 2
CARRERA 15
CARRERA 13
CARRERA 11
8 Andrés D.C.
CALLE 90
Monte Napoleone
ZONA ROSA
CALLE 86
CALLE 82
6 Amelia Toro
Caribbean Sea
PANAMA
Atlantic Ocean
VENEZ.
Pacific Ocean
Bogotá
COLOMBIA
ECUADOR
PERU
BRAZIL

THE BASICS

Taxis are plentiful and inexpensive, but make sure the driver turns on the meter.

Bogotá Marriott
Avenida El Dorado No. 69b-53
57-1-485-1111
marriott.com
$$
Bright colors, plenty of amenities, and modern rooms.

Hotel de la Opera
Calle 10 No. 5-72
57-1-336-2066
hotelopera.com.co
$$
Book a room in the colonial wing, with its heritage furniture, tiled floors, and pastel walls.

Hotel Ambalá
Carrera 5 No. 13-46
57-1-342-6384
hotelambala.net
$
Budget choice in Candelaria, with clean and functional rooms.

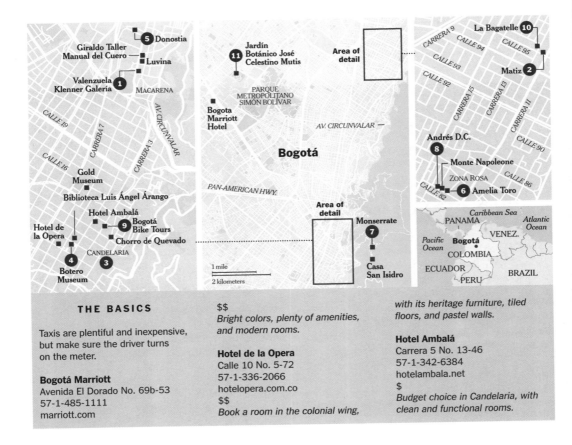

Cartagena

With its cocaine days in the past, the Colombian seaport of Cartagena has emerged as the belle of the ball. This tropical city on the Caribbean is pulsating like a salsa party, drawing well-heeled Latin Americans and European socialites to its restored colonial mansions, fancy fusion restaurants, and Old World–style plazas. Other rhythms can be heard, too. Guitar players stroll through the cobblestone alleyways. Beauty pageants and dance festivals keep the city swinging after dark. And techno dance clubs keep Cartagena's revelers up till dawn. But this stunningly beautiful city also has its quiet side. White sand beaches and crystal-clear water are just a short hop away. — BY ERIC RAYMAN

FRIDAY

1 *Storming the Walls* 4 p.m.

Cartagena is a city for walking, and its **Old City**, or Ciudad Vieja, a historic walled district, feels like a Moroccan medina, with 300-year-old Spanish colonial buildings huddled along brick streets. The palette is saturated with deep blue, dusty rose, burnt orange, and ochre. Cool sea breezes and plenty of shade make this area quite comfortable even in the 90-degree heat. To get your bearings, wave down one of the horse-powered taxis and take a 15-minute ride across the Old City. The coachman will point out sites as you clip-clop along and, at sunset, will light the candles in the headlamps.

2 *Romancing the Stones* 6 p.m.

The 400-year-old stone walls encircling the city are surprisingly well preserved and stretch for more than two miles. Walk west along the wide plaza on top of the wall; the Caribbean is on your right and the lovingly restored medieval streets on your left. For a sunset cocktail, stroll over to **Café del Mar** (Baluarte de Santo Domingo; 575-664-6513; cafedelmarcartagena.com), grab an outdoor seat near the rusty cannons that once guarded the city, and order a Colombian piña colada.

3 *Bon Appétit* 8 p.m.

Cartagena features a rich culinary palate, combining flavors and ingredients from the Caribbean, Europe, Africa, and even Asia. For a sumptuous but atypical meal, dine at **El Santísimo** (Calle del Torno 39-62; 575-660-1531; elsantisimo.com; $$$), where French-trained chefs prepare classic Colombian dishes with modern sauces. You might find prawns in a tamarind coconut sauce. Don't skip dessert or, as the menu calls it, "the Sins of the Nun."

SATURDAY

4 *Touring at Dawn* 8 a.m.

There are few reasons to leave the Old City, but one of them is to climb the massive **Castillo de San Felipe** (fortificacionesdecartagena.com), a huge fort built during the 17th and 18th centuries by the Spanish (or, more precisely, their slaves) to defend the port's terrestrial flank. The fortress contains an ant farm of hidden tunnels that you can explore with or without a guide and that adventurous kids will love. Start early before the sun broils everything, and later, when your taxi returns you to the city center, recharge with fresh fruit from one of the women peddling it there. Nearly all of it will be in nature's protective wrappers: bananas, mangos, papayas, guamas, ciruelas, coconuts, and guayabas. Try a níspero, a kiwi-shaped fruit with the texture of pear

OPPOSITE The Cartagena Cathedral, in the Old City.

BELOW A carriage ride (with serenade) in the Old City.

and the heavenly taste of chocolate, caramelized sugar, and blackberry.

5 *Art and Inquisition* 11 a.m.

Three must-see museums are within a block of one another and can be seen in under 30 minutes each. The **Museo de Arte Moderno** (Plaza San Pedro Claver) shows works by Colombian artists including bronzes by Enrique Grau. The **Gold Museum** (Plaza de Bolívar; 575-660-0778), in a Baroque mansion, exhibits jewelry that eluded the conquistadors. And, for those with strong constitutions, there's the **Palacio de la Inquisición** (Plaza de Bolívar), where rusted instruments of torture document the Catholic Church's efforts to root out heresy in the New World.

6 *What's in a Name?* 1 p.m.

The working-class neighborhood of **Getsemaní** has two popular restaurants said to be feuding over the rights to a name: **La Casa de Socorro** and **La Cocina de Socorro**. La Cocina (Carrrera 8 B 24-38; 575-660-2044) is the fancier of the two. Locals seem to prefer La Casa (Calle Larga 8E-112; 575-664-4658; restaurantelacasadesocorro.com; $$$), a diner that serves big portions of traditional Colombian seafood like shrimp and crab claws with coconut rice or red snapper with fried plantains.

7 *Try These On* 5 p.m.

Native crafts like hammocks, clay figurines, and colorfully painted wooden masks are available everywhere. For more unusual items, head to the stores along Calle Santo Domingo and Calle San Juan de Dios. Even if you're not female and size 4, check out the wares of **Silvia Tcherassi** (Calle San Juan de Dios 31-11; 575-664-9403; silviatcherassi.com), a leading fashion designer. The **Abaco** bookstore (Calle de la Iglesia 3-86; 575-664-8338; abacolibros.com) stocks photography books featuring local architecture and artisans.

8 *Wedding Crashers* 7 p.m.

One of the best times to visit the city's magnificent cathedrals is at sundown, the wedding hour. And one of the most romantic is the 16th-century **Church of San Pedro Claver** (Plaza San Pedro Claver; 575-664-7256; cartagenainfo.net/saintpeterclaver). Guests start arriving around 6 p.m., dressed in white linen or formal wear. Follow them into the cavernous nave, lighted by candles and decorated with bouquets of fragrant white flowers. The strains of "Dona Nobis Pacem" resonate along the vaulted ceiling from the choir in the balcony while the bride and groom exchange their vows.

9 *Revolution Stops Here* 9 p.m.

Beg or steal your way into **La Vitrola** (Calle Baloco No. 2-01; 575-664-8243; $$), a stylish restaurant that draws sophisticated Colombians. The atmosphere is 1940s Cuban, with high ceiling fans, mahogany wine racks, and sepia photographs of the owners'

ABOVE The skyline along Cartagena Bay is the face of modern Cartagena, today's iteration of a city founded on this harbor by the Spanish in 1533.

BELOW The Castillo de San Felipe was part of the fortifications protecting Cartagena when it was a bastion of Spanish supremacy in the New World.

friends. The food is nueva Colombiana, with specials like onion soup with pimento, cheese, and crema de leche and a baked grouper in a mango and passion fruit sauce.

10 *Cartagena Social Club* 11 p.m.

Cartagena is a musical city. In the late evening, a sea breeze freshens the air and the rhythm of trotting horses blends with the laughter and singing of friends gathered in bars, clubs, and public squares. Take a table outside **Donde Fidel** (Plaza de los Coches 32-09; 575-664-3127) and order a Club Colombia beer. Then again, to hear live music, there's no reason to leave La Vitrola, where on most nights a talented combo performs merengue, salsa, and Cuban music. Sit at the bar and sip an aguardiente, the anise-flavored drink that's a national favorite.

SUNDAY

11 *Back to Nature* 9 a.m.

Slip back into nature at **La Ciénega**, a mangrove forest that teems with wildlife. Tours on a wooden canoe are available through the Turinco tour company (575-665-6325; turincoctg.com) and meet near the Hotel Las Américas. You'll see kingfishers, herons, and pelicans on one side of your boat, and Cancún-style high rises on the other. Cross the road to **La Boquilla**, a popular beach along the sea. Find an umbrella, a hammock, and a cool coconut lemonade.

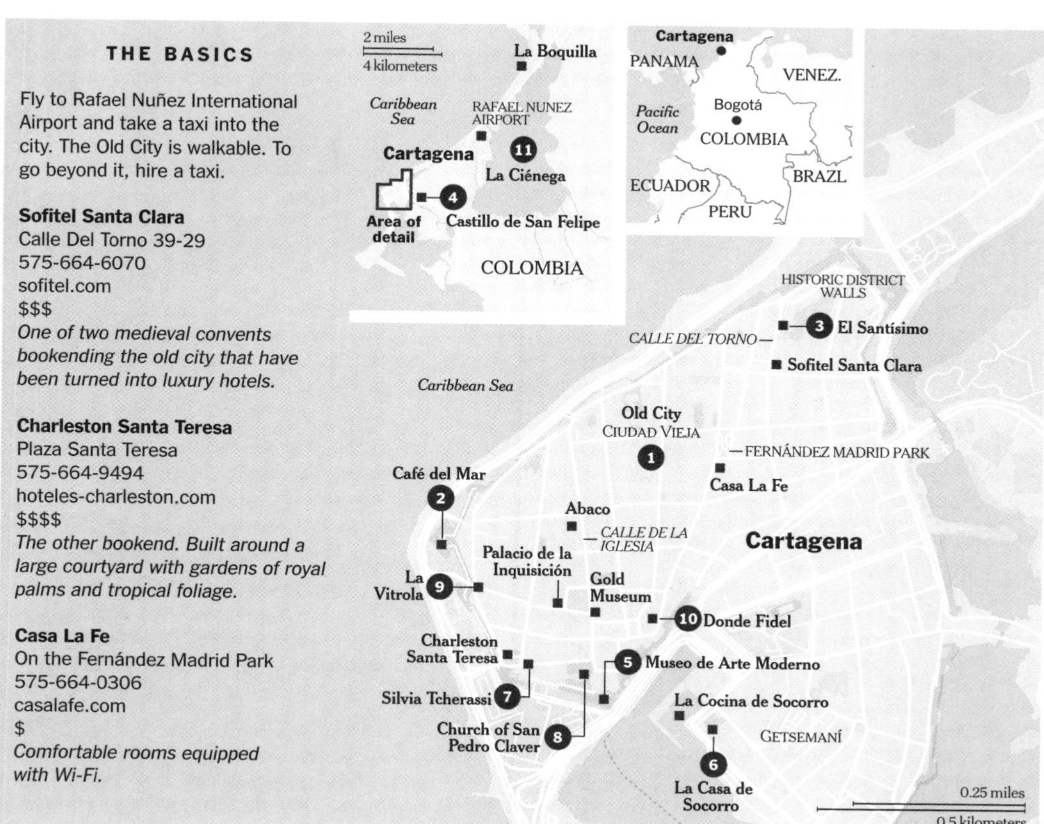

THE BASICS

Fly to Rafael Nuñez International Airport and take a taxi into the city. The Old City is walkable. To go beyond it, hire a taxi.

Sofitel Santa Clara
Calle Del Torno 39-29
575-664-6070
sofitel.com
$$$
One of two medieval convents bookending the old city that have been turned into luxury hotels.

Charleston Santa Teresa
Plaza Santa Teresa
575-664-9494
hoteles-charleston.com
$$$$
The other bookend. Built around a large courtyard with gardens of royal palms and tropical foliage.

Casa La Fe
On the Fernández Madrid Park
575-664-0306
casalafe.com
$
Comfortable rooms equipped with Wi-Fi.

Villa de Leyva

Villa de Leyva, founded in a high mountain valley in 1572, meets contemporary life on its own terms. Declared a national monument in 1954, it's an aggressively preserved colonial city, so the clank of the modern rarely interrupts the séance with the past. Long a weekend destination for Bogotá residents seeking a respite from the city, Villa de Leyva, which now has about 4,000 residents, has become a place where Europeans and the occasional American visit to see what made the Spaniards plant a flag there in the first place. — BY DAVID CARR

FRIDAY

1 *Cobblestone Amble* 3 p.m.

The tranquil comforts of Villa de Leyva, with its mix of people in traditional hats and ponchos walking next to kids in jeans and T-shirts, project an alluring kind of welcome. Spend a couple of hours ambling along the narrow streets lined by red-tile-roofed, whitewashed houses, many featuring balconies decorated with flower pots overflowing with bougainvilleas and geraniums. (Wear shoes compatible with rough cobblestones.) Abundant fossils from the surrounding area are embedded into plaster walls, and massive front doors are flanked by carvings, some alluding to the occupations of the original residents. Once you leave the old city and venture into the more modern part of town, don't be surprised to see a yard full of chickens or goats next to an Internet cafe.

2 *A Square to Reckon With* 5 p.m.

At first glance, the vast, empty expanse of the **Plaza Mayor** seem designed to reduce the onlooker to a contemplation of his or her own insignificance. One of the largest town squares in South America, the plaza lacks the decorative playfulness of so many of its smaller siblings in Colombia and elsewhere, with only the paving stones giving it shape and form. But as the sun begins to drop down toward the nearby mountains, the plaza can quietly dazzle. Step into its vastness, with an expanse framed by the remarkable colonial buildings that define its perimeter, and the centuries past seem near. By sundown, tourists—mostly Colombian—and locals begin to traverse its length to fetch dinner or take in the view. Sit on the steps of the church to watch the people and the sunset.

3 *Risotto of the Andes* 7 p.m.

Food is mostly fuel in Villa de Leyva (and everything is inexpensive by global standards), but some menus are better than others. Go Italian at **La Ricotta** (Carrrera 10, 11-49; 57-313-312-7598; villaleyvanos.com/moreno; $), for the local twist on familiar favorites like spaghetti Bolognese, four-cheese ravioli, seafood risotto, and pizzas.

4 *Rum and Warblers* 9 p.m.

Evenings here are as seductive as the sunsets, though the pleasures are low-key. Don't expect a disco, but ask around to find out where the music is playing. Or just wander until you find a patio bar where guitars and harmonicas are accompanying the European and Colombian patrons warbling Spanish love songs. Be careful if you're going back to your hotel on foot. The town's uneven streets threaten even the hardiest vehicle, and darkness and a bit too much of the local rum can make walking a hazard as well.

OPPOSITE The timeworn streetscape of Villa de Leyva.

RIGHT Spanish Colonial-era architecture on the Plaza Mayor, with an Andean backdrop.

SATURDAY

5 *How Were the Curubas?* 9 a.m.

Head to the **Plaza de Mercado**, where there is an extensive Saturday farmers' market. It's a busy place, with moments of joy bubbling through; families that truck in fruits and vegetables from the surrounding mountains sit on crates and drink perico, a tiny cup of the local coffee with a dash of milk, or shared beers. The market is also jammed with stalls selling fruits that look colorful and intriguing, but may not be immediately recognizable: lulos, staples for juicing, are abundant here, as are granadillas and curubas. At a corner of the market one Saturday, a farmer sliced open giant avocados and salted them for on-the-spot consumption.

6 *Name That Soup* 10 a.m.

You won't have to venture far for brunch. In another part of the market, huge wood-fired pots contain mysterious but tasty soups. (Near as one visitor could tell, a particularly delicious batch included the hoof of a cow.) A word about language: This isn't Spain or Mexico, so the American traveler's practice of just speaking in Spanish until you run out of palabras and then switching to English will be met with quizzical stares. The local people are incredibly friendly and helpful, but they don't hear a lot of English.

7 *Cloud Forest* 11 a.m.

Villa de Leyva also serves as a base camp for outings in the surrounding hills. For a hike above the tree line at **Iguaque Sanctuary and National Park** (parquesnacionales.gov.co), arrange a car or taxi through your hotel for the half-hour drive and a scheduled return. Plan on at least two and a half hours for the hike up, an hour at the top, and an hour-and-a-half descent. On the path upward, you might think you were walking through a butterfly exhibit, the air is so thick with fluttering wings. Over a path that is mostly roots and rocks, you will make your way from a subtropical forest up into the clouds and the lakes and past the hairy, otherworldly frailejón plants that decorate the top of the mountain. The descent has its own perils, so don't let a combination of fatigue and impatience push you faster than you should go, and leave plenty of time to be back before dark. Dress in layers; the temperature is lower at this higher altitude.

8 *Banish the Hunger* 7 p.m.

If you're hankering for a hearty dinner after all that exercise, take a table at **Carnes y Olivas** (Carrera 10, 11-155 centro; 57-310-316-9262; $$), where the steaks are huge and juicy. Or go for big portions of a different ilk at **Restaurante Savia** (Casa Quintero, Local 20; 57-8-732-1778; villaleyvanos.com/savia; $), which serves vegetarian plates, pastas, chicken, and fish, none of which will leave you hungry.

SUNDAY

9 *Sweet Eye-Opener* 10 a.m.

Villa de Leyva has an impressive array of hotels that are relatively cheap and often spectacular on a small scale — particularly the courtyards, which are so inviting and restful that it can be difficult to get

ABOVE A corner of the vast, stone-paved, and usually quiet Plaza Mayor attracts young visitors on a festival weekend.

motivated and hit the streets. One inducement to leaving the comfort behind is the local custom of coffee and pastries in small cafes. A tempting spot is **La Galleta** (Calle 13, 7-03; lagalleta.com.co), where you might try millojas, a dessert made with arequipe, a sweetened milk similar to the Portuguese dulce de leche. Another place, one where some of the fare may seem a little more traditional for breakfast, is **La Waffleria** (Carrera 9, 14-14; 57-313-412-9007; lawaffleriadelavilla.co).

10 *Back to Prehistory* 11 a.m.

El Fósil (57-310-570-0243; museoelfosil.com), a small museum about three miles from town, lives up to its name with an almost complete kronosaurus, a giant and prehistoric gatorlike marine reptile that lived in this neighborhood about 110 million years ago. Difficult as it may be to imagine, what is now the Villa de Leyva area was then a shallow sea. You can take a cab or bus to the museum. By bus, head toward Santa Sofía and tell the driver you want to get off at El Fósil; from the roadside, the museum is about a 10-minute walk.

ABOVE Local fare at a restaurant in Villa de Leyva: beans, plantains, and tiny Andean potatoes.

THE BASICS

Fly to Bogotá and take a bus for the three-and-a-half-hour trip to Villa de Leyva on mountain roads. Or work with your hotel to hire a car service.

Hotel la Posada de San Antonio
Carrera 8, 11-80
57-8-732-0538
hotellaposadadesanantonio.com
$
Just a block off the main square. Lovely courtyard, reliable restaurant.

Duruelo Inn
Carrera 3, 12-88
57-8-732-0222
duruelo.com.co
$$
In the hills, with grand vistas.

Hotel Boutique Villa Roma
Calle 8, 10-166
57-8-732-1343
hotelvillaroma.com
$
Ten-minute walk to the town center.

Suriname

Just 500,000 people live in Suriname, a small country on the northeastern shoulder of South America, but the variety of cultures they represent rivals those of much larger countries. The official language is Dutch, in a nod to Suriname's past as a colony of the Netherlands, but on the streets of Paramaribo, the Atlantic Ocean port that is the country's capital, one hears languages like Hindi and Javanese as well as Sranan Tongo, the local lingua franca, which borrows from English, Dutch, and Portuguese. Chinese characters decorate signs on casinos and corner stores. Motorized rickshaws called tuk-tuks speed past mosques and Hindu temples. Inland, Dutch vacationers explore the jungle and fish for piranha. But the capital has its own appeal, with colonial architecture, compelling history, friendly people, and phenomenal food.

— BY SIMON ROMERO AND DAVID SHAFTEL

FRIDAY

1 *This Is South America?* 3 p.m.

Paramaribo, which has about 250,000 residents, ranks as one of South America's safest and tidiest capitals, good for walking and bicycling. With its white clapboard mansions and brick buildings, it seems to belong to another continent, if not another era. Surveying the buildings surrounding **Independence Square**, one could be forgiven for mistaking the scene for a quad at a New England college, especially while taking in the red-brick Finance Ministry, complete with its Doric columns, hipped roof, dormers, and clock tower. Take a stroll through nearby streets, and more evidence of Suriname's pre-1975 colonial past comes into view: Lutheran churches, street names with vast streams of consonants and vowels (try Zwartenhovenbrugstraat on for size). Colorful minibuses gliding through the streets show a different face. Drivers adorn them with hand-painted illustrations of the religious temples, musical subcultures, outlaws, and heroes that beguile this nation, from Bollywood stars and Gandhi to Bob Marley, Malcolm X, Nelson Mandela, George W. Bush, and Saddam Hussein.

2 *Mixed Heritage* 4 p.m.

Parts of the city became a Unesco World Heritage Site in 2002, and with around 250 listed monuments, there are plenty of highlights. These include **Fort Zeelandia**, a 17th- and 18th-century cluster of buildings on the Suriname River that was the debarkation point for arriving colonials, and the white, veranda-surrounded **Presidential Palace**, which has a stately dignity that is snuffed out at sundown when it becomes irradiated by green floodlights, giving it an air of ethereal pretense. Don't miss the **Neve Shalom Synagogue**, which, completed in 1839, looks more like a cross between a North American plantation house and a small-town bank than a place of worship. Surinamers are fond of boasting of its harmonious proximity to the **Central Mosque**, whose minarets climb in stark contrast to the earthly synagogue.

3 *Weighing In* 7 p.m.

Just up the river from the historic district is a cluster of hotels, bars, and restaurants that challenge the city's post-sunset repose. The establishments surrounding the **Café-Bar 't Vat** (Kleine Waterstraat 1; hetvatsuriname.com), a beer garden-like restaurant, resemble any tourist center found on the backpacker trail, where early '90s hip-hop mingles with the smell of stale pilsner. Opt instead for a riverside sundowner and an Italian dinner at **De Waag** (Waterkant 5; 597-474-514; $$), a restaurant in the former weighing house where sugar and coffee were inventoried

OPPOSITE Dutch colonial architecture in Paramaribo, Suriname's ethnically diverse capital and major town.

RIGHT The dock at Frederiksdorp, a restored coffee plantation accessible only by boat.

before being shipped to Europe. The building's antique scales have been preserved, and the restaurant is now one of the more elegant establishments in town.

4 *Suriname Sounds* 10 p.m.

Save room for beer and a snack, and make your way to **Joke's Crab House** (108 Verlengde Gemenelandsweg; 597-532-024) to keep the night going. It's a great place to hear live jazz by local artists.

SATURDAY

5 *Jungle Wares* 10 a.m.

At the markets along the elegant **Waterkant**, or Waterfront, dozens of stalls offer a window into Suriname's astonishing diversity. At the Freedom Market, Maroons, descendants of slaves who escaped into the jungles, and Arawaks, one of the country's indigenous tribes, sell all kinds of goods from the country's interior—from bush meat to live monkeys and bottles of casiri, a brew made from cassava. At the adjacent Central Market, there are a variety of stalls selling knickknacks, fresh produce, and ready-made delights like curry egg and sardines with onions and peppers. One day a stall specializing in Javanese cuisine was offering rice cubes stewed in coconut, brown sugar, and spicy pepper and served in a banana leaf. Other vendors sell pirated Bollywood movies, and Rastafarians offer reggae CDs and tapestries of the Ethiopian emperor Haile Selassie.

6 *Lunch in a Warung* Noon

Explore **Blauwgrond**, an ethnically mixed district famed for its great restaurants and for the most part calmer than other areas favored by tourists here (mostly Dutch travelers). Blauwgrond is renowned for its Javanese restaurants called warungs. Look for drinks made of lemongrass, milk, and coconut, and order saoto, a soup of fried potato, bean sprouts, egg, chicken, and spices with astounding potency. Another local treat to seek out is the West Indian fast food at several **Roopram Roti** shops around town.

7 *New Amsterdam South* 2 p.m.

Suriname's colorful history owes something to an island called Manhattan. Learn how at **Fort Nieuw Amsterdam** (597-322-225; fortnieuwamsterdam.com). Exhibits at the complex explain that in the 17th century the Dutch traded what later became New York City to the English in return for Suriname, with its lucrative sugar and coffee plantations. For decades, it seemed as if the Dutch had gotten the better end of the deal. Soon, though, they were under attack from escaped slaves who had organized into a formidable opposition, mounting raids on plantations. Built as a bastion to ward off the attackers, Fort Nieuw Amsterdam now stands as testament to the resilience of the rebellious slaves and their descendants, with whom the Dutch were ultimately forced to sign peace treaties. After slavery ended in 1863, Javanese, East Indian, and some Chinese laborers were brought in to fill the labor shortage, ultimately producing the cultural mash-up that is today's Suriname.

8 *African Plates* 7 p.m.

At the open-air **Log House** (Anton Drachtenweg 134; 597-840-3408; theloghouserestaurant.net; $$$) on the Suriname River, Kenyan and Swahili dishes are

ABOVE Dutch colonial architecture in Paramaribo.

BELOW A Hindu festival at a Paramaribo temple. Suriname is proud of its ethnic diversity, a legacy of colonialism.

served alongside European and Caribbean cuisine (the fish dishes stand out), and the bar serves up wines and fruity cocktails. The restaurant has a commitment to nurturing local jazz; call to see if there are any performances on the schedule.

SUNDAY

9 *Spice Brunch* 10 a.m.

Spice Quest (107 Nassylaan, Paramaribo; 597-520-747; $$) serves excellent Surinamese fusion cuisine and Japanese food under the direction of the chef and owner Patrick Woei. On Sunday it's open for brunch. The specialty is dim sum, but lovers of pancakes and eggs will find there are dishes for them as well.

10 *That Asian Feeling* 11 a.m.

Have your hotel or a local tour company arrange a trip for you to nearby plantation country. Once outside the city, you will be struck by the similarities between coastal Suriname and Southeast Asia. The connection isn't just topographical, in the muddy rivers and lowland farming, but also cultural. Your tour may take you to **Frederiksdorp** (597-680-4403; frederiksdorp.com), a faithfully restored coffee plantation, now primarily a hotel and restaurant, on the Commewijne River, which joins the Suriname River near the sea. Frederiksdorp is reachable only by boat, and you may find that yours resembles the outboard-powered sampans that do similar duty in parts of Asia.

THE BASICS

Direct flights from Amsterdam land in Paramaribo. From other cities, expect a stopover, often in Trinidad.

The Royal Torarica
10 Kleine Waterstraat
597-473-500
royaltorarica.com
$$
Comfortable hotel within walking distance of the beer garden at 't Vat and the colonial buildings of Independence Square. Pool and casino.

Hotel Krasnapolsky
39 Domineestraat
597-475-050
krasnapolsky.sr
$$
In the middle of the capital's bustle, with 84 guest rooms.

Best Western Elegance
Frederick Derbystraat 99
597-420-007
bestwesternsuriname.com
$$
Modern and pleasant; away from the tourist district.

Quito

Nestled amid snowcapped Andean peaks, Ecuador's capital has long been overlooked by travelers on their way to the country's most famous destination, the Galápagos Islands. But visitors who bypass this lively historic city of some two million people are missing out. At 9,350 feet above sea level, on the eastern slopes of the Pichincha Volcano, Quito offers breathtaking vistas around nearly every corner. Its historic center, a Unesco World Heritage site, is one of the largest in South America, with 40 colonial churches and chapels, 16 convents and monasteries, and picturesque plazas. In recent years, museums have been inaugurated; mansions restored; hotels, restaurants, and cafes opened; and safety improved. — BY MICHELLE HIGGINS

FRIDAY

1 *Sunset Over the City* 5:30 p.m.

Parque Itchimbía (Calles José María Aguirre N4-108 and Concepción) offers panoramic views of Quito's historic center and, in the distance, the winged *Virgin of Quito* statue. Check out the Art Nouveau **Itchimbía Cultural Center** (Itchimbía Centro Cultural, 593-2-258-4362; centrocultural-quito.com). The glass and steel structure, imported from Hamburg in 1889, was on the other side of the city until it was moved to Itchimbía hill in 2004. Venture below the observation deck to find a **Pim's**, part of an Ecuadorean chain. Order a cocktail and find a seat near one of the heat lamps on the outdoor deck to watch the lights come on in the city below.

2 *With a Latin Twist* 7:30 p.m.

Theatrum Restaurant & Wine Bar (Teatro Nacional Sucre, Calle Manabi between Guayaquil and Flores; 593-2-257-1011; theatrum.com.ec; $$$), on the second floor of the National Theater, serves Mediterranean cuisine with a Latin twist in a high-vaulted room draped in red velvet curtains. The five-course tasting menu includes specials like grilled octopus with olives and fava beans or crab ravioli and rabbit risotto, and a refreshing sorbet as a palate cleanser. The restaurant will arrange free transportation to and from your hotel, if you wish.

3 *Party Plaza* 10 p.m.

If the food and altitude haven't sapped your energy, head to **Plaza Foch** at the intersection of Calle Reina Victoria and Mariscal Foch in northern Quito, where young people gather before hitting nearby night spots. A noticeable police presence makes it safe to explore the immediate area, but if you plan to party beyond the three-block radius of Calama, Juan León Mera, and Pinto Streets, take a taxi. On Fridays, you'll find live music after 10 p.m. at **Q**, a restaurant and bar at the base of the Nü House boutique hotel (Calles Mariscal Foch E6-12 and Reina Victoria; 593-2-255-7840; quitoq.com). Across the plaza, **La Boca del Lobo** (Calles Calama 284 and Reina Victoria; 593-2-254-5500; labocadellobo.com.ec) has a red lounge and a glassed-in patio with funky chandeliers, hanging birdcages, and ceiling tiles featuring religious iconography. It serves a selection of fried appetizers for midnight snacking.

SATURDAY

4 *After Hours* 3 a.m.

Most bars close by 3 a.m. One after-hours option is the **Metro Café** (Avenida Orellana at the corner of Rábida; 593-2-255-2570), which prepares diner fare around the clock. It's also a good breakfast option, serving up stacks of pancakes and greasy-spoon

OPPOSITE Modern Quito climbs up the hillsides from the old city, which Unesco calls the "best-preserved, least altered historic center in Latin America."

RIGHT Dancers on the Plaza San Francisco, a downtown spot where musicians and performers gather crowds.

dishes like cheddar scrambled eggs with hash browns and bacon. During the day, families with restless children will appreciate the outdoor playground.

5 *Into Thin Air* 9 a.m.

Take the dizzying **Teleférico** aerial tram up to the Cruz Loma viewpoint, some 13,000 feet above sea level (Avenidas Occidental and Fulgencio Araujo; 593-2-222-2996). Take a hat (temperatures drop as you climb to the top), and pay a bit extra for the express line. At the top, stroll the nature paths threaded amid waving grasses. To help counteract the effects of the altitude, buy coca tea at the tea shop in the mountain lodge.

6 *Art With a Message* 11:30 a.m.

La Capilla del Hombre (Calles Lorenzo Chávez EA18-143 and Mariano Calvache; 593-2-244-8492; capilladelhombre.com), which means Chapel of Man, is an impressive cultural complex conceived in 1985 by Oswaldo Guayasamín, one of Ecuador's greatest artists, as a tribute to the resilience of the Latin American people. The three-story museum, in the Bellavista neighborhood, houses a heart-wrenching sequence of paintings, murals, and sculptures that captures the miseries and victories of people struggling against political oppression.

7 *A Taste of the Coast* 1 p.m.

Settle in for lunch on the leafy patio of **La Chillangua Verde Esmeralda** (Calles Zaldumbie

ABOVE The Gothic Basilica del Voto Nacional incorporates distinctly New World touches. Its gargoyles are based on iguanas, pumas, and Galápagos tortoises.

RIGHT A painted figure at Folkore Olga Fisch, a boutique that no serious shopper should miss. Its handcrafted merchandise also includes tapestries and straw fedoras.

N25-165 and Toledo; 593-2-222-5313; $$), which specializes in coastal Ecuadorean cuisine, including tasty ceviches and camarones encocadas, a rich seafood dish prepared with coconut juice.

8 *Folkore and Foraging* 3 p.m.

Folklore Olga Fisch (Avenidas Colón E10-53 and Caamaño; 593-2-254-1315; olgafisch.com) is a boutique with a selection of indigenous and Ecuadorean art, including handwoven tapestries, silver jewelry, straw fedoras, and pottery. It's a must-stop for shoppers. The small museum upstairs displays pre-Columbian artifacts and post-colonial art. Next, hone your haggling skills at **El Ejido** park, a short taxi ride away, where artisans in indigenous garb line the northern end on most weekends with stalls featuring handmade jewelry, alpaca scarves, wooden flutes, and other craft items. Nearby, the **Mercado Artesanal La Mariscal** (Calle Jorge Washington between Reina Victoria and Juan León Mera) has about another hundred stalls of similar souvenirs.

9 *Above the Clouds* 8 p.m.

Hold tight for a bumpy ride up the potholed gravel road to **Hacienda Rumiloma** (at the end of Obispo de la Madrid; 593-2-320-0953; haciendarumiloma.com; $$), more than 10,000 feet up the slopes of the Pichincha Volcano, literally above the clouds. The jarring ride is well worth it for a romantic dinner overlooking the city. Outfitted in a hodgepodge of Baccarat chandeliers, booths made of thick slabs of worn wood, and antique chairs covered in woven fabrics, the restaurant offers a luxurious rustic feel, with a wood-burning stove in one corner and a baby grand piano in another. Specialties like the Asian-influenced camarones Rumiloma and cordero La Cantera, a savory lamb dish, are served on heavy metal platters. Head downstairs to the Irish Pub for an after-dinner drink next to the fireplace. (There are also luxurious suites with fireplaces.)

ABOVE A room at Hacienda Rumiloma. If you're not staying at this high-altitude hotel, go for dinner.

SUNDAY

10 *Swiss Breakfast* 10 a.m.

Grab a pastry at the **Swiss Corner**'s deli/bakery (at the corner of Avenida De los Shyris N38-41 and El Telégrafo; 593-2-246-8007; $) or sit down in its cheery restaurant next door for yogurt and fruit parfaits or eggs and hash browns.

11 *Old Town* 11 a.m.

The cobblestone streets of Quito's historic center are closed to traffic from 8 a.m. to 2 p.m. on Sunday — an ideal opportunity to explore. Start

at the **Basílica del Voto Nacional**, (Calle Carchi 122 and Venezuela), Ecuador's largest Gothic cathedral, adorned with gargoyles inspired by the country's iguanas, pumas, and Galápagos tortoises. Then take Calle García Moreno to the **Plaza de la Independencia**, Quito's main square, surrounded by the cathedral, the Presidential Palace, the Archbishop's Palace, and City Hall. Take a break at the **Hotel Plaza Grande**'s cafe (Calles García Moreno and Chile; 593-2-251-0777; plazagrandequito.com) and order a creamy cup of Ecuadorean hot chocolate. Continuing on Calle García Moreno, you will pass **La Compañía de Jesús,** which has a gold-leaf altar inside. On Calle Sucre, head uphill to the **Plaza San Francisco**, dominated by a church and convent, where musicians gather and locals spontaneously break into dance. For a last taste of town, make your way to the pedestrian street La Ronda (also known as Calle Morales), where balconies are decorated with flowers and flags, children play hopscotch, and tiny restaurants serve up Ecuadorean specialties.

ABOVE The winged Virgin of Quito, perched high above the city, is a familiar backdrop to the streetscape, rising beyond roof peaks and church towers.

OPPOSITE A woman carries plants and flowers on her back, a traditional figure moving amid the utilitarian elements of a modern street.

THE BASICS

Take taxis to get around, especially at night; prices are low. The official currency in Ecuador is the United States dollar.

Hotel Patio Andaluz
García Moreno 6-52
593-2-228-0830
hotelpatioandaluz.com
$$
In Old Town, 32 rooms decorated with antique-style furniture.

Hotel Plaza Grande
Calles García Moreno and Chile
593-2-251-0777
plazagrandequito.com
$$$$
Elegant lodging in a restored Spanish-colonial mansion.

Casa Gangotena
Calle Bolivar 541
593-2-400-8000
casagangotena.com
$$$$
Historic mansion overlooking Plaza San Francisco.

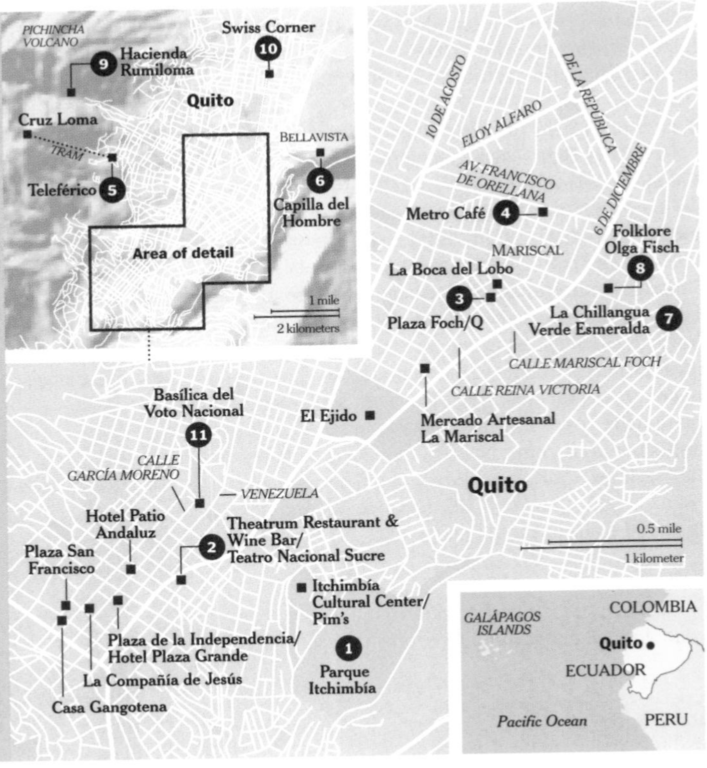

PICHINCHA VOLCANO
9 Hacienda Rumiloma
10 Swiss Corner
Quito
Cruz Loma
TRAM
5 Teleférico
BELLAVISTA
6 Capilla del Hombre
Area of detail
1 mile
2 kilometers
10 DE AGOSTO
DE LA REPÚBLICA
ELOY ALFARO
AV. FRANCISCO DE ORELLANA
6 DE DICIEMBRE
4 Metro Café
8 Folklore Olga Fisch
MARISCAL
La Boca del Lobo
3 Plaza Foch/Q
7 La Chillangua Verde Esmeralda
CALLE MARISCAL FOCH
CALLE REINA VICTORIA
11 Basílica del Voto Nacional
El Ejido
Mercado Artesanal La Mariscal
CALLE GARCÍA MORENO
VENEZUELA
Quito
Hotel Patio Andaluz
Plaza San Francisco
2 Theatrum Restaurant & Wine Bar/ Teatro Nacional Sucre
0.5 mile
1 kilometer
Itchimbía Cultural Center/ Pim's
Plaza de la Independencia/ Hotel Plaza Grande
La Compañía de Jesús
Casa Gangotena
1 Parque Itchimbía
GALÁPAGOS ISLANDS
COLOMBIA
Quito
ECUADOR
Pacific Ocean
PERU

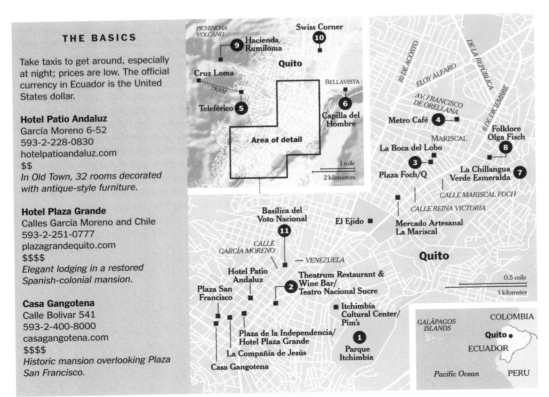

Cuenca

To call Cuenca picturesque would be an understatement. Surrounded by Andean peaks and crisscrossed by four rivers, this city in Ecuador's southern highlands exudes natural beauty as well as Spanish colonial charm. The city center, a pedestrian-friendly district of terra-cotta roofs, domed churches, attractive plazas, and cobblestoned streets, is a Unesco World Heritage Site, and many of its old houses have been restored and turned into upscale guesthouses, restaurants, and galleries. Thanks to preservation efforts and strong cultural roots, Cuenca has retained its rich ancestral heritage as well as its buildings: visitors can sample traditional cuisine and barter for handmade goods in outdoor markets, buying from vendors wearing traditional indigenous garb. Outside the city, there are mountain lakes, thermal baths, and Incan ruins to explore. — BY MICHELLE HIGGINS

FRIDAY

1 *View From Above* 4:30 p.m.

With its white church perched atop a hill, **Mirador a Turi** (at the top of Camino a Turi) is a vantage point affording breathtaking views of the city and surrounding mountains. The best time is dusk, when the sky turns pink, the church lights up, and the city begins to twinkle. Take a taxi just south of the city to the end of Fray Vicente Solano Avenue and up the winding Camino a Turi. Leave early so that you can stop on your way up the hill at **Galeria Vega** (Vía a Turi 201; 593-7-288-1407; eduardovega.com), the workshop and gallery of Eduardo Vega, Cuenca's most famous ceramicist and designer. (It closes at 5:30 p.m.) On display and for sale are original ceramic vases, murals, and jewelry.

2 *New Andean Fare* 8 p.m.

Las Monjas (Borrero 6-41, between President Córdova and Juan Jaramillo; 593-7-282-2750; $) was named for the convent across the street — "monjas" means "nuns." Rich dark woods, papal-red walls, and whimsical paintings of cornette-wearing sisters playfully evoke the name. But the décor leans more toward minimalism than religious iconography, with clean lines and a trickling fountain. The food, described as novoandina, or new Andean, blends traditional ingredients like chamburo, babaco, jícama, and quinoa with more common fare. Everything is fresh and organic. Be sure to try the llapingachos (cheese-filled potato patties), a typical Ecuadorean dish, and empanadas de viento, which contain cheese and are sprinkled with sugar.

3 *Expat Saturday Night* 10 p.m.

For night life, there are a variety of bars along Calle Larga. **Wunderlust** (Hermano Miguel 3-43 and Calle Larga at the Escalinata; 593-7-283-1274; wunderbarcafe.wordpress.com), a funky German-owned cafe, is popular among expats and locals alike for its laid-back vibe, cozy rooms, international food, and cheap drinks.

SATURDAY

4 *Pines Over the Plaza* 10 a.m.

Parque Abdón Calderón (Benigno Malo and Mariscal Sucre), the city's central square, marked by eight towering Chilean pine trees that were planted in the 19th century, is a good place to begin taking in the city's Spanish architecture (cuenca.com.ec/cuencanew/en/node/162). On one side of the plaza is the **Iglesia del Sagrario**, also known as the Old Cathedral, built in 1567. On the other is the massive **Catedral de la Inmaculada Concepción**, begun in 1885 in the Neo-Gothic style with rose-colored marble

OPPOSITE Outside the Immaculate Conception Cathedral on the Parque Abdón Calderón, Cuenca's central square.

RIGHT Making Panama hats, which originated in Ecuador.

floors and three sky-blue domes that dominate Cuenca's skyline. It was completed in 1967 as the New Cathedral, the name more commonly used by locals. You can tour the churches or take in the sights from a shaded park bench.

5 *Flowers and Foraging* 11 a.m.

On the southern side of the New Cathedral, along Mariscal Sucre near Padre Aguirre Street, find the **Plaza de las Flores** and its lovely outdoor flower market. In front of the carved stone facade of the Church of El Carmen de la Asunción, you can watch skillful vendors, some who still wear traditional dress, create tightly bound bouquets and elaborate centerpieces. From there, take Padre Aguirre street to **Plaza de San Francisco**, where artisans of the indigenous Otavalo people offer handmade blouses, sweaters, ponchos, alpaca scarves, wooden flutes, and other crafts. Stick to the covered sidewalk for some of the more traditional options. Across the plaza, **Casa de la Mujer**, the Municipal Handicraft Center (General Torres and President Córdova streets; 593-7-284-5854), offers more souvenirs at indoor stalls and artisan workshops; goods range from maracas to jewelry made from the tagua nut (also called vegetable ivory), which grows in the region.

6 *Lunch by the Brook* 1 p.m.

Take a half-hour taxi ride from downtown Cuenca, through scenic mountain passes and grassy slopes dotted with grazing cattle and alpacas, to **Hostería Dos Chorreras** (Via al Cajas, Km 21; 593-7-404-1999; hosteriadoschorreras.com). Located at roughly 12,000 feet above sea level, near the entrance to Cajas National Park, this rustic restaurant serves farm-raised trout; canelazo, a strong hot drink often made with sugar cane alcohol, cinnamon, and citrus juice; and other local specialties. Designed to bring the natural environment inside, the restaurant has large windows overlooking a trickling brook that at one point runs through the building itself, past moss-covered boulders. Guided hiking, horseback riding, kayaking, and other outdoor adventures are also available here.

7 *Panamas in Ecuador* 3 p.m.

Find out how the Panama hat (the real thing is made in Ecuador, not Panama) got its name at the **Panama Hat Museum** and workshop (Museo del Sombrero Paja Toquilla; Calle Larga 10-41, between Padre Aguirre and General Torres; 593-7-283-1569; barrancospanamahats.com). It's in the shop of the Paredes Roldán family, which has been producing the hats for more than 60 years. Tour the workshop and try on the different styles, which can be modified to fit you. A well-made Panama hat, woven from locally grown fine toquilla straw, is so flexible that it can be rolled up into a small cylindrical bundle for easy traveling. The finer the weave, the higher the quality (and price) of the hat.

8 *Riverbank Stroll* 4:30 p.m.

More museums, galleries, and artisan shops can be found along Calle Larga. When you've finished examining the wares, take one of several sets of stairs down to the tree-lined **Barranco**, where Old-World houses with wrought-iron balconies cling to the bank above the swiftly flowing Rio Tomebamba, one of Cuenca's four rivers.

9 *Gazebo Dining* 7 p.m.

Casa Alonso (Bolívar 12-55 between Tarqui and Juan Montalvo; 593-7-282-3889; mansionalcazar.com; $$), the restaurant at the boutique hotel Mansión Alcázar, offers fine dining in an intimate setting. Ask

for a table in the glass gazebo that overlooks the beautiful gardens in the rear of the hotel.

SUNDAY

10 *Take the Waters* 10 a.m.

Roughly 10 minutes from Cuenca by taxi, the village of **Baños** (not to be confused with the major spa town in the Central Sierra) is home to several thermal resorts. Heated by volcanic activity underground, the springs lack the sulfur smell typical of many such places. **Piedra de Agua** (Parroquia Baños, Paseo de la Guadalupana and Calle S/N; 593-7-289-2496; piedradeagua.com.ec) is among the most luxurious of the spas, yet has extremely reasonable rates. Built from volcanic limestone found on its site, it offers a series of indoor and outdoor thermal pools, volcanic-mud treatments, steam baths, and massages in underground caves.

OPPOSITE ABOVE Old-World houses of the Barranco.

OPPOSITE BELOW The lobby at the Mansión Alcázar.

ABOVE Domes of the Immaculate Conception cathedral.

THE BASICS

Flights from Quito land in Cuenca several times a day. Taxis are inexpensive, and prices on everything from souvenirs to hotel rooms are often negotiable.

Mansión Alcázar
Bolívar 12-55
593-7-282-3889
mansionalcazar.com
$-$$$
Luxury boutique hotel with antique décor, balconies overlooking a central courtyard, and a lovely landscaped garden.

El Dorado Hotel
Gran Colombia 7-87
593-7-283-1390
eldoradohotel.com.ec
$-$$
Business hotel a block from the New Cathedral.

Casa del Aguila
Mariscal Sucre 13-56
593-7-283-6498
hotelcasadelaguila.com
$-$$
Restored colonial mansion with big windows and a leafy setting.

CAJAS NATIONAL PARK
ECUADOR
2 miles
4 kilometers
Hostería Dos Chorreras 6
Cuenca
Piedra de Agua
Area of detail
Baños 10
Cathedral of the Immaculate Conceptión
El Dorado Hotel
Plaza de las Flores 5
Parque Abdón Calderón 4
BORRERO
Casa de la Mujer
Church of El Carmen de La Asunción
Iglesia del Sagrario
Plaza de San Francisco
PRESIDENT CÓRDOVA
2 Las Monjas
1 mile
2 kilometers
Casa de Aguila
Area of detail
9 Casa Alonso/ Mansión Alcázar
8 Barranco
7 Panama Hat Museum
CALLE LARGA
3 Wunderbar
Cuenca
Rio Tomebamba
FRAY VICENTE SOLANO AVENUE
Mirador a Turi 1
Galeria Vega
CAMINO A TURI
COLOMBIA
Quito
ECUADOR
Cuenca
Pacific Ocean
PERU
BRAZIL

Lima

Lima has long been a cosmopolitan city hesitant to embrace its diversity. A capital founded by Spanish conquistadors that subsequently exploded with influxes from Asia and then from Peru's own Andean highlands, it has remained a city of fairly segregated neighborhoods. But led by Lima's cuisine — which has gained worldwide renown for its freshness and creativity — the city is changing. Sushi and ceviche chefs are learning from one another. A popular street food is "five flavors" a rice and pasta dish with Italian, Chinese, Andean, Japanese, and African influences. For the tourist, the diversity means days of exploring neighborhoods with distinct cultures and histories, interspersed with the spicy, sweet, and subtle gastronomic experience of how it all comes together.
— BY ETHAN TODRAS-WHITEHILL

FRIDAY

1 *Sins of the Sea* 4 p.m.

In Lima, food rules. And in the cocina limeña, seafood is king, an especially popular choice for the kind of long, leisurely lunch that Peruvians love. Just a block or two from the ocean, with ceramic tile floors and an open-air foyer, **Pescados Capitales** (Avenida La Mar 1337; 51-1-421-8808; pescadoscapitales.com; $$) combines the relaxation of the beach with an air of upper-crust refinement. "Pecados capitales" refers to the seven deadly sins, all of which can be ordered from the menu. Start off with a little Freudian lust (lujuria freudiana, grilled baby calamari), and then chow down on some creamy, indulgent greed (avaricia sole Rockefeller) or simple infidelity (infidelidad grilled swordfish) if you fear that your stomach may not forgive so easily.

2 *Park It in the Parks* 6 p.m.

Far from the city center but right up against the beach is the upscale neighborhood of Miraflores, which roughly translates as "look at all the pretty flowers." Miraflores's parks of irises, cactuses, and palms make for a good stroll and introduction to Lima. Start off at **Parque Kennedy**, at the heart of the neighborhood, which often hosts spoken-word poetry and outdoor art exhibitions. Cross the Diagonal to **Café Haiti** (Diagonal 160; 51-1-446-3816), an old-school hangout of the Lima literati with bamboo chairs and a sidewalk cafe. Do some people-watching and sample a lemony-sweet nonalcoholic hierba luisa, one of Peru's signature beverages.

3 *Sweet Archaeology* 9:30 p.m.

For dessert, take a quick cab to **La Bodega de la Trattoria** (General Borgoño 784; 51-1-241-6899), the casual wing of La Trattoria, where the chef in charge of sweets is the South American television dessert diva Sandra Plevisani. Get a table out on the patio and have a bocanera de chocolate, a fudge-filled chocolate soufflé, while you look out at **Huaca Pucllana**, the complex of pre-Incan structures across the street.

SATURDAY

4 *Heart of the City* 9 a.m.

Stroll up the pedestrian-only Jirón de la Unión, past modish shops and colorful 200-year-old colonial facades, and emerge in the **Plaza Mayor**, the main square, which is surrounded by some of Lima's finest architecture. This is the spot in which Francisco Pizarro founded the city in 1535 and in which Peruvians declared their independence in 1821. Tour the gold-leaf altars and paintings of the **Lima**

OPPOSITE The Church of San Francisco, built in the Baroque style in the 17th century, is part of Lima's legacy from the days when Peru was a Spanish colony.

RIGHT Huaca Pucllana, a complex of ancient Incan structures still standing in central Lima.

Cathedral on the eastern edge, and if you have the time, visit the **Church of San Francisco** a couple of blocks northeast to see its 17th-century convent and network of catacombs (Plaza San Francisco; 51-1-427-1381; museocatacumbas.com).

5 *Chifa, Chifa Everywhere* Noon

From the city center, walk to **Calle Capón**, Lima's Chinatown. Peru has a large ethnically Chinese population and a profusion of chifa (Peruvian-Chinese) restaurants. Chifa is spicier than traditional Chinese food, relying more on seafood and sauces and less on vegetables. One of the best spots is **Salon Capón** (Jirón Paruro 819; 51-1-426-9286; $), where you might try steamed langostino dumplings with tamarind sauce and spicy garlic-fried calamari. Afterward, stroll through the pedestrian zone with the classic Chinatown arch on either end, stopping to have your palm read, the smell of sandalwood incense filling the air.

6 *X-Rated Pottery* 1 p.m.

The **Gold Museum** (museoroperu.com.pe) is a popular tourist choice, with its ancient gold headdresses, ornaments, and jewelry. But glimpse another side of pre-Columbian culture in the erotic pottery collection at the **Museo Rafael Larco Herrera** (Avenida Bolívar 1515; 51-1-461-1312; museolarco.org). Its display of artifacts and reproductions, dating from the first millennium A.D., begins with giant phalluses and moves on to detailed depictions of sexual acts that are otherwise unviewable outside seedy video stores and surreptitiously visited corners of the Internet.

7 *Desert Worship* 3 p.m.

Lima is a city built by and for the Spanish conquerors, but Inca sites remain. Take a cab to **Pachacamác** (pachacamac.net), an archaeological site that housed an important oracle for more than 1,500 years, and which has a beautifully restored Temple of the Moon. Skip the tour loop unless you pay your cabbie to drive you around, but shell out the extra fee for a guide, since you can't get into some areas without one. Bring a hat and sunglasses, because a visit to Pachacamác reminds you that Lima is one of the world's largest desert cities.

8 *Make Mine a Maki* 6 p.m.

Matsuei (Manuel Bañon 260; 51-1-422-4323; $$), a restaurant in San Isidro co-founded by Nobuyuki Matsuhisa of Nobu fame, is a premier spot for sushi. Like the Chinese, the Japanese settled in Peru in the early 20th century. Fish as fresh as Lima's makes ideal ingredients in maki acevichado, a Japanese roll with the classic Peruvian ceviche sauce and ingredients like fried calamari with shrimp, salmon, and rice.

9 *Pisco Crawl* 9 p.m.

The pisco sour, Peru's national drink (it even has its own national day of celebration), is worth some serious sampling. The key ingredient, Peruvian pisco, is a brandy made from a single distillation of young wine. The sour marries it with Peruvian lime, egg white, and bitters derived from the bark of a Peruvian tree. You can get them all over town, but start with a traditional version at **Bar Inglés** (Los Eucaliptos 590, San Isidro; 51-1-611-9000; hotelcountry.com); the mixologist promises to produce one that is exactly like the original that was served in the 1930s in Lima. Then try a creatively updated pisco sour at the **Huaringas Bar** (Calle Bolognesi 472, Miraflores; 51-1-447-1133; huaringasbar.com.pe), the first bar to add fruit flavors, like passion fruit.

SUNDAY

10 *Bohemian Life* 10 a.m.

Barranco, home to Lima's bohemian upper crust, including the novelist Mario Vargas Llosa, is a neighborhood filled with art galleries, European-style parks, and pubs. From the marigold-studded **Plaza de Armas**, walk west down to the **Bridge of Sighs**, an old wooden bridge over a bougainvillea-lined walkway that, when accompanied by guitar players and women selling single roses, manages to be both touristy and romantic. Wind your way over to the **Lucia de la Puente** gallery (Paso Sáenz

Peña 206A; 51-1-477-9740; gluciadelapuente.com), which has changing contemporary art exhibitions. One featured an Incan ruin constructed out of old computer keyboards.

11 *Getting Crafty* 1 p.m.

Walk across the street from Lucia de la Puente to the artisans' collective **Dédalo** (Paseo Sáenz Peña 295; 51-1-477-0562; dedaloarte.blogspot.com/). Each room in the labyrinthine century-old mansion houses a different type of craft, from jewelry and picture frames to lamps and leatherwork, from more than 1,000 different local artists. A cafe in the back serves coffee, tea, and selections from a decent wine list. It's a nice spot to sit and figure out how to explain to your partner the beautiful but useless blown-glass vase you just bought.

OPPOSITE Miraflores, an upscale neighborhood right up against the Pacific Ocean beach. With its parks and cafes, it's a good place to begin exploring.

ABOVE The Archbishop's Palace, built in 1924, sits on the same site that the conquistador Francisco Pizarro allocated to the city's highest-level priest in 1535.

THE BASICS

Take a taxi from Jorge Chávez Airport into the city. Miraflores makes the best base for a visit, with a wide range of quality hotels and a beachfront location.

Hotel Señorial
José Gonzáles 567
51-1-445-0139
senorial.com
$
A lovely, relaxed place with a flowery courtyard and hearty breakfast at a nice price.

Miraflores Park Hotel
Avenida Malecón de la Reserva 1035
51-1-610-4000
mira-park.com
$$$$
For upscale lodging, you can't do better.

Sonesta Hotel El Olivar
Pancho Fierro 194
51-1-712-6000
sonesta.com/lima
$$
In a tranquil section of Miraflores, with views of the Olivar Forest park.

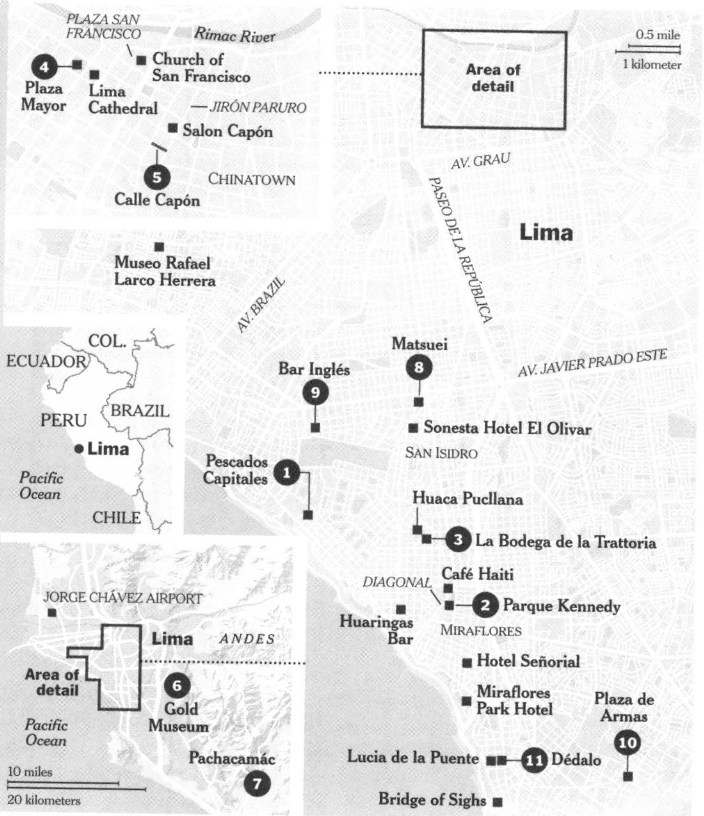

PLAZA SAN FRANCISCO
Rimac River
Church of San Francisco
4 Plaza Mayor
Lima Cathedral
JIRÓN PARURO
Salon Capón
5 Calle Capón
CHINATOWN
Museo Rafael Larco Herrera
Area of detail
0.5 mile
1 kilometer
AV. GRAU
PASEO DE LA REPÚBLICA
Lima
AV. BRAZIL
COL.
ECUADOR
PERU
BRAZIL
Lima
Pacific Ocean
CHILE
Matsuei 8
Bar Inglés 9
AV. JAVIER PRADO ESTE
Sonesta Hotel El Olivar
SAN ISIDRO
Pescados Capitales 1
Huaca Pucllana
3 La Bodega de la Trattoria
Café Haiti
DIAGONAL
2 Parque Kennedy
Huaringas Bar
MIRAFLORES
Hotel Señorial
Miraflores Park Hotel
Plaza de Armas 10
Lucia de la Puente
11 Dédalo
Bridge of Sighs
JORGE CHÁVEZ AIRPORT
Lima
ANDES
Area of detail
6 Gold Museum
Pacific Ocean
Pachacamác 7
10 miles
20 kilometers

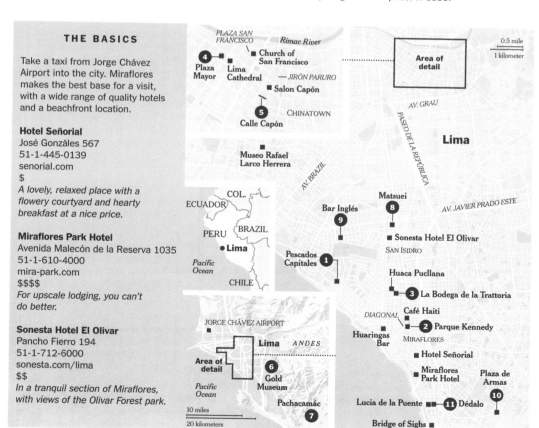

Rio de Janeiro

You don't have to go for Carnaval to see Rio de Janeiro. You'll probably see more of the city if you don't—and also more of its residents, the Cariocas, since many of them flee the tourist onslaught for vacation homes and other cities' Carnavals. And you won't really miss the party, because it never stops. There's always the samba, always caipirinhas, and always the beach. Rio is glued to its sandy shoreline. When the sun fails to appear, Cariocas can become flustered and confused—sort of like ants whose hill was just destroyed by an 8-year-old.

— BY SETH KUGEL AND ARIC CHEN

FRIDAY

1 *Ride Up, Look Down* 3 p.m.

Throw anti-cliché caution to the wind and take the cog railway to the top of **Corcovado** (Rua Cosme Velho 513; 55-21-2558-1329; corcovado.com.br). This is where the iconic statue *Christ the Redeemer* presides over Rio. You can see the famous Sugarloaf Mountain, the island-pocked Guanabara Bay, and the beaches outlining the coast like links of white sausages. Even better, you can make fun of the inevitable sightseer aping the statue's outstretched arms for a photo. "Turistas chatos" means "annoying tourists" in Portuguese, should that phrase come to mind.

2 *Caipirinha Lessons* 7 p.m.

The caipirinha, a cocktail of muddled lime, sugar, ice, and the sugar-cane liquor known as cachaça, has become a global bar standard. Try it on its home turf, at the **Academia da Cachaça** (Rua Conde Bernadotte 26; 55-21-2529-2680; academiadacachaca.com.br; $$) in the upscale neighborhood of Leblon. You can choose among hundreds of artisanal brands, including Lua Cheia, a fruity, intense cachaça aged for two years. After a couple of caipirinhas, you might want to turn to the place's appetizer menu. An escondidinho, a traditional dish of dried beef served under cheesy mashed manioc, makes for a good warm-up for dinner later.

3 *Gourmet Alley* 9:30 p.m.

The peacocks of Rio flock to the Leblon area for dinner, specifically Rua Dias Ferreira. On a one-block stretch, you can choose from the always busy **Sushi Leblon** (No. 256; 55-21-2512-7830; sushileblon.com; $$), with its sometimes exotic sushi offerings (think quail egg and truffles), and **Quadrucci** (No. 233; 55-21-2512-4551; quadrucci.com.br; $$), with its Brazilian-inflected Italian dishes like shrimp risotto with mango, mascarpone, and arugula. For other nouvelle concoctions, head for **Zuka** (No. 233b; 55-21-3205-7154; zuka.com.br; $$$) and try the white fish and pepper ceviche and rack of lamb with passion-fruit mashed potatoes.

4 *A Local Draft* 11 p.m.

You could head to one of Leblon's chic and expensive clubs, but try a more traditional Rio setting: the ultra-social, old-fashioned bars known as botequins, where locals young and old gather for conversation and drinks. The beverage of choice is the Brazilian style of draft beer known as chopp (SHOW-pee), and that usually means a Brahma Pilsener. For a bit more variety, head to **Botequim**

OPPOSITE Christ the Redeemer, the symbol of Rio de Janeiro, overlooks the city from high atop Corcovado peak. Ride up on the cog railway and share his view.

RIGHT Take one of Rio's beloved streetcars uphill to explore the shops and cafes of the St. Teresa neighborhood.

Informal (Rua Conde Bernadotte 26, Leblon; 55-21-2540-7561; and other locations) which serves darker chopp as well.

SATURDAY

5 *The UFO Across the Bay* 9 a.m.

Get up early and take a 20-minute ferry ride (Barcas/SA; 55-21-2620-6756) across Guanabara Bay to the **Niterói Museum of Contemporary Art**, also known as the MAC (Mirante de Boa Viagem; 55-21-2620-2400; macniteroi.com.br). Designed by Brazil's most famous architect, Oscar Niemeyer, who also designed the modernist capital city, Brasília, the museum resembles a flying saucer. It offers excellent views of the bay and Rio, and its exhibitions emphasize Brazilian artists.

6 *Anti-Rio Rio* 1 p.m.

Climb up most hills in Rio and you end up in a favela, one of the city's squatter slums long ruled by drug gangs but also legendary as sources of artistic and musical talent. The police have now largely reclaimed the favelas and broken the power of the gangs, especially near tourist areas. But **Santa Teresa** was always the picturesque exception anyway, a hilltop neighborhood that is considered Rio's artsy anti-beach. Arrive on a tram and stroll its twisting streets filled with great little restaurants and unusual gift shops. Wander the main drag, Rua Almirante Alexandrino, and have lunch there, or continue uphill to the thatched-roof pavilions of **Aprazível** (Rua Aprazível 62; 55-21-2508-9174; aprazivel.com.br; $$$) for the spectacular views and bacalhau do pai, a cod pastry dish filling enough for two.

7 *Old Books, Modernist House* 4 p.m.

With its charming garden and three floors filled with art and furniture, the **Chácara do Céu Museum** (Rua Murtinho Nobre 93; 55-21-2507-1932, museuscastromaya.com.br) feels like someone's house. And, in fact, it is. The name means Country Estate in the Heavens, and the building, a Modernist structure, is the former home of the French-born industrialist Raymundo Ottoni de Castro Maya, who was an avid collector of Brazilian, European, and Asian art. Equally fascinating is his impressive library of old Portuguese and French books.

8 *Starck and Seafood* 8 p.m.

Continue the architectural ogling over dinner at the Philippe Starck–designed **Hotel Fasano** (Avenida Vieira Souto 80; 55-21-3202-4000; fasano.com.br), right on Ipanema beach. Its seafood restaurant,

ABOVE The Niterói Museum of Contemporary Art, designed by Brazil's most famous architect, Oscar Niemeyer.

Fasano Al Mare ($$$$), serves dishes like crispy tuna with white beans, cream, and red onions, while its breezy interior sheds a flattering light on the glamorous clientele within. Afterward, head to the hotel's London-themed bar, **Baretto-Londra**, for a nightcap.

9 *Lapa Crawl* 11 p.m.

Have a second wind? This city parties late, so join the students, bohemians, yuppies, and just plain locals reveling in the streets of **Lapa**. This historic, charmingly shabby neighborhood in central Rio goes late into the night with plentiful street food—and cheap drinks. Duck into popular samba clubs like **Rio Scenarium** (Rua do Lavradio 20; 55-21-3147-9005; rioscenarium.com.br) and the intimate **Carioca da Gema** (Rua Mem de Sá 79; 55-21-2221-0043; barcariocadagema.com.br). Or just barhop your way to tomorrow.

SUNDAY

10 *Juicing Up* 10 a.m.

Juice stands are a way of life in Rio, and they offer a dizzying Portuguese menu of fruits like caqui (persimmon) and graviola (soursop). You can't go

ABOVE Street food and samba clubs keep things lively in Lapa.

BELOW Leblon and Morro Dois Irmãos (Two Brothers Hill).

wrong with tangerine juice and a grilled ham-and-cheese sandwich at **Polis Sucos**, a popular chain that has a stand in the middle of the Ipanema neighborhood (Rua Maria Quitéria 70A, Ipanema; 55-21-2247-2518). For a supposedly healthier, if more caloric, start, order a shake made from açai, the high-energy purple palm fruit from the Amazon.

ABOVE Street art in Santa Teresa.

OPPOSITE Futevolei, a hands-free hybrid of soccer and volleyball, on the soft sand of Ipanema Beach.

11 *Palms and Circumstance* 11 a.m.

In Rio, your station in life is pretty much defined by which beach you go to for a suntan. Unless you're looking for young prostitutes and their balding admirers, skip Copacabana Beach. Instead, go to **Ipanema Beach**, its equally famous neighbor one cove over. The beach is delineated by lifeguard stations, or postos, and anywhere near Posto 9 makes for good beautiful-people-watching. Settle into a rented beach chair, buy a bag of the crunchy snacks called Biscoitos Globo, and catch a bit of the amazing hybrid of soccer and volleyball known as futevolei.

THE BASICS

The metro has only two lines but is easy to use. It runs from Ipanema through Copacabana and to most attractions in the city center.

Hotel Fasano
Avenida Vieira Souto 80
55-21-3202-4000
fasano.com.br
$$$$
Philippe Starck's splashy contribution to Ipanema's waterfront, with Brazilian modernist furniture and a rooftop infinity pool.

Ipanema Plaza
Rua Farme de Amoedo 34
55-21-3687-2000
ipanemaplaza.com.br
$$
Fashionable favorite near the gay section of Ipanema Beach.

Cama e Café
Rua Paschoal Carlos Magno
55-21-2225-4366
camaecafe.com.br
$
A booking service that matches travelers with bed-and-breakfast hosts in Santa Teresa.

Brasília
BOLIVIA
BRAZIL
Rio de Janeiro
ARGENT.
URUGUAY
Atlantic Ocean

2 Academia da Cachaça
4 Botequim Informal
LEBLON
3 Sushi Leblon
Quadrucci/ Zuka

To Niterói Museum of Contemporary Art 5
Rio Scenarium
SANTOS DUMONT AIRPORT
Carioca da Gema 9
LAPA
SANTA TERESA
7 Chácara do Céu Museum
Cama e Café
6 Aprazível
Guanabara Bay
FLAMENGO
Rio de Janeiro
SUGARLOAF MOUNTAIN
1 Corcovado
TIJUCA NATIONAL PARK
BOTAFOGO
URCA
Lagoa Rodrigo de Freitas
COPACABANA
AVENIDA ATLÂNTICA
10 Polis Sucos
Atlantic Ocean
Ipanema Plaza
IPANEMA
Area of detail
LEBLON
8 Hotel Fasano/ Fasano al Mare/ Baretto-Londra
11 Ipanema Beach
1 mile
2 kilometers

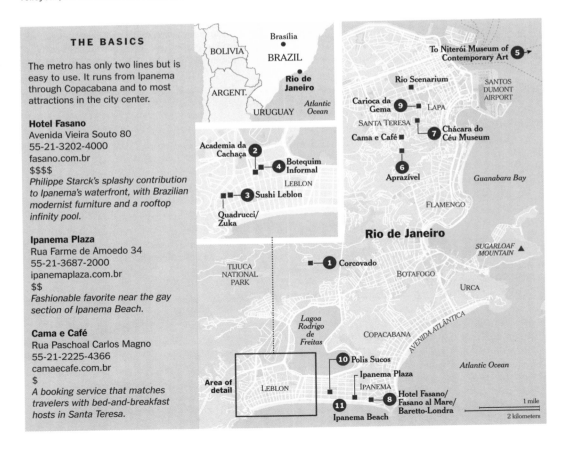

São Paulo

A city of high-rises and traffic jams in a country of rain forests and beaches, São Paulo, South America's biggest metropolis, is a Brazilian freak of nature, except without the nature. But the city's flaws — high prices, street crime, incessant drizzle — are no match for its strengths: artistic and economic energy, relentless night life. Sometimes, it even manages to turn its flaws into assets, as when celebrated architects take ugly concrete and create post-Brutalist masterpieces, like Isay Weinfeld's sleek bookstore Livraria da Vila on Alameda Lorena. São Paulo's 11 million-plus inhabitants do their part by infusing the din with contagious Brazilian energy; flashing smiles and thumbs-up signs are among the few things the city shares with the rest of the vast country whose booming economy it anchors. — BY SETH KUGEL

FRIDAY

1 *Grimy Glory* 3 p.m.

The elite may snap up luxury apartments as far from the heart of the city as possible, but São Paulo's historic center still bustles with government employees and other office workers who have a nice secret on their hands. Sure, parts of the center could use a rinse in a giant urban bathtub, but much of the former glory is intact, including the city's most beautiful art museum, the **Pinacoteca** (Praça da Luz, 2; 55-11-3324-1000; pinacoteca.org.br), housed in a former high school. Don't miss the adjacent sculpture garden before hopping a subway to São Bento to get lost in the busy street commerce on **Rua 25 de Março** (25demarco.com.br) and stroll the pedestrian-only streets near the **Centro Cultural Banco do Brasil**, a glorious old bank building turned exhibition space (Rua Álvares Penteado, 112; bb.com.br/cultura).

2 *Cocktails or Caffeine?* 6 p.m.

When the business bustle dies down, make your way past the grand old **Teatro Municipal** (Rua Líbero Badaró, 377) toward one of the classic works by Brazil's best-known architect, Oscar Niemeyer: the marvelously undulating 38-story **Copan** apartment building (Avenida Ipiranga, 200; www.copansp.com.br), now home to a diverse community of residents. Choose your pick-me-up at the ground-floor shopping center: a creamy espresso at the old-school, standing-room-only **Café Floresta** (55-11-3259-8416; cafefloresta.com.br) or a creative caipirinha cocktail at the classy and ballyhooed **Bar da Dona Onça** (55-11-3129-7619; bardadonaonca.com.br).

3 *Vertical Jungle* 8 p.m.

Enough grime. Find the nearest ponto de táxi (taxi stand) and flee to upscale Vila Olímpia to dine with the elite at **Kaá** (Avenida Juscelino Kubitschek, 279; 55-11-2045-0043; kaarestaurante.com.br; $$$$). Stepping through the barely marked entrance into the Arthur Casas–designed restaurant is like entering an alternative universe. The showstopper is the 4,300-square-foot vertical garden, a wall draped in plant species from the Mata Atlântica — the rapidly disappearing rain forest that São Paulo used to be a part of. The contemporary cuisine — Brie tortellini with fig jam in sage butter, for example, or squid stuffed with crayfish and black risotto — is worth the steep price.

4 *House Party* 11 p.m.

In Vila Olímpia, high-end nightclubs come and go, but the conspicuously consuming playboys and the surgically enhanced women they buy Champagne for are, alas, forever. Forgo that scene and head to **Casa 92** (Rua Cristovão Gonçalves, 92, Largo da Batata;

OPPOSITE South America's largest city, with 11 million people, São Paulo is the anchor of Brazil's economy, alive with business deals by day and partying at night.

RIGHT The upscale buffet line at Santinho.

55-11-3032-0371; casa92.blogspot.com), a nightspot in what surely must have been the home of someone's grandmother. As you wander from room to room and through the pleasant outdoor spaces, you might find yourself crashing a birthday party, striking up a caipirinha-fueled conversation, or hitting the upstairs dance floor where recently formed couples make out.

SATURDAY

5 *Breakfast and Bed* 4 a.m. or 9 a.m.

Ending a long night on the town or starting a big day on the town at a padoca (the informal term for bakery) are two mutually exclusive São Paulo traditions. You can do either at **Bella Paulista** (Rua Haddock Lobo, 354; 55-11-3214-3347; bellapaulista.com; $$), a padoca on steroids where the late-night crowd feasts on everything from pastries (very good) to oversize hot sandwiches (good) to salads (decent) to pizza (not so much). Starting at 7 a.m., there's also a breakfast buffet with breads and pastries, fruit, eggs, and cold cuts. For a cheaper option, ask your hotel for directions to a neighborhood padoca and order fresh orange juice and a pão na chapa, a roll buttered and grilled until crisp.

6 *Art Run* 11 a.m.

Plan a tour through São Paulo's energetic gallery scene using the widely available, excellent Mapa das Artes. You might start at funky **Choque Cultural** (Rua João Moura, 997; 55-11-3061-4051; choquecultural.com.br), a crumbling old house that is always showing something surprising or provocative, then walk to the slick **Zipper Galeria** (Rua Estados Unidos, 1494; 55-11-4306-4306; zippergaleria.com.br), which features 23 young Brazilian artists. A step up in class is **Nara**

BELOW Art of the moment in contemporary surroundings at Galeria Leme.

Roesler (Avenida Europa, 655; 55-11-3063-2344; nararoesler.com.br). Then hop a taxi just across the Pinheiros River to **Galeria Leme** (Avenida Valdemar Ferreira, 130; 55-11-3814-8184; galerialeme.com). Note: those prostitutes hanging out on the nearby street corner are not a performance art installation.

7 *BIA Awaits* 2 p.m.

Saturday is for feijoada, the classic Brazilian dish of black-bean stew brimming with every part of a pig you can imagine. **Feijoada da Bia** (Rua Lopes Chaves, 105; 55-11-3663-0433; $$) is hidden away in a homey setting in the Barra Funda neighborhood (but within walking distance of the Marechal Deodoro subway stop). Lunch includes all you can eat and an easygoing chorinho band.

8 *Theater Scene* 8 p.m.

The language barrier may make seeing a play untenable, but that doesn't mean you can't dive into the hip alternative theater scene around Praça Roosevelt. Mingle with the pre- and post-theater crowd at nearby bars like **Rose Velt** (Praça Franklin Roosevelt, 124; 55-11-3129-5498; rosevelt.com.br), a cozy spot with quirky décor, like the patch of tiled São Paulo sidewalk on one wall. It carries Colorado brand pale ale (brewed in São Paulo state), a nice change when the corporate swill you'll get at most bars around town grows old.

SUNDAY

9 *All's Fair* 10 a.m.

Weekends bring out lovers of all things vintage to antiques fairs. One of the best starts at 8 a.m. on Sundays at **Praça Dom Orione** in the Italian neighborhood of Bixiga. It attracts a São Paulo mishmash

ABOVE The undulating Copan apartment building, a classic work by Brazil's great architect Oscar Niemeyer, makes an inspiring home for a diverse group of residents.

RIGHT A caipirinha cocktail, ready for the sampling, at Bar da Dona Onça on the ground floor of the Copan building.

of gay and straight, old and young, families and couples, all checking out old-fashioned cameras, antique walking canes, and posters, and rummaging through piles of bossa nova LPs and vintage clothes. Several antiques stores also line the park to satisfy indefatigable shoppers.

10 *Artful Cuisine* 12:30 p.m.

From afar, the red-striped skyscraper known as the **Instituto Tomie Ohtake** (Avenida Faria Lima, 201; 55-11-2245-1900; www.institutotomieohtake.org.br) resembles a contemporary tribute to the candy cane, though from street level, its oddball curves and colors become mesmerizing. And the creative range of exhibits inside — including paintings by the Brazilian-Japanese Ohtake — are well worth the trip. Also inside is **Santinho** (55-11-3034-4673; restaurantesantinho.com; $$), a restaurant from the well-regarded chef Morena Leite, whose Capim Santo (capimsanto.com.br) has long been a stop for upscale Brazilian cuisine. Here, she has put together a super-fresh lunch buffet of gorgeous cold dishes (from quinoa to salads of unusual combinations like banana and raisin or tuna tartare mixed with tapioca pearls), main courses (wild duck in blackberry sauce, the Brazilian classic dried beef with abóbora squash), and desserts including a crepe-like tapioca filled with the decadent cocoa-and-condensed-milk dessert called brigadeiro.

OPPOSITE Sinuous works at the Tomie Ohtake Institute.

THE BASICS

Taxis are plentiful, but don't expect your driver to speak English.

Emiliano
Rua Oscar Freire, 384
55-11-3069-4369
emiliano.com.br
$$$$
A top boutique hotel (complete with helipad) on luxurious Oscar Freire Street, home to some of the city's best restaurants and shops.

Hotel Pergamon
Rua Frei Caneca, 80
55-11-3123-2021
pergamon.com.br
$$
Brazilian art in the lobby and stylish touches in the rooms. In a vibrant, gay-friendly neighborhood.

Unique
Avenida Brigadeiro Luís Antônio, 4700
55-11-3055-4710
hotelunique.com.br
$$$$
Chic hotel in the affluent Jardim Paulista district.

ESCULTURAS

Salvador

Outside of Carnaval week each February, when the emphasis is decidedly on the present, the coastal city of Salvador, capital of Bahia state, seems almost obsessed with its African past. Nowhere in Brazil is the deep influence of three and a half centuries of slavery so obvious, from the color of people's skin to the color of the food (often orange, from the ubiquitous use of dendê, or red palm oil); from the deep influence of the African-derived religious traditions of candomblé to the musical beats of axé and samba. In the Rio Vermelho neighborhood, home to the hottest night life in this city on the Bay of All Saints, even the cool kids often shun the chicest bars and restaurants to hang out in the public plazas, drinking beer and eating the traditional, African-inspired black-eyed pea fritters called acarajé. — BY SETH KUGEL

FRIDAY

1 *Past and Present* 3 p.m.

The state-run **Modern Art Museum of Bahia**, or MAM (Avenida Contorno; 55-71-3117-6141; mam.ba.gov.br), features contemporary artists, yet is inextricably tied to the Bahian past. MAM is set along the coast in the **Solar do Unhão**, a 17th-century colonial complex that now houses cultural institutions and events. The museum's collection includes prominent 20th-century Brazilian artists like Tarsila do Amaral and Di Cavalcanti.

2 *Battle of the Baianas* 6 p.m.

Spend your first evening in the **Rio Vermelho** neighborhood, where the action starts at happy hour. Choose a plaza and grab one of the tables tended by waiters from nearby bars. Then send a friend to wait in line at one of the stands where women in traditional Bahian dress make acarajé, frying balls of dough in dendê oil until crispy, splitting them in half, and slathering them with sauces, shrimp, and wicked malagueta peppers. The stands are known by the names of their founders. Direct your friend to **Dinha**, where the stand has outlived the maitre d'acarajé but the food still lives up to her name (Largo de Santana; 55-71-3334-4350; casadadinhadoacaraje.com.br; $).

3 *Africa via Brazil* 8 p.m.

The interior of the lovely Bahian restaurant **Dona Mariquita** (Rua do Meio 178; 55-71-3334-6947; donamariquita.com.br; $$) is fashioned after a candomblé terrace (where religious ceremonies are performed), with a thatched roof, whitewashed walls, and splashes of color doled out sparingly. Leila Carreiro, the owner, has studded the menu with African-influenced traditional dishes that were fading into obscurity, like arroz de hauçá, a mound of sweet coconut rice topped with a salty smoked shrimp sauce and surrounded by a moat of hearty shredded dried beef.

4 *Alley Bar* 10 p.m.

Have a drink at the **Boteco do França** (Rua Borges dos Reis, 24A; 55-71-3334-2734), but don't sit indoors. Find an empty table in the narrow alleyway between the bar and the evangelical church next door. Passers-by dodge tables to use the alley as a shortcut between two main streets.

OPPOSITE A seaside walk in the sculpture garden at the Modern Art Museum of Bahia, or MAM. Salvador, the capital of Bahia state, is a place of both African-inspired traditions and updated sophistication.

RIGHT At the Nosso Senhor do Bonfim church, a ferry ride away from the main city, a fence is covered by "wish ribbons" left in hopes of good fortune.

SATURDAY

5 *Pelourinho Ramble* 11 a.m.

You can easily spend most of a day in the cobbled, hilly streets of the **Pelourinho** district. It was revived from its decayed, crime-ridden, red-light reputation in the 1980s and turned into its current touristy but irresistible self. Wander into the dazzling gold-plated Baroque interior of the **São Francisco Church and Convent** (Terreiro de Jesus; 55-71-3322-6430), buy a coconut treat from a street vendor, and browse at the design and crafts shops, which vary in quality. One you can count on is **Didara Design** (Rua Gregório de Matos, 20; 55-71-3321-9428; didara.com.br), featuring Goya Lopes's famed African-themed prints — people, animals, abstract — on shirts, dresses, aprons, pillows, and fabric bought by the meter. Upscale but not unaffordable, her work is about as genuinely Salvador as acarajé, but much easier to wrap up for the trip home.

6 *Cafe With a View* 5 p.m.

It's easy to forget you're in the Cidade Alta, the upper tier of the city, but you'll quickly remember if you wander over to **Cafelier** (Rua do Carmo, 50; 55-71-3241-5095; cafelier.com.br) in the Santo Antônio neighborhood of the historic center. The cafe, which looks more like an antiques store than a coffee shop, has a stunning view of the bay. Take a picture; you can Photoshop out any gaudy cruise ships later.

7 *Defensive Maneuvers* 7:30 p.m.

The white-washed **Forte Santo Antônio Além do Carmo** (end of Largo de Santo Antônio; 55-71-3117-1488), a former fort and prison, is now known as the Forte da Capoeira, a center for the martial arts and dance form that emerged from the traditions of African

TOP Drums and percussion are the theme at this shop in irresistible Pelourinho, a hilly district of cobbled streets, intriguing stores, and inviting cafes.

ABOVE Martial arts at Forte da Capoeira.

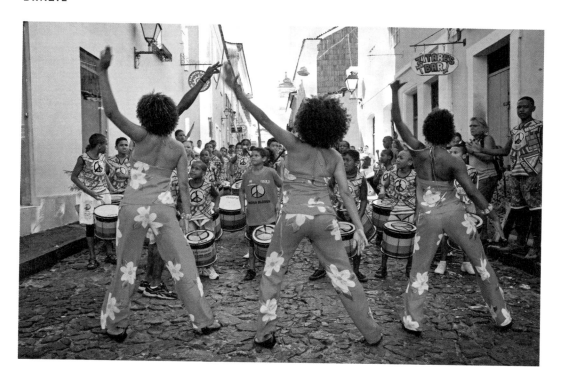

slaves. On a Saturday evening at 7:30 you can head inside the fort and follow the rhythms to the classroom where the master and students practice.

8 *Under the Frangipani* 9 p.m.

The grungy chaos of Pelourinho disappears as you step into the garden of **Maria Mata Mouro** (Rua da Ordem Terceira, 8; 55-71-3321-3929; mariamatamouro.com.br; $$) and sit down under the flowering frangipani tree (jasmin-manga in Portuguese). The menu is so international that you might be tempted to skip the fish moqueca, a traditional stew. But make sure at least one in your party tries it. The restaurant's take on the dish is lighter than many and executed to perfection.

9 *Nightcap Infusion* 10 p.m.

Pelourinho is no Rio Vermelho when it comes to night life, but you can stop for a beer and live music just about anywhere, or have a nightcap at **O Cravinho** (Terreiro de Jesus, 3; 55-71-3322-6759; ocravinho.com.br), a dark bar with heavy wooden tables that serves infused cachaça, the Brazilian sugar-cane liquor. The namesake infusion is the one with cloves, but there's something for everyone —orange peel or ginger, for example. There are times to err on the side of caution in Pelourinho—it can be dangerous at night—but in the central square, taxis are waiting to take you home.

SUNDAY

10 *Creative Reuse* Noon

It's worth the 20- or 30-minute cab ride to **Boca de Galinha** (Rua da Estação, 58; 55-71-3398-1232; $) to check out the recipe for success that its owner, Nilton Souza, has stumbled upon: Find a run-down neighborhood. Set up some tables on a balcony

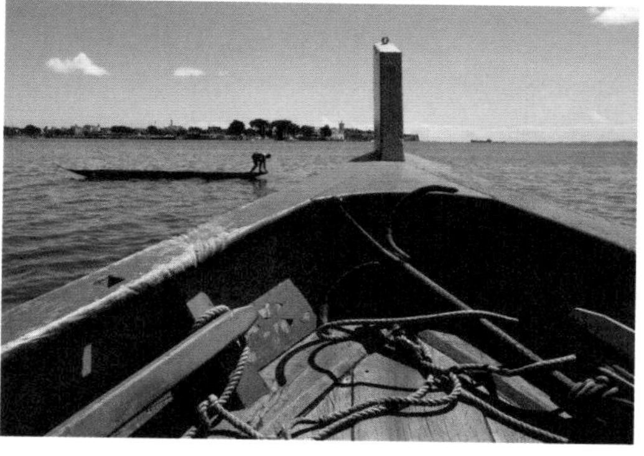

ABOVE Performers from the Olodum Creative School.

RIGHT A ferry crossing the bay to the Ribeira neighborhood. Take the trip to see Nosso Senhor do Bonfim church and its Room of Miracles.

overlooking the bay. Write out the daily menu of moquecas and fried fish longhand in school notebooks. (To avoid a wait, arrive by noon.)

11 *Dessert and Miracles* 2 p.m.

No need to call a cab back to town. Ask for directions to the nearby ferry that will take you across the bay to the **Ribeira** neighborhood. Stop off at the **Sorveteria da Ribeira** (Largo da Ribeira, 87; 55-71-3316-5451; sorveteriadaribeira.com.br) and take a stab at deciding which exotic mystery fruit you think makes the best ice cream: Siriguela? Graviola? Umbu? Cupuaçu? Then hop a quick cab (or walk about a mile and a half) to Salvador's most famous church, **Nosso Senhor do Bonfim** (Praça Senhor do Bonfim; 55-71-3316-2196), where models of body parts left as thanks are on display in the Room of Miracles.

ABOVE The proprietor at an acarajé stand. Women in traditional Bahian dress sell the acarajé, balls of fried dough slathered with sauces, shrimp, and peppers.

OPPOSITE The ornately decorated Baroque-era San Francisco Church in the Pelourinho district.

THE BASICS

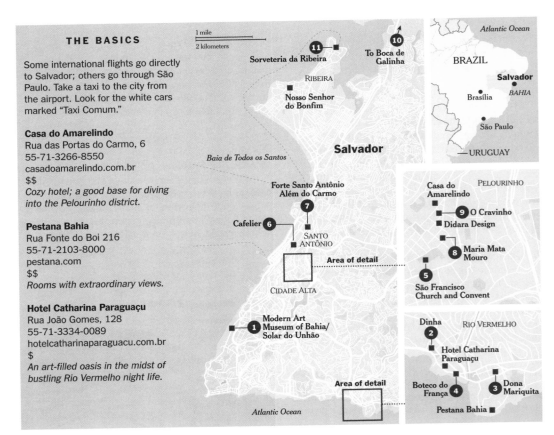

Some international flights go directly to Salvador; others go through São Paulo. Take a taxi to the city from the airport. Look for the white cars marked "Taxi Comum."

Casa do Amarelindo
Rua das Portas do Carmo, 6
55-71-3266-8550
casadoamarelindo.com.br
$$
Cozy hotel; a good base for diving into the Pelourinho district.

Pestana Bahia
Rua Fonte do Boi 216
55-71-2103-8000
pestana.com
$$
Rooms with extraordinary views.

Hotel Catharina Paraguaçu
Rua João Gomes, 128
55-71-3334-0089
hotelcatharinaparaguacu.com.br
$
An art-filled oasis in the midst of bustling Rio Vermelho night life.

PROJETO
SÃO FRANCISCO
RESTAURAÇÃO E
REVITALIZAÇÃO
da Igreja e Convento
Eletrobrás

Bahia

The Paulistanos—São Paulo residents—trickling into Bahia in the 1970s were mostly hippies and artists who created a kind of bohemian village life in the sunshine and sand of this coastal Brazilian state. Well-heeled vacationers soon followed, transforming choice parts of the windswept shore into a playground for a glamorous, carefree crowd. Now private helicopters whisk billionaires to beachfront homes, while the not-so-rich stay in swanky but discreetly eco-conscious hotels in Trancoso, a former fishing village that functions as the chic coastal strip's town center. Beneath all the glitter, the original charm remains (at least when the disco music isn't resounding): unspoiled beach fringed by coconut groves and rain forest, villages with an aura of history and a simpler past, and a surrounding diverse culture with its own laid-back spirit.

— BY ALEXEI BARRIONUEVO

FRIDAY

1 *Beach Natives* 2 p.m.

Bahia's beaches remain pristine, with a few inns and beach clubs and only a smattering of homes, most set back from the water. Building restrictions have prevented taller condos and hotels, preserving, for now, the sense of the natural. Take a walk or a dip at **Praia Nativos**, the beach at Trancoso and a favorite spot of the beautiful people, who venture out for the waves, the sunbathing, and each other. Few will flinch as a steady stream of private planes and helicopters zip above the water.

2 *Cobblestone Chic* 4 p.m.

Trancoso, with its uneven cobblestone streets and dirt roads, still looks like the hippie getaway that first drew vacationers' attention a quarter-century ago. Colorfully painted small wooden houses are still the norm, even though some of them are now shops selling $35 wineglasses and $3,000 paintings. Make your way to the **Quadrado**, a grassy, open quadrangle near a cliff overlooking the beach. It's flanked by the town's nicest restaurants and boutiques, deceptively humble in their traditional buildings. Anchoring the far end is an old white church, São João Batista, a reminder that the town was founded by Jesuits and dates back to the 1500s. During the peak season, which goes from about December through February, the Quadrato is eerily quiet for most of the day and starts waking up at about 3 p.m., when shops and restaurants open.

3 *Shop by Night* 5 p.m.

Browse through the boutiques on the Quadrado for creative takes on the essentials of the good life. If you're looking for sexy Brazilian swimwear, or for something light and fetching to wear for dancing, you've come to the right place. Interesting objets d'art and home accessories are also well represented: coconut jewelry boxes, carved wooden furniture, clay sculptures, ceramics. There's plenty of time to linger. Shops and galleries are open until midnight or later.

4 *Quadrado Dining* 9 p.m.

Along the Quadrado as the evening wears on, multicolored lights sparkle from low-hanging trees and friends sit at outdoor tables on the dusty edge of the grass, clinking the ice in their drinks or digging into the local seafood. **El Gordo** (Praça São João 7,

OPPOSITE Praia Rio Verde, one of the gorgeous beaches that bring Brazil's jet setters to Bahia's coastline around the picturesque town of Trancoso.

RIGHT Relaxing at Praia do Espelho.

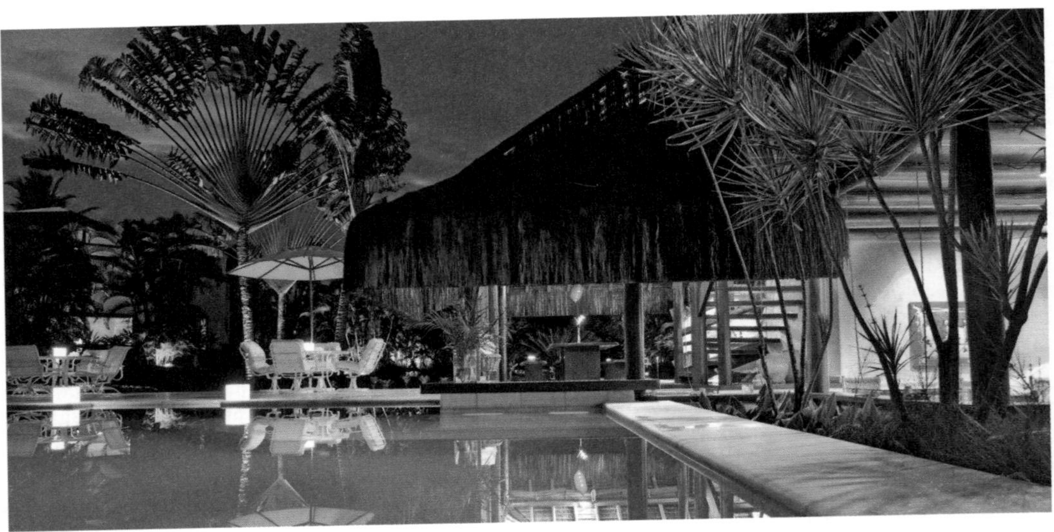

Quadrado; 55-73-3668-1193; elgordo.com.br; $$$), the restaurant at the small hotel of the same name, offers international cuisine, great service, and a romantic setting around a serene pool.

5 *Cocktails and Breezes* 11 p.m.

The sculptured 20- and 30-somethings you saw earlier on the beach — models and actors sprinkled in with São Paulo's elite professionals — are now sipping colored martinis in the open-air bars as gentle nighttime breezes tickle their skin. Select a likely-looking spot and join in, or move from bar to bar. Some places feature forró, traditional Brazilian dance music. During the heart of the summer holidays this mellow scene is transformed as "pop-up" clubs and hard-partying revelers move in. Young women in revealing party dresses and men in body-hugging Italian shirts and Bermuda shorts dance to thumping music until dawn.

SATURDAY

6 *Discoveries* 1 p.m.

The Brazilian government calls this area the Discovery Coast because it was where Portuguese sailors first landed in South America. Set out today to do your own exploring on the beaches beyond Trancoso — miles of pristine sand stretching in both directions. To the north are **Praia Rio da Barra**, walkable from Nativos and far less populated, and **Praia do Taipe**, which is reached via a long boardwalk strung between towering cliffs. Closest to the south are Praia dos **Coqueiros** and Praia do **Rio Verde**, still gorgeous and mostly untamed, despite a fair number of beach bars. Have lunch at one of the waterside restaurants, and make an afternoon of it.

7 *African Flavors* 9 p.m.

O Cacau (Praça São João, Quadrado; 55-73-3668-1266; $$$), one of the more popular restaurants on the Quadrado in Trancoso, specializes in Bahian cuisine, which mixes African and Portuguese influences and is famous all over the country. Some of its most prominent ingredients, now identified with this part of Brazil, are African in origin, including hot chili peppers called malagueta and a strongly flavored orange palm oil called dendê. This is a good place to try moqueca, a spicy fish stew that is the center of many a Bahian meal, or acarajé balls (mashed beans fried in oil) with vatapá, a garlicky paste of shrimp and coconut.

SUNDAY

8 *In the Mirror* 11 a.m.

One of the best Bahia spots is **Praia do Espelho**, about a half-hour car ride from Trancoso over

BELOW A beachside lounge in Trancoso.

a winding dirt road and past grazing cows. A sprawling, wide ribbon of powdery sand, it's known for water as smooth as a mirror (espelho in Portuguese) on calm days — the perfect antidote for young Brazilians recovering from a night of clubbing. Pass the beachgoers lounging on brightly colored pillows at the Pousada e Restaurante do Baiano (pousadadobaiano.com.br), a colonial-style inn where daytime D.J.'s play a down-tempo mix, and swim out in the transparent water toward the clearly visible coral formations offshore.

9 *Who Needs a Menu?* 1 p.m.

Pull yourself away from the water long enough to walk over for lunch at **Restaurante da Silvinha** (55-73-9985-4157), a small and simple but sophisticated restaurant masquerading as a rustic beach hut. Sip a passion-fruit caipirinha or a bright green caipivodka, and order whatever they're cooking — there's no menu. Don't be anxious about what will arrive on the plate. You're in good hands.

OPPOSITE ABOVE The pool at Villas de Trancoso, one of the luxury hotels on the Bahia coast.

ABOVE Cycling on the Quadrado, a square lined with preserved buildings that hold upscale shops and restaurants.

THE BASICS

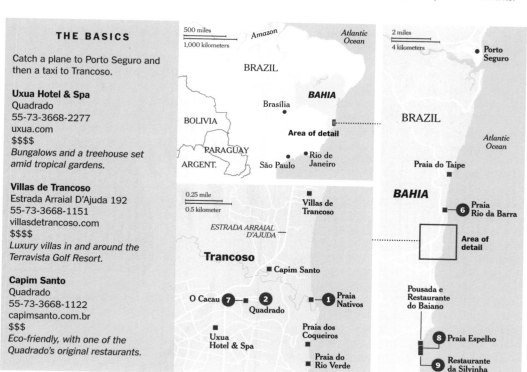

Catch a plane to Porto Seguro and then a taxi to Trancoso.

Uxua Hotel & Spa
Quadrado
55-73-3668-2277
uxua.com
$$$$
Bungalows and a treehouse set amid tropical gardens.

Villas de Trancoso
Estrada Arraial D'Ajuda 192
55-73-3668-1151
villasdetrancoso.com
$$$$
Luxury villas in and around the Terravista Golf Resort.

Capim Santo
Quadrado
55-73-3668-1122
capimsanto.com.br
$$$
Eco-friendly, with one of the Quadrado's original restaurants.

500 miles
1,000 kilometers
Amazon
Atlantic Ocean
BRAZIL
BAHIA
Brasília
BOLIVIA
Area of detail
PARAGUAY
ARGENT.
São Paulo
Rio de Janeiro

2 miles
4 kilometers
Porto Seguro
BRAZIL
Atlantic Ocean
Praia do Taipe
BAHIA
6 Praia Rio da Barra
Area of detail
Pousada e Restaurante do Baiano
8 Praia Espelho
9 Restaurante da Silvinha

0.25 mile
0.5 kilometer
Villas de Trancoso
ESTRADA ARRAIAL D'AJUDA
Trancoso
Capim Santo
O Cacau 7
2 Quadrado
1 Praia Nativos
Uxua Hotel & Spa
Praia dos Coqueiros
Praia do Rio Verde

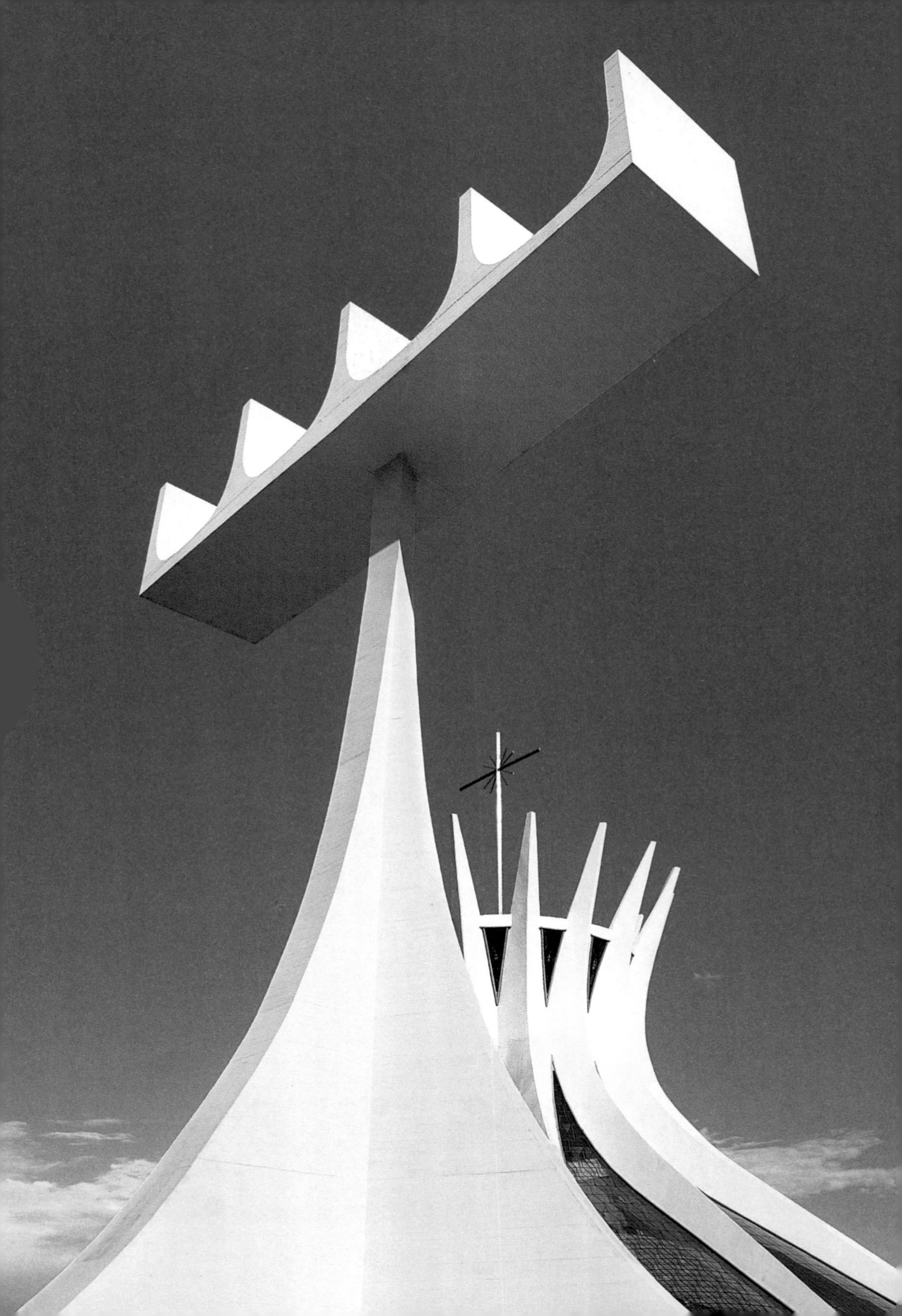

Brasília

Despite the modern architectural monuments by the legendary Oscar Niemeyer, Brazil's retro-futuristic capital city—erected on an expanse of dry plains in central Brazil in the 1950s and '60s—has generally drawn few visitors who didn't have business with the federal government. But as Brazil's economy booms and its world influence increases, Brasília is coming of age, gaining a new museum here, a cool bridge there, top-shelf restaurants everywhere. Brasília is also safer and calmer than Rio de Janeiro or São Paulo, unless you count the stress of trying to understand its maddening address system. Adding to the charm are awe-inspiring sunsets, samba hot spots, and something even the greatest urban planners in the world couldn't have given the city upon its inauguration in 1960: a half-century of tradition and history.

— BY SETH KUGEL

FRIDAY

1 *Congress of Niemeyer* 4 p.m.

Start in the heart of the "Pilot Plan," the original planned city, where three Niemeyer-designed buildings house the three branches of Brazilian government around **Praça dos Três Poderes** (Three Powers Square). They're all classic, curvy Niemeyer: the Planalto Palace, where Brazil's president works; the Federal Supreme Court; and towering over both, two sky-scraping office towers and the accompanying convex and concave domes where the National Congress sits. Stroll up the esplanade past the pale green ministry buildings to one of the most recent works by Niemeyer: the 2006 **Honestino Guimarães National Museum** (SCS, Lote 2; 55-61-3325-5220) where you can see the work of contemporary artists from around the world. Niemeyer died in 2012 at a few days shy of age 105, after continuing to work past his 100th birthday.

2 *Sunset From a Shrine* 6 p.m.

The sunset in Brasília is beautiful from just about anywhere, but the best place of all to catch it is at the **Ermida Dom Bosco** (QI 29, Lago Sul), a Niemeyer-designed shrine across the artificial Lake Paranoá from the Pilot Plan. The lookout attracts a daily crowd that melts away once the sun is gone. Don't follow the masses: stick it out with the stray couples (and coconut-water vendors) and catch the stunning oranges and reds and lavenders that fill the sky about 20 minutes later.

3 *Bar Hopping* 8 p.m.

The most popular evening activity for all local residents is to eat, drink, and talk at the hyper-social bars that serve young and old, straight and gay, beer lovers and caipirinha aficionados alike—at pub prices. Perhaps the most traditional of all the watering holes is **Beirute** (CLS 109, Bloco A; 55-61-3244-1717), seamlessly mixing the older regulars with a young gay crowd; the food, as you might expect, runs Middle Eastern, including the football-shaped minced-meat-and-bulgur snacks known in Portuguese as kibes. Two other favorite spots are **Libanus** (CLS 206, Bloco C, Loja 36; 55-61-3244-9795), younger and a bit more raucous, and **Boteco** (CLS 406, Bloco D, Loja 35; 55-61-3443-4344), a spirited Rio de Janeiro–style bar erected, in classic Brasília juxtaposition, across the parking lot from a supermarket. Waiters bring around trays bearing snacks to choose from; the most famous is the coxinha de camarão, a shrimp version of Brazil's staple bar snack, chicken croquettes.

OPPOSITE The bell tower at the Cathedral of Brasília, one of the futuristic buildings by the architect Oscar Niemeyer that define the city. Brasília, a planned capital city, sprang up on an expanse of dry plains in the mid-20th century.

BELOW The stained glass of the Dom Bosco Sanctuary, designed by Carlos Alberto Naves, glows in shades of blue.

SATURDAY

4 *Soupie, Anyone?* 9 a.m.

"Soupie" is how the Brazilians pronounce SUP, the abbreviation for stand-up paddle surfing, a sport involving you, a surfboard, and a paddle. And you'll need to pronounce it the way they do if you want the staff member at the gate of the **Clube Naval** (SCES, Trecho 2, Conjunto 13; clubenavaldf.com.br) to let you through to the lakeside base of **Clube do Vento** (55-61-3532-5009; clubedovento.com). You'll soon be paddling out into Lake Paranoá toward the stunning Juscelino Kubitschek Bridge with its three criss-crossing arches, which opened in 2002 and immediately became a city landmark.

5 *Northeastern Buffet* Noon

Just about every Brazilian city outside the northeast has a healthy number of migrants from that cuisine-rich and financially poor region, but Brasília also has a branch of the northeast-based **Mangai** (SCE Sul; 55-61-3224-3079; mangai.com.br; $$), a palace of regional cuisine where diners pick and choose from a buffet of 80 or so main dishes (heavy on the pork and squash and manioc) and 40 or so desserts. Fill a plate, and have a dessert and a fresh fruit juice. Also included: hammocks on the porch overlooking Lake Paranoá to take a postprandial rest.

6 *Modernist Worship* 2 p.m.

No colonial-era churches in this town. Instead, Brasília's houses of worship fit right in with the modernist theme. You've already caught a glimpse of Niemeyer's National Cathedral near the ministries, now it's time for a visit to what must be the bluest church in the world, the **Dom Bosco Sanctuary** (SEPS, Quadra 702; 55-61-3223-6542; santuariodombosco.org.br), completed in 1970. Its 50-foot-high Gothic arches are filled in with 12 tones of blue stained glass, casting the interior (and its 2.75-ton chandelier and cedar cross) in haunting submarine tones. From there, continue south to the drastically more modest **Igrejinha de Fátima** (EQS 307/308; igrejinhadefatima.org), the city's first church, also a Niemeyer special.

7 *Sunset Samba* 4 p.m.

Late-afternoon samba is a Saturday tradition in town, and while the bars that host it may not be much to look at, cold beer, a warm crowd, and a hot band render the soulless venues atmospherically irrelevant. One hopping place is **Cadê Tereza** (CLS 201, Bloco B, Loja 1; 55-61-3225-0555; cadeterezabar.com.br), named after a Jorge Ben Jor song whose title means "Where's Tereza?" The likely answer to that question: If she didn't get there early enough, she's probably in line. Another choice is the longtime classic **Calaf** (SBS, Quadra 2, Bloco S; 55-61-3325-7408; calaf.com.br), which brings unexpected weekend life to the otherwise abandoned Southern Banking Sector.

8 *Copenhagen on Paranoá* 9 p.m.

Dress up and head to one of Brasília's most elegant and unusual restaurants. **Aquavit** (SMLN, Trecho 12, Conjunto 1, Casa 5; 55-61-3369-2301; restauranteaquavit.co; $$$$). There, the chef and owner Simon Lau Cederholm, a native of Denmark, will greet you as if you were attending a dinner party at his house. And in fact, you are: he opened the restaurant in his own home (which he designed;

ABOVE The Niemeyer-designed National Congress building.

RIGHT A full plate at Mangai, where diners choose regional cuisine from a buffet of 80 main dishes and 40 desserts.

he's also an architect) in 2005. The set menu is a mix of Danish cuisine, French technique, and Brazilian ingredients. One night's five-course prix fixe included both a cold soup of cucumber with smoked salmon and a locally made cheese, which the chef whipped and served with both nuts and fruit of the cashew tree, an abundant crop in the region.

SUNDAY

9 *Petit Déjeuner* 9 a.m.

The idea of a true French patisserie on the bland commercial blocks in Brasília is almost as counterintuitive as having a McDonald's on the Champs-Élysées. But they both exist. The superior of the two is **Daniel Briand Pâtissier & Chocolatier** (SCLN 104, Bloco A, Loja 26; 55-61-3326-1135; cafedanielbriand.com; $$), a breakfast- and brunch-lover's dream. Order a breakfast platter or elegant pastries, buttery croissants with house-made jams, fresh-made quiche, or varied pâtés à la carte.

10 *President's Palace* 10:30 a.m.

Head back to the Praça dos Três Poderes for a tour of the **Planalto Palace**, the work space of Brazil's president. The public spaces are filled with Brazilian art and modernist furniture by the celebrated Brazilian designer Sérgio Rodrigues. But that's not all: you can also see the room where the cabinet meets, and even peek into the president's office.

THE BASICS

Brasília, designed for an automobile culture, is not a walking city. Get around by taxi or bus. There's also a metro, but its reach is limited.

Meliá Brasil 21
SHS, Quadra 6, Conjunto A, Bloco F
55-61-3218-4700
melia.com.br
$$
One of many perfectly comfortable business-style hotels.

Hotels Sector
Brasília Palace
SHTN, Trecho 1, Conjunto 1
55-61-3306-9100
plazabrasilia.com.br
$$
Style and history. Looks as if it had stepped right out of the '60s, though the rooms have been renovated.

Royal Tulip Brasília Alvorada
SHTN, Trecho 1,Conjunto 1B
55-61-3424-7000
royaltulipbrasiliaalvorada.com
$$$$
Large hotel on the shore of Lake Paranoá with pools, spa, tennis courts, and fitness center.

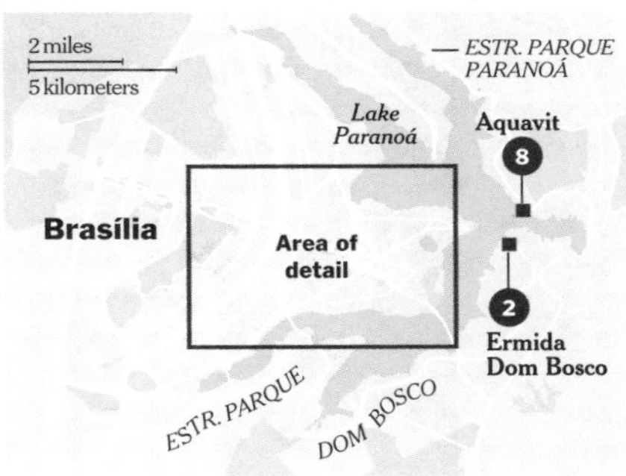

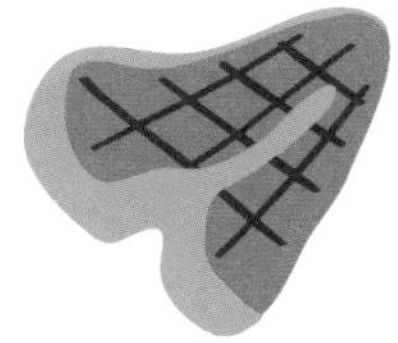

Montevideo

Montevideo may be overshadowed by its flashier neighbors Punta del Este and Buenos Aires, but it does not suffer from an inferiority complex. As Uruguay's capital and its commercial hub, Montevideo follows its own nonchalant pace. Its 1.3 million residents are at ease with their timeless pleasures; those leather cases slung over their shoulders, for example, hold thermoses and gourds for making mate tea. And although Montevideo's skyline is punctuated by few skyscrapers, the city is home to charming small museums and a lively old town. You will compete for attention with only a handful of other tourists. Montevideanos are happy to keep their city under wraps. — BY SETH KUGEL

FRIDAY

1 *Hot Dogs and Cake* 4 p.m.

Dive into downtown life at the **Plaza Fabini** (18 de Julio and Rio Negro; also called Plaza del Entrevero), a manicured, fountain-filled square that's perfect for soaking in late afternoon rays and for people watching. The outdoor cafe **La Pasiva** is famous for its "panchos," hot dogs served with a secret-recipe spicy mustard and best washed down with a bottle of Paso de los Toros, Uruguay's contribution to the great grapefruit sodas of the world. You still have many hours until Montevideo's late dinner hour, so make your way next to **Cake's** (José Ellauri 1067; 598-2-707-6207; cakes.com.uy) in the upscale Pocitos neighborhood. It's a wonderful place to have tea and a gargantuan dessert. Try the Uruguayan-style mille-feuille, with loads of dulce de leche; or the Ramón Novarro, a chocolate cake with loads of dulce de leche; or the alfajores, cookies filled with loads of dulce de leche. (They do have some items without dulce de leche, but why bother?)

2 *Muzzarela and Fainá* 9 p.m.

Casual restaurants in Montevideo have strikingly similar menus, based around chopp (draft beer), muzzarelas (tasty Sicilian pizza slices), fainá (flatbread made with chickpea flour), and chivitos (steak sandwiches). For an old-school spot that's a cut above the rest, try **Pizzería Trouville** (21 de Septiembre 3104; 598-2-711-2598; pizzeriatrouville.com.uy; $), a popular place in Pocitos that's somewhere between a diner and a bar. Its muzzarelas are dripping with cheese (unless you just order "pizza," which comes cheeseless) and taste especially good if you can snag an outdoor table.

3 *Double Your Fun* 11 p.m.

Montevideo is not on the radar of many celebrities (or not yet) but **Baar Fun Fun** (Ciudadela 1229, Mercado Central; 598-2-915-8005; barfunfun.com), a bar founded in 1895 and now a hot spot for tango and local candombé music, has attracted a few, as evidenced by the photographs on the wall. Among the wall-worthy: the Canadian rocker Bryan Adams; the American actor Danny Glover; and Michelle Bachelet, the former president of Chile. Uruguayans of all ages pack into this place to drink uvita, a super-sweet wine-based concoction; listen to live performances; and, to the extent the cramped space allows, dance.

SATURDAY

4 *Morning Market* 10 a.m.

Though taxis are cheap, Montevideo's center is manageable on foot, and a good place to start is **Mercado de los Artesanos** (Plaza Cagancha 1365; 598-2-901-0887), a crafts market where artists work in shifts selling each other's candles, leatherwork, ceramic lamps, and finger dolls. Next, walk down 18

OPPOSITE The Palacio Salvo in downtown Montevideo.

RIGHT Flowers for sale on a city street.

de Julio to gawk at the **Palacio Salvo**, the tallest building in South America when it was built in the 1920s. Then wander into the old city, seeing how pleasant a historic district can be when you remove the tourists and install residents going about their daily business.

5 *From Gurvich to Figari* Noon

Montevideo venerates at least two of its country's artists enough to dedicate museums to them. The **Museo Gurvich** (Ituzaingó 1377, Plaza Matriz; 598-2-915-7826; museogurvich.org), shows art of José Gurvich, who died in 1974. The man did just about everything — paintings, sculptures, collages, murals, coffee sets — with subjects from the seven deadly sins portrayed by barnyard animals to a Where's Waldo-like montage. The **Museo Figari** (Juan Carlos Gómez 1427; 598-2-915-7065; museofigari.gub.uy) houses work by Pedro Figari (1861–1938), a folk modernist painter — and a lawyer and politician — who depicted African-Uruguayans, slavery, gauchos, and Indians.

6 *Meet for Meat* 3 p.m.

Saturday afternoons take on a party atmosphere at the **Mercado del Puerto** (Piedras and Yacaré; 598-2-915-4178; mercadodelpuerto.com), a grand 19th-century port market that is a carnivore's delight. The traditional routine: start at the bar of Roldós with a bottle of Medio y Medio, a revelry-inducing mix of sparkling and dry wines. Then switch to a Uruguayan red when you sit down for a meal at one of the parrillada (mixed grill) restaurants, while skilled grill masters roast hunks of meat and, probably just for show, the occasional green pepper.

BELOW The sidewalk serves as a stage for tango dancers performing at lunchtime.

7 *Sharing Straws* 7 p.m.

Remember when weekend evenings meant hanging out on the waterfront with your thermos of hot water, drinking yerba mate through a shared metal straw? You don't? Then you're clearly not from Pocitos, where a stretch of the **Rambla**, a beachfront promenade, fills up with couples and groups of friends. The crowd skews young but is by no means exclusively so. The owner of the mate, or gourd, pours in the water, and passes it to one friend after another. It's a bring-your-own affair, so if you want to join, be sure to pick up a mate and thermos earlier in the day. They're easy to find.

8 *Sushi Break* 10 p.m.

Try as they might, Montevideanos cannot live on meat alone, and one place they take a break from the beef culture is at **Café Misterio** (Costa Rica 1700, Carrasco; 598-2-601-8765; cafemisterio.com.uy; $$), a sushi bar that has for years been one of the hippest spots in town. Retro meets modern in the ever-changing décor, 30-somethings meet 60-somethings at the bar, and octopus sashimi meets mojitos on the menu.

9 *Round (Like a Record)* 2 a.m.

At 2 a.m. it is almost too early to arrive at a dance club like **Lotus** (World Trade Center; 598-2-628-1379; lotus.com.uy), but there are plenty of jam-packed bars in the area like **El Pony Pisador** (José Iturriaga 3497; 598-2-622-1885; elponypisador.com.uy) for a previa, or warm-up. Lotus itself is almost disturbingly round, like a disco on a 1970s Martian spaceship, but it creates a flowing transition between wallflowers on the outside, flirters one ring in, and dancers sweating to house music on the inside.

SUNDAY

10 *Market Makers* 11 a.m.

Looking for fresh onions, candy-coated peanuts, comfy sweaters, well-worn books, flowers, a used remote control, and a puppy? You'll find those and lots of other things at the **Tristán Narvaja** street fair, which takes over blocks and blocks around the thoroughfare of the same name on Sundays. Even if you're not in the market for anything besides a stroll through an interesting market, you are guaranteed satisfaction.

11 *The National Lunch* 1 p.m.

If you've made it this far without having a chivito, the Uruguayan steak sandwich that even in its plainest form comes loaded with lettuce, tomato, egg, and cheese, you may have set a Montevidean record. **Paponita** (18 de Julio 1649; 598-2-408-4840; $), an old-school diner filled with cute old couples, will end your streak. The Canadian chivito comes with ham, lettuce, tomato, and tons of other stuff; the copa melba is a sky-high ice-cream concoction that is nearly as much of an architectural accomplishment as some of the surrounding buildings.

ABOVE A cook at Papoñita constructs a chivito, Uruguay's favorite comfort food. The foundation is a sandwich made with the succulent local steak, and the ingredients stacked on top are limited only by the imagination — and gravity.

Mercado del Puerto 6
Mercado de los Artesanos 4
Papoñita 11
18 DE JULIO
BULVAR GENERAL ARTIGAS
Lotus/ World Trade Center 9
Museo Figari
CENTRO
Tristán Narvaja 10
Montevideo
The Don Hotel
Plaza Fabini/ La Pasiva 1
El Pony Pisador
Palacio Salvo
Rambla 7
Cake's
PALERMO
POCITOS
Gurvich Museum 5
Baar Fun Fun 3
Ermitage Hotel
0.5 mile
1 kilometer
21 DE SEPTIEMBRE
Café Misterio 8
Pizzería Trouville 2
Montevideo
CARRASCO
COSTA RICA
TROUVILLE
The Belmont House
Area of detail
Río de la Plata
2 miles
4 kilometers
BRAZIL
Río Paraná
URUGUAY
Montevideo
Buenos Aires
ARGENTINA
Atlantic Ocean

THE BASICS

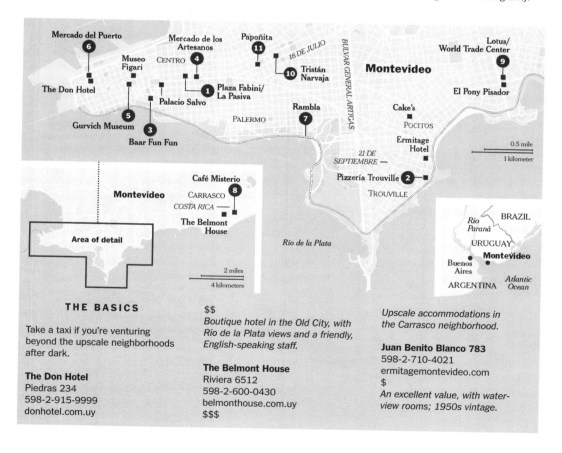

Take a taxi if you're venturing beyond the upscale neighborhoods after dark.

The Don Hotel
Piedras 234
598-2-915-9999
donhotel.com.uy
$$
Boutique hotel in the Old City, with Rio de la Plata views and a friendly, English-speaking staff.

The Belmont House
Riviera 6512
598-2-600-0430
belmonthouse.com.uy
$$$
Upscale accommodations in the Carrasco neighborhood.

Juan Benito Blanco 783
598-2-710-4021
ermitagemontevideo.com
$
An excellent value, with water-view rooms; 1950s vintage.

Casino

Punta del Este

Punta del Este, a sandy peninsula jutting into the Atlantic at the mouth of the Rio de la Plata, has a long history as a fashionable summer retreat. These days it's also an international party spot where glitterati from Argentina, Brazil, and well beyond arrive from December to March to chill at trendy bars and stock up on Gucci and Valentino. But Punta is also a holiday spot for middle-class families, sport fishermen, gamblers, cruise-ship passengers, and tourists. There are jazz festivals, film festivals, rodeos, outdoor fashion shows, and tournaments for golf, rugby, and polo. The beaches that form a blond, boulder-flecked halo around the city are lined with glinting Miami-esque towers, immaculate old stucco hotels, and modernist glass summer homes. Farther inland, rolling hills are carpeted with stands of pine and green-golden pastures for cattle as tasty as Argentina's (tastier, Uruguayans claim).

— BY MATT GROSS AND LARRY ROHTER

FRIDAY

1 *Gold Coast* 3 p.m.

Take an orientation drive to get acquainted with your surroundings. The town of Punta del Este itself covers the peninsula and has miles of beach, a port crowded with yachts, plenty of shopping, and a seaside promenade, **La Rambla**, along its coastal avenue. Driving northeast from there on Route 10, cruise along a crowded shoreline of hotels, condominiums, sports clubs, marinas, nightclubs, and restaurants, and after about 10 minutes you'll hit **La Barra**, a hip, tiny suburb. Some of the young, carefree crowd who populate this place may still be rubbing the sleep out of their eyes, since the typical routine is to rise around noon or 2 p.m., wander to the beach, and head out after a midnight dinner to go clubbing until 6 a.m. About 10 miles farther on is José Ignacio, an exclusive enclave where Porsches crowd the narrow streets, beauties in microbikinis blow kisses on the beach, and celebrities have quiet hideaways inland from the famous lighthouse.

2 *Beefy Architecture* 6 p.m.

To call a chivito a cheese-steak sandwich may be accurate, but it misses the point. Chivitos are grilled slices of juicy beef tenderloin on a roll, but more important, they're delivery devices for toppings: mozzarella, bacon, egg, lettuce, tomatoes, mushrooms, onions, hot peppers, sweet peppers, olives, pickles, several different blends of mayonnaise. Fresh ingredients are key, but just as important are the architectural talents of the chef. Back in Punta del Este, find a chivito for your pre-dinner supper at **La Pasiva** (Avenida Gorlero and Calle 28; 598-4244-1843; pasivadepuntadeleste.com). Don't be afraid to eat heartily. Your actual dinner is hours away.

3 *Sun Show* 8 p.m.

For in-town sunset viewing, amble out to the peninsula's tip. You'll have a good look as the sun casts rainbows onto clouds and sinks into the sea. When darkness falls, you can stroll along the Rambla, dark waves crashing just below, or check out the perennially popular bar **Moby Dick** (Rambla Artigas 650; 598-4244-1240; mobydick.com.uy) for pre-dinner drinks.

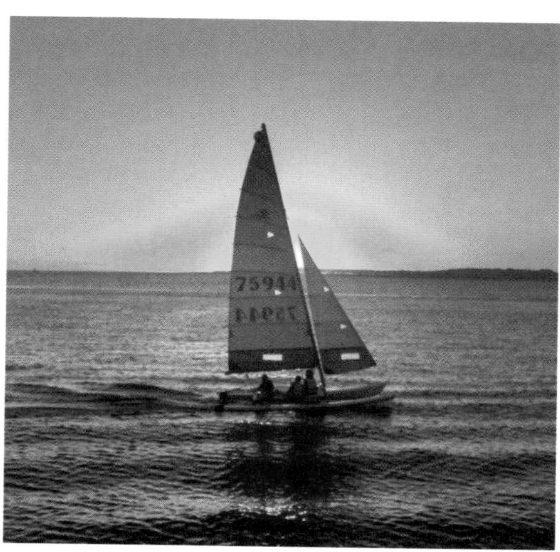

OPPOSITE Bright lights in Punta del Este, a traditional summer beach retreat where casinos, marinas, high-rise hotels, and nightclubs now draw the glitterati from all over South America and beyond.

RIGHT Sailing off Playa Mansa, or Tame Beach, on the sheltered side of the Punta Del Este peninsula.

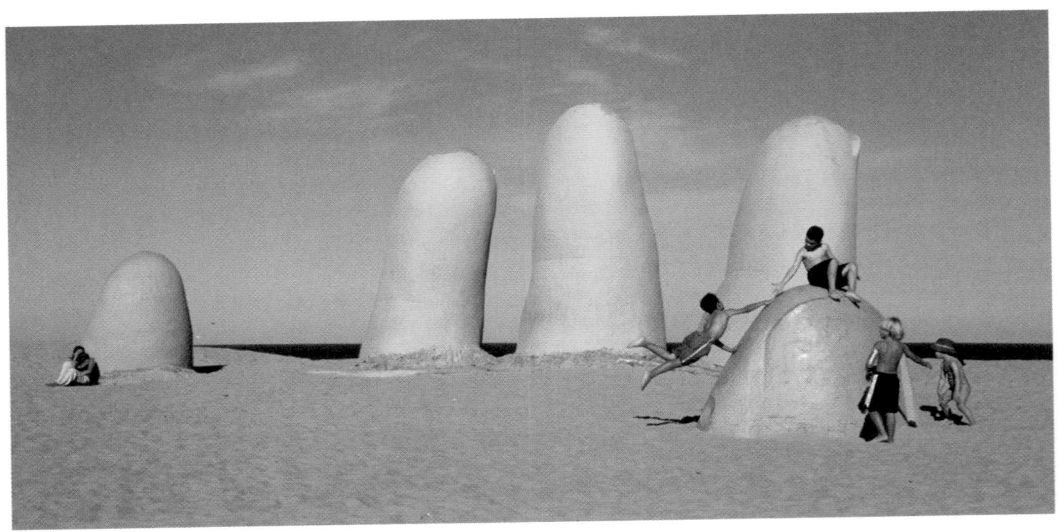

4 *Fish Course, Cheese Course* 11 p.m.

Lo de Charlie (819 12th Street, Punta del Este; 598-4244-4183; $$), an intimate bistro with pale violet walls and an open kitchen, specializes in seafood and knows what to do with it. On one visit, dinner consisted of a pile of chipirones, or baby squid, sautéed with onions; an orgy of side dishes like pommes lyonnaises; and pan-seared stingray with an aromatic saffron sauce. For dessert, the perennial favorite is the cheese-flavored ice cream.

5 *Dance Till Dawn* 2 a.m.

The big clubs are open, and within an hour they'll be packed with heaving, gyrating bodies. The younger crowd congregates in La Barra at places that come and go, depending what's hot this year. **Space**, one that may last a while, is a huge, warehouse-sized place with five bars. A slightly older set gravitates to **La Plage**, at Parada 12 on the Playa Brava beach, with the sound of crashing waves just outside competing with the thunderous music inside. In La Barra, the action spills out into the streets, and in both areas, dancing continues until dawn.

SATURDAY

6 *Hand Me the Sunblock* Noon

Grab your sunglasses and head for the beach. In town and close by, you can choose between two distinct experiences. The **Playa Mansa**, or Tame Beach, faces the calm, broad estuary of the Río de la Plata. Some families have frequented the same placid patches of this seashore for generations, using the old numbered bus stops, known as paradas, as markers of their favored spots. Surfers and adventurous (some might say foolhardy) swimmers prefer the rougher Atlantic Ocean side of the peninsula, starting with the **Playa Brava**, or Wild Beach, close to downtown and stretching up toward the nearby town of La Barra. Playa Brava is the site of one of Punta's famous landmarks—a sculpture of part of a giant hand, its digits protruding from the sand. A 1982 creation of the Chilean sculptor Mario Irarrázabal, it's often called "La Mano," or "The Hand," and it feels playful—a popular photo op and a magnet for children. Its actual title, however, suggests a whole different interpretation: it's called *Monument to the Drowned.*

7 *Undersea Relics* 5 p.m.

Get out of the sun and plunge into the deep at **Museo del Mar** (La Barra; 598-4277-1817: museodelmar.com.uy), a warehouse-sized museum chock-full of marine ephemera: 30-foot whale skeletons, fetal dolphins in formaldehyde, giant turtle shells, a stuffed manta ray. It's quirky, chaotic, obsessively detailed, and, without question, unique.

8 *Artisan Fair* 7 p.m.

There's cool boutique shopping on the main street (Route 10) in La Barra, and its jewelry stores and antiques shops are a refreshing departure from the Louis Vuitton and Valentino shops off Avenida Gorlero in downtown Punta. But there's an alternative in Punta, too, at the **Feria Artesanal**, an evening artisan street market on the Plaza Artigas, the town's central square. You'll find interesting souvenirs here: folkloric art, handmade silver and leather crafts, hand-knit woolens, and gourds for drinking yerba mate tea.

9 *Uruguayan French* 10 p.m.

La Bourgogne (Avenue del Mar at Calle Pedragosa Sierra; 598-4248-2007; labourgogne.com.uy; $$$$), in the El Bosque neighborhood, has often been called the best restaurant in Uruguay. It is affiliated with the Relais & Châteaux restaurant group, and the cuisine is French. Perfectly mannered waiters deliver homemade breads, Argentinian wines, and entrees like rabbit with Uruguayan caviar.

SUNDAY

10 *Castle in the Air* 11 a.m.

Allow plenty of time to gawk at **Casapueblo** (Punta Ballena; 598-4257-8041; carlospaezvilaro.com.uy), a rambling, shockingly white structure high on the cliffs northwest of Punta that looks like a villa imported from the *Star Wars* planet Tatooine. Built piecemeal by the Uruguayan artist Carlos Páez Vilaró as his workshop, studio, and museum, it spills down toward the wide Rio de la Plata in a surrealist tumble of honeycombed stucco, all curves, angles, domes, gleaming swimming pools, and artistic flourishes. You can go inside this "habitable sculpture," as its creator christened it, to see galleries of his paintings, and you can wander around parts of the fantasyland exterior. Casapueblo is also a hotel and has a restaurant, **Las Terrazas** (598-4257-8611).

OPPOSITE Children see a plaything, but this sculpture's title, *Monument to the Drowned*, suggests a darker meaning.

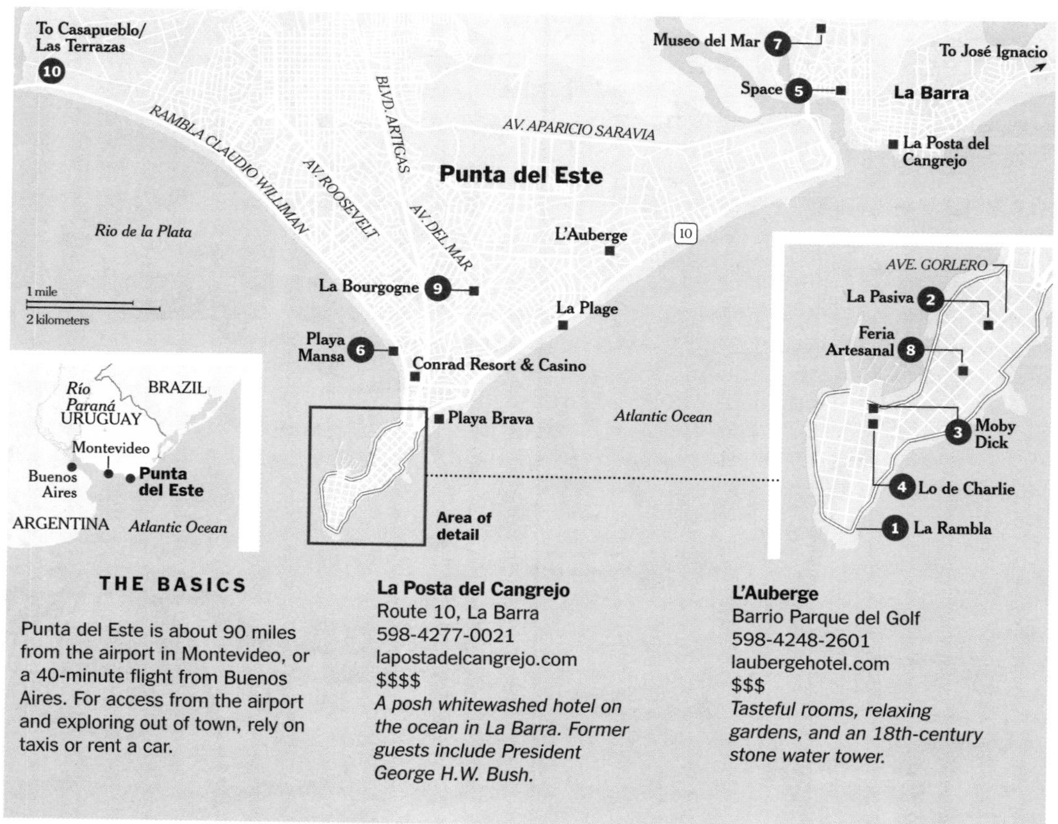

THE BASICS

Punta del Este is about 90 miles from the airport in Montevideo, or a 40-minute flight from Buenos Aires. For access from the airport and exploring out of town, rely on taxis or rent a car.

La Posta del Cangrejo
Route 10, La Barra
598-4277-0021
lapostadelcangrejo.com
$$$$
A posh whitewashed hotel on the ocean in La Barra. Former guests include President George H.W. Bush.

L'Auberge
Barrio Parque del Golf
598-4248-2601
laubergehotel.com
$$$
Tasteful rooms, relaxing gardens, and an 18th-century stone water tower.

PAX

Buenos Aires

Contemporary Argentine history is a roller coaster of financial booms and busts and gripping political soap operas. But through all the highs and lows, one thing has remained constant: Buenos Aires's graceful elegance and cosmopolitan cool. This attractive city continues to draw food lovers, design buffs, and party people with its riotous night life and fashion-forward styling. The creative energy and enterprising spirit of Porteños (as the residents of this port city are called) are always on display—just look to the growing ranks of art spaces, boutiques, restaurants, and hotels. And the city's classic character lives on, as well—in tango, cafe culture, and the never-ending obsession with soccer.
— BY PAOLA SINGER AND MICHAEL T. LUONGO

FRIDAY

1 *Recoleta Ramble* 3 p.m.

Mingle with affluent Argentine shoppers in the upscale Recoleta neighborhood. Argentina, with its expansive cattle ranches, is known for stylish leather goods, and you'll find many of them at the shops here. Browse at **Rossi y Caruso** (Posadas 1387; 54-11-4811-1965; rossicaruso.com) and **Humawaca** (Posadas 1380; 54-11-4811-5995; humawaca.com). This is also a neighborhood for boutiques filled with designer fashions. For Argentine wines, drop in at **Grand Cru Degustaciones** (Rodriguez Peña 1886; 54-11-4816-3975; grandcru.com.ar). When conspicuous consumption palls, walk into **Recoleta Cemetery** (Calle Junín 1790, at Plaza Frances; 54-11-4804-7040; cementeriorecoleta.com.ar) to join the pilgrims at the grave of Eva Perón.

2 *Don't Skip Tea* 6 p.m.

Sirop Folie (Vicente Lopez 1661; 54-11-4813-5900; siroprestaurant.com; $), on a quaint alley in Recoleta, serves a very British afternoon tea that includes fresh scones, homemade marmalades, finger sandwiches, cakes, and fragrant blends by Tealosophy. Well-dressed families show up after 5 p.m., filling the comfy, pastel-colored window banquettes. For Asian-inspired tea, try the **Tea Connection** (Avenida Cerviño 3550, 54-11-4807-5034; teaconnection.com.ar). Whatever you do, don't skip this meal; dinnertime is ages away.

3 *Jazz It Up* 9:30 p.m.

Live music is one of Buenos Aires's top attractions, and contemporary jazz is stealing the spotlight thanks to a new generation of talented musicians who developed their own style. Check out a live show at **Thelonious Jazz Club** (Salguero 1884, first floor; 54-11-4829-1562; theloniousclub.com.ar), a lounge with vintage black leather sofas, battered hardwood floors, and a back-lit bar. You may catch a performance by the celebrity Argentine saxophonist Ricardo Cavalli.

4 *Midnight Meal* 11:30 p.m.

On weekend nights, Porteños take late-night dining to the extreme. Mingle with stylish night owls at intimate **Tegui** (Costa Rica 5852; 54-11-5291-3333; tegui.com.ar; $$$$), a glamorous hidden restaurant. The entrance to this au courant spot in the outskirts of the Palermo neighborhood is camouflaged by a wall of graffiti art. An ambitious, locally sourced menu of dishes is prepared in an open stainless-steel

OPPOSITE Recoleta Cemetery, resting place of many of Argentina's rich and famous, including Eva Perón.

RIGHT The Casa Rosada, where Eva Perón used to speak from the balcony and Madonna, playing her in the film *Evita*, sang "Don't Cry for Me, Argentina."

kitchen. One night's selections included slow-cooked tenderloin with poached egg and toasted manioc flour.

SATURDAY

5 *The Coffee Époque* 11 a.m.

Café Tortoni (Avenida de Mayo 825; 54-11-4342-4328; cafetortoni.com.ar; $), founded in 1858, is the most famous of the cafes from Buenos Aires's belle époque. It has attracted a literary clientele including Jorge Luis Borges, and it is still full of atmosphere and a good place for breakfast. (You might also find a tango show there at night.) A bit out of the way but even more more magnificent is **Las Violetas** (Avenida Rivadavia 3899; 54-11-4958-7387; lasvioletas.com; $), a 123-year-old French-style cafe with gorgeous stained glass. The classic breakfast is café con leche with three croissants.

6 *Where Evita Looms Large* 1 p.m.

Few historical figures have caught the world's imagination like Evá Peron. The wife of President Juan Perón, Evita, as she was known, died of cancer in 1952, at age 33, but not before becoming one of the most controversial and influential women in the Western world. At the presidential palace, the **Casa Rosada** (Calle Balcarce, overlooking Plaza de Mayo), visitors can walk out onto the balcony where she used to address throngs of her supporters, known as "the shirtless ones" because many were poor laborers. In the musical *Evita*, the balcony is the setting for the song "Don't Cry for Me, Argentina." The **Museo del Bicentenario** (54-11-4344-3802; museo.gov.ar) behind the palace holds Perón relics. But a more impressive memorial is on the **Health Ministry Building** (Avenida Nueve de Julio 1925 between Belgrano and Moreno): two enormous steel sculptures of Evita's likeness soldered to the soaring exterior.

7 *Chimichurri* 2 p.m.

Get your steak fix at **Miranda** (Costa Rica 5602; 54-11-4771-4255; parrillamiranda.com; $$), a bustling parrilla, or grill, where the décor is cool and the staff is hip but the food remains traditionally no-frills. This loftlike industrial space manages to feel cozy thanks to potted plants, wall textiles, wood accents, and a steady stream of film executives who work in nearby studios (the surrounding area is aptly named Palermo Hollywood). Order classics like provoleta, a char-grilled, herb-seasoned slice of thick cheese, and bife de chorizo, a juicy sirloin strip steak. This timeless favorite comes with excellent house-made fries and a side of chimichurri marinade.

ABOVE Las Violetas, a cafe from Argentina's belle époque.

8 *House of Xul* 5 p.m.

The painter, sculptor, and writer Alejandro Xul Solar is Argentina's answer to Paul Klee. Before his death in 1963, he selected paintings to be exhibited in the museum he envisioned; now the **Museo Xul Solar** (Laprida 1212; 54-11-4824-3302; xulsolar.org.ar) is a reality. Glimpse a singular world: reinvented tarot cards, a piano with three rows of rainbow-colored keys. For many more artists' views of the world, pay a visit to **Malba**, short for Museo de Arte Latinoamericano de Buenos Aires (Alcorta 3415; 54-11-4808-6500; malba.org.ar), which has one of the finest Latin American art collections in the world.

9 *Little Italy, Argentina* 10 p.m.

More than a third of Argentina's population is of Italian descent, which probably explains why Buenos Aires has such delightful pastas and gelati. **Sottovoce** (Libertador 1098; 54-11-4807-6691; sottovoceristorante.com.ar; $$) is a classic family restaurant that always gets it right. Most pastas are handmade. Pair them with any sauce: the Sottovoce, made of tomato, basil, oregano, garlic, olive oil, and Parmesan, is delicately flavorful. For dessert, try the delectable dulce de leche ice cream, or walk a few blocks to gelato galore at **Un' Altra Volta** (Quintana 502; 54-11-4783-4048; unaltravolta.com.ar). Good luck choosing among the 60 flavors.

ABOVE Looking over the bottles at Grand Cru Degustaciones in the Recoleta neighborhood. Stop in here for a wide selection of Argentine wines.

BELOW The Buenos Aires landmark 9 de Julio Avenue, named for Argentina's Independence Day.

SUNDAY

10 *Boutiquey Barrio* Noon

Cobbled **San Telmo** is known for old-school tango shows, staid antiques shops, and a Sunday street fair packed with vintage finds. But there's new life in this old barrio. Check out the contemporary art galleries that have moved to the neighborhood, displaying a variety of artists including some who have exhibited at fairs like the Venice Biennale.

11 *Catch a Match* 2 p.m.

To see archenemies River Plate and Boca Juniors battle it out on the field in this soccer-crazed town, book a seat through an established tour operator like **Go Football** (54-11-4816-2681; gofootball.com.ar). A guide will pick you up at the hotel, stay with you during the game, and teach you the local cheers. Not here on a game day? Then go for a leisurely stroll in **El Rosedal**—a romantic rose garden inside the 400-acre **Parque Tres de Febrero**. If the mood strikes, rent a paddle boat and ride around the park lake.

ABOVE Wooden bathtubs at the wine-themed Hotel Mio.

OPPOSITE A dappled street in the Palermo neighborhood.

THE BASICS

The easiest way to get around is by taxi. If you want to try the subte (subway), buy a Guía T transit and street map or check guiat.site88.net.

Hotel Mio
Avenida Quintana 465
54-11-5295-8500
miobuenosaires.com
$$$
A wine-themed hotel, with large and theatrical rooms featuring carved wooden bathtubs and doors made of wine barrels.

Algodon Mansion
Montevideo 1647
54-11-3530-7777
www.algodonmansion.com
$$$$
Luxury in a renovated mansion in Recoleta.

Vitrum
Gorriti 5641
54-11-4776-5030
vitrumhotel.com
$$$
In Palermo Hollywood. Colorful glass facade and spacious, retro-futuristic rooms.

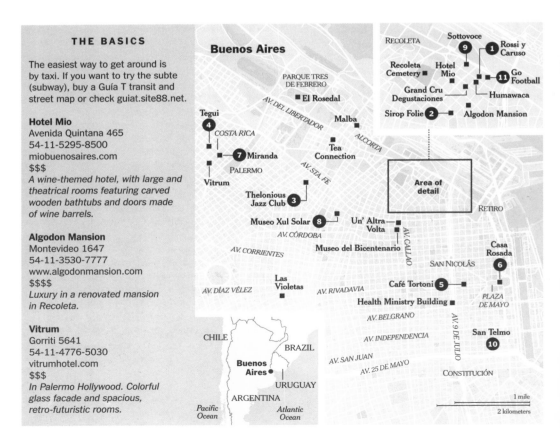

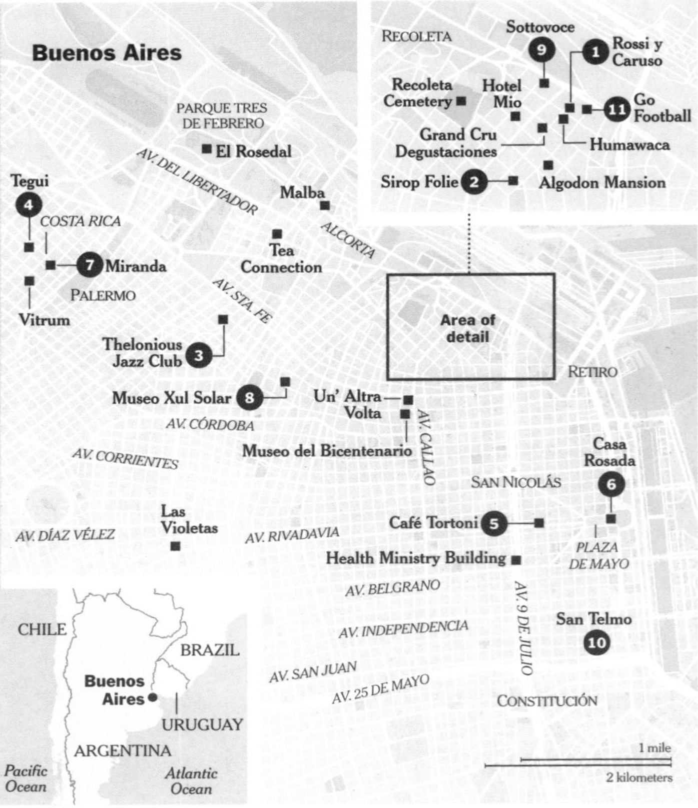

Buenos Aires
Recoleta
Sottovoce 9
1 Rossi y Caruso
Recoleta Cemetery
Hotel Mio
11 Go Football
Grand Cru Degustaciones
Humawaca
Sirop Folie 2
Algodon Mansion
Parque Tres de Febrero
El Rosedal
Av. del Libertador
Malba
Alcorta
Tegui 4
Costa Rica
7 Miranda
Tea Connection
Palermo
Vitrum
Av. Sta. Fe
Area of detail
Thelonious Jazz Club 3
Retiro
Museo Xul Solar 8
Un' Altra Volta
Av. Córdoba
Av. Callao
Av. Corrientes
Museo del Bicentenario
Casa Rosada 6
San Nicolás
Las Violetas
Café Tortoni 5
Av. Díaz Vélez
Av. Rivadavia
Plaza de Mayo
Health Ministry Building
Av. Belgrano
Av. 9 de Julio
Av. Independencia
San Telmo 10
Av. San Juan
Av. 25 de Mayo
Constitución
1 mile
2 kilometers
Chile
Brazil
Buenos Aires
Uruguay
Argentina
Pacific Ocean
Atlantic Ocean

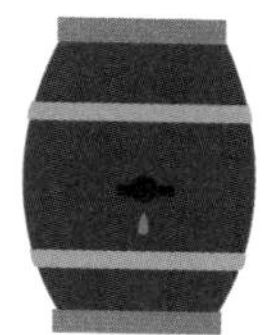

Mendoza

Six hundred miles west of Buenos Aires, hugging the Andes Mountains, the high, dry fields of Mendoza open themselves to the sun with ideal conditions for growing grapes. Often compared to the Napa Valley of California but in a much earlier stage of wine-country evolution, Mendoza took off after 2002, when a devalued peso gave Argentina an advantage in international markets. It's now home to hundreds of wineries, and new vintners and wine-loving tourists are both still pouring in. The result is a vibrant wine scene with a great array of bottles for different budgets and palates, cutting-edge eco-sustainable cantinas, and a new generation of innovative winemakers. The city of Mendoza, capital of Mendoza province, makes a good base for a visit, with comfortable hotels and a mix of architecture that showcases Art Deco alongside '60s modern (the vintage pickup trucks are also a throwback to another era). Just a short drive away are the vineyards, as well as adventure sports and resorts. — BY ONDINE COHANE

FRIDAY

1 *Prepping Your Palate* 6 p.m.

Start your tour of the city with a wine sampling at **Vines of Mendoza** (Belgrano 1194; 54-261-438-1031; vinesofmendoza.com). The tasting room features about 100 producers, and it is the only spot in the city where you can try so many in one place. The multi-lingual servers are well trained and knowledgeable. Samplings include a flight of malbecs, made from Mendoza's most famous grape, and an overview of the varietals from the region, like torrontés, merlot, and bonarda. The tasting room is owned by Michael Evans and Pablo Gimenez Riili, whose 1,000-acre cooperative vineyard in the Uco Valley gives those who dream of making their own wine the possibility of owning as little as three acres of vines, with access to a state-of-the-art facility and an excellent in-house oenologist. Tours and barbecues can be arranged at the vineyard.

OPPOSITE Vineyards in the province of Mendoza, a capital of Argentinian wine, against the hazy blue peaks of the Andes.

RIGHT Two-wheeled touring in the high, dry country that fosters Mendoza's grapes and its hundreds of wineries.

2 *The Art of Grilling* 9 p.m.

This being Argentina, the city's most famous chef, Francis Mallmann, is a master of the simple art of wood-fired meat grilling. In the courtyard of his flagship restaurant **1884** (Belgrano 1188; 54-261-424-2698; 1884restaurante.com.ar; $$), an array of different cast-iron grills (like the parrilla, a barbecue grill, or the plancha, a cast-iron griddle) and wood-fired ovens are on sizzling display. The seven-hour-grilled lamb (cooked in a mold on the grill) with mashed potatoes brings new meaning to the term tender.

3 *Night Birds* Midnight

After-hours in Argentina gets going late, so don't be surprised if most people don't show up until after midnight for empanadas and cocktails at **El Palenque** (Aristides Villanueva 287; 54-261-15-429-1814), a bustling restaurant and bar based on an Argentine pulpería, or tavern, on Aristides Villanueva, the city's night-life artery. Well-heeled Mendocinos at outdoor tables sip on wine out of pinguinos, penguin-shaped pitchers.

SATURDAY

4 *Parading the Plazas* 9 a.m.

Much of Mendoza was reduced to rubble during a devastating earthquake in 1861, and the city's five airy plazas were built to provide some safe open spaces in the event of another disaster. They have become the cornerstones of the city, especially on the weekends. At the most popular, the **Plaza Independencia**, ice cream and yerba mate vendors

sell their goods while kids run around and adults relax on park benches listening to the bands that congregate. Wander from here to the other four plazas to get a good sense of the city's layout. The Plaza San Martín, in the Financial District, is dominated by a statue of General José de San Martín, who led Argentina to independence. Plaza Chile has the best children's playground. Plaza Italia is dedicated to a country that gave Mendoza many immigrants (there is a statue of Romulus and Remus and a fountain with 1,400 ceramic tiles from the Cathedral of Bologna). And Plaza España, with lovely green spaces, may be the most beautiful of all.

ABOVE A florist's wares in the city of Mendoza. The downtown is a walkable agglomeration of five airy plazas.

BELOW Munching on a lomo — a steak, cheese, and egg sandwich — is a traditional method of rebuilding depleted energy after a grueling night out on the town.

5 *Morning Tipple* 11 a.m.

About a 50-minute drive from Mendoza, past smaller towns and along country roads lined with vines, **Achaval Ferrer** (Calle Cobos 2601, Perdriel; 549-261-553-5565; achaval-ferrer.com) started out as a side project for three wine-loving friends, including the Italian winemaker Roberto Cipesso. But their wines, particularly their three malbec crus (each from different soils and altitudes) have quickly gained acclaim. The tour and tasting offer an informed overview of a small, high-quality wine estate.

6 *Twin Pairings* 1 p.m.

Bodega Ruca Malen's surprisingly elegant restaurant (Ruta Nacional, Kilometer 7, Luján de Cuyo; 54-261-413-8909; bodegarucamalen.com; $$$$) faces the Andes at the edge of one of the property's vineyards and involves a five-course daily tasting menu pairing the vineyard's wines (as well as some other favorites of the owners) with seasonal and local plates. A small plate of chorizo with criolla sauce and Argentine cereal, for example, came with a glass of

Yauquen malbec cabernet sauvignon, and a medallion of grilled beef came with Ruca Malen malbec.

7 *Deep Detox* 4 p.m.

Even if you are not staying at the **Entre Cielos** resort and vineyard (Guardia Vieja 1998, Vistalba; 54-261-498-3377; entrecielos.com), it's worth stopping at the spa and the six-station hammam, 20 minutes from the city center. After multiple steams and scrubs, your skin will glow and most of the alcohol you've consumed at tastings and lunch will exit your system. If you want to continue the vineyards tour instead, stop at **Bressia** (Cochabamba 7725, Agrelo, Luján de Cuyo; 54-261-524-9161; bressiabodega.com), home to distinctive, more Old World–style blends.

8 *Regional Staple* 9 p.m.

Think of the lomo as Mendoza's answer to the Philadelphia cheesesteak—a grilled-sirloin sandwich with melted cheese, fried egg, and mayo. At the old-school city institution **Don Claudio** (Tiburcio Benegas and Aristides Villanueva; 54-261-423-4814), the dish is served in a bright, canteen-like space, with large

bottles of ice-cold Quilmes, the country's favorite beer. Later, head to Plaza Pellegrini and watch locals perform tango alfresco.

SUNDAY

9 *Brunch Stop* 10 a.m.

The fresh, seasonal dishes found on the menu at **Maria Antonieta** (Belgrano 1069; 54-261-420-4322; mariaantonietaresto.com) are a refreshing change from the ubiquitous steak. Besides house-made muffins and freshly squeezed juices like strawberry and grapefruit, breakfast choices include huevos al agua (poached eggs). The cheerful whitewashed

TOP Tango on the dance floor at the Park Hyatt.

ABOVE Proving that Mendoza isn't all about wine, a beer accompanies a lomo at Don Claudio.

interior and sidewalk seating are good for whiling away an hour with coffee and the paper, and there's free Wi-Fi.

10 *Green Escapes* 11 a.m.

Rent bikes at **Bikes and Wines** (54-261-410-6686; bikesandwines.com) and head to **Parque General San Martín**, a green oasis of more than 1,200 acres designed by the landscape architect Carlos Thays in 1896. On Sundays, picnicking families stream through the huge cast-iron gates and head to spots like Cerro de La Gloria, which has a glorious view across the city and foothills of the Andes. Want to get closer to the mountains themselves? **Argentina Rafting** (54-261-429-6325; argentinarafting.com) has kayaking, mountain biking, and hiking day trips for $73, and **Discover the Andes** (54-261-156-571-967; www.discovertheandes.com) offers hikes like the Vallecitos trek, with stunning views.

ABOVE A cocktail in preparation at 1884, a restaurant where the dinner fare is meat grilled over a wood fire.

OPPOSITE Civic spirit burning bright — and on a large scale — at the Plaza Independencia.

THE BASICS

Fly to El Plumerillo Airport in Mendoza and rent a car.

Park Hyatt Mendoza
Chile 1124
54-261-441-1234
mendoza.park.hyatt.com
$$$
The city's most luxurious hotel, with a great central location and a good wine bar.

Casa Lila
Avellaneda Nicolás 262
54-261-429-6349
casalila.com.ar
$$
Sweet bed-and-breakfast run by a friendly couple.

Cavas Wine Lodge
Calle Costaflores s/n, Alto Agrelo
54-261-410- 6927
cavaswinelodge.com
$$$$
In the shadow of the Andes. A popular spot for honeymooners and people on wine tours.

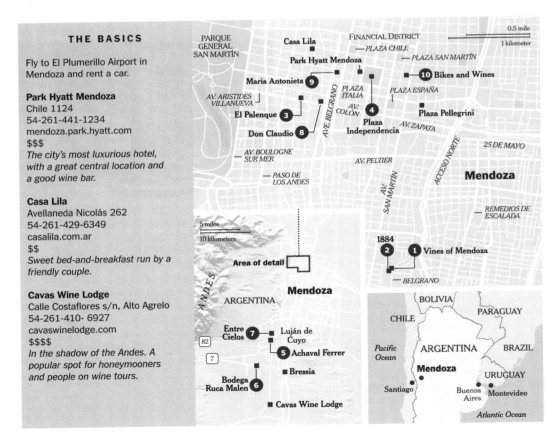

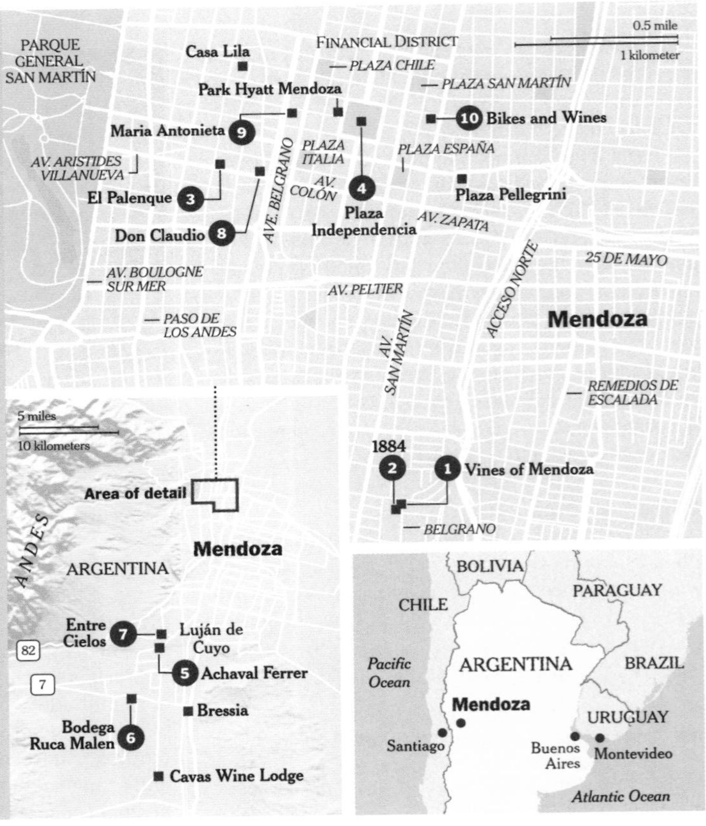

PARQUE GENERAL SAN MARTÍN
Casa Lila
FINANCIAL DISTRICT
PLAZA CHILE
PLAZA SAN MARTÍN
0.5 mile
1 kilometer
Park Hyatt Mendoza
Maria Antonieta 9
10 Bikes and Wines
PLAZA ITALIA
PLAZA ESPAÑA
AV. ARISTIDES VILLANUEVA
AV. COLÓN
El Palenque 3
4 Plaza Independencia
Plaza Pellegrini
AVE. BELGRANO
Don Claudio 8
AV. ZAPATA
25 DE MAYO
AV. BOULOGNE SUR MER
AV. PELTIER
ACCESO NORTE
PASO DE LOS ANDES
AV. SAN MARTÍN
Mendoza
REMEDIOS DE ESCALADA
5 miles
10 kilometers
1884
2
1 Vines of Mendoza
Area of detail
BELGRANO
ANDES
Mendoza
ARGENTINA
BOLIVIA
PARAGUAY
CHILE
Entre Cielos 7
Luján de Cuyo
82
5 Achaval Ferrer
7
Pacific Ocean
ARGENTINA
BRAZIL
Mendoza
URUGUAY
Bressia
Bodega Ruca Malen 6
Santiago
Buenos Aires
Montevideo
Cavas Wine Lodge
Atlantic Ocean

Ciudad de Mendoza

helados
tortas

Salta

Argentina's northwestern Salta province has long been famous for its spectacular scenery of Andean peaks, red-rock valleys, and vineyards, but its central metropolis, the city of Salta, has emerged only in the last few years as a bright spot on the tourist map. Founded in 1582 by the Spanish commander Hernando de Lerma, the city has traditionally served primarily as a commercial center for the province's mining and agricultural enterprises. A concerted effort to encourage new hotels, restaurants, and shops is now paying off in a stream of visitors attracted to Salta's updated colonial charm. Today, the old city center is recognized as a jewel-box-size getaway, made for exploring on foot and appreciated for its rich cultural offerings, grand neo-Classical buildings, and thriving after-dark life. — BY SHIVANI VORA

FRIDAY

1 *1,000 Steps (or a Ride)* 4:30 p.m.

Get a view of the city and nearby valleys from **San Bernardo Hill** (Avenida Uruguay and Paseo Güemes), east of the town center. If you're feeling energetic, climb more than 1,000 stairs to the top from the path behind the equestrian statue of Martín Miguel de Güemes, who led Salta's rebels in the Argentine War of Independence. Along the way, admire more than a dozen shrines and the hardy locals sprinting up through the low scrub as a way to get in their daily exercise. If the climb sounds uninviting, there's an easier way. A leisurely cable-car ride from San Martín Park leads to the same panorama.

2 *The Local Vibe* 7:30 p.m.

After you make it back down to flat ground, walk over to the tree-lined **Plaza 9 de Julio**, which is the main square and Salta's heartbeat. Come evening, the plaza and the streets around it are alive with Salteños congregating at cafes and bars to unwind from their day. One popular spot is the Argentine-Italian deli **Casa Moderna** (España 674; 54-387-422-0066), which despite its name first opened in the early 1900s. To indulge your oenophile side, order by the glass from the selection of wines produced in the high-altitude vineyards nearby.

3 *Llama Stroganoff* 9 p.m.

Get a taste of the Salta region's cuisine at the perpetually packed **El Charrua Restaurante Parrilla** (Caseros 221; 54-387-432-1859; parrillaelcharrua.com.ar; $), a casual place with brick and stone walls and a lively ambience. While the menu has the usual array of beef cuts standard at any Argentine parrilla, the real stars here are the dishes made with tender llama meat. While most menus around town offer it in a carpaccio style, here you will find it in dishes like llama stroganoff.

SATURDAY

4 *Suburban Cloud Forest* 9 a.m.

Just outside **San Lorenzo,** an affluent suburban village four miles away from the city, the **Quebrada de San Lorenzo** (San Lorenzo Gorge) nature reserve is tucked at the foot of the sub-Andean mountains. It preserves a section of the fragile environment called Yungas forest, which is found on the eastern side of the Andes. With an uphill hike here, you can immerse yourself among the green ferns, creeks, moss, and colorful fauna of a tropical cloud forest. Along the way, you may bump into native farmers, descendants of the ancient Inca, riding down on horseback from their homes in the hills.

OPPOSITE Lights at dusk in the Andean town of Salta.

RIGHT Lunch at El Solar del Convento, a local restaurant. Fare of the Salta region includes the usual Argentine beef, but some menus also list llama steaks.

5 *Jasmine Lunch* Noon

The American actor Robert Duvall made the 250-acre ranch called **House of Jasmines** famous when he bought it to use as a vacation home. New owners have since turned it into a luxury hotel with a restaurant, **La Table de House** (Ruta Nacional N 51, Kilometer 6, La Merced Chica; 54-387-497-2002; houseofjasmines.com; $$), that's a good place to refuel after your morning of activity. The midday menu lists selections like gnocchi arrabiata and salad with tomatoes, avocado, and grilled llama or chicken. Stroll a bit on the sprawling grounds, which are fragrant with scents of jasmines, eucalyptus trees, roses, and herbs.

6 *Ice Children* 3:30 p.m.

The hours when much of the city is shut down for siesta are the ideal time to explore a museum, and the **Museum of High Altitude Archaeology**, or MAAM (Mitre 77, on the Plaza 9 de Julio; 54-387-437-0592; maam.gob.ar) remains open all afternoon. The archaeology of the Andes is largely the story of the Inca, and the museum's artifacts trace their culture, and those of the tribes that preceded them, over thousands of years. The best known items are the 500-year-old frozen bodies of three Incan children killed in a ritual sacrifice, which are displayed in rotation, one at a time, in a case kept at zero degrees Fahrenheit. They were discovered in 1999, amid a treasury of objects made of gold, textiles, and other materials, atop 22,000-foot Mount Llullaillaco at the border of Salta Province and Chile. In the cold and dry air at the top of the mountain, the bodies were naturally mummified, and the children look eerily as if they had just gone to sleep.

7 *Crafts to Take Home* 5:30 p.m.

The city is littered with touristy stores selling run-of-the-mill goods, but a few shops stand out for their uncommon wares. **Samponia** (Caseros 468; 54-387-422-8333) sells brightly colored frames, pillows, ottomans, and bowls that are handmade using traditional Incan techniques but have a distinct contemporary look. **Rio del Valle Luracatao** (Leguizamón 515; 54-387-431-0082; riodelvalleluracatao.com) has rugs, throws, and handbags made of hand-spun llama and alpaca wool. At **El Gauchito Salteño** (Caseros 760; 54-387-432-9459), pick up dulce de leche made with the extra-creamy milk from the mountain cows.

8 *Warmth and Good Cooking* 9:30 p.m.

The elegant candlelit atmosphere and the high thatched ceilings at **El Solar del Convento** (Caseros 444; 54-387-421-5124; $) combine with warm service and simply but thoughtfully prepared food to make dinner here a solid choice. Every meal starts with a free glass of local sparkling wine, and the extensive menu includes grilled meats such as steaks and chorizo as well as choices like rabbit in pineapple sauce and trout roasted with lemon, butter, and wine.

9 *Folkloric Night Life* Midnight

The Salta region is famed for its peñas, traditional folk music halls where locals come with guitars and take turns playing and singing as bystanders clap along. The action starts around midnight and

ABOVE Take the cable car to the top of San Bernardo Hill for views toward the Andes. Or, if that is too easy, walk up on a pathway with more than 1,000 stairs.

BELOW Native costumes with 21st century updating still survive in Salta, where the descendants of the Inca dominate many areas outside of town.

stretches nonstop well past 4 a.m. Arrive on the early side at **La Casona del Molino** (Luis Burela 1; 54-387-434-2835), a five-minute cab ride from the city center, to get a table in one of the five rooms or the spacious courtyard. Order a bottle of Argentine beer, sit back, and listen to the catchy music.

SUNDAY

10 *Faith Tour* 11 a.m.

Catch the peaceful mood of the city as it wakes by strolling to some of its picturesque church buildings. Start with the neo-Classical **Catedral Basílica de Salta** on the Plaza de Julio. Then walk over to the **Convento San Bernardo** (Caseros 73) to admire the attractive carved door, an example of aboriginal art. Finish with the **Iglesia San Francisco** (Cordoba 33), which has a rich purple façade and a 170-foot bell tower that is said to be the tallest in South America.

11 *Empanada Overload* Noon

Salteños staunchly believe they invented the empanada. There is a raging debate in town about where the tastiest ones can be had, but if you want to try a selection, end your visit to the city at **Patio de la Empanada** (San Martín and Malvinas; 54-387-431-4484). In half a dozen stalls on a covered terrace, empanada makers serve up their own takes on the city's favorite snack.

THE BASICS

Aerolíneas Argentinas and other local carriers offer flights from Buenos Aires to Martín Miguel de Güemes International Airport in Salta.

Kkala Boutique Hotel
Las Higueras 104, Tres Cerritos
54-387-439-6590
hotelkkala.com.ar
$$
Six-room upscale hotel with a personable staff and a mixture of antique and modern handicraft décor.

Bloomers Bed and Brunch
Vicente Lopez 129
54-387-422-7449
bloomers-salta.com.ar
$
Small inn in a prime location a few blocks from the Plaza 9 de Julio. The brunch is a highlight.

Legado Mitico Salta
Bartolomé Mitre 647
54-387-422-8786
legadomitico.com
$$$
Nicely decorated hotel with themed rooms; in a renovated mansion.

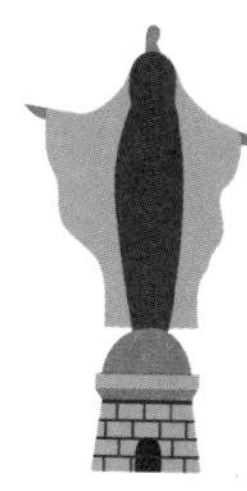

Santiago

Six million Chileans, half the country's population, live in the cosmopolitan capital city of Santiago, an old Spanish settlement in the strip of land wedged between the snowy Andes and the Pacific Ocean. Pablo Neruda, the Nobel prize–winning poet, once described Santiago as "asleep for eternity," and a couple of decades ago, many travelers seemed to agree, stopping just long enough to change planes for adventures elsewhere. All of that has changed with the rapid growth of the Chilean economy, government initiatives to create a Silicon Valley of the South, and artistic and cultural energy electrifying the city. Now there's more than enough to discover here over a weekend: a thriving culinary scene, new museums and parks, renovated Beaux-Arts neighborhoods, and blocks of stylish galleries and cafes clustered near "Sanhattan," the soaring financial district.

— BY FINN-OLAF JONES AND LIZA FOREMAN

FRIDAY

1 *With the Conquistador* 4 p.m.

The **Plaza de Armas** was the birthplace of Santiago, founded in 1541 by the conquistador Pedro de Valdivia, and it still seems to be the center of the action. The conquistador keeps watch over the plaza from his equestrian statue while below him a virtual opera of preachers, performers, pigeons, pedestrians, and palm trees plays out against a dramatic backdrop of neo-Renaissance government buildings and a colonial-era cathedral. Nearby, the Royal Customs House holds the small but outstanding **Museum of Pre-Columbian Art** (Bandera 361; 56-2-928-1500; precolombino.cl). To get into the metropolitan rhythm, take a seat at one of the cafes bordering the plaza and order a snack and a pisco sour, the house cocktail for the entire country.

2 *Avenida Shopping* 6 p.m.

You can't say you've been shopping in Santiago without heading to the luxury-store-lined **Avenida Alonso de Córdova**. Explore designer outlets and upscale stores like **Wool** (No. 4098; 56-2-208-8767; alfombraswool.com), where square carpet samples are displayed on the wall like fine works of art. Contemporary art galleries have also taken root in this affluent neighborhood, Vitacura. **Galería Animal** (Avenida Nueva Costanera 3731; 56-2-371-9090; galeriaanimal.com), around the corner from Alonso de Córdova, displays mostly Chilean art. **Galería Patricia Ready** (Espoz 3125; 56-2-953-6210; galeriaready.cl) is an art complex with a secluded courtyard and cafe.

3 *Adventurous Dining* 10 p.m.

Diners can't go wrong with any of the high-end restaurants along the section of Avenida Nueva Costanera near the popular Peruvian restaurant **La Mar** (3922 Nueva Costanera). But young Vitacura restaurateurs have also staked out locations farther afield. One to try is **Casamar** (Avenida Padre Hurtado Norte 1480; 56-2-954-2112; casamarchile.cl; $), which features sustainable seafood in a glass- and bamboo-framed space. Look for dishes like grilled octopus with tomato marmalade or a warehou ceviche.

4 *The Local Salsa* Midnight

No matter where you have dinner, and no matter what time you finish up, the night is still young and the party scene beckons. Santiago is bursting with boisterous bars and discos, but the ubiquitous salsa dance halls seem to attract just about everyone. Don't worry if you can't salsa: many places have nightly lessons (and if not, other patrons are not shy about giving them). You can even get away with just stepping in place at popular spots like **Maestra Vida**

OPPOSITE AND RIGHT Downtown and a viewpoint on San Cristóbal Hill. Squeezed between the Andes and the Pacific, Santiago is home to half of Chile's population.

(Pio Nono 380; 56-2-777-5325; maestravida.cl). For a low-key alternative to the salsotecas, sample wine by the glass at **Baco Vino y Bistro** (Santa Magdalena 113/Nueva de Lyon 116; 56-2-231-4444), a wine bar in the bustling downtown district of Providencia. It draws a mixed crowd of well-dressed residents and serious wine connoisseurs.

SATURDAY

5 *New Collections* 11 a.m.

Part of Santiago's recent energy has gone into establishing new museums. One of them is **Museo de la Chilenidad** (Padre Hurtado Sur 1155; culturallascondes.cl), which displays a permanent collection including works by Chilean master painters from the 19th and early 20th centuries. Another, the **Museo de la Moda** (Avenida Vitacura 4562; 56-2-218-5500; museodelamoda.cl), is devoted to fashion and to the memory of the founder's mother, Raquel Bascuñán Cugnoni, a socialite with a penchant for haute couture. Its approximately 10,000 garments include a Jean Paul Gaultier conical bra designed for Madonna and a tutu worn by Margot Fonteyn. The Museo de la Moda also has a delightful cafe called El Garage.

6 *House of Neruda* 3 p.m.

The Nobel Prize–winning poet Pablo Neruda was a serious politician (his socialist sympathies offended Chilean right-wing governments, sending him into exile for years), but he certainly knew how to have fun, as evidenced in his marvelously eccentric home **La Chascona** (Fernando Marquez de La Plata 192; 56-2-737-8712; fundacionneruda.org). Call in advance for an English-language tour of this meandering compound that clings to the slope of Cerro San Cristóbal, the big mountain overlooking town. The poet lived, loved, and conspired here with his fiery third wife, Matilde Urrutia. The house was built to resemble both a ship and a lighthouse, and it incorporates a secret passageway behind Neruda's dinner table, a bewildering collection of knickknacks gathered from his travels as a diplomat, and paintings by his famous friends. Look for the two-faced portrait of Urrutia by Diego Rivera, with Neruda's profile hidden in her hair.

7 *Mountaintop Virgin* 5 p.m.

Head up to the park on top of San Cristóbal, where families and romantic couples head to enjoy the epic view. Board the **Funicular San Cristóbal** at the edge of Bellavista (Pio Nono 445) for a 10-minute ride to the top, where a few last steps lead up to the 72-foot statue of the Virgin Mary that casts an eye over the cityscape. Look for one of the carts selling cups of mote con huesillo, a concoction of wheat and peaches that makes for a delicious syrupy sunset cocktail.

8 *Tudor Temptations* 10 p.m.

For a local dining experience somewhat removed from the high-end restaurants of Vitacura, **Casa Lastarria** (Lastarria 70; 56-2-638-3236; casalastarria.cl; $$), in the artsy downtown district of Lastarria, offers home-cooked meals in a 1930s Tudor-style building that is filled with vintage furniture. Expect dishes like conger eel in almond sauce or chicken with Cognac.

9 *All in One Place* Midnight

Multifaceted nightspots, combining entertainment, dancing, drinks, and food, have become popular in Santiago. Try one out at **Bar Constitución** (Constitución 61; 56-2-244-4569; barconstitucion.cl), which has indoor and outdoor spaces including a bar, terrace, lounge, and dining area. It features live music and attracts a young, fun-loving, casual crowd.

SUNDAY

10 *Memorials for the Missing* 9:30 a.m.

The **Museum of Memory and Human Rights** (Matucana 501; 56-2-365-1165; museodelamemoria.cl), a contemporary concrete, glass, and copper structure designed by the Brazilian architect Marcos Figuero, covers an entire downtown block. Inside are photographs of victims of General Augusto Pinochet's brutal dictatorial rule, video footage of protesters, and other documentation of Pinochet's 17 years (1973–1990) in power, when more than 3,000 people lost their lives or disappeared during his crackdown on dissent. Another memorial site is Londres 38 (londres38.cl), a building that was the municipal headquarters for the Socialist government of Salvador Allende before it became a torture center under the Pinochet regime.

11 *On Two Wheels* 11 a.m.

Santiago's long boulevards, hillside lanes, and leafy parks are a bicyclist's paradise, especially during the weekends, when the streets are thronged by spandexed bikers. Rent a bike at **La Bicicleta Verde** (Santa María Avenida 227, Office 12; 56-2-570-9338; labicicletaverde.com), which also offers daily three-hour bicycle tours. If you have the time and the ambition, take a cycling tour in the nearby vineyards of the Maipo—a region of winding roads and wineries some 30 miles from the city.

OPPOSITE The Plaza de Armas, laid out in 1541.

ABOVE A bar at La Chascona, the playfully designed home of the Nobel Prize-winning poet Pablo Neruda.

Funicular San Cristóbal 7
The Aubrey
Maestra Vida 4
6 La Chascona
SANTA MARÍA AV.
PIO NONO—
Plaza de Armas 1
11 La Bicicleta Verde
9 Bar Constitución
8 Casa Lastarria
Museum of Pre-Columbian Art
SAN CRISTÓBAL
Museum of Memory and Human Rights 10
MATUCANA—
Area of detail
1 mile
2 kilometers
Mapocho River
Casamar
AV. PADRE—HURTADO NORTE
VITACURA
—AV.VITACURA
Galería Patricia Ready
La Mar 3
Galería Animal
Museo de la Moda
Wool
Santiago
W Santiago
2 Avenida Alonso de Córdova
Museo de la Chilenidad 5
Baco Vino y Bistro
PROVIDENCIA
Hotel Boutique Le Rève
↓ To Maipo Wineries
CHILE
ARGENTINA
Mendoza
URUGUAY
Santiago
Buenos Aires
Pacific Ocean
Atlantic Ocean

THE BASICS

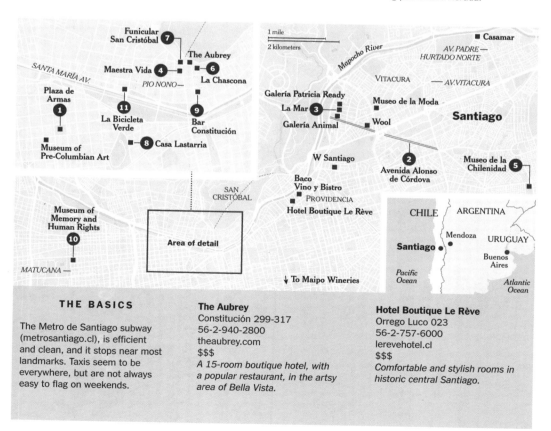

The Metro de Santiago subway (metrosantiago.cl), is efficient and clean, and it stops near most landmarks. Taxis seem to be everywhere, but are not always easy to flag on weekends.

The Aubrey
Constitución 299-317
56-2-940-2800
theaubrey.com
$$$
A 15-room boutique hotel, with a popular restaurant, in the artsy area of Bella Vista.

Hotel Boutique Le Rève
Orrego Luco 023
56-2-757-6000
lerevehotel.cl
$$$
Comfortable and stylish rooms in historic central Santiago.

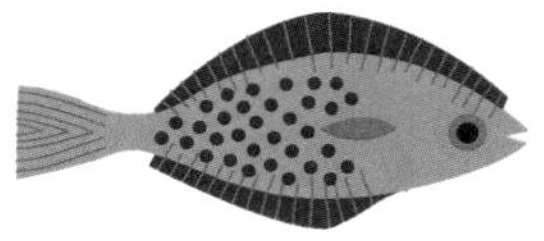

Viña del Mar

Its name means "vineyard by the sea," and Chileans call it simply "Viña," or sometimes "Garden City," but these days Viña del Mar is better known for surf breaks and gorgeous beaches than for its manicured parks and boulevards. Among the largest resorts on the South American Pacific coast, with a population of about 300,000, Viña lures Argentines and Brazilians who come for its family-friendly atmosphere, cruise-ship passengers who wander in for a few hours, and plenty of Chileans, including media stars and the cultural elite from Santiago, just an hour and a half's drive away. Beyond the beach, Viña offers seafood restaurants, night life, shopping, vineyard tours, and an array of festivals including the summer International Song Festival, where rock, pop, and salsa stars perform. — BY MICHAEL T. LUONGO

FRIDAY

1 *Presidential Hill* 4 p.m.

Take a walk in the oldest part of the city, near where the palm-lined inlet Estero Marga Marga meets the ocean. Viña began in the 1870s as a small resort and expanded, with new architecture transforming its seaside cliffs, after an earthquake in 1906 damaged nearby Valparaíso. One structure from that era is **Castillo Wulff**, a Germanic turreted granite castle on a rocky point (it now houses municipal offices). The castle has become a symbol of Viña del Mar, as has the nearby giant floral clock that spells out the city's name and offers a brilliant greeting to passing ships. This neighborhood is **Cerro Castillo**, or Castle Hill. Other century-old whimsical homes jut from the cliffs, and one choice piece of real estate is occupied by a mansion used as the Chilean president's summer palace. The Marga Marga is lined with midcentury towers faceted by balconies looking toward the sea. Today Viña is the center of the Chilean Riviera, a strip of sandy coast filled with high-rise condos and suburban-style houses.

2 *Surf City* 5 p.m.

Walk down to the beach for some sun worship. Beaches are arrayed for miles — Playa Caleta Abarca, Playa Los Artistas, Playa Casino, Playa Blanca, Playa El Sol — less crowded as you head north up the coast toward the popular surfing town of Reñaca, but inviting everywhere. For now, you can stay near Cerro Castillo to soak up some rays or dip your toes. Viña's climate is warm, but the water is cold, and treacherous currents make swimming a chancy activity. Half the fun for many beachgoers is watching the surfers. You might see skimboarders, dressed in wet suits against the cold, standing on the sandy embankment at the end of the inlet, waiting to dash out to the perfect wave on their small, finless boards.

3 *Italian Tradition* 8 p.m.

Go Italian at **Ristorante San Marco** (Avenida San Martín 597; 56-32-297-5304; ristorantesanmarco.cl; $$), a fixture in Viña since 1957. A squad of bow-tied waiters serves pastas and other Italian and seafood specialties in a cozy dining room, and the customers keep coming back.

4 *Gamblers and Dancers* 10 p.m.

As one might expect from a resort town, Viña offers a variety of night life, much of it centered at the city's 1930s-era casino, **Enjoy Viña del Mar Casino & Resort** (199 Avenida San Martín; 56-32-284-6100; enjoy.cl), set in a palm-lined oceanfront park. The most glamorous nightclub in town, the **Ovo** disco, is

OPPOSITE Surf breaks and glorious stretches of sand, the Pacific Ocean's gifts to Viña del Mar, bring vacationers from Argentina and Brazil as well as Chile. Cruise ships stop in, too. This crowd is at Reñaca, north of town.

BELOW A pool at the Hotel del Mar, a resort that also has a spa, restaurants, and a nightclub.

inside the resort. If you'd like something a little less see-and-be-seen, there are options like **Bar Spartako** (Avenida Valparaíso 90; 56-32-297-0883), a rock bar popular with young locals, or **Café Journal** (Variante Agua Santa 4; 56-32-266-6654; cafejournal.cl), a quiet place by day that hosts D.J.'s at night.

SATURDAY

5 *Beach Market* 10 a.m.

In need of a fitness fix? Join health-conscious locals jogging on the waterfront promenade, which has been refurbished with beachside fitness areas. If you'd rather walk than run, you're also in luck. The promenade is a great place for a leisurely seaside stroll. While you're in the area, take a walk through the **Feria Marga Marga**, a big Saturday morning street market that brings the locals out in force. Shop for handicrafts and sample the fresh fruits and vegetables grown by local producers.

6 *Slow Food, Viña-Style* Noon

Though it has familiar chains like McDonald's and Starbucks on its main restaurant strip, Avenida San Martín, Viña also offers semi-hidden culinary spots. In the cluster of narrow dead-end streets called **Pasajes**, several blocks from the casino, you'll find family restaurants like the lunch-only **Donde Willy** (6 Norte 353, No. 17; 56-32-269-7971; $), run by Miguel Valdivia. "People in Viña eat too many fast things," he told one lunchtime customer. "The idea was to have a place where people could eat traditional food of Chile." At Donde Willy, that means dishes like cazuela de vacuno, a simmered beef stew with potatoes, pumpkin, green beans, corn on the cob, rice, oregano, and cumin.

7 *Valley of Sauvignon* 1:30 p.m.

Head inland to see some of Chile's famous wineries. The **Casablanca Valley** wine region, noted for sauvignon blanc, is 45 minutes from Viña. Blessed with sunny days and ocean breezes, the valley is a good home for grapes and not bad for touring, either. One famous — and notably successful — winery here is **Veramonte** (Ruta 68, Kilometer 66; 56-32-232-9924; veramonte.com). Another is **William Cole** (Tapihue Road, Kilometer 4; 56-32-215-7777; williamcolevineyards.cl). Call ahead to make sure the wineries you want to visit are open.

8 *Pacific Coast Highway* 5:30 p.m.

Drive north on the **Avenida Borgoño**, the shore-hugging coastal road. The vistas of crashing waves, cliffs, lighthouses, and sea lions will make you want to take your time. "This is a real Chilean view," Isabella Castro Freudenthal, a college professor living in Viña, told one visitor who asked about the sights from the road. "There's the beach, then a hill, a valley, then the mountains in the distance." Stop at **Reñaca** to see the thundering waves of its prime surfing beach, and then continue on to the small beach resort of **Concón**. You will still be just a few miles north of Viña.

9 *Special Delivery* 7 p.m.

In Concón, fish are caught offshore in small boats and brought to **Restaurante La Gatita** (Avenida Borgoño at Higuerillas; 56-32-32-811-352; $), built on a rocky outcrop overlooking the ocean. The pretty dining room, with red and blue tablecloths, has windows with broad ocean views. Gatita's fresh fish makes it a very popular place, and it doesn't take reservations; in high season you might have to wait two hours for a table. So have your name added to the list and take a walk. Even though Concón, like Viña and Renaca, has attracted dense development, this is still a prosperous small town in a spectacular natural setting, hardly a bad place to kill that pre-dinner downtime.

SUNDAY

10 *La Hacienda* 10 a.m.

The collection of European and Chilean paintings in the **Museo de Bellas Artes** (Parque Quinta Vergara; 56-32-225-2481), is worth a look, but the real attraction here is the surroundings. The museum building is a Venetian-style white confection of a palace, built in 1910, that was the home of the locally prominent Vergara/Alvarez family (their art collection was the museum's core). The ornate palacio, decked out in arches and balustrades, was the centerpiece of their hacienda, and the land is now the lovely **Parque Quinta Vergara**, an oasis of towering palms and manicured gardens. Its amphitheater is the setting for the annual International Song Festival, and classical music concerts take place here all summer. Check the performance schedule to see if anything is on today.

OPPOSITE The Castillo Wulff, one of several whimsical homes built in the early 20th century, flaunts its turrets on a conspicuous rocky point and has become a symbol of Viña del Mar. Take a walk in its cliffside neighborhood, Castle Hill.

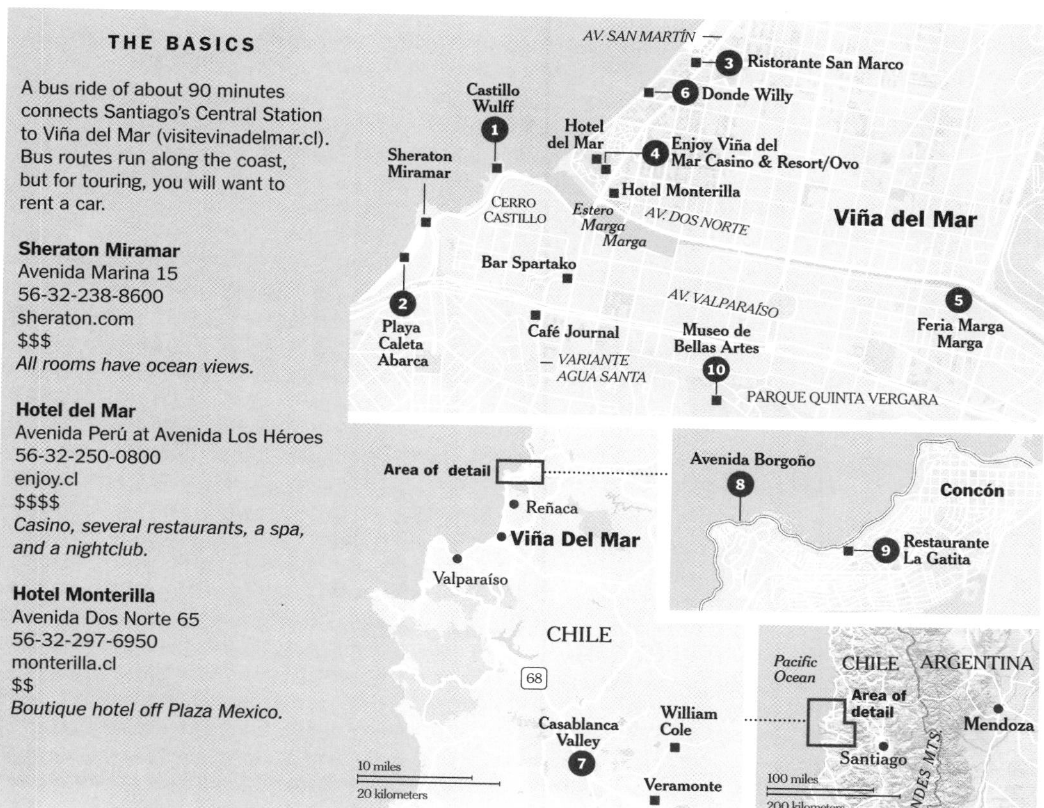

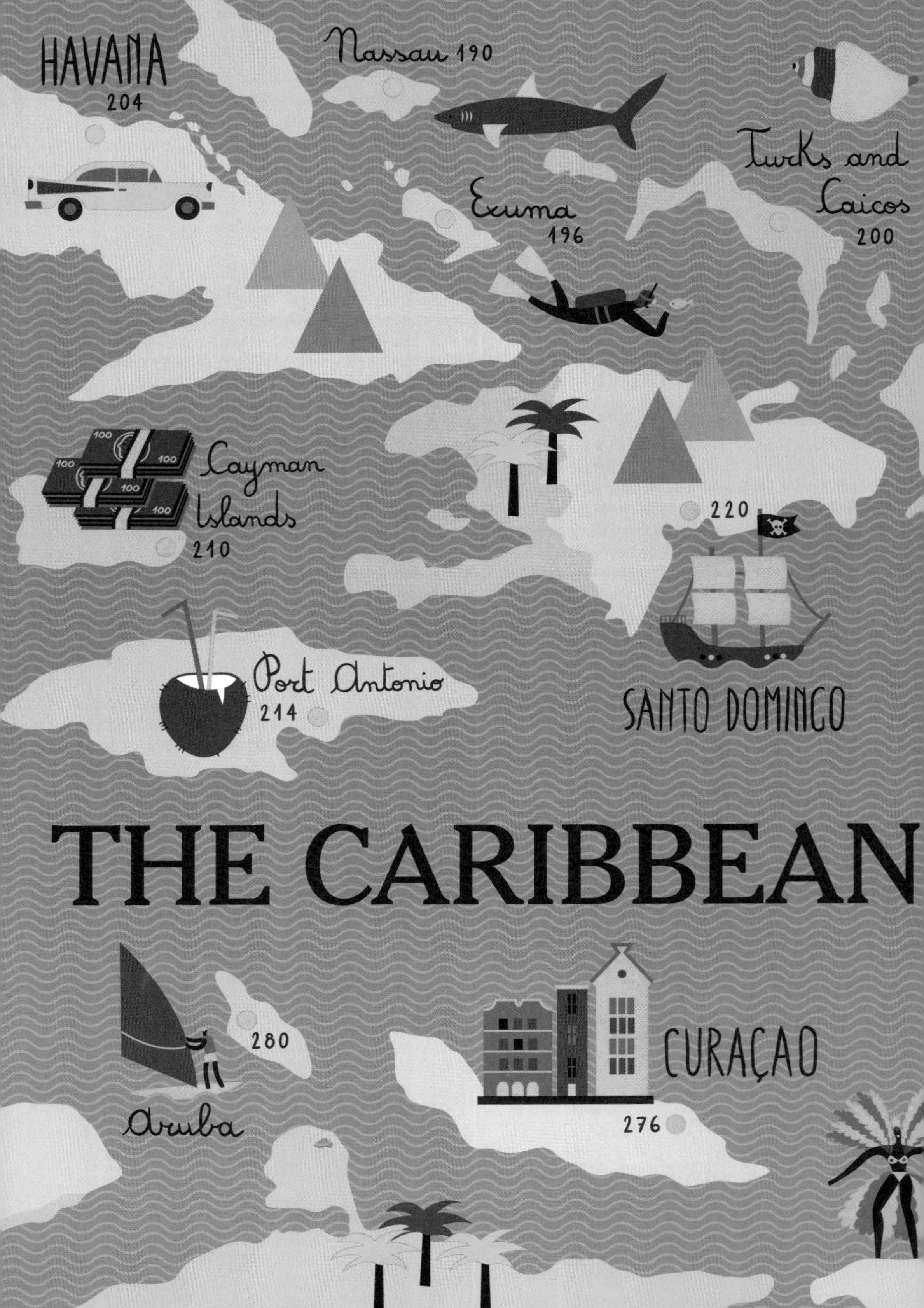
HAVANA
204
Nassau 190
Turks and
Caicos
200
Exuma
196
100
Cayman
Islands
210
220
Port Antonio
214
SANTO DOMINGO
THE CARIBBEAN
280
CURAÇAO
Aruba
276

ST. THOMAS
236

St. John
240

184
BERMUDA

SAN JUAN
224
Vieques
232
ANGUILLA
246
228
Ponce
St. Martin / St. Maarten
250
ST. BARTS
254

Antigua
258

St. Lucia
262
BARBADOS
268
Bequia
272
nidad
284

Bermuda

Bermuda, a British overseas territory east of North Carolina, has long been a favorite getaway for the sort of American East Coast bluebloods who sail their yachts in the biannual 635-mile Newport-to-Bermuda race. Current local homeowners include Michael Bloomberg, Silvio Berlusconi, and Michael Douglas. And even those millionaires and billionaires who don't keep homes in Bermuda often headquarter their companies here; the island's reputation as a tax haven lures businesses whose chief investors are as diverse as Mitt Romney and George Soros. But this breezy archipelago also makes room for tourists on less rarefied budgets who come to play the golf courses, relax on the pink-sand beaches, and experience the quirky charms of an Atlantic Ocean outpost with a personality all its own. — BY DAVID LAHUTA

FRIDAY

1 *Tea in Shorts* 4 p.m.

In a country with a Union Jack on its flag, it's no surprise that many British traditions endure. Tuck in for afternoon tea at **Heritage Court** (76 Pitts Bay Road; 1-441-295-3000; fairmont.com/hamilton; $$$), a white-tablecloth dining room in the Fairmont Hamilton Princess, a hotel that first opened in 1885. Nibble on cucumber sandwiches, petits fours, and fresh-baked apricot and fig scones served with kumquat jam and Devonshire clotted cream. And yes, you may see men in the classic local attire of Bermuda shorts, knee socks, and suit jackets.

2 *Happiest Hour* 6 p.m.

Bermudians are serious about Friday happy hour, when the island clocks out and rum-punches in for the weekend. Well-dressed locals make their way to the **Newstead Belmont Hills Golf Resort & Spa** (27 Harbour Road; 1-441-236-6060; newsteadbelmonthills.com), which hosts a weekly outdoor fiesta, live band and all, on its harborfront patio. Try a Dark 'n' Stormy: rum and Bermuda stone ginger beer.

3 *Fish on Front Street* 9 p.m.

Most guests at **Port O Call** (87 Front Street; 1-441-295-5373; portocall.bm; $$) stick to the specials —typically, fresh local fish simply pan-seared and served with a citrus vinaigrette. From September through March, try the spiny lobster, split and finished on the grill. The place is cozy and smart, with half-moon banquettes, wood-paneled walls, and a granite-topped bar that's usually jammed with island power brokers.

SATURDAY

4 *Dive a Wreck* 8 a.m.

When Peter Benchley was researching his novel *The Deep*, he found inspiration underwater in the *Constellation*, a four-masted schooner that sank off Bermuda in 1943. Even neophytes can explore the well-preserved wreck, which is in a mere 30 feet of water, with an introductory dive given by **Blue Water Divers & Watersports** (Robinson's Marina, Somerset Bridge; 1-441-234-1034; divebermuda.com). In a great two-for-one deal, about 50 feet from the *Constellation* is the wreck of the *Montana*, an English steamer that sank 80 years earlier. Spot pieces of its cargo like shattered china, glass bottles, even a pool table, among thick schools of damselfish, grouper, and barracuda.

5 *Chowder Showdown* 1 p.m.

It's hard to find a restaurant that doesn't serve Bermuda fish chowder, a spicy seafood-and-vegetable

OPPOSITE An undersea pathway of coral reefs leads to the hook-shaped island of Bermuda.

BELOW Tucker's Point on the quiet east end.

stew traditionally eaten with a dash of Gosling's Black Seal rum and Outerbridge's Original Sherry Pepper sauce. Two of the island's favorite chowder spots, both in Hamilton, are the **Hog Penny Restaurant & Pub** (5 Burnaby Hill; 1-441-292-2534; hogpennypub.com; $$), a classic English pub, and the **Lobster Pot** (6 Bermudiana Road; 1-441-292-6898; lobsterpot.bm; $$), a nautically themed cafe with an outdoor patio. When you're done, catch some rays at sweeping **Elbow Beach**, minutes away in Paget Parish.

ABOVE A lobster dinner at Port O Call on Front Street.

BELOW Diving at the wreck of the *Montana*, a steamship that sank in shallow water off Bermuda in 1863.

6 *Island Artists* 2 p.m.

The **Masterworks Museum of Bermuda Art** (183 South Road; 1-441-236-2950; bermudamasterworks.com) displays works from its collection of island-inspired art, including paintings by Georgia O'Keeffe, Winslow Homer, and Marsden Hartley, in its modern museum building in the **Bermuda Botanical Gardens**. Check the current exhibition and then take a walk in the gardens, which hold more than 1,000 varieties of plants and flowers, including hibiscus, oleander, and orchids, arrayed in park, woodland, and greenhouses. The Garden for the Sightless is planted with fragrant species like lemon, lavender, and geranium.

7 *Grab a Gift* 4 p.m.

For designer handbags and shiny baubles, take your wallet to Hamilton, Bermuda's port capital. For authentic Bermudiana, however, head to quieter **St. George's**, on the island's east end. The **Book Cellar** (Tucker House Basement, Water Street;

1-441-297-0448) specializes in historical, nautical, and architectural books about Bermuda. Sniff handmade scents at the **Bermuda Perfumery** (5 Queen Street; 1-441-293-0627; bermuda-perfumery.com), housed in an 18th-century cottage with coral-stone walls and exposed cedar beams. And buy authentic Bermuda shorts at the **English Sports Shop** (30 Water Street; 1-441-297-0142), where you'll find them in all colors of the rainbow.

8 *Outdoors or In?* 8 p.m.

If it's dining with sea spray you're after, head to **Mickey's Beach Bistro & Bar** (60 South Shore Road; 1-441-236-9107; mickeys.bm; $$$-$$$$), an open-air restaurant at the Elbow Beach Bermuda hotel that serves pasta and seafood. Prefer indoor dining with a view? Sit near the window at **Ocean Echo** in the Reefs Hotel (56 South Shore Road; 1-441-238-0222; thereefs.com; $$) and sample inventive spins on local favorites, like Bermuda fish cake in black plum sauce.

9 *Night's Still Young* 11 p.m.

There are plenty of hotel lounges for after-dinner cocktails. But for more local action, head to Front Street in Hamilton. There you'll find the **Pickled Onion** (53 Front Street; 1-441-295-2263; thepickledonion.com), with a rollicking dance floor, large outdoor balcony, and locally brewed beers from the Dockyard Brewing Company. When you're done checking out the handsome 30-something crowd there, head down the street to **Café Cairo** (93 Front Street; 1-441-295-5155), an Egyptian-themed nightclub that's open until 3 a.m.

SUNDAY

10 *Water Hazards* 7:30 a.m.

Originally designed by Robert Trent Jones, then redesigned by Jones colleague Robert Rulewich in 2009, **Port Royal** (5 Port Royal Drive; 1-441-234-0974;

ABOVE Happy hour, a ritual faithfully observed on Fridays. This one is at the Newstead Belmont Hills resort.

BELOW The Masterworks Museum of Bermuda Art.

portroyalgolf.bm) is Bermuda's finest golf course, with water views from nearly every hole. Don't forget your camera on the 16th. Regarded by many as the greatest hole in golf, this 235-yard, crescent-shaped par three hugs the Atlantic coast with nothing but the ocean between the tee and the green.

11 *Go to Church* 11 a.m.

The small cove called **Church Bay** has some of the island's prettiest snorkeling, with blue angels, parrotfish, and thriving coral just 100 yards offshore. Rent gear from the dive shop at the nearby **Fairmont Southampton Hotel & Resort** (101 South Shore Road; 1-441-238-2332; fairmont.com/southampton). When you're done, avoid the cruise-ship crowds at Horseshoe Beach and head for quieter **Warwick Long Bay**. In this stretch of fine pink sand more than half a mile long, you're bound to find a slice to call your own.

ABOVE A swim in the inifinity pool at the Newstead Belmont Hills resort, with the ocean beyond.

OPPOSITE For many a repeat visitor, golf is Bermuda's raison d'etre. This course, one of several, is Port Royal.

Hamilton
Hog Penny Restaurant & Pub
Port O Call
Lobster Pot
Heritage Court/ Fairmont Hamilton Princess
FRONT ST.
Café Cairo
Pickled Onion
2 miles
4 kilometers
Area of detail
BERMUDA INTERNATIONAL AIRPORT
Atlantic Ocean
Tucker's Point Hotel & Spa
Harrington Sound
BERMUDA
SOUTH RD.
St. George's
Bermuda Perfumery
Book Cellar
English Sports Shop
Blue Water Divers & Watersports
Somerset Bridge
Great Sound
Area of detail
Bermuda Botanical Gardens
Masterworks Museum of Bermuda Art
Mickey's Beach Bistro & Bar
Fairmont Southampton Hotel & Resort
Elbow Beach
Newstead Belmont Hills Golf Resort & Spa
Church Bay
Warwick Long Bay
Port Royal
Ocean Echo/Reefs Hotel
New York City
PA.
N.J.
300 miles
600 kilometers
VA.
Atlantic Ocean
N.C.
S.C.
BERMUDA

THE BASICS

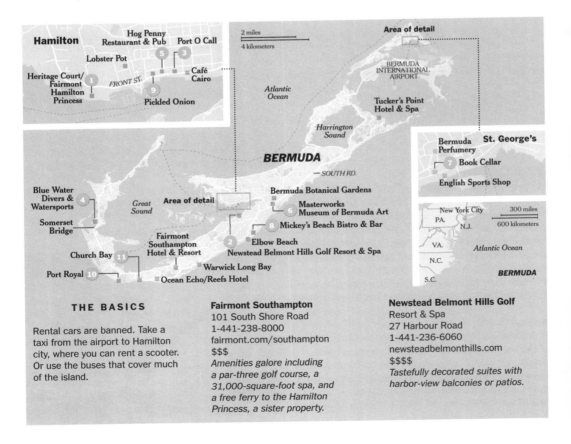

Rental cars are banned. Take a taxi from the airport to Hamilton city, where you can rent a scooter. Or use the buses that cover much of the island.

Fairmont Southampton
101 South Shore Road
1-441-238-8000
fairmont.com/southampton
$$$
Amenities galore including a par-three golf course, a 31,000-square-foot spa, and a free ferry to the Hamilton Princess, a sister property.

Newstead Belmont Hills Golf Resort & Spa
27 Harbour Road
1-441-236-6060
newsteadbelmonthills.com
$$$$
Tastefully decorated suites with harbor-view balconies or patios.

Nassau

Since at least the ninth century, when the Arawak Indians arrived, the Bahamas have lured people to their shores. The Spanish came in the 15th century and the British in the 17th, and in the 1600s Blackbeard created a pirate paradise of drinking and prostitution on New Providence Island, the patch of sand and sun now half occupied by the Bahamian capital city of Nassau. A glitzy era began in the 1960s when the revolution in Cuba diverted tourists from Havana, quickly making Nassau a tourist hot spot. Now the less populated "out islands" of the Bahamas have stolen away the attention of a new generation of adventuresome tourists. But Nassau is more than a port of call for cruise ships or an island hop on the way to somewhere else. Spend a weekend here, and you will find an appealing blend of cosmopolitan and uniquely Bahamian experiences. — BY DAVID G. ALLAN

FRIDAY

1 *A Dip and a Drop* 5 p.m.

Give yourself a dose of what you came for with a swim and a frozen cocktail at **Compass Point Beach Resort** (West Bay Street, Gambier; 1-242-327-4500; compasspointbeachresort.com), a tiny cluster of fruit-colored bungalows that welcomes nonguests to take a dip in the private cove. Dry off while sipping drinks in the outdoor bar. The cocktails are properly tropical: the frozen hurricane is a frothy concoction featuring peach schnapps, grenadine, and rum.

2 *Island Italian* 8 p.m.

Nassau's restaurants often fall into one of two categories: slipshod local fresh-fish places of uneven quality, and overpriced celebrity-chef chains that pack in so many resort guests they need to ship in seafood. **Café Matisse** (Bank Lane; 1-242-356-7012; cafe-matisse.com; $$$), a charming Italian restaurant in a century-old house in the heart of colonial Nassau, happily falls into neither category. The attentive staff serves diners in the leafy, candlelit backyard and in intimate interior rooms adorned with Matisse prints. The menu at one visit included cold cream of tomato soup with goat cheese and cilantro, grilled lobster with daikon in an orange bisque, and millefoglie alla papaya — puff-pastry layers filled with fresh papaya.

3 *A Smoke and a Snifter* 10 p.m.

The Old World charm of brandy snifters and local hand-rolled cigars awaits you at **Graycliff** (West Hill Street; 1-242-302-9150; graycliff.com), a hotel that began in the 1740s as the home of John Howard Graysmith, pirate captain of the schooner Graywolf. Visit the parlor, a haven of plump sofas and marble tables with a piano player at a baby grand and white-jacketed waiters who can suggest a perfect pairing of Cognac and Bahiba Reserva cigars.

SATURDAY

4 *Man About Town* 9 a.m.

Avoid the afternoon heat and crowds with an early self-guided tour that avoids the kitschy museums and duty-free shops on Bay Street. A good place to start is the **Christ Church Cathedral** (George and King Streets) with a stunning interior and impressive stained glass that belie its simple facade. Then head up Market Street to Trinity Place, stopping into **Bahamian Kitchen** (1-242-325-0702; $) for sweetened sour-orange-juice "lemonade" before entering the pink colonial buildings of **Parliament Square**. Walk past the Senate and the Supreme Court building to the square's north end, where you can climb the stairs in the octagonal former

OPPOSITE The Compass Point Beach Resort, where nonguests can drop in for a drink and take a dip in the private cove.

RIGHT A match at the Haynes Oval cricket field.

jail, now a public library. Head uphill one block to East Hill Street and veer right toward the grounds of **Government House**, the official residence of the Bahamas' governor-general, where you will be greeted by epaulet-decorated guards. Continue on West Hill Street to **Graycliff Cigar Company** and find a dozen or so industrious hand-rollers and a dimly lighted, well air-conditioned smoking lounge.

5 *Support Local Arts* 10:30 a.m.

One museum worth your time is the **National Art Gallery of the Bahamas** (West Hill Street; 1-242-328-5800; nagb.org.bs), set in the serene former home of the first chief justice of the Bahamas. An impressive, eclectic collection of local art includes photos from the late 1800s of Nassau streets you just explored; Stanley Burnside's bold and vivid *Solomon*; and interesting temporary installations.

6 *Swimming With Sharks* 12:30 p.m.

A man aptly named Stuart Cove found in the original set of the 1996 Elijah Wood film *Flipper* an attractive base for his **Dive Bahamas** operation (South Ocean Boulevard; 1-242-362-4171; stuartcove.com). The company, which will pick you up from your hotel, offers snorkeling, underwater scooters, and diving, including dives that put you in touch with reef sharks.

7 *Jolly Good Show* 4 p.m.

One of the few reminders that the Bahamas are still part of the British Commonwealth can be found at the **Cricket Club** (1-242-326-4720; bahamascricket.com) at Haynes Oval cricket field between British-built Fort Charlotte and Arawak

BELOW The Cloisters gazebo on Paradise Island, a popular location for weddings.

OPPOSITE ABOVE Cricketers at rest, at Haynes Oval.

Cay. Grab a seat on the balcony and ask the excited Indian and British fans to explain the rules.

8 *Nautical Nosh* 8 p.m.

Near the bridge leading to Paradise Island is the popular **Poop Deck** (East Bay Street; 1-242-393-8175; thepoopdeck.com; $$), where the food is fresh and the view of the harbor idyllic. Try the lightly battered cracked conch and end with the rich guava duff, a local specialty. If you'd prefer to eat like (and with) the locals, head to the row of glorified seafood shacks on **Arawak Cay** collectively known as the fish fry. The leader of the pack is **Twin Brothers** (1-242-328-5033; twinbrothersbahamas.com; $$), where you will want to forgo the cramped interior and find a palm-covered spot out front by the stands serving fluffy, spicy conch fritters, milkshake-thick daiquiris, and a sweet, high-octane cocktail of condensed milk, coconut water, and gin known as sky juice.

9 *Shaken, Not Stirred* 10 p.m.

Change from your beach shirt into a tailored jacket for cocktails at Paradise Island's cinematic **One & Only Ocean Club Resort** (1-242-363-2501; oneandonlyresorts.com), with a lobby and bar that was transformed into the title setting for the James Bond film *Casino Royale*. But why drink among the plush couches inside when you can stroll across the lawn to the open-air bar perched on the sea cliff? **Dune** restaurant's outdoor bar, with its natural wave soundtrack, feels more like the set of a sexy spy thriller. Bond purists should skip the fruity Casino Royale cocktail and get a martini the way 007 likes it—three measures (ounces) gin, one of vodka and half a measure of vermouth with a lemon twist.

SUNDAY

10 *Private Island* 9 a.m.

If you really want to escape the clamor, charter a boat or take a cruise to **Rose Island**, nine miles

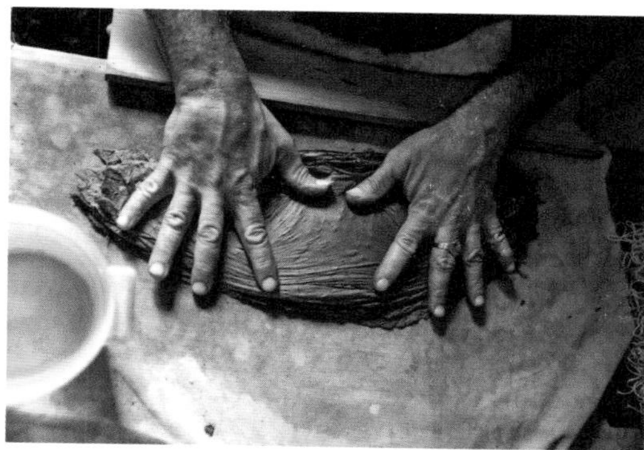

RIGHT Shaping tobacco leaves at Graycliff Cigar Company.

east. One option (most practical if you can muster a crowd to share the cost) is **High Seas Bahamas** (highseasbahamas.com), which takes its passengers to a private stretch of beach for snorkeling, drinking, lounging, and feasting on fresh conch salad and more.

11 *Say 'I Do'* 10 a.m.

If you lack the time or funds for the Rose Island escape, head to Paradise Island instead. It's easy to see why the manicured **Versailles Gardens** and pretty waterside **Cloisters** gazebo (off Paradise Drive) are the sites of about 150 weddings a year. Once you've walked up a sweat, take the first road west of the One & Only resort until you reach the unmarked path that leads to the powdered-sugar sands and teal expanse of **Cabbage Beach**.

ABOVE On Paradise Island, just offshore from Nassau, sun worshippers can find their Eden in the powdered-sugar sands and teal expanse of Cabbage Beach.

OPPOSITE Crystalline waters near Nassau make for good visibility in the reefs and shallows. Some snorkelers reach deep enough to grab conch for lunch.

Northeast Providence Channel
ARAWAK CAY
PARADISE ISLAND
One & Only Ocean Club Resort/Dune 9
Cabbage Beach
Christ Church Cathedral 4
Twin Brothers
Graycliff Cigar Company
2 Café Matisse
Comfort Suites Paradise Island
11 Versailles Gardens
Cloisters
7 Cricket Club
Parliament Square
Nassau Harbor
National Art Gallery of the Bahamas 5
Bahamian Kitchen
EAST HILL ST.
Poop Deck 8
EAST BAY ST.
Graycliff 3
Government House
Nassau
0.5 mile
1 kilometer
A Stone's Throw Away
British Colonial Hilton
Area of detail
10 Rose Island
1 Compass Point Beach Resort
NEW PROVIDENCE ISLAND
6 Dive Bahamas
4 miles
8 kilometers
FLORIDA
GRAND BAHAMA
ABACO
THE BAHAMAS
Miami
Nassau
ELEUTHERA
ANDROS
NEW PROVIDENCE
CAT
Atlantic Ocean
EXUMA

THE BASICS

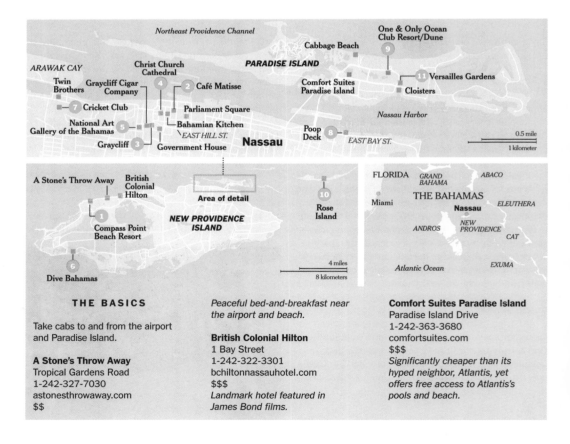

Take cabs to and from the airport and Paradise Island.

A Stone's Throw Away
Tropical Gardens Road
1-242-327-7030
astonesthrowaway.com
$$
Peaceful bed-and-breakfast near the airport and beach.

British Colonial Hilton
1 Bay Street
1-242-322-3301
bchiltonnassauhotel.com
$$$
Landmark hotel featured in James Bond films.

Comfort Suites Paradise Island
Paradise Island Drive
1-242-363-3680
comfortsuites.com
$$$
Significantly cheaper than its hyped neighbor, Atlantis, yet offers free access to Atlantis's pools and beach.

Exuma

The real Exuma, a Bahamian island southeast of Nassau, is a do-it-yourself place, best discovered with sand between your toes. On its unspoiled beaches, the only footprints are probably your own, and the clear Atlantic waters dance before you like a kaleidoscope of jades, purples, and blues. It is also a place where street addresses are nonexistent and where you will have to slow down in spite of yourself: there is regular time, and there is Bahamian time, and the more you try to hurry, the longer it will take you to get there. — BY ABBOTT COMBES

FRIDAY

1 *Into the Drink* 6 p.m.

If you're staying at the **Club Peace and Plenty** hotel in George Town (1-242-336-2551; peaceandplenty.com), attend the manager's Friday-night reception; if you're not staying there, crash it. Crashing is O.K.; you just should forgo the complimentary rum punch and pay for your own drinks, served up with plenty of gusto poolside and in the former slave quarters that are the main bar. There are two reasons you want to be there. One is the allure of tropical libations with names like Reef Wrecker and Goombay Smash. The other is to meet the regulars.

2 *High Life* 7 p.m.

Luxury resorts are few and far between on Exuma, but you can sample the ambience at one of them, the posh **Grand Isle Resort**, by having dinner at its restaurant, **Palapa Pool Bar and Grill** (Queen's Highway, Emerald Bay; 1-242-358-5000; grandisleresort.com; $$-$$$). You could order one of the "American-style" entrees, but it's more fun to sample the local grouper or Bahamian barbecue.

SATURDAY

3 *Grouper Breakfast* 8 a.m.

Join the locals for a Bahamian breakfast at one of the "shacks" on the old United States Navy base a half-mile west of town. **Tino's** (1-242-336-2277; $$) is where you'll see the most cars; have a breakfast of "stew fish" (grouper), grits, and bread.

4 *Roads Less Traveled* 9:30 a.m.

Technically, Exuma is an archipelago of 365 cays and islands that uncoils for 150 miles or so southeast of Nassau, but for the purposes of this weekend, it's just two islands—one named Great and the other Little, linked by a single road (the Queen's Highway) and one bridge. To begin a morning of scattershot exploration, grab a map and head east to **Little Exuma**. Keep your eyes open along the way. Exuma has a rich history of ship wrecking, blockade breaking, rum-running, and drug trafficking, and you never know when you'll happen upon a secluded cove where Captain Kidd once anchored or even see a brick of marijuana washed up on the shore, as has happened. After you cross the bridge onto Little Exuma, find the **Tropic of Cancer Beach** (so called because it's practically on it) between Forbes Hill and Williams Town, and loll awhile. Or be impulsive: take an unmarked road (street signs on the island are as rare as neckties) left toward the water and see what you find. Beaches in the Bahamas are public property up to the high-tide mark, but you should respect private property in reaching them.

OPPOSITE A quiet beach near George Town, the capital of the sparsely populated Exuma island chain.

RIGHT Crafting a basket for sale at the straw market.

5 *Cotton Picking* 11:30 a.m.

Return to the Queen's Highway, drive into Williams Town and meander through the ruins of the **Hermitage Plantation**, a reminder of how British loyalists tried—and eventually failed—to establish a plantation economy on the island after the American Revolution. Another reminder, incidentally, is the wild cotton you see the entire length (about 60 miles) and breadth (about 7 miles) of Great and Little Exuma. For lunch, stop at **Santanna's** roadside stand in Williams Town (1-242-345-4102; $$) for a plate of cracked lobster. On your way back to George Town, take a right in the middle of the big bend leading into **Forbes Hill** and put some more sand between your toes at the sweeping beach there.

6 *To Market, to Market* 1:30 p.m.

Back in the middle of George Town, under the spreading ficus tree, survey the intricate weaving and other handicrafts of the women of the **straw market**, whose salesmanship, by the way, can be fierce. And up the road, **Sandpiper Arts & Crafts** (1-242-336-2084; sandpiperexuma.com) features Bahamian artwork and a smart selection of clothing, jewelry, books, toys, and souvenirs.

7 *Nature's A.T.M. Machine* 3 p.m.

Westward! Back on the Queen's Highway, the 22-mile jaunt to **Cocoplums Beach** is a pleasant drive through small towns and postcard-pretty ocean vistas. After Steventon but before Rolleville, turn right at the Cocoplums sign. Stroll the beach and withdraw a few sand dollars.

RIGHT Waterside golf at the Four Seasons Resort.

8 *Let Them Eat Steak* 8 p.m.

Have a steak (well, O.K., the seafood is a good choice, too) at **Eddie's Edgewater** (1-242-336-2050; $$) on Lake Victoria in the center of George Town. The kitchen defines Bahamian time, and you will undoubtedly be hungry by the time the meal arrives. After dinner, ask around about where the Saturday-night action is: there's usually a band playing at one of the hotels or bar-restaurants or, shades of culture implosion, a karaoke machine. Or maybe opt for the sounds of silence and let a slow boat ride around the starlit harbor be your good-night serenade.

SUNDAY

9 *Sporting Life* 9 a.m.

Take to the sea for an adventurous morning of scuba diving, snorkeling, fishing, and/or boating, but don't wait until Sunday to make the arrangements: reserve in advance with **Dive Exuma** (1-242-336-2893; dive-exuma.com); **Starfish** (1-800-893-8622; in Exuma, 1-242-336-3033; starfishexuma.com); or

Minns Water Sports (1-242-336-3483; mwsboats.com). Drop anchor almost anywhere, jump in the water, and you'll think you're swimming in the pages of *National Geographic*, surrounded by chromatic tropical fish and flowerlike coral reefs. The island is a magnet for bonefishermen (many of whom swear by the flats just before the bridge to Little Exuma), though some anglers prefer going after barracuda, tarpon, grouper, or even sharks.

10 *Take a Hike* 10 a.m.

As an alternative to participatory sport, take a water taxi across the harbor to **Stocking Island** from the Club Peace and Plenty dock. Stocking Island's trails, blue holes, hidden cave, and beaches, particularly on the unprotected Atlantic side, can bring out the nature lover in even the slickest of city slickers.

OPPOSITE ABOVE Clothes hung out to dry and flapping in the wind, a sight along the Queen's Highway.

ABOVE Leaving the dock at sunset. The linked main islands of Great and Little Exuma are part of a chain with many smaller islands and calm, shallow channels.

5 miles
10 kilometers
Cocoplums Beach 7
Grand Isle Resort 2
Palappa Pool Bar and Grill
Emerald Bay
GREAT EXUMA
EXUMA INT'L AIRPORT
QUEEN'S HWY.
Sandpiper Arts & Crafts 6
1 Club Peace and Plenty
Minns Water Sports
Straw market
George Town
Lake Victoria
Starfish
Eddie's Edgewater 8
FLORIDA
GRAND BAHAMA
ABACO
THE BAHAMAS
Miami
Nassau
ELEUTHERA
ANDROS
NEW PROVIDENCE
CAT
Atlantic Ocean
Area of detail
Palm Bay Beach Club
Coral Gardens
10 Stocking Island
Area of detail
9 Dive Exuma
3 Tino's
Atlantic Ocean
Little Exuma 4
Forbes Hill
Santanna's
Tropic of Cancer Beach
Williams Town
Hermitage Plantation 5

THE BASICS

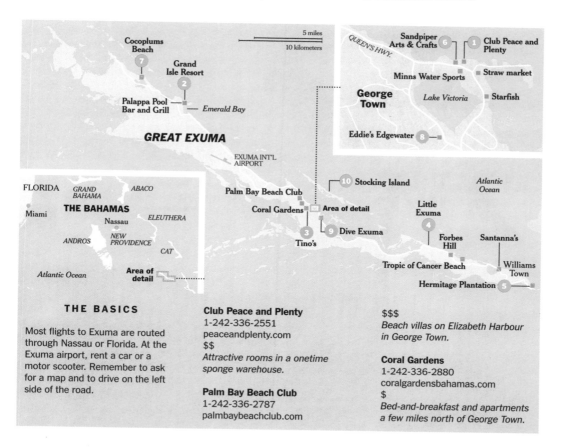

Most flights to Exuma are routed through Nassau or Florida. At the Exuma airport, rent a car or a motor scooter. Remember to ask for a map and to drive on the left side of the road.

Club Peace and Plenty
1-242-336-2551
peaceandplenty.com
$$
Attractive rooms in a onetime sponge warehouse.

Palm Bay Beach Club
1-242-336-2787
palmbaybeachclub.com
$$$
Beach villas on Elizabeth Harbour in George Town.

Coral Gardens
1-242-336-2880
coralgardensbahamas.com
$
Bed-and-breakfast and apartments a few miles north of George Town.

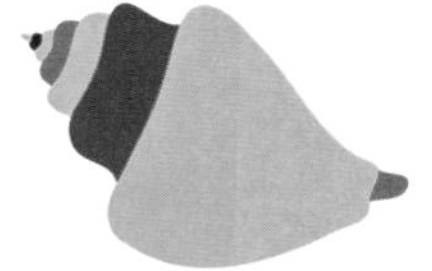

Turks and Caicos

Dangling at the southern end of the Bahamas island chain like an afterthought, Turks and Caicos was often overlooked as a Caribbean destination. But thanks to the arrival of some of the swankiest names in hotels — Regent, Aman Resorts, and Meridian, for example — Turks and Caicos is now firmly on the map of those seeking a beach vacation with heavy pampering and a splash of indulgence. It is the kind of place where hotel staff members adjust your beach-chair umbrella as the sun shifts and pass out cool towels to keep you from overheating. The moderately priced hotels have maid service a mere two times a day, instead of providing guests with a small army of personal servants. Technically, the islands are in the Atlantic, but with this level of coddling — not to mention some of the bluest waters in the world — who cares? — BY JEREMY W. PETERS

FRIDAY

1 *Sunset Show* 5:30 p.m.

Chances are your hotel is somewhere on **Grace Bay**, with its stunning stretch of satin-soft white sand curving along the northeastern edge of Providenciales, the main island. The beach gently slopes into the ocean, which reveals bands of blue and green that are so brilliant that no postcard could do them justice. This must be one of the loveliest beaches anywhere in the tropics. Time your stroll with the setting sun when the orange light reflects off the blue water.

2 *Conch-ed Out* 8 p.m.

Grace Bay is also home to a surfeit of restaurants, some better than others. For something less touristy, venture about 15 minutes by car into the Blue Hills along the northwestern coastline. **Da Conch Shack** (Blue Hills Road; 1-649-946-8877; conchshack.tc; $$) stays true to its name, serving up conch from a beach hut with heaps of the mollusk's glistening pink shells outside. Sit down at a picnic table just a few steps from the water, take off your shoes, dip your feet into the sand, and decide how you want your conch. Curried? Sautéed? Diced up and served ceviche-style? Definitely don't skip the conch fritters, which are golden brown, moist, and chewy.

3 *Know When to Fold 'Em* 11 p.m.

Las Vegas it's not. But Providenciales does offer charming, if low-key, gaming, from slots to blackjack to craps. Its two tourist-geared casinos are both situated in nondescript buildings that could easily be mistaken for medical offices or insurance agencies. But consider that a good thing. The lack of any flashy appointments at the **Casablanca Casino** (Grace Bay Road; 1-649-941-3737; thecasablancacasino.com) lends a low-stakes atmosphere that won't make you feel like a chump for heading straight for the $10 blackjack table.

SATURDAY

4 *Eat What?* 9 a.m.

After laying eyes on Grace Bay, you'll probably want to stay put. But then you'll miss the nearby islets like Iguana Island, a nature preserve where the scaly little lizards scamper through the brush, and Water Cay, home to stunning Half Moon Bay, whose crescent of powdery white sand is framed by limestone cliffs. **Silverdeep** (Leeward Highway; 1-649-946-5612; silverdeep.com) offers three-hour

OPPOSITE The beach at Grace Bay, a stunning stretch of soft white sand, wraps around the northeastern edge of Providenciales, the main island of Turks and Caicos.

RIGHT The beach lounge at the Seven Stars Resort on Grace Bay. Providenciales has no shortage of hotels eager to pamper and indulge their paying guests.

excursions that include rum punch and a local delicacy—but you have to earn it. Your captain will shell and clean as much conch as you can pluck from the ocean floor, before mincing and marinating it in lemon and lime. Oh, and what is that translucent, spaghetti-shaped appendage purported to have aphrodisiac powers? That's the conch penis, and you should be prepared to eat it.

5 *Rooms at the Top* Noon

You may think you've seen luxury on Providenciales, but **Amanyara** (Northwest Point; 1-649-941-8133; amanresorts.com) makes the Regent look like a Holiday Inn. The price of a stay there during the winter is stratospheric; dropping in for lunch is a more affordable way to marvel at the resort's airy, pagodalike pavilions and reflecting pools, and even that is no bargain. Expect to pay handsomely for the jerk chicken garnished with avocado and pawpaw salad. But what better way to forget about the perils of the global economy than to lounge on one of the poolside canopied beds, nursing a cocktail?

6 *Infinite Mojitos* 7 p.m.

Like much of the Caribbean, Providenciales has no shortage of beach bars outfitted in full-on tropical kitsch. Tiki torches, thatch umbrellas, and coconut shells abound. But for something less conventionally beachy, try the Infiniti Bar at the **Grace Bay Club** (Grace Bay Road; 1-649-946-5050; gracebayclub.com), where drinks are served from a 90-foot oblong slab of black granite stretching toward the water. The club claims that it's the Caribbean's longest bar. It is impressive, as are the cocktails, all made with tropical flair, like the raspberry mojito, and the appetizers, which should tide you over until dinner.

7 *Under the Palms* 8:30 p.m.

It's hard to imagine a nicer dinner setting than Grace Bay Beach. But a five-minute drive inland takes you to **Coco Bistro** (Grace Bay Road; 1-649-946-5369; cocobistro.tc; $$$), about the prettiest place you can hope to find away from the water. Set underneath a canopy of soaring palm trees, this outdoor restaurant offers hearty alternatives to the steady diet of conch and fish. Here is the place to find prime rib, rack of lamb, and a Caesar salad served with bacon and a peppery dressing. You might even inquire about taking a palm tree home with you from the nursery right next door.

8 *Split-Level Bars* 11 p.m.

Despite Providenciales's tropical locale, night life here is more martini glasses than plastic cups. But if you insist on tiny umbrellas in your drink, head to the **Ports of Call** mall, a strip mall near the resorts along Grace Bay Road that has two fun-loving bars: **Jimmy's Dive Bar & Grill** downstairs (1-649-946-5282; jimmysdivebar.com), and upstairs, predictably, the **Upstairs Bar and Grill** (1-649-941-8914; upstairsbarandgrill.com). The distance between the two is just a flight of stairs, so patrons can easily wander back and forth depending on the crowd and the live music offerings.

SUNDAY

9 *Sunday Blues* 10 a.m.

The blues that surround Turks and Caicos are so vivid that you'll want to consult a color wheel. Is that cyan? Cobalt? Azure? But the water in **Chalk**

BELOW The Amanyara resort. To glimpse its luxury without paying the room rates, have lunch in its restaurant.

Sound, an inlet surrounded by national park on one side and sprawling villas on the other, is the most unusual shade of blue anywhere on the island. A touch lighter than turquoise and not quite sky blue, it appears something like the color of the United Nations flag. A camera-ready road snakes down the peninsula that runs along the southern end of the sound, providing sweeping views of the vivid water and the hillsides.

10 *Sea-View Sandwiches* Noon

In one corner of Chalk Sound sits **Las Brisas** (At Neptune Villas, Chalk Sound Drive; 1-649-946-5306; neptunevillastci.com; $), a cafe that offers inexpensive sandwiches (shredded pork, chicken and, of course, conch) and even more spectacular views. The restaurant is perched at a slight elevation and faces the water. One day's menu included a fried-plantain cup filled with grilled shrimp and topped with a Creole sauce. Work off your lunch by renting one of the sea kayaks from the bartender and paddling it around Chalk Sound. On an island this luxe, it's probably the only real work you'll do yourself for the entire trip.

OPPOSITE ABOVE On excursions with the Silverdeep boat company, guests dive for conch and the staff cleans and marinates it for a conch salad lunch.

ABOVE A walk at Grace Bay. The beach here slopes gently into an ocean colored in bands of blue and green.

THE BASICS

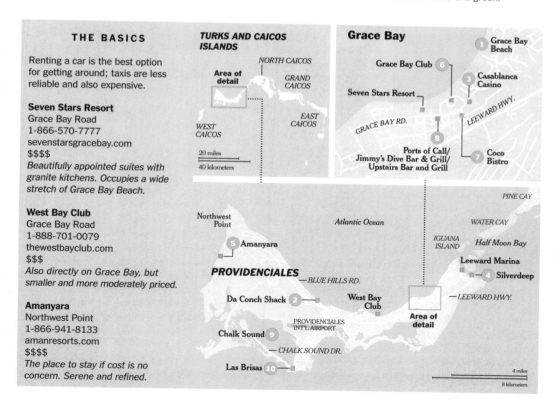

Renting a car is the best option for getting around; taxis are less reliable and also expensive.

Seven Stars Resort
Grace Bay Road
1-866-570-7777
sevenstarsgracebay.com
$$$$
Beautifully appointed suites with granite kitchens. Occupies a wide stretch of Grace Bay Beach.

West Bay Club
Grace Bay Road
1-888-701-0079
thewestbayclub.com
$$$
Also directly on Grace Bay, but smaller and more moderately priced.

Amanyara
Northwest Point
1-866-941-8133
amanresorts.com
$$$$
The place to stay if cost is no concern. Serene and refined.

PARE
52

Havana

There's nothing else in the Caribbean quite like Havana, the Cuban capital and cultural hotspot. A 40-minute flight from Miami whisks the visitor to a city that seems an era and a continent apart from the United States, though it's only about 100 miles away. Europeans, Canadians, and South Americans already know Havana well, and Americans, while still a novelty here, are starting to join them as travel restrictions begin to loosen. What they all find here are a thriving contemporary-arts scene, ancient narrow streets plied by immaculately maintained vintage American cars, and fun-loving inhabitants who seem not to walk but to sway to a musical beat that rolls over the city every night like the mist over the Malecón. No wonder this glamorous city so beguiled earlier generations. It has enough new panache and passion to seduce a 21st-century world as well.

— BY FINN-OLAF JONES

FRIDAY

1 *A Capital Living Room* 4 p.m.

Introduce yourself to Havana, and vice versa, by strolling the **Malecón**, Havana's dramatic oceanfront boulevard, fishing spot, and hangout zone. Start from Habana Vieja, Old Havana, and curve your way down the bay, listening to the waves pounding against the seawall as you go. Head for the old **Hotel Nacional**, a landmark perched on a promontory above the Art Deco buildings of the Vedado district. If you can make it that far, reward yourself with a mojito in the Nacional's gorgeous Moorish lobby. You'll be in the same space where the hotel once welcomed famous guests from Winston Churchill to Fred Astaire to the American gangster Lucky Luciano.

2 *Capitalist Dinner* 8 p.m.

You can literally taste Cuba's nascent experiment with a free-market economy in the thriving paladares—homes and apartments turned into private restaurants—that have revolutionized the country's dining scene. Havanaphiles will argue which paladare is best, but **La Guarida** (Concordia 418; 53-7-866-9047; laguarida.com; $$) still tops many lists. Wander up a dilapidated stairway in Habana Vieja to a suite of ornate rooms and a balcony. Lobster tacos, ajiaco, or whatever can be procured in Cuba's heavily regulated food markets that day is served up with admirable flair.

3 *Beat Street* 10 p.m.

Obispo Street is a lively pedestrian thoroughfare cutting through the heart of Habana Vieja and lined with bars jumping to some of Cuba's best mambo and jazz bands. Start on the southern end of the street at **El Floridita** (557 Obispo; 53-7-867-1300; floridita-cuba.com), which claims to be the birthplace of the daiquiri. It was Ernest Hemingway's favorite watering hole for two decades; his usual discreet spot at the end of the bar is now marked by an indiscreet life-size statue of him. Perhaps an even better stop is **La Lluvia de Oro** (316 Obispo; 53-7-862-9870), where the Cuba libres are served up with lobster snacks and outstanding live music. When you're ready to move on, just wander out and stop at whichever bar makes your foot tap the most.

SATURDAY

4 *Chez Hemingway* 10 a.m.

The mutual love affair between Ernest Hemingway and Cuba still finds expression in the

OPPOSITE La Habana Vieja, or Old Havana. Even with its Communist overlay, Havana remains a city of glamour, with ancient narrow streets, colonial and Art Deco buildings, and its own unique passion and panache.

RIGHT Street art in Old Havana. One of the oldest cities in the New World, Havana was founded in 1519.

Finca La Vigía (Calle Vigía, San Francisco de Paula; 53-7-691-0809), or Lookout Farm, his home for 21 years, nine miles south of Havana. Hemingway's nomadic lifestyle is evident from the African game trophies and hordes of multilingual books in the rooms. His mail is on the bed and his clothes are in the closet, almost as if he had just stepped out for another fishing trip in the Gulf Stream. (He left in 1960, after the Cuban revolution, and never returned; he committed suicide in Idaho in 1961.) The Finca's authentic appearance is largely thanks to an ongoing restoration project conducted jointly by the Boston-based Finca Vigía Foundation, which provided preservation experts, and the museum's Cuban staff, who seem to revere this hilltop man cave as if it were a shrine.

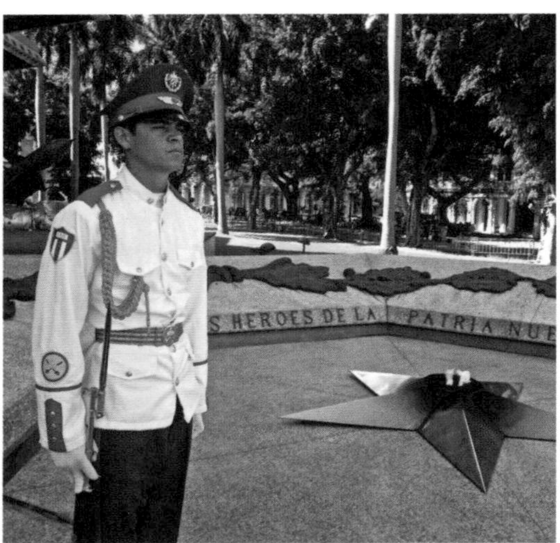

5 *Lunch at the Cathedral* 1 p.m.

Make sure to reserve a table in advance at one of Havana's most stylish and popular paladares, **Doña Eutimia** (Callejon del Chorro 60; 53-7-861-1332; $), on a corner street off Plaza de la Catedral. The restaurant is squeezed into three cozy parlors, but if it's not too hot, grab a table outside on the cobblestones. Have a mojito frappé and enjoy ropa vieja, grilled shrimp, or other Cuban delicacies.

6 *Legal Cubanos* 2 p.m.

The sweet scent of dried tobacco leaves wafting outside the picturesquely dilapidated **Partagás Factory** (Calle Industria 520; 53-7-862-4604) leaves little doubt

ABOVE The old buildings of Central Havana, from the terrace of the Parque Central Hotel. In the background are mid-20th-century high-rise buildings and the seafront.

LEFT Outside the Museum of the Revolution, which before the Cuban Revolution in 1959 was the presidential palace. Bullet holes remain in the marble stairway.

what used to go on here. Now most of the cigar rolling takes place in more modern facilities outside of town. But the store and bar adjoining the entrance are Old School and sell some of the finest cigars on the planet, including the rare Cohiba Behike, rolled from a blend of scarce leaves responsible for its famed "creamy" taste. Stick around for an espresso or aged rum.

7 *Hypercapitalist Outpost* 3 p.m.

A wooden rooster? Nude portraits? Che wear? Few markets are as lively as the **Centro Cultural Antiguos Almacenes de Depósito San José**, which operates in a harborfront warehouse at the corner of Avenida Desamparados and Calle San Ignacio. Socialist practices are dropped here in favor of lively haggling amid a cacophony of vendor stalls. The market also has a couple of pleasant open-air grill cafes where you can watch the ships sail by.

8 *Che's Killing Field* 5 p.m.

The imposing fortress of **San Carlos de la Cabaña** (Carretera de la Cabaña) has been sheltering Havana beneath its towering hilltop cannons since the 18th century, and it still affords an epic view into town, especially at dusk. The fortress is next door to Che Guevara's former home and served as his post-revolutionary headquarters when he was the head of the army. Here he personally supervised firing-squad executions in the dried-out moat. Despite its grim history, the fort is a romantic spot. When colonial re-enactors shoot off the ceremonial cannon over the rampart at 9 p.m., the sound can be heard all over Havana.

ABOVE Obispo Street, a pedestrian walkway in Old Havana, bursts with life at sunset. Choose from its many bars with live music by Cuba's best mambo and jazz bands.

9 *On Your Toes* 7:30 p.m.

Look up the schedule for the glorious six-tiered neo-Baroque **Gran Teatro de La Habana** (458 Paseo de Martí; 53-7-861-3077). If the Ballet Nacional de Cuba (www.balletcuba.cult.cu) is performing, you're in luck. Not only is the ballet world-class, but the discreet socializing, flirting, and gossiping among Havana's chic set in the back rows and galleries during the performance and intermission are right out of *Anna Karenina*.

SUNDAY

10 *Caribbean Louvre* 11 a.m.

The sprawling **Palacio de Bellas Artes** (Trocadero; 53-7-861-3858; www.bellasartes.cult.cu) displays the works of Cuba's superstars like the Picasso protégé Wilfredo Lam and the Afro-folkloric painter Manuel Mendive. There's also a fascinating

section of 16th- to 19th-century Cuban landscapes and portraits, many of which were confiscated from their private owners during the revolution.

11 *Paging Al Pacino* 2 p.m.

Cross the street from the Bellas Artes to see a loudly propagandistic depiction of Cuba's 1959 revolution in the **Museo de la Revolución** (Calle Refugio 1; 53-7-862-4091). Appropriately enough, the museum is housed in the exquisite Tiffany-glassed, Beaux Arts interiors of the pre-1959 presidential palace, which still has bullet holes in its marble stairway. The displays include bloody uniforms and garish caricatures of American presidents in the "Cretin Corner." For fans of *The Godfather: Part II* there's a special parting treat: the original gold-plated telephone given to the dictator-president Fulgencio Batista by the ITT Corporation.

ABOVE Many of the cars speeding past old city buildings are carefully kept American models from before 1959.

OPPOSITE A musician at El Floridita, famous as a favorite hangout of Ernest Hemingway in his days in Cuba. The bar claims to be the birthplace of the daiquiri.

0.5 mile
1 kilometer
TUNEL DE LA HABANA
8 San Carlos de la Cabaña
Malecón
1
Hotel Nacional
CALLE REFUGIO
Hotel Palacio O'Farill
Museo de la Revolución 11
TROCADERO
HABANA VIEJA
5 Doña Eutimia
VEDADO
La Guarida 2
Palacio de Bellas Artes 10
La Lluvia de Oro
SAN LAZARO
CONCORDIA
OBISPO
Hotel Raquel
NEPTUNO
Gran Teatro de La Habana 9
3
CALLE AMARGURA
CALLE INDUSTRIA
El Floridita
Gulf of Mexico
FLA.
Miami
THE BAHAMAS
Straits of Florida
Havana
CUBA
Caribbean Sea
6
Partagás Factory
Havana
Centro Cultural Antiguos Almacenes de Depósito San José
7
TO JOSE MARTÍ INTERNATIONAL AIRPORT
4 To Finca La Vigía

THE BASICS

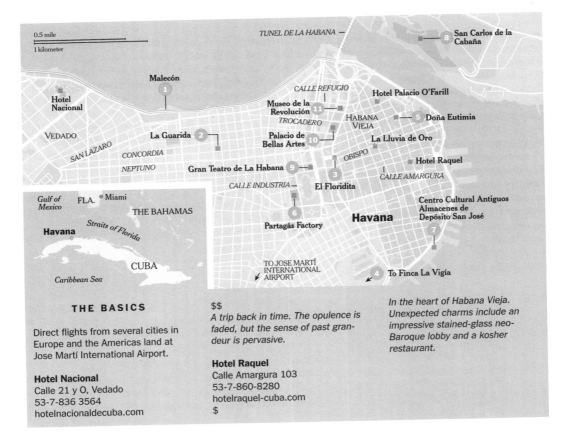

Direct flights from several cities in Europe and the Americas land at Jose Martí International Airport.

Hotel Nacional
Calle 21 y O, Vedado
53-7-836 3564
hotelnacionaldecuba.com
$$
A trip back in time. The opulence is faded, but the sense of past grandeur is pervasive.

Hotel Raquel
Calle Amargura 103
53-7-860-8280
hotelraquel-cuba.com
$
In the heart of Habana Vieja. Unexpected charms include an impressive stained-glass neo-Baroque lobby and a kosher restaurant.

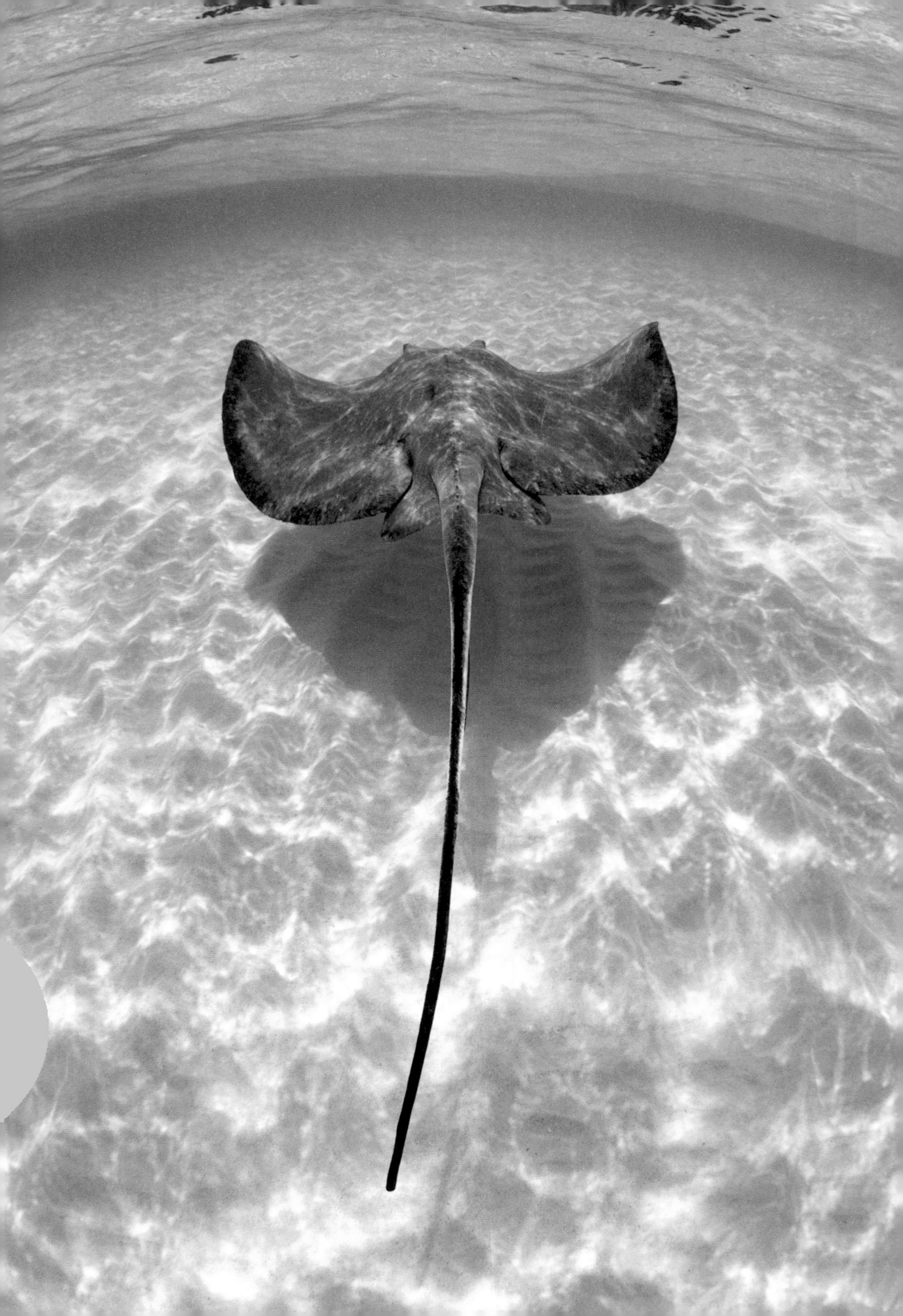

Cayman Islands

Signs of wealth and extravagance in the Cayman Islands, a British Overseas Territory 270 miles south of Havana, are difficult to miss. From the mansions along the southern shore of Grand Cayman, the main island, to a Ritz-Carlton resort so large it straddles the major thoroughfare, travelers know they have arrived in the Caribbean's kingdom of offshore finance. But if dropping $4,500 a night on a suite at the Ritz is not in your budget, you'll be relieved to learn that the Caymans have more economical options to offer, like modest but pleasant hotels and tasty jerk chicken from a roadside shack. And regardless of the condition of your credit card, the beach sand will still be sugary fine, and the snorkeling will still be great.
— BY JEREMY W. PETERS

FRIDAY

1 *Take the Cake* 2 p.m.

Brave the cruise-ship crowds in George Town, the main town, to get your shopping done early. The Tortuga Rum Company (tortugarumcakes.com) is Grand Cayman's version of Starbucks; with more than a dozen of them across the island, it's not much of an exaggeration to say there is one on nearly every corner. There are even two in the airport's tiny, five-gate main terminal. The rum cake comes in several flavors, from coffee to banana to Golden Original. Instead of going for the shrink-wrapped boxes, buy one of the freshly baked cakes at the company's **Tortuga Duty Free and Cake Factory** (South Church Street, George Town; 1-345-949-7701). You'll probably have to eat it while you're in the Caymans, but that's why they have the wrapped ones to take back home.

2 *Plenty of Mileage* 3 p.m.

Beaching on Grand Cayman does not require much effort, forethought, or cost, since all the beaches are free. Chances are you'll be staying on or very close to Seven Mile Beach — the gorgeous natural jewel and tourism profit center of Grand Cayman — which is lined with hotels and condominium developments. So you probably need not stray very far to lounge on one of the Caribbean's finest stretches of sand. The "seven-mile" moniker is a bit generous (the odometer on my rental car clocked the length at around five miles). But be assured that there is enough space to visit a different section each day of your visit and feel as if you've ventured onto a new beach. The far northern section is typically least crowded. About at the beach's midpoint, there is fine people-watching to be done along the stretch where the Westin and the Ritz-Carlton are located.

3 *Cayman Curry* 7 p.m.

The multicultural population of Grand Cayman, a byproduct of its international banking industry, has produced a diverse culinary scene. This may have been the last place where you were expecting to find a nice spicy plate of Indian food, but **My Bar** at the **Sunset House** (390 South Church Street; 1-345-949-7111; sunsethouse.com; $$), overlooking the ocean a few minutes' drive south of George Town, has excellent curry dishes and other Indian specialties. For inexpensive sushi with a hint of tropical influence (think rolls accented with mango and papaya) try **Yoshi Sushi** (Falls Plaza, West Bay Road; 1-345-943 9674; yoshisushicayman.com; $$).

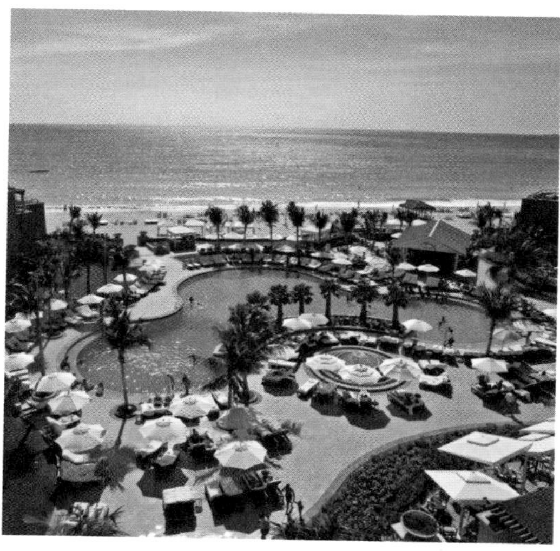

OPPOSITE A resident of Stingray City, a series of sandbars in the North Sound of Grand Cayman Island.

RIGHT A pool at the Ritz-Carlton. Inside the hotel is Blue, a restaurant run by the chef of Le Bernardin in New York.

4 *Pirate Cocktails* 9 p.m.

Grand Cayman is not as liberal with its alcohol-serving laws as some of the other Caribbean islands. On Friday nights, most establishments close at 1 a.m. And on Saturdays, all the bars have to be shut down and emptied out by midnight, which means that last call can arrive at the teetotaling hour of 11:30. So if you want to pack in a full evening of partying, you'd better start early. Drinking here seems to be closely associated with pirates, especially the notorious Calico Jack Rackam (or Rackham), who terrorized these islands in the early 18th century. **Rackam's Waterfront** (North Church Street, George Town; 1-345-945 3860; rackams.com) is a low-key bar on the harbor, and **Calico Jack's Bar & Grill** (118, Seven Mile Beach; 1-345-945-7850) sometimes has D.J.'s. **Pirates of the Caymans** (George Town Harbor; 1-345-945-7245; piratesofthecaymans.com) offers cocktail cruises with an open bar.

SATURDAY

5 *Meet the Rays* 8:30 a.m.

The island's most popular recreational activity is diving. If you're a scuba enthusiast, head for the renowned Bloody Bay Wall dive site off Little Cayman, one of the "sister islands." But there's a more accessible thrilling experience at **Stingray City**, a series of sand bars in the North Sound of Grand Cayman where touchingly gentle and friendly stingrays swim in shallow water. Numerous companies ferry tourists out to snorkel and to visit the stingrays, which allow people to pet and feed them. One reasonably priced option is a three-hour tour with **Captain Marvin's** (two locations; 1-345-945-6975; captainmarvins.com). Nonalcoholic beverages and snorkel gear are provided onboard.

6 *Chicken Without Pretensions* 1 p.m.

On Grand Cayman, there is no shortage of pricey dining. Even fast-food outlets charge lofty prices. Spend your lunch money on a better deal: the jerk-chicken plate at **Seymour's Jerk Centre** (Shedden Road, in the parking lot of Roy's Boutique; 1-345-945-1931; $), which locals regard as some of the best chicken on the island. Seymour's isn't much to look at — it's just a shed in a gravel parking lot with a couple of picnic tables — but the food will leave you satisfied.

7 *Idle Pleasure* 3 p.m.

Although you might see little reason ever to leave Seven Mile for another beach, **Rum Point**, on the other side of North Sound, has a small, lovely beach with calm, clear water perfect for swimming. Lie in a hammock or recline in a lounge chair under its great pine trees, or take a dip in the clear blue sea. While you're there, grab a beer or slurp a fast-melting daiquiri at the **Wreck Bar** (rumpointclub.com).

8 *Beach Bernardin* 8 p.m.

Sample the grander side of Grand Cayman with a gourmet dinner at the Ritz-Carlton. Eric Ripert, the chef at Le Bernardin in New York, runs a restaurant here, **Blue by Eric Ripert** (1-345-815-6912; ritzcarlton.com/GrandCayman; $$$$) that he has described as "the equivalent of Le Bernardin by the beach." Prepare yourself for fare like seared local tuna with picholine olive puree, marcona almond, and sherry emulsion, or perhaps house-made tortellini with pumpkin, arugula pistou, and Parmesan. For dessert, how about something like a caramel mousse with caramelized popcorn, praline cream, and popcorn sorbet? For a real splurge, order the four-course chef's tasting menu, with accompanying wines.

SUNDAY

9 *Brake for Iguanas* 9 a.m.

Take a walk amid palms and parrots at the **Queen Elizabeth II Botanic Garden** (Frank Sound Road, North Side district; 1-345-947-9462; botanic-park.ky). The garden, most of which is a 65-acre natural

ABOVE The blue iguana, a favorite example of the local fauna, receives some extra coloration in this fanciful beach sculpture at Rum Point.

preserve, is serious about flowers, especially tropical orchids, and also protects habitats for a variety of other native plants, as well as exotic animals like rare butterflies and the blue iguanas that may be basking in your path.

10 *Mideast Brunch* 11 a.m.

By now you should have regained enough appetite after last night's feast to think about eating humbler food again. For a brunch that will help balance your budget, drive to **Al La Kebab** (Marquee Plaza; 1-345-943-4343; kebab.ky; $). Despite its location in the parking lot of a strip mall, it has a pleasant outdoor patio and friendly table service. Break your fast with falafel, fruit, and yogurt parfait, or the signature kebabs with beef and lamb, chicken, or vegetables. The food has an ambitious flair that reaches beyond the Middle East, with a multitude of sauces to choose from, like spicy chili, peanut satay, and red curry.

ABOVE Lounging at Seven Mile Beach. Although the "seven-mile" name may not be quite accurate, the beach is long and varied enough to allow for visiting a different section every day in a short trip and feeling you have found a new place.

THE BASICS

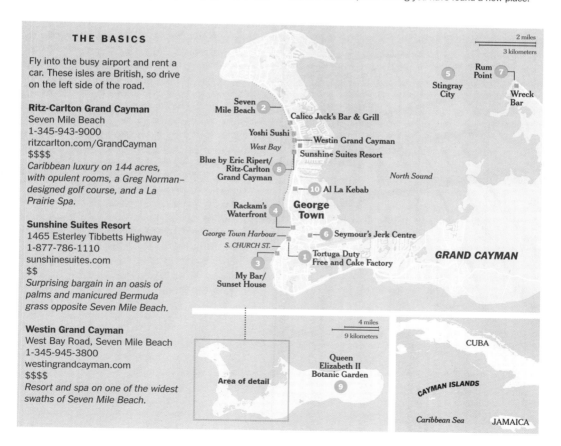

Fly into the busy airport and rent a car. These isles are British, so drive on the left side of the road.

Ritz-Carlton Grand Cayman
Seven Mile Beach
1-345-943-9000
ritzcarlton.com/GrandCayman
$$$$
Caribbean luxury on 144 acres, with opulent rooms, a Greg Norman–designed golf course, and a La Prairie Spa.

Sunshine Suites Resort
1465 Esterley Tibbetts Highway
1-877-786-1110
sunshinesuites.com
$$
Surprising bargain in an oasis of palms and manicured Bermuda grass opposite Seven Mile Beach.

Westin Grand Cayman
West Bay Road, Seven Mile Beach
1-345-945-3800
westingrandcayman.com
$$$$
Resort and spa on one of the widest swaths of Seven Mile Beach.

2 miles
3 kilometers
5 Stingray City
Rum Point 7
Wreck Bar
Seven Mile Beach 2
Calico Jack's Bar & Grill
Yoshi Sushi
Westin Grand Cayman
West Bay
Sunshine Suites Resort
Blue by Eric Ripert/ Ritz-Carlton Grand Cayman 8
North Sound
10 Al La Kebab
Rackam's Waterfront 4
George Town
George Town Harbour
6 Seymour's Jerk Centre
S. CHURCH ST.
1 Tortuga Duty Free and Cake Factory
GRAND CAYMAN
3 My Bar/ Sunset House
4 miles
9 kilometers
Area of detail
Queen Elizabeth II Botanic Garden 9
CUBA
CAYMAN ISLANDS
Caribbean Sea
JAMAICA

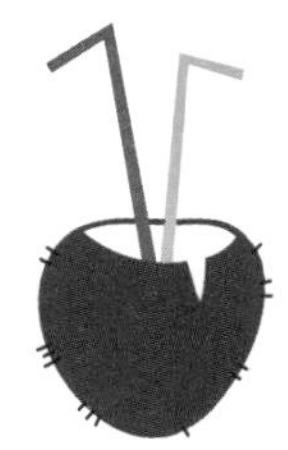

Port Antonio

In the 1950s and '60s, movie stars and European royalty arrived by helicopter and yacht to spend the winter months in their villas near Port Antonio, on the northeastern coast of Jamaica. In this lush land of reef-blocked beaches and palm-shrouded mountains, Errol Flynn bought thousands of acres near Boston Bay; Queen Elizabeth once checked in to the Frenchman's Cove Resort; and Robin Moore reportedly wrote The French Connection *at his house near the Blue Lagoon, the 200-foot-deep cerulean pool where the movie* The Blue Lagoon *was later filmed. By the 1970s, Negril and Montego Bay were grabbing the tourist trade, and then a series of devastating hurricanes struck Port Antonio, wrecking roads and hotels. Porty, as the town is known, is attempting a comeback, but not venturing into glitz. It remains a lovely, almost genteel getaway, where high-end vacationing intermingles easily with day-to-day rural Jamaican life.* — BY MATT GROSS AND DAVID KAUFMAN

FRIDAY

1 *Yacht-Ready Harbor* 2 p.m.

Port Antonio's elegant Georgian courthouse contrasts sharply with the crumbling (and frequently hurricane-battered) concrete edifices that make up much of the city's downtown. On the edge of town sits Folly, the ruins of a late-19th-century Classical Revival mansion built for a Tiffany heiress. Masons mixed the cement with saltwater, and there was no one to keep up the building after the heiress left in 1920, so it began to fall apart. Head across town for a seaside walk at the picturesque **Errol Flynn Marina** (errolflynnmarina.com), built in 2002 at a cost of $14 million and complete with helipad. Shiny yachts are in evidence, though the international mega-yachters that Port Antonio hoped to attract have been slow to drop in.

2 *Celebrity Sands* 3 p.m.

Each beach in Portland parish, the district of which Port Antonio is the capital, has its own atmosphere. One of the most restful and secluded is at **Frenchman's Cove Resort**, a 42-acre compound that has faded since the glamorous days when Queen Elizabeth was a guest but endures in its beautiful location. Pay the small entry fee for the beach, which offers chair rentals and waiter service, and spend a few relaxing hours. Near Frenchman's Cove, other relics from the midcentury heyday remain: Errol Flynn's sprawling seafront cattle ranch, which his much younger wife took over after his death; Trident Castle, a grandiose private chateau now offered as a location for weddings; and Tiamo Spa Villas, the former compound of Princess Nina Aga Khan.

3 *Callaloo and a View* 7 p.m.

Take the uphill road to the **Hotel Mocking Bird Hill** (off Route A4 between Boston Bay and Port Antonio; 1-876-993-7267; hotelmockingbirdhill.com), above Frenchman's Cove, for dinner at **Mille Fleurs** (1-876-993-7134; $$$), where expansive views of the coast and the sea come with the meal. The food is a sophisticated take on Caribbean flavors: callaloo and feta-stuffed chicken breast, steak with rum sauce and grilled bananas; jerk-spiced pimento-encrusted tofu. If you're a bird lover, you may want to come back in the daytime. The hotel has six and a half acres of grounds lush with tropical vegetation and claims to be one of the best bird-watching spots in Jamaica.

SATURDAY

4 *Market Music* 10 a.m.

At the lively **Musgrave Market** in the heart of town (West Street between Port Antonio Square

OPPOSITE A bamboo raft on the Rio Grande river.

RIGHT Carvings for sale at the market.

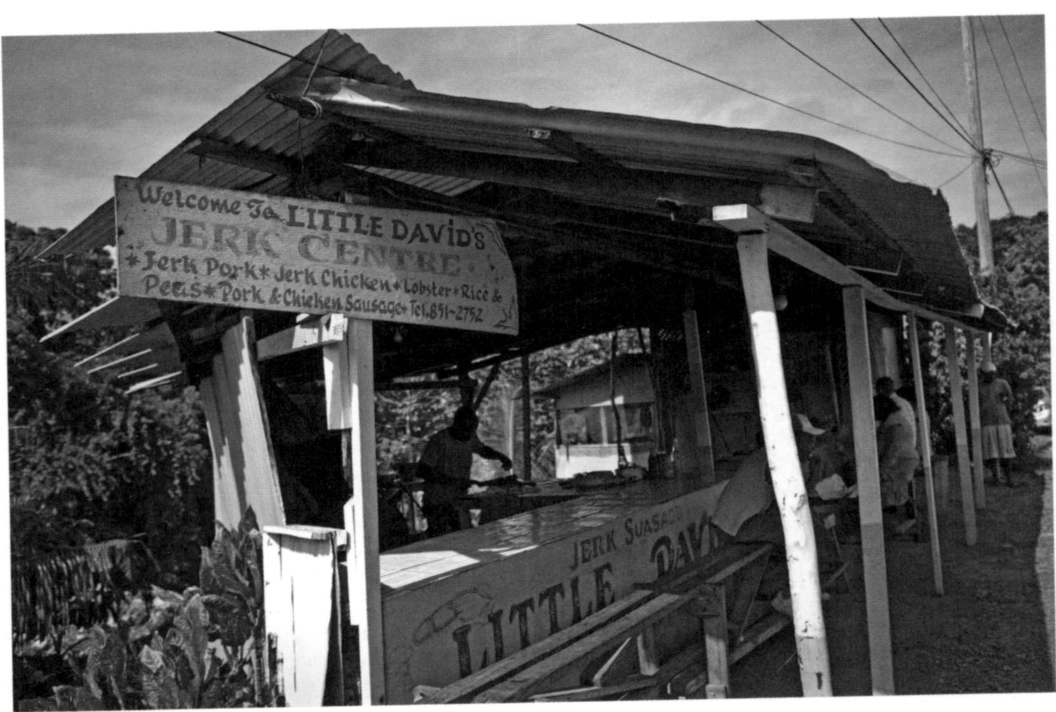

and Main Square), wares range from local farmers' produce to artfully carved and painted wooden fish sculptures. Find the tiny shops where you can hunt for recordings of reggae, ska, and an older genre, mento, which has been rediscovered in and outside of Jamaica. Rooted in African slave melodies, mento is laden with sexual innuendo and yet manages to be folksy and feel-good. The best known mento musicians are the Jolly Boys, who became popular in Port Antonio in the 1950s; Errol Flynn gave them their name. Still making music well into their 70s, the Jolly Boys have found unlikely worldwide fame in the 21st century. Browse for mento and other island genres at the market, and check **Pieyaka Muzik** (5 West Street; 1-879-897-0879) across the street. At **Dekal Internet Cafe** (No. 4 City Center Plaza; 1-876-297-7566), take a break for buttery croissants with strong coffee from beans grown in the nearby Blue Mountains.

5 *Jerk at the Source* 1 p.m.

Drive southeast along the coast about half an hour to **Boston Bay**, where—according to local lore—the spice-rub preparation known as Jamaican jerk was born in the 1950s. Whether or not that's true, local cooks have successfully exploited the association. Clustered just above the beach are nearly a dozen jerk shacks selling sliced chicken and pork spiked with rubs of Scotch-bonnet pepper, lime juice, and ginger. Grilled over coals in steel drums, the jerk is sold by the pound and served simply on newspaper and paper plates. Pair your choice with festival bread (deep-fried hushpuppies) and hand-pressed fruit juices.

6 *Choose Your Shore* 2 p.m.

If you like your seacoast with plenty of wave action, stay where you are and park your blanket at **Boston Beach**, where the surging swells have long lured surfers. For something calmer, work your way back northwest a couple of miles to **Winnifred Beach**, which is protected by a reef. There's plenty of space on the sand for stretching out, trees to shade you when you've had enough sun, and beach shacks selling food and Red Stripe, the popular Jamaican beer. Both beaches, Boston and Winnifred, are gorgeous—in other words, normal for the Portland coast.

7 *Precipitous Repast* 7 p.m.

Hanging off the edge of a cliff, **Dickie's Best Kept Secret** (Route A4 about one mile west of Port Antonio; 1-876-809-6276; $$) puts the "shack" in ramshackle, but that hasn't kept generations of celebrity patrons from dropping in at its precarious

ABOVE A stand at Boston Beach, home of jerk cooking.

location. It's decorated with hand-carved wooden figurines that (sort of) illustrate Jamaica's emergence from slavery and colonialism, and the floors slope at odd angles. The excellent food is a throwback to the high-end resort cuisine of the 1970s: fruit plates, grilled lobster, crêpes suzette. Meals must be ordered in advance; Dickie's orders only the supplies needed for the day.

8 *Mento Onstage* 9 p.m.

Bushbar, a restaurant and watering hole at the high-end **GeeJam** resort (1-876-561-8600; geejam.com) in the upscale San San area, offers live music in a jungle-shrouded setting. It's the natural home, when they're in town, of the Jolly Boys; Jon Baker, an owner of GeeJam and a longtime music-industry executive, orchestrated their unlikely comeback, and the GeeJam studio is on this property. If you're able to catch the Jolly Boys, don't pass up the chance. At one performance here, the band's nattily dressed lead singer, Albert Minott, slunk sensually across the stage as he delivered a soulful, gravelly-voiced set that included Jolly Boys originals and covers of the Velvet Underground and Amy Winehouse.

SUNDAY

9 *One Last Beach* 10 a.m.

South of Boston Bay, a mile-long shoreline of nearly deserted white sand fronts the aptly named

ABOVE Smoking ganja (marijuana), not unusual in Jamaica.

BELOW Fish for sale from a bicycle in town.

Long Bay. Like nearly all of Portland's beaches (Frenchman's Cove is the notable exception), it is publicly owned and free. Wander at will, and then find refreshment away from the water at one of the small bars or restaurants among the palms.

10 *Mountain Splash* Noon

If beaches grow tiresome, there are easy, light hikes into the John Crow Mountains, which invariably end with a dip into the deep, cold, crystal-clear waters of **Reach Falls**, about a 90-minute drive from Port Antonio. The falls is a series of cascades, caves, and waterfalls, popular on Sundays with local families. Join them for a splash in the cool pools. Closer to Port Antonio, there's low-key river rafting on the languid Rio Grande.

ABOVE The Jolly Boys on stage at GeeJam. The group has been performing since the 1950s and was named by Errol Flynn, who had a cattle ranch nearby.

OPPOSITE Trident Castle, a grandiose private chateau offered as a palatial location for weddings, businesess conferences, and film and video shoots. Sprawling over a long stretch of coast, it is a legacy of Portland parish's glory days.

THE BASICS

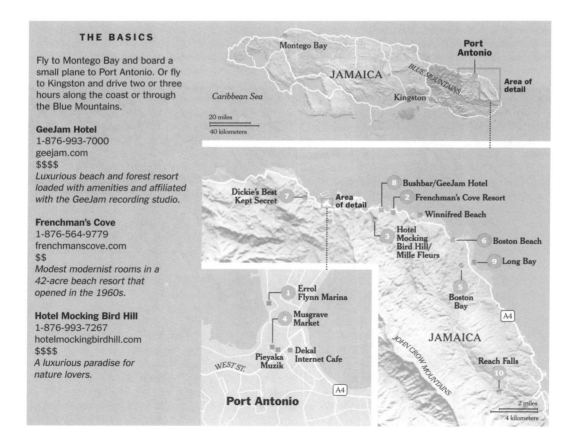

Fly to Montego Bay and board a small plane to Port Antonio. Or fly to Kingston and drive two or three hours along the coast or through the Blue Mountains.

GeeJam Hotel
1-876-993-7000
geejam.com
$$$$
Luxurious beach and forest resort loaded with amenities and affiliated with the GeeJam recording studio.

Frenchman's Cove
1-876-564-9779
frenchmanscove.com
$$
Modest modernist rooms in a 42-acre beach resort that opened in the 1960s.

Hotel Mocking Bird Hill
1-876-993-7267
hotelmockingbirdhill.com
$$$$
A luxurious paradise for nature lovers.

Montego Bay
Port Antonio
JAMAICA
BLUE MOUNTAINS
Area of detail
Caribbean Sea
Kingston
20 miles
40 kilometers
8 Bushbar/GeeJam Hotel
Dickie's Best Kept Secret 7
Area of detail
2 Frenchman's Cove Resort
Winnifred Beach
3 Hotel Mocking Bird Hill/ Mille Fleurs
6 Boston Beach
9 Long Bay
5 Boston Bay
1 Errol Flynn Marina
4 Musgrave Market
Pieyaka Muzik
Dekal Internet Cafe
WEST ST.
A4
Port Antonio
JAMAICA
JOHN CROW MOUNTAINS
Reach Falls 10
2 miles
4 kilometers

vintage

Santo Domingo

Whether one believes it was Columbus who actually discovered America or not, he clearly left his mark on Santo Domingo, the breezy capital of the Dominican Republic and the most vibrant of Caribbean cities. Columbus's remains are said to be here, and a bronze statue honoring him sits in Zona Colonial, where one can retrace his steps and find solace in an otherwise chaotic city. Exploring, after all, is what Columbus did, and you'll find plenty of reasons to keep wandering. Here in the oldest European city in the New World are the oldest church in the Americas, the first paved road, and even the first sewer system. But Santo Domingo also offers plenty that's new, including an elegant restaurant in a pirate's cave and a seaside walkway with towering condos on one side and the ocean that carried Columbus to the island on the other.

— BY MARC LACEY

FRIDAY

1 *Columbus's Corner* 4 p.m.

If Santo Domingo has a nerve center, it may be the always crowded **El Conde Restaurant** (Calle El Conde at Arzobispo Meriño; 1-809-688-7121). Order a cold Presidente beer and take in the sights (including the pigeons) of the **Parque Colón**, a leafy square in the heart of the Zona Colonial. Across the square is the **Cathedral of Santa María la Menor** (Calle Arzobispo Meriño, Parque Colón), completed in 1540 and also called La Catedral Primada de América—America's first church (by most accounts, it is the New World's oldest surviving one). Also nearby, on the Plaza de la Hispanidad, is the **Museo Alcázar de Diego Colón** (1-809-682-4750, rsta.pucmm.edu.do/ciudad/alcazar/website), a museum in a palace that was constructed for Christopher Columbus's son Diego in 1517, when Diego was a Spanish viceroy.

2 *Out With the Crowd* 6 p.m.

Santo Domingo's traffic is an infuriating mess. Find yourself stuck in it and you might wish you'd stayed home. But foot traffic is another thing entirely, and no place packs in more bodies than **El Conde**, a street closed to vehicles and filled with pedestrians and merchants of all stripes. There are too many knickknacks for sale, but the people-watching is first-rate and there are plenty of surprises along the way, like the facials that are sometimes given on the sidewalk.

3 *Colonial Dining* 8 p.m.

When hunger calls, duck into **Mesón D'Bari** (Calle Hostos 302; 1-809-687-4091; $$), a Dominican restaurant in a restored colonial home. To start things off, order the empanadas, which come filled with seafood or vegetables. Then try the grilled crab, a specialty here, or a plate of spicy shrimp that will have you thirsting for a cocktail. Enjoy the live bands, which play anything from salsa to jazz.

4 *Frying to the Beat* 10 p.m.

Work off your meal by walking the safe streets of this area to **El Sartén** (Calle Hostos 153; 1-809-686-9621), a tiny bar where you'll find some first-class Dominican joie de vivre. There are far glitzier nightspots, with velvet ropes, burly doormen, and revelers dressed like it's New Year's Eve. But

OPPOSITE Curbside gamesmanship in Santo Domingo, the breezy capital of the Dominican Republic and the oldest European-founded city in the New World.

BELOW The Columbus Lighthouse, a museum said to house the remains of Christopher Columbus.

no place has the energy of El Sartén, whose name means "The Frying Pan" and which can feel like one when everyone is packed together, dancing to loud merengue and bachata music. Plop down in a curbside plastic chair and look inside as gray-haired Dominicans show off their old-time steps. Or better yet, grab a partner and join in the fun.

SATURDAY

5 *Mining Above Ground* 10 a.m.

Amber and larimar, a sea-blue stone, are found on the island and are carved to make beautiful figurines and jewelry. For stunning examples, check out the small shops in the colonial area. Or drop in at the **Museo Mundo de Ambar** (452 Arzobispo Meriño; 1-809-682-3309; amberworldmuseum.com) and learn about the uses of amber resin through the ages.

6 *Cigar Rolling* 1 p.m.

You don't have to be a smoker to enjoy watching the Dominican Republic's beloved cigars being rolled. At a cigar shop called **Museo del Tabaco** (El Conde 101; 1-809-689-7665), you can witness all the stages in the entire painstaking process, from moist leaves to hand-rolled beauties. You can see it from the sidewalk, but for a whiff of the pungent leaves, step inside. Don't buy the Cuban cigars that are sold along the sidewalk; most are fakes.

7 *Rediscover Columbus* 3 p.m.

A cab ride away on the other side of the Ozama River is the **Columbus Lighthouse** (Parque Mirador del Este, 1-809-591-1492; turismosantodomingo.com/faro-a-colon.html), a museum built 10 stories high and in the shape of a giant cross. The lighthouse, which was inaugurated in 1992 to mark the 500th anniversary of Columbus's arrival in America, is equipped with high-powered beams that can blast the night sky. But it's rarely turned on, partly to save power and partly because neighbors did not take kindly to looking out of their darkened hovels and seeing the government streaming light into the heavens. Inside, you'll find artifacts from throughout the Americas and, if the Dominican tradition is to be believed, the remains of Columbus himself.

8 *Down-Under Dining* 8 p.m.

Caves are thought to be dank, bat-infested, and lacking in glamour. But not **El Mesón de la Cava** (Avenida Mirador del Sur 1; 1-809-533-2818; elmesondelacava.com; $$), an underground restaurant that shines. Well-heeled capitalinos enjoy seafood Dominican-style inside this limestone hideaway, which is said to have served as a redoubt for pirates centuries ago. The service is impeccable and the offerings diverse and delicious, especially the traditional shrimp in cilantro cream sauce, a Dominican delicacy that will have you longing for more. This is spelunking in style, so remember that after polishing off that bottle of rum, you will have to climb back up those narrow stairs.

SUNDAY

9 *A Scrunched Sandwich* 10 a.m.

Eating at **Hermanos Villar** (Avenida Independencia at Esquina Pasteur; 1-809-682-1433; $) is not necessarily relaxing, but this popular

ABOVE Santa María la Menor, built from 1512 to 1540, is by most accounts the oldest church in the Americas.

RIGHT On the Malecón walkway, the views on one side are of condominiums and, on the other, of nothing but blue sea.

diner does not disappoint. The house specialty is sandwiches made of flattened baguettes and served piping hot with a variety of meat, cheese, and vegetable fillings. If you come with a group, order one extra-long sandwich for all and munch away to your heart's content.

10 *Not All Attics Are Equal* 11 a.m.

In the small plaza in front of the Sofitel hotel is the **Pulga de Antiguedades** (Plaza María de Toledo), a Sunday-only flea market that offers attention-getting artwork, crafts, and bric-a-brac that could have been taken from Caribbean attics. The sellers are a motley crew, and so are their wares. Bargain hard for that aging map, gem-studded dagger, or necklace made from shells. Nearby is the seaside walkway, the **Malecón**, which is closed to traffic on Sundays and fills with revelers who sip rum and other mysterious liquids out of paper bags, as they soak in the breeze. Peer out into the ocean, away from the sky-high condominiums, and you'll see nothing but blue.

ABOVE The Alcázar de Colón palace, now a museum, was built in 1517 for Christopher Columbus's son Diego.

THE BASICS

Multiple international airlines serve Santo Domingo. Taxis are plentiful and inexpensive.

Sofitel Nicolás de Ovando
Calle Las Damas
1-809-685-9955
sofitel.com
$$
Named after one of the first governors of the Americas. Elegant rooms, lap pool, views of the port.

Boutique Hotel Palacio
Calle Duarte 106
1-809-682-4730
hotel-palacio.com
$
Converted mansion in the Zona Colonial, with comfortable and quiet rooms overlooking a courtyard.

Hotel Doña Elvira
Calle Padre Billini 207
1-809-221-7415
dona-elvira.com
$
Bed-and-breakfast with a dozen cozy rooms, some overlooking a mosaic-tiled plunge pool.

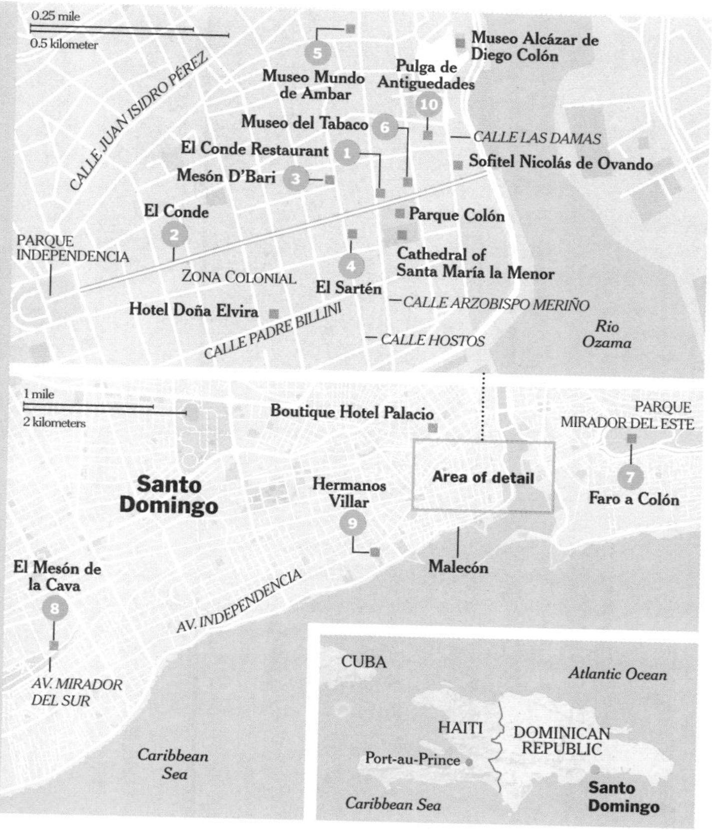

0.25 mile
0.5 kilometer
CALLE JUAN ISIDRO PÉREZ
5 Museo Mundo de Ambar
Museo Alcázar de Diego Colón
Pulga de Antiguedades 10
Museo del Tabaco 6
CALLE LAS DAMAS
El Conde Restaurant 1
Sofitel Nicolás de Ovando
Mesón D'Bari 3
El Conde 2
Parque Colón
PARQUE INDEPENDENCIA
Cathedral of Santa María la Menor
ZONA COLONIAL
4 El Sartén
CALLE ARZOBISPO MERIÑO
Hotel Doña Elvira
CALLE PADRE BILLINI
CALLE HOSTOS
Rio Ozama
1 mile
2 kilometers
Boutique Hotel Palacio
PARQUE MIRADOR DEL ESTE
Santo Domingo
Hermanos Villar 9
Area of detail
7 Faro a Colón
Malecón
El Mesón de la Cava 8
AV. INDEPENDENCIA
AV. MIRADOR DEL SUR
Caribbean Sea
CUBA
Atlantic Ocean
HAITI
DOMINICAN REPUBLIC
Port-au-Prince
Santo Domingo
Caribbean Sea

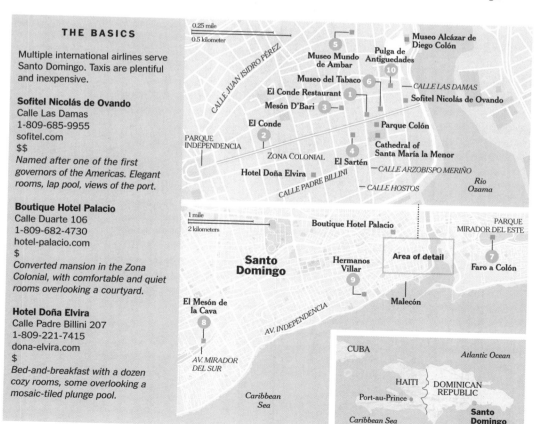

San Juan

Trying to sample the pleasures of some cities over a weekend can be a bit like entering a pie-eating contest. Sounds like a madcap lark, but after a while you're likely to feel overstuffed, foolish, and maybe a little sick. San Juan, the capital of Puerto Rico, poses no such problems. True, you could pass a week in the city and still not probe all its corners. But the major highlights can fit easily into a Friday-to-Sunday visit, even accounting for the leisurely pace that seems appropriate to the tropics. — BY CHARLES ISHERWOOD

FRIDAY

1 *Buy a Hat* 4 p.m.

A walk through the central streets of **Old San Juan** reveals a city in ferocious competition to become the most souvenir-clogged metropolis on the planet. Perhaps because it's a popular stop on Caribbean cruise tours, the central city is chockablock with stores selling tacky gewgaws. (There's even a shop that calls itself the Tourist Trap.) But since a hat is necessary on a steamy afternoon, visit the tiny, old-fashioned emporium called **Olé** (105 Fortaleza Street; 1-787-724-2445), which sells hand-fitted Panama hats that you can customize yourself. The proprietor, Guillermo Cristian Jeffs, will describe the history of the Panama hat in effusive detail, and assure you that none of his hats — in contrast to the piles to be found filling shelves elsewhere — are made in China.

2 *Cool Oasis* 7 p.m.

Make your way to the famous **Hotel El Convento** (100 Cristo Street; 1-787-723-9020; elconvento.com), an Old San Juan institution. The name derives from the grand building's history: founded as a convent — the first in Puerto Rico — it housed Carmelite nuns for 250 years before entering a period of tumultuous decay, for a time becoming a flophouse and eventually (ay dios mío!) a parking lot for garbage trucks. The structure was rebuilt beginning in 1959 on the foundations of the original, reopening three years later as a hotel. The bar and restaurant overlooking the grand open-air courtyard ($$-$$$) is the perfect spot for dinner.

SATURDAY

3 *Pick-Me-Up* 10 a.m.

Breakfast is served all day at **Caficultura** (401 San Francisco Street; 1-787-723-7731; $$), a bustling coffeehouse that sits on a corner of the Plaza Colón, near the eastern end of Old San Juan. Black glass chandeliers hang from the high ceilings, and marble floors magnify the convivial sound of locals and tourists lingering over a morning meal. Although sandwiches are on the menu, the range of breakfast options, with local twists like banana pancakes with rum, is most appealing, along with local pastries. A table with a view of the passing scene is recommended, since as in many restaurants in San Juan, the byword here is not necessarily efficiency.

4 *Look Upward* 1 p.m.

Old San Juan is justifiably cherished for its beautifully preserved buildings and its sleepy charm.

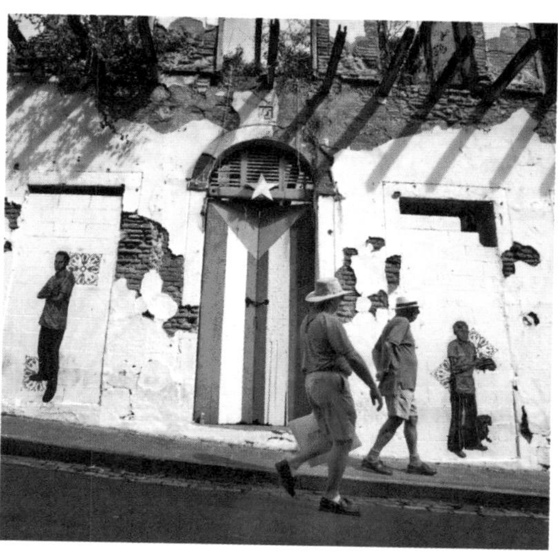

OPPOSITE A turret on the ramparts of the Castillo San Felipe del Morro, one of the two great fortresses at the north end of Old San Juan, Puerto Rico. Construction of El Morro began in 1539.

RIGHT Outdoor art on the walls of a dilapidated building in Old San Juan includes the Puerto Rican flag, a potent symbol of identity on this island.

Wander its streets with their distinctive blue-glazed cobblestones: check out the cathedral on Cristo Street, stop for a rest in the slightly seedy central **Plaza de Armas** on San Francisco Street, stroll along Fortaleza Street until you come to the western end, where the grand governor's mansion sits. For relief from the sometimes dreary spectacle of souvenir shops, cast your eyes upward to the ornate balconies or let the myriad colors of the buildings collect into a sort of visual kaleidoscope.

5 *History With a View* 5 p.m.

Just before dusk is a prime time to visit the **Castillo San Felipe del Morro** (www.nps.gov/saju) at the north end of Del Morro Street, one of the two historic fortresses that more or less bookend the north side of Old San Juan. The majestic structure takes on a soft glow as the sun falls over the horizon, and it offers views of the bay and the ocean that are best savored when pink and orange bands of light begin to settle over the water. Construction on the castle began in 1539, when Spain was in control of San Juan. It's from here that the Spanish forces fended off various maritime attacks, and you can peek through windows where cannons once stood.

6 *Local Cooking, High Style* 8 p.m.

After exploring the old town, set off for a new neighborhood that feels almost like another city entirely. **Condado** hugs the beach to the east of Old San Juan and has the glittery feel of Miami Beach. Here's where high-end hotels, most with casinos, attract night-life-seeking locals and tourists alike. **Casa Lola** (1006 Ashford Avenue; 1-787-998-2918; casalolarestaurant.com; $$), in a stand-alone house painted a festive pink, is the flagship of a small local restaurant empire established by the chef Roberto Treviño, a native of the San Francisco Bay area. The stylish main dining room has a view of the city across the lagoon. The fare includes dishes like mahi mahi with sweet plantains and local sausage or a risotto with pork loin and chimichurri sauce.

7 *Nighttime Beach Beauties* 10 p.m.

For a late drink, and a stronger dose of the white-clothes-tanned-skin ambience, stroll down the Condado strip to **Oceana** (1853 Mcleary Avenue; 1-787-728-8119; oceanapuertorico.com), where the patio tables at the restaurant and bar practically sit right on the beach. That's one of the virtues of this prime people-watching spot: when you tire of the human spectacle swirling around the bar, you can cast your eyes up at a star-filled night sky, let the pounding of the music subside, and tune your ears to the gentle sound of the surf pounding at the shore seemingly right beneath your table.

SUNDAY

8 *Cultural Fiber* 11 a.m.

Take in two of the city's major art museums, both outside the tourist circuits of Old San Juan and the strips along the beach. Start at the **Museo de Arte de Puerto Rico** (299 Avenue de Diego; 1-787-977-6277; mapr.org), where the history of local art is laid out in handsome galleries on two floors. (José Campeche, the 18th-century painter considered the first notable Puerto Rican artist, has a room to himself.) Pay particular attention to the rich history of the country's poster art. Walk 10 minutes from there, absorbing the atmosphere of the city as locals experience it, to

ABOVE Riding a wave near the hotel strip at Condado.

BELOW Pastel-hued buildings and narrow cobblestone streets add to the sleepy charm characteristic of Old San Juan.

the **Museo de Arte Contemporáneo de Puerto Rico** (Avenue Ponce de Leon and Avenue Roberto H. Todd; 1-787-977-4030; museocontemporaneopr.org), which opens at 1 p.m. Its exhibitions of works by local and locally born artists are arrayed around a courtyard.

9 *Fill Up on Mofongo* 2 p.m.

Another reasonable walk from the museums brings you back to the Condado strip, which has a far sleepier aspect during the day. For dependable classic local fare, the **Café del Angel** (1106 Avenue Ashford; 1-787-643-7594; $$) is a stalwart. Eat your fill of the indispensable mofongo—the fried plantain dish that is the mainstay of the local cuisine—for a reasonable price. The sandwiches are excellent, too, and the décor is, ahem, authentically unglamorous: at lunchtime one day, the most noticeable fixture in the indoor dining room was the abuela (grandmother) slumbering away on a chair in a corner.

10 *Time Out, With Surf* 3 p.m.

Exit the urban vibe and slouch onto the sand in **Isla Verde**, where most of the big hotels are. Happily, you don't have to be staying at one of them to enjoy the surf. The beaches at Carolina are dotted with pale-skinned visitors working on their winter tans, but locals come here, too, to enjoy the light surf. It's the perfect place to wind down your visit and recharge your batteries.

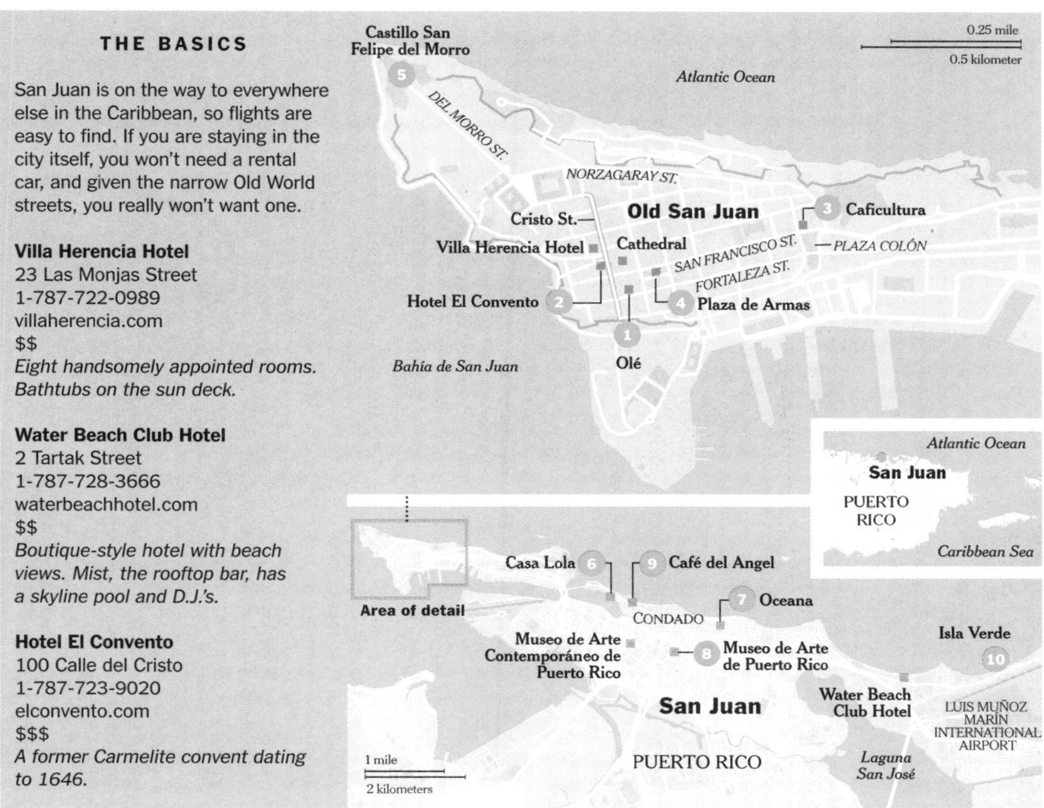

THE BASICS

San Juan is on the way to everywhere else in the Caribbean, so flights are easy to find. If you are staying in the city itself, you won't need a rental car, and given the narrow Old World streets, you really won't want one.

Villa Herencia Hotel
23 Las Monjas Street
1-787-722-0989
villaherencia.com
$$
Eight handsomely appointed rooms. Bathtubs on the sun deck.

Water Beach Club Hotel
2 Tartak Street
1-787-728-3666
waterbeachhotel.com
$$
Boutique-style hotel with beach views. Mist, the rooftop bar, has a skyline pool and D.J.'s.

Hotel El Convento
100 Calle del Cristo
1-787-723-9020
elconvento.com
$$$
A former Carmelite convent dating to 1646.

MUSEO DEL ANTIGUO
PARQUE DE BOMBAS

Ponce

Ever since it was founded in 1692 on the southern coast, between a mountain range and the Caribbean Sea, Ponce, Puerto Rico's second-largest city, has been overshadowed by San Juan, the island's center of government and commerce, and later, of its tourist trade. But with the active assistance of the Puerto Rican government, which has rebranded the entire southern region Porta Caribe, Ponce's profile is rising. New apartments and condos have taken shape. Spanish colonial, Art Deco, and neo-Classical buildings have been restored. And the city has renovated and expanded its cultural crown jewel, the Ponce Museum of Art, which claims to have the most extensive art collection in the Caribbean. For the traveler, Ponce is also important as a jumping-off point for more tourist experiences, from beaches and snorkeling to tours of the famous Arecibo observatory and a spectacular complex of caves.

— BY JEREMY W. PETERS AND HENRY FOUNTAIN

FRIDAY

1 *A Collector's Vision* 1 p.m.

For an art lover, the **Ponce Museum of Art** (Avenida Las Americas 2325; 1-787-848-0505; museoarteponce.org) alone is worth a trip here. The core of the collection — thousands of works by European old masters and modern and contemporary artists from the Americas and Africa — was purchased by the museum's founder, Luis A. Ferré, a Puerto Rican businessman and politician who studied at both the Massachusetts Institute of Technology and the New England Conservatory of Music, and died in 2003 at age 99. Originally opened in 1959, the museum reopened in 2010 after a three-year renovation and an expansion that created space for hundreds of new works. Spend some time with the likes of Goya, Van Dyck, and Rubens, as well as Latin American artists like the Puerto Rican painters José Campeche, Francisco Oller, and Miguel Pou.

2 *Spanish Inflection* 4 p.m.

Puerto Rico is, of course, an American commonwealth, but on a downtown stroll, you could be forgiven for thinking you were in Spain. The buildings are a hodgepodge of ambitious designs: Spanish colonial row houses, a neo-Classical-style high school modeled after New York's Grand Central Terminal; a red and black candy-striped wooden firehouse on the **Plaza Las Delicias**, the idyllic main square. Stop for ice cream at **King's Cream** (Plaza Las Delicias; 1-787-843-8520).

3 *Harbor Walk* 6 p.m.

Ponce's downtown is actually about three miles north of the sea. For a waterfront scene, head to the pretty boardwalk along the harbor, **Paseo Tablado La Guancha**, or La Guancha for short. Tall palm trees, sea vistas, friendly pelicans, music, and small stands selling food and drinks make this a popular spot. Sit on a bench and have a beer while you gaze out at the blue Caribbean.

4 *Plates for Carnivores* 7 p.m.

The waterfront **Hilton Ponce Golf and Casino Resort** (Avenida Caribe 1150; 1-877-464-4586; hiltoncaribbean.com/ponce) has the feel of a big beach resort, complete with a 27-hole golf course, even though it's in town. Among its several restaurants, **La Cava** ($$$) is the most ambitious, a fine-dining establishment in a modern-looking space decorated with flowing red draperies and high-backed chairs. The menu covers most of the serious protein eater's favorite food groups — beef in several incarnations, lamb, venison, duck. An occasional touch of the Caribbean

OPPOSITE The firehouse on Ponce's main square.

BELOW A tour of the spectacular caverns carved out by an underground river at Rio Camuy Cave Park.

creeps in: one night's choices included adobo-spiced pork with pigeon peas and dark rum sauce.

SATURDAY

5 *Rapid Rise* 10 a.m.

The natural setting around the city is one of the less promoted but most appealing parts of visiting Ponce. It is well worth a drive up Route 10, a corkscrew of a highway that winds north through the island's verdant interior, to see how quickly the landscape changes from urban and flat to rural and mountainous. Suddenly, it feels as if you've somehow crossed into Guatemala.

6 *Spectacular Descent* Noon

Keep driving north and west to the **Río Camuy Cave Park**, about 50 miles from Ponce (Route 129, Arecibo; 1-787-898-3100; seepuertorico.com/destinations/porta-atlantico; closes when it's raining). The Río Camuy is a subterranean stream traveling for seven miles under the limestone terrain known as karst, and the park sits in the middle of an extensive cave system. A concrete walkway into Clara Cave leads to a series of spectacular chambers, including a 173-foot-high central room filled with huge stalagmites and other limestone features. At the Tres Pueblos sinkhole, 650 feet in diameter and draped in jewel-green vegetation, the pathway is a ledge with the Río Camuy 160 feet below. Even more spectacular, though, is the view upward, 250 feet to the surface. A gentle mist seems suspended in the sunlight, and long tendrils hang down 100 feet along the sides — roots of the cupey tree.

7 *Channel Jodie Foster* 2 p.m.

From Rio Camuy, it's a 15-minute drive across rugged countryside to the **Arecibo Observatory** (Route 625; 1-787-878-2612, naic.edu), a giant radio telescope operated by Cornell University. Its builders took advantage of the karst terrain, suspending its aluminum reflector over a shallow sinkhole to save construction costs. The reflector functions as a mirror — but for radio waves, not light. Viewed from the observation deck of the visitor center, it looks like the world's largest spaghetti strainer with a mad scientist's death-ray machine floating on cables above it, a vision that may have contributed to its use as a prop for the villain in the James Bond film *GoldenEye*. Jodie Foster hung out here as a scientist in the movie *Contact*, but don't expect to replicate her trip through a wormhole to meet friendly aliens. The telescope may be better appreciated as a testament to the ability of humans to build anything they can dream up. With its yawning bowl 1,000 feet in diameter, made of 39,000 sheets of perforated aluminum; its 300-foot concrete towers; and its 700-ton receiving array suspended from 18 cables, it's a heck of a piece of equipment.

8 *Dining Central* 8 p.m.

Back in Ponce, have dinner in the center of things, close to the stone lions of the fountain on the Plaza Las Delicias. **Lola** (Calle Reina; 1-787-813-5050; ramadaponce.com; $$) is at the Ramada Hotel, which occupies an arresting yellow 19th-century building on the square. Choose from an unsurprising but satisfying selection of entrees, like shrimp with risotto, strip steak, or spinach ravioli.

SUNDAY

9 *Cayo Gilligan* 10 a.m.

Ponce is not known for its beaches, but the coast to the west of it is. Drive about 40 minutes to

Guánica, which has a downtown so small it makes Ponce feel like San Juan, and rent a kayak or take a short ferry ride to get to uninhabited **Gilligan's Island** (portadelsolpuertorico.com/gilligans-island) just offshore. The island, properly called Cayo Aurora, is part of the Guánica Biosphere Reserve and has been preserved from development. Take a picnic and snorkeling gear.

10 *Underwater Stars* 1 p.m.

If you have time to tour farther beyond Ponce, push on west for more beaches and some underwater adventures in the warm, caressing Caribbean. **Paradise Scuba and Snorkeling Center** (787-899-7611; paradisescubasnorkelingpr.com) in the small fishing village of La Parguera, runs snorkeling and diving trips that will get you out to a shallow reef where sea life congregates. Spend some time exploring amid the coral, angelfish, and sea cucumbers. Then, for an experience you won't forget, take Paradise Scuba's nighttime excursion to a bioluminescent bay, where plankton produce a blue-green light when disturbed. When you leap off the boat, the sea flashes around you as though hundreds of fireflies had taken the plunge, too. Every move produces more sparks, and even floating quietly face down with mask and snorkel, you'll feel as if a glittering rain were cascading by.

OPPOSITE ABOVE AND BELOW Wildlife and waterfront commerce in Ponce at the Paseo Tablado La Guancha (La Guancha for short), a walkway hugging the Caribbean. Towering palm trees, blue sea vistas, friendly pelicans, music, and small stands selling food and drinks all make this a popular spot.

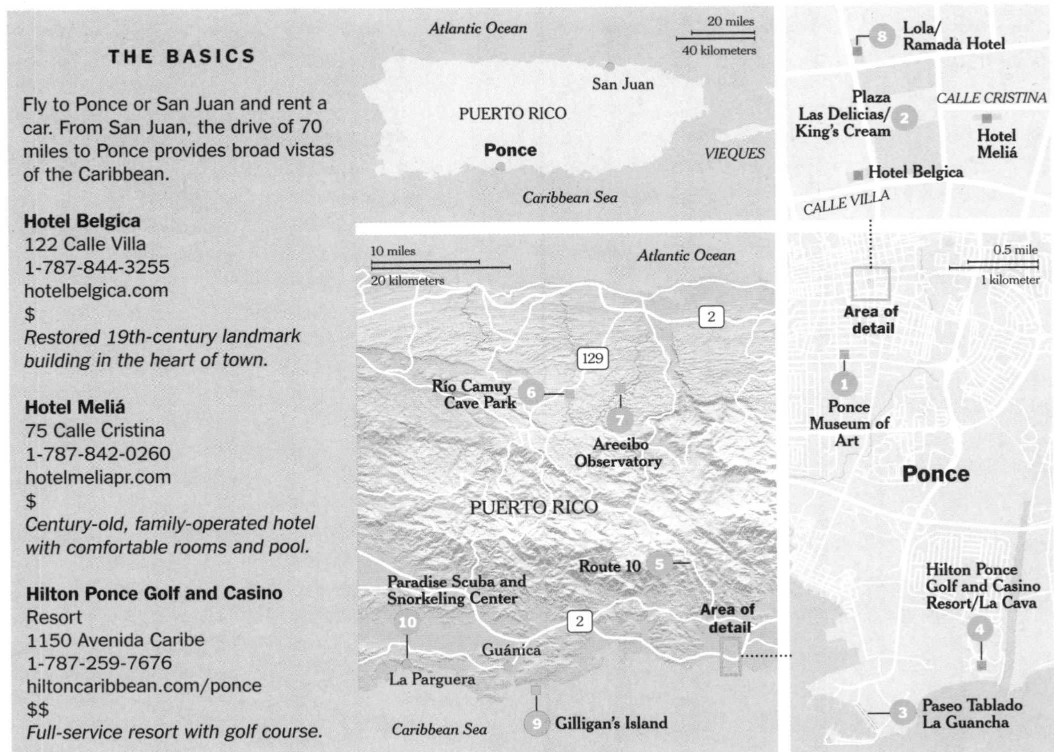

THE BASICS

Fly to Ponce or San Juan and rent a car. From San Juan, the drive of 70 miles to Ponce provides broad vistas of the Caribbean.

Hotel Belgica
122 Calle Villa
1-787-844-3255
hotelbelgica.com
$
Restored 19th-century landmark building in the heart of town.

Hotel Meliá
75 Calle Cristina
1-787-842-0260
hotelmeliapr.com
$
Century-old, family-operated hotel with comfortable rooms and pool.

Hilton Ponce Golf and Casino Resort
1150 Avenida Caribe
1-787-259-7676
hiltoncaribbean.com/ponce
$$
Full-service resort with golf course.

Vieques

The mascot of Vieques seems to be the coquí, a tiny frog whose image adorns everything from T-shirts to hot-sauce bottles. Yet, given the island's rapid metamorphosis from military testing ground to upscale beach resort, perhaps a tropical butterfly would be better suited. Since the United States Navy ceased military operations in 2003, this small island just off the east coast of mainland Puerto Rico has seen a boom in restaurants, galleries, and hotels, including a W resort. It's a testament to the island's natural beauty, with its white-sand beaches, coral reefs, and bioluminescent bay. — BY HUGH RYAN

FRIDAY

1 *Beach Revival* 4 p.m.

Vieques has worked to improve many of its beaches; access roads to some were in shambles when the Navy left. **Red Beach**, along a wide-mouthed cove on the island's warmer Caribbean side, features open-walled wooden cabanas and ample parking. The beach gets a little crowded in the afternoons, but in the evenings the crowds are gone, and this spot has some of the clearest azure-blue water on the island—with terrific snorkeling along the eastern end.

2 *Upscale Dinner* 7 p.m.

Venture out to the **W Retreat & Spa** (State Road 200, Kilometer 3.2) for dinner at **Sorcé** (1-787-741-7022; sorcevieques.com; $$), an open-air seaside restaurant named for an archaeological site on the island. The successor to an Alain Ducasse spot that remained at the W for a couple of years after the resort's opening in 2010, Sorcé emphasizes local dishes including fresh-caught fish, Caribbean lobster, and sopa de marisco, a Vieques version of seafood soup. Ducasse may have departed, but this is still an attractive space offering upscale dining.

OPPOSITE [illegible] horses on the Puerto Rican island of Vieques. Long do[illegible]ed by a United States Navy testing ground, Vieque[illegible]aimed its beaches and terrain for recreation and t[illegible] after the military left in 2003.

RIGHT [illegible]p into the Caribbean from an old fishermen's pier [illegible] lively town of Esperanza.

3 *Downscale Drinks* 10 p.m.

Al's Mar Azul, just steps from the ferry dock in Isabel Segunda (1-787-741-3400), is a turquoise-painted dive bar decorated with international license plates, old signs from the island, and other flotsam. It has Foosball, dart boards, air-hockey tables, slot machines, and the requisite pool table. Order a piña colada, a stiff margarita, or the local beer, Medalla, and kick back.

SATURDAY

4 *Smooth Souvenirs* 9 a.m.

Beaches on the Atlantic side of Vieques are often overlooked—after all, no one talks about going to an "Atlantic island" for vacation. But **Glass Beach**, a tiny stretch of sand at the end of Calle Regimientio 65 de la Infanteria, has a special attraction: perfectly smooth stones, seashells, and sea glass polished by the ocean and sand. Local jewelry makers walk along the beach, eyes cast downward, to gather supplies for their craft. It's a great place to spend some time and pick up a souvenir.

5 *Scene by the Sea* Noon

Calle Flamboyán in Esperanza is also called the **Malecón**, Spanish for seafront. The Caribbean laps right up against the street's rampart, which

on Saturday afternoons is the site of a continuously changing market. Artists sell jewelry and clothing, farmers display organic produce, and food carts grill spicy kebabs of shrimp and chicken. Pick up a gift for back home, sample the sidewalk cuisine, and do some people watching.

6 *See Turtles* 1 p.m.

The waters off Vieques are home to aquatic wonders, including manatees, dolphins, eagle rays, nurse sharks, barracuda, and sea turtles that come up on the beaches to lay their eggs in January and February. A number of companies offer two-hour snorkeling trips around **Cayo Afuera**, a small scrub island with a large coral reef on its eastern side. A reliable outfitter is **Abe's Snorkeling** (1-787-741-2134; abessnorkeling.com), which offers a tour that includes snorkeling equipment and knowledgeable guides. If you prefer to go on your own, pick up a mask from **Black Beard Sports** (101 Calle Muñoz Rivera; 1-787-741-1892; blackbeardsports.com), a local emporium that can offer helpful tips on good spots for snorkeling off Vieques itself.

7 *Tropical Forest Ruins* 4 p.m.

Channel your inner Tomb Raider by exploring the ruins of **Central Playa Grande**, one of the 19th-century sugar plantations that once dominated Vieques. A dozen stone and brick ruins lie hidden in the forest, obscured by ceiba trees and bougainvillea vines. The adventurous—and those with four-wheel drive—can explore on their own. Look for a small sign that reads "Sleeping giant, witness to our history," marking the trailhead off PR-201. If you would rather have a guide, the **Vieques Conservation and Historical Trust** (138 Calle Flamboyán; 1-787-741-8850; vcht.org) runs tours.

8 *Fresh Catches* 8 p.m.

In much of Puerto Rico, "fried" seems to be the most popular food group, but there is a new wave of tablecloth-and-candlelight restaurants on Vieques—and not just at the W resort. **El Quenepo** in Esperanza (148 Calle Flamboyán; 1-787-741-1215; $$) elevates native Caribbean ingredients like breadfruit, calabaza squash, and limón to a higher culinary plane. One menu offered line-caught dorado, grilled and wrapped in pancetta and served over a seafood risotto.

9 *Swimming With Stars* 10 p.m.

The otherwordly bioluminescent bay on the Caribbean side of the island lives up to its reputation. But until recently, the usual way of getting close to this magical mass of glowing microorganisms was to strip down to your swimming suit and get wet. Tour operators will still take you out for that magical dip in the shining water. But another approach is to take a kayak tour with **Vieques Adventure Company** (1-787-692-9162; viequesadventures.com), which has a fleet of translucent kayaks. Whomever you go with, make sure they're licensed. Portions of the license fees go to Puerto Rico's Department of Natural Resources, to protect the wondrous ecosystem.

SUNDAY

10 *Downward Doggy-Paddle* 9:30 a.m.

What better place to do your sun salutations than on the white sands of **Sun Bay**? Local yogi MariAngeles (1-787-435-7510) leads 90-minute

BELOW Going eye to eye with the local sea life, in this case a Caribbean lobster, at the Marine Life Exhibit of the Vieques Historical and Conservation Trust.

alini-style classes on the eastern end of the . (Sun Bay is the Caribbean cove right outside wn of Esperanza on PR-997.) Call ahead for a the class, or take a mat and go through the s on your own.

ots, Not Flip-Flops 11 a.m.

rs, horses, scooters, skateboards — Vieques s to discourage walking. But for hiking siasts, there is hope still. On the western edge Bay, a land bridge leads to **Cayo de Tierra**, ded atoll a quarter mile off the island's coast. trails crisscross the cay, which is uninhabited t by birds, geckos, and the occasional iguana. the rocky promontory, you get a breathtaking view of Vieques, and manatees have been known to splash in the shallow waters below.

OPPOSITE ABOVE A vendor on Flamboyan Street, the main strip of the southern Vieques town of Esperanza, shows off his wares by slicing up a coconut.

ABOVE An electric-blue streak marks the path of a swimmer in Vieques's otherworldly bioluminscent bay. Its microorganisms emit flashes of light when disturbed.

Atlantic Ocean
Juan
CULEBRA
RTO
O
Area of detail
VIEQUES
Caribbean Sea
Area of detail
200
VIEQUES
W Retreat & Spa/ Sorcé 2
Red Beach 1
Hix Island House
Central Playa Grande 7
Area of detail
10 Sun Bay
Cayo Afuera 6
11 Cayo de Tierra
meters
Isabel Segunda
Al's Mar Azul 3
Casa de Amistad
CALLE MUÑOZ RIVERA
4 Glass Beach
Black Beard Sports
Esperanza
Vieques Adventure Company 9
CALLE FLAMBOYAN
El Quenepo 8
Malecón 5
Vieques Conservation and Historical Trust

THE BASICS

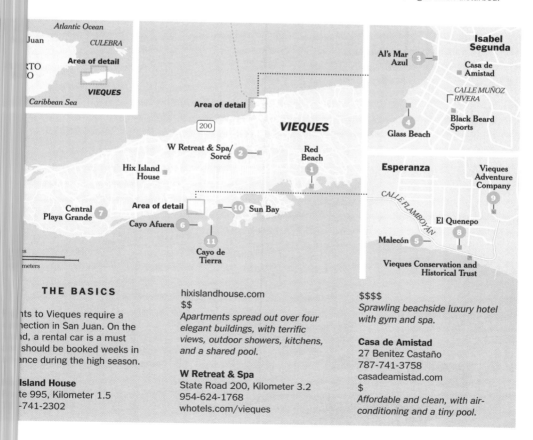

nts to Vieques require a nection in San Juan. On the nd, a rental car is a must should be booked weeks in ance during the high season.

Island House
te 995, Kilometer 1.5
-741-2302
hixislandhouse.com
$$
Apartments spread out over four elegant buildings, with terrific views, outdoor showers, kitchens, and a shared pool.

W Retreat & Spa
State Road 200, Kilometer 3.2
954-624-1768
whotels.com/vieques
$$$$
Sprawling beachside luxury hotel with gym and spa.

Casa de Amistad
27 Benitez Castaño
787-741-3758
casadeamistad.com
$
Affordable and clean, with air-conditioning and a tiny pool.

HEAVENLY DAYS

St. Thomas

ıost garishly lush, with fat sugary beaches that ːt its steep green slopes from the surrounding ıanse of blue ocean glow, the island of St. Thomas is ssic Caribbean, a getaway for swimming and snorkel-, sipping rum drinks, and snoozing in the shade swaying palms. But it also has an authentic urban ıter: Charlotte Amalie, the capital and largest city the United States Virgin Islands. Restaurants, ops, and quirky bars line the city's historic streets, d cruise ships are a fixture in its harbor, which cupies the crater of an ancient volcano. A major gar producer and slave port in its days as a Danish lony, St. Thomas was purchased, along with its ster islands, by the United States in 1917 and served r a while as a naval base. The sailors you're likely see today are the sort who will sell you an afternoon ruise on a catamaran. — BY NICK KAYE

FRIDAY

Beach of Dreams 2 p.m.

First, leave some footprints at St. Thomas's ıarquee attraction, **Magens Bay Beach** (Route 35; -340-777-6300; magensbayauthority.com), on the sland's north side. One of the world's most visited ınd most photographed stretches of sand and water, t is almost a textbook example of a perfect Caribbean beach. The sand is white and curves in a heart shape; the shallow water is Technicolor turquoise in the sun; and it's all a public park. With pelicans and gulls riding trade winds above, the warm-water bay makes a giant bathtub of the Atlantic. Take a swim and a walk, and get into the spirit of the relaxed, happy clusters of smiling vacationers.

2 *Milkshake Moderation* 4:30 p.m.

The caloric hazards of overindulging in ice cream are well known, but the milkshakes at the **Udder Delite Dairy Bar** (1-340-777-6050), a small shack on Magens Bay Road near the beach, add a new reason to go easy: they're spiked with alcohol. Step up to the dairy bar and try one, perhaps a Jamocho, with chocolate and coffee ice creams and Kahlua. Then grab a seat on the patio, where workers play dominos in the afternoons, shaded by a big genip tree. Udder Delite is an island institution beloved by all, and if you're under age or the designated driver, don't despair: it also offers virgin varieties of its shakes.

3 *Scan for Sails* 5:30 p.m.

A mandatory detour on the drive to Charlotte Amalie is the lookout at **Drake's Seat**, perched above the bay on Route 40, where Sir Francis himself is said to have watched his fleet in the late 16th century. Today you'll see green hills dotted with houses before an endless blue horizon. By this time in the afternoon, the tourist crowds that clog the parking lot should be cleared out, and as daylight fades toward dusk, the view only gets lovelier.

4 *Local Lobsters* 8 p.m.

While away the evening in **Frenchtown**, an old fishing village just southwest of Charlotte Amalie. It's an enclave of tiny pastel houses, numerous restaurants, and streets safe for ambling around at night. A popular spot for dinner is **Oceana** (8 Honduras; 1-340-774-4262; oceanavi.com; $$$). Its small wooden building was the Russian consulate in the days of Danish rule, and its outdoor tables occupy a choice spot on the water. Try the Caribbean lobster. Afterward, move on to **Epernay** (Frenchtown Mall, 24-A Honduras; 1-340-774-5348), a small, dimly lighted bistro and wine bar that stays open late.

OPPOSITE Hills and harbor in St. Thomas.

RIGHT Magens Bay Beach, a textbook example of a perfect Caribbean beach, is the eagerly anticipated first stop for many travelers in St. Thomas.

SATURDAY

5 *Take Home the Hot Sauce* 10 a.m.

St. Thomas has long been a free port, and the Danes demanded that it remain as such after the United States took over, so goods are imported inexpensively. Loads of T-shirt shops (don't even think about buying anything with "Mon" on it) and plenty of high-end stores can be found, but the best places to browse are on and around **Dronningens Gade**, or Main Street, between Market Square and the Emancipation Garden. Look for salvaged nautical goods, rare black-coral jewelry, and Caribbean-flavored art. A good gift to take home is some of the local hot sauce; two good brands are Pepper J. and Jerome's.

6 *Simply West Indian* Noon

A few blocks from the water in Charlotte Amalie is **Cuzzin's Caribbean Restaurant and Bar** (7 Back Street; 1-340-777-4711; $$), one of the best spots on the island for West Indian fare. Simple yet exciting dishes like curried shrimp and conch creole, with island staples like fungi, a polenta-like dish made with cornmeal, keep both tourists and locals dropping in.

7 *Plunge In* 2 p.m.

The splendor of Magens Bay draws crowds, but on the East End you'll find quieter beaches with beauty of their own. **Lindquist Beach**, off Route 38 between the Wyndham and Sapphire resorts, is a local favorite, secluded and shaded by sea grape and palm trees. **Sapphire Beach**, reached through the Sapphire resort's free parking lot, may be an even better choice. Along with the requisite blue water and unlittered sand, it offers cheap rental gear that you can use to snorkel the rich waters offshore, where you may see everything from baby sea turtles to four-foot-long barracudas.

8 *Sunset in the East* 5:30 p.m.

A curving bay endows the Secret Harbour Beach Resort with a sunset view, and you may as well take advantage of it. Watch the fading rays tint the sea while you're ordering dinner at the **Sunset Grille** (Secret Harbour Beach Resort; 1-340-714-7874; sunsetgrillevi.com; $$$), close to the water's edge. Expect creative cocktails, an interesting wine list, and a menu that makes use of local bounty.

9 *A Bowlful of Rum* 8 p.m.

Switch gears with a stop at the party-hearty **Duffy's Love Shack** (6500 Red Hook Plaza; 1-340-779-2080; duffysloveshack.com) in the town of Red Hook. Part of the appeal of the drinks here is the vessels they're served in: souvenir mugs, pineapples, model cars, and, for serious drinkers who want to share the rum-and-liqueurs special, a 64-ounce fishbowl. A young crowd dances as reggae and hip-hop stick to the thick air.

SUNDAY

10 *Toast With Gladys* 9 a.m.

Hidden down a winding alley off Main Street in Charlotte Amalie is brick-lined **Gladys' Cafe** (Royal Dane Mall West; 1-340-774-6604; gladyscafe.com; $), where breakfast lovers start gathering at 7 a.m. Along with your extra-thick French toast and

ABOVE Volcanoes formed much of the landscape of St. Thomas, creating harbors set into ancient craters.

RIGHT Gladys' Cafe in Charlotte Amalie, the main town.

ggs, get a sense of the past in these surroundings. The Royal Dane Mall is a converted 18th-century building said to have been used as a pump house or a water well. Across the street from its entrance is the boyhood home (14 Dronningens Gade) of the Impressionist painter Camille Pissarro, who was born on St. Thomas in 1830 and, while making his lasting reputation living and painting in France, remained a Danish citizen until his death in 1903.

11 *Morning Danish* 10 a.m.

Colonial history is in plain sight in Charlotte Amalie. Start a walking tour at **Emancipation Garden**, a small park near the water where the Danes announced freedom for the island's slaves on July 3, 1848. Many of today's Virgin Islanders are descended from the people freed that day. Just north, up Government Hill near manicured gardens with basking iguanas, are the vine-draped **99 Steps**, constructed partly of old ballast bricks from Danish ships. A sweaty climb to the top leads to the tower at **Blackbeard's Castle** (1-340-776-1234; blackbeardscastle.com), which was built in the 1660s — not by a pirate, but by the Danish military. Your hamstrings may object, but you can't end your historical hike before seeing the **St. Thomas Synagogue** (340-774-4312; synagogue.vi), on a steep hill on Crystal Gade. The oldest synagogue in continuous use on United States soil, it houses a congregation formed in 1796. Inside, the pews are made from native mahogany and the floor is island sand.

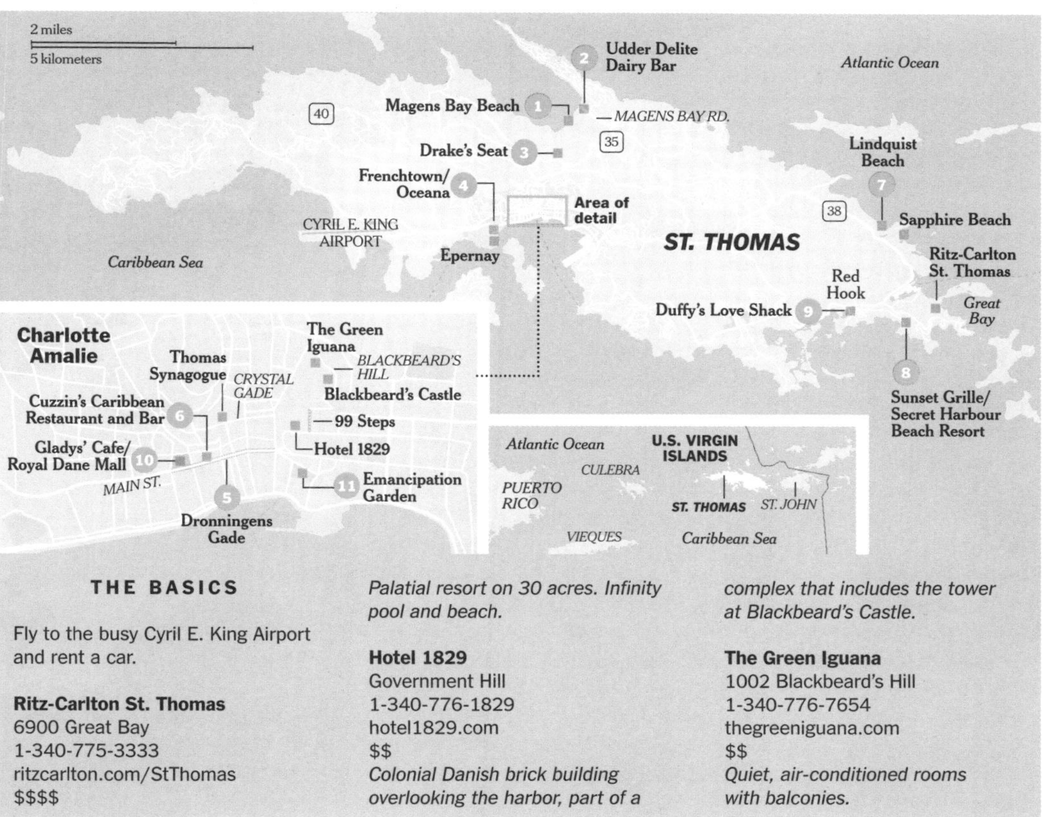

THE BASICS

Fly to the busy Cyril E. King Airport and rent a car.

Ritz-Carlton St. Thomas
6900 Great Bay
1-340-775-3333
ritzcarlton.com/StThomas
$$$$
Palatial resort on 30 acres. Infinity pool and beach.

Hotel 1829
Government Hill
1-340-776-1829
hotel1829.com
$$
Colonial Danish brick building overlooking the harbor, part of a complex that includes the tower at Blackbeard's Castle.

The Green Iguana
1002 Blackbeard's Hill
1-340-776-7654
thegreeniguana.com
$$
Quiet, air-conditioned rooms with balconies.

St. John

In a Caribbean increasingly defined by development and high prices, much of St. John remains an exception. It does have expensive, tony places, like Caneel Bay and the Westin, but it also has campgrounds with well-equipped and comfortable tents and cottages. There are only a few roads, and most wind up at one or another of the island's gorgeous white-sand beaches, framed by the tropical forests of Virgin Islands National Park, which covers more than half the island. Thousands more acres of the surrounding waters — traversed in 1493 by Christopher Columbus, who christened the Virgin Islands — have been declared a national monument.

— BY JON RUST AND WENDY PLUMP

FRIDAY

1 *Your Ship Comes In* 3 p.m.

The ferry bringing you to St. John from St. Thomas, home to the nearest airport, arrives at **Cruz Bay**. This is also the usual spot for getting acquainted with St. John, which has a year-round population of just 5,000 people. Stroll around **Wharfside Village**, the small commercial area near the pier, and check out the shops. It's not too soon to pick up a souvenir.

2 *Island Rhythm* 4 p.m.

Settle into paradise with happy hour at **Joe's Rum Hut** (1-340-775-5200; joesrumhut.com). The bar and the adjacent Cruz Bay Pizza Shop are in Wharfside Village, but the Virgin Islands Pale Ale comes with free views of the harbor. Try a mojito, and as the sun goes down and the boats come and go, start getting used to island time.

3 *Seafood Saloon* 7:30 p.m.

At **Woody's Seafood Saloon** (a block from the pier in Cruz Bay, 1-340-779-4625; woodysseafood.com; $$), people spill out into the street as they gather to kick off a night on the town. The conch fritters and corn-crusted scallops are great starters, and the seafood platter of grilled fish, shrimp, and scallops goes well with the Jimmy Buffett tunes and the dancing servers. If this place is too crowded, head to the nearby **Beach Bar** (1-340-777-4220; beachbarstjohn.com) for mahi sandwiches and live music. Have a nightcap next to the still waters and the moonlight shining off the bay.

SATURDAY

4 *North Beach* 8:30 a.m.

Pick up fruit or pastries and bottled water, and at the west end of Wharfside Village, under a shade tree in front of Low Key Watersports (divelowkey.com), find **Noah's Little Arks** (1-340-693-9030). Rent one of the small yellow craft and motor out through the idled sailboats in Cruz Bay toward the other aquamarine bays — Caneel, Hawksnest, Trunk, Cinnamon; there are dozens of coves, cays, and beaches. In 1952 the financier and conservationist Laurance S. Rockefeller came to St. John on a sailing trip and fell in love with the place. He bought thousands of acres of land to preserve it from development. He built a small, swanky resort, a sort of eco-tourism prototype, at an old plantation at Caneel Bay. But he donated most of his purchase to the U.S. National Park

OPPOSITE Trunk Bay in the Virgin Islands National Park, which occupies more than half of St. John.

BELOW A school of fish surrounds a pair of snorkelers in the warm, clear waters of Trunk Bay.

Service. Pull the boat up onto a beach and dig into your picnic breakfast.

5 *Inside the Aquarium* 11 a.m.

While you're exploring, don't neglect the snorkeling. St. John stands out in the Caribbean for its variety and quality of snorkeling spots. The government's protection extends out to offshore reefs, restricting boating and fishing, and all beaches are public to the vegetation line. Under the surface, join schools of silverfish, shimmeringly psychedelic parrotfish, foot-long starfish, and the occasional nurse shark. If you're a beginner, start at **Trunk Bay**, where a snorkel trail features markers on the sea floor explaining what you see. More experienced snorkelers often head for **Waterlemon Cay**.

ABOVE Paddleboarding on the pristine south side of St. John, part of Virgin Islands National Park.

BELOW A campground at Maho Bay in the national park.

6 *Bar and Grill* 1 p.m.

On the other side of the island is **Coral Bay**, which has one of the best-protected harbors in the Caribbean and was the commercial center for sugar plantations in the early 18th century. Now it bustles with sailors who anchor in the bay, many of them flocking to **Skinny Legs** (Route 10; 1-340-779-4982; skinnylegs.com; $-$$), said by some to be the best bar and grill on St. John. Burgers are a specialty, and the bar is open all evening.

7 *South Beach* 3 p.m.

There are three reasons most people come to St. John: beaches, beaches, and beaches. Now it's time for the beaches of the south coast, where the coves are calm, protected from winter swells. At **Salt Pond Bay**, a few miles down Route 107 from Coral Bay, is St. John's prettiest beach, the quintessential creamy Caribbean shoreline. A short walk away is a brackish lake where birds abound and another beach where the Atlantic Ocean crashes onto a cobblestone shoreline. A bit farther is **Ram's Head**, a stark and windswept cliff jutting into the ocean. Down the road is isolated and beautiful **Lameshur Bay**. If you're feeling vigorous, hike the **Reef Bay Trail**, practically a requirement for vacationing on St. John (trailhead at Centerline Road 4.9 miles east of Cruz Bay, or catch a ride from the national park visitor center in Cruz Bay). It is about five miles round trip, with a steep, 937-foot descent to the valley floor, but it rewards the hardy with a chance to see petroglyphs probably carved by the pre-Columbian Taino people.

8 *Conch on the Bay* 7 p.m.

At **Miss Lucy's** (Route 107, Friis Bay; 1-340-693-5244; $$), outside Coral Bay, the food is fabulous, and, according to the head chef, the restaurant pulls in people from St. Thomas. Start with a thick, creamy conch chowder or a goat-cheese salad with romaine, apples, and almonds. Entrees have included dishes like ponzu tuna, sushi-grade fish sliced thin and served with seasoned soba noodles, wasabi, and ginger; jumbo lump crab cakes with lobster sauce; and a flavorful vegetarian platter. As you drive away sated, watch out for the wild goats and chickens that congregate along the road, perhaps attracted to the smells wafting from the kitchen.

SUNDAY

9 *A Walk in the Ruins* 9 a.m.

Long before the United States bought the Virgin Islands from Denmark in 1917, sugar cane was the raison d'être for life on St. John. At the eastern end of the north shore road, the **Annaberg ruins** (1-340-776-6201; nps.gov/viis), in the national park, offer a glimpse into the island's past. Wander among the stone-and-coral remains of old structures and

BELOW A bus stop on St. John. The island has few roads, and most wind up at one or another of the gorgeous beaches.

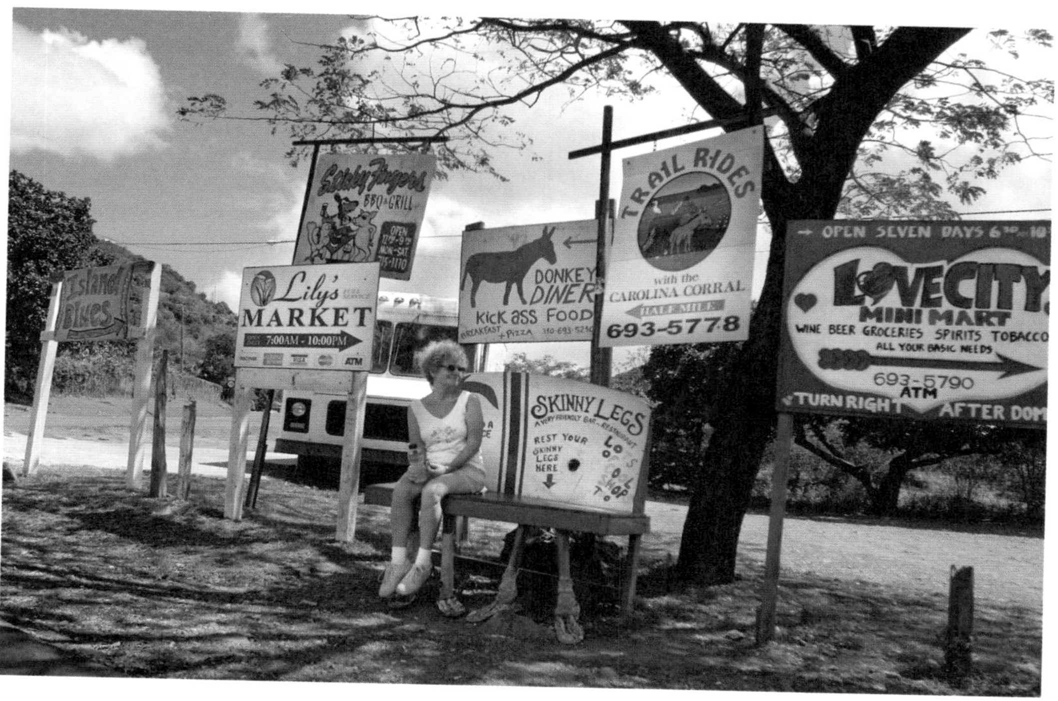

a windmill; imagine the scent of crushed cane, molasses, and rum; and enjoy the spectacular views of Tortola and Jost Van Dyke in the British Virgin Islands, while in the distance sailboats ride the breeze in Sir Francis Drake Passage. Seeing what's left of the slave quarters, one gets a hint of the cruelty that led to revolts against the plantation owners.

10 *Stand Up and Paddle* 11 a.m.

The clear, calm waters of St. John's coves make it a great location for paddleboarding, a form of an ancient Polynesian sport that was repopularized in Hawaii in the early 2000s. It was taken up by surfers with brand names like Laird Hamilton and Gerry Lopez, who were looking for a way to train when the surf was flat. Rent a board from **Arawak Expeditions** (Mongoose Junction, Cruz Bay; 1-340-693-8312; arawakexp.com), which will also provide a lesson if you need one. (You stand on the board, and make your way along with a paddle.) SUP, as it is known, is a 360-degree experience, with vistas of land and sea spread around you, and more wide-ranging views of the fish beneath your board than you could get from an afternoon of snorkeling. Pass over spotted rays and turtles, schools of colorful fish, and colonies of black sea urchins huddled below.

OPPOSITE Maho Bay on the north shore. Much of the sea around St. John is protected as a national monument.

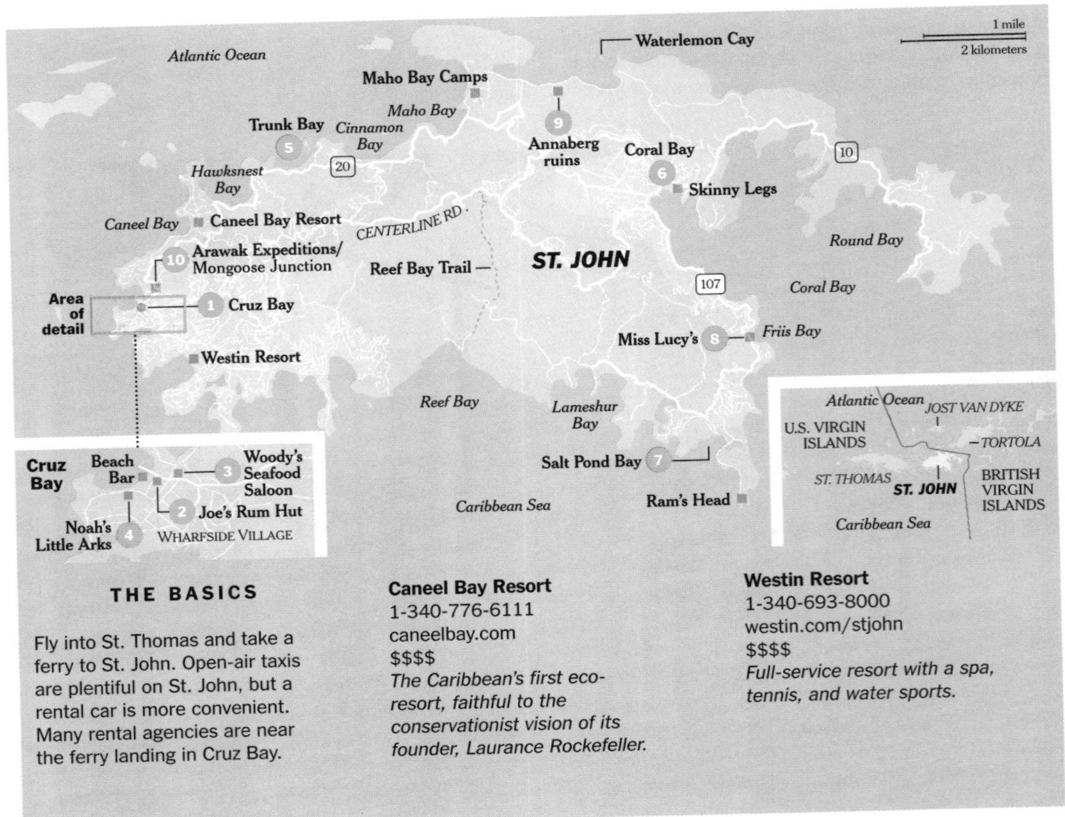

THE BASICS

Fly into St. Thomas and take a ferry to St. John. Open-air taxis are plentiful on St. John, but a rental car is more convenient. Many rental agencies are near the ferry landing in Cruz Bay.

Caneel Bay Resort
1-340-776-6111
caneelbay.com
$$$$
The Caribbean's first eco-resort, faithful to the conservationist vision of its founder, Laurance Rockefeller.

Westin Resort
1-340-693-8000
westin.com/stjohn
$$$$
Full-service resort with a spa, tennis, and water sports.

Anguilla

Though celebrity sightings at its fabulous resorts long ago became gossip-column fare, Anguilla has not sacrificed its low-key, egalitarian character to the demands of the high-end tourist trade. Goats still outnumber limos, quaint bed-and-breakfasts remain open, and anyone can go to any beach. A sinuous 16-mile-long sliver of limestone and coral just three miles wide at its widest point, Anguilla is said by some to have been christened by Christopher Columbus (its name is Italian for "eel"), but its European settlers were English, and it is still English, a British dependent territory with its own twist. Its 15,000 residents live with all the modern comforts, and everyone has a car. But no one has a street address — people just know where to find one another.

— BY EMILY S. RUEB AND SHERRY MARKER

FRIDAY

1 *Hill and Valley* 3 p.m.

Have a look around The Valley, Anguilla's capital. It's an agglomeration of government buildings; low concrete houses; and churches, including the artfully eccentric St. Gerard's, which has a facade of uneven stones and pebbles. **Wallblake House** (Wallblake Road), the 18th-century plantation house next to St. Gerard's, gives a sense of Anguilla's past, when cotton was raised here. A few blocks away, the Valley's most charming street, Crocus Hill Road, runs steeply uphill through an avenue of mahogany trees. Along the way are a cluster of early-20th-century gingerbread cottages, several old-fashioned bake ovens, and gardens edged with pink conch shells. At the top of the hill is Anguilla's oldest hotel, **Lloyd's Guest House**, a canary-yellow building perched on the island's highest point.

2 *Harbor Talk* 5 p.m.

Other towns are scattered across the island, and fishing boats go out from villages like Island Harbor and Blowing Point. **Sandy Ground**, on the north coast, has a deep natural harbor where cargo boats can put in and sleek yachts and sailboats anchor near a string of harborside bars and restaurants. Sandy Ground wraps willing visitors in a kind of timeless island charm. Dogs bark and roosters crow; meandering goats seem to have the right of way. Join the evening crowd sipping rum punch at the beachside outdoor tables at **Johnno's** (1-264-497-2728), and let the locals and the longtime Anguilla visitors regale you with their stories. Ask about the national sport, boat racing — a passion that brings everyone together to cheer favorite crews. Remember the route that got you to Johnno's. You may want to return on Sunday for its jazz brunch.

3 *Homegrown Chef* 7 p.m.

Local chefs trained at the island's most expensive resorts sometimes graduate to running their own kitchens. Vernon Hughes, who began his career as a dishwasher at Cinnamon Reef and rose to executive chef there, runs **E's Oven** (South Hill; 1-264-498-8258; $$) on the site of his mother's old stone oven. Anguillan foodies make the restaurant a regular stop, and satisfied vacationers come back year after year for dishes like pan-fried whole snapper, salmon and capers in cream sauce, and pineapple-glazed chicken.

4 *Driftwood Reggae* 9:30 p.m.

Night life on easygoing Anguilla sways more than it pulses, but there are many spots where you can bury your toes in the sand and take in local bands. If you like Caribbean music, the place to go is **Dune Preserve** (Rendezvous Bay; 1-264-729-4215;

OPPOSITE A frangipani in bloom on Anguilla.

RIGHT Pastel facades of abandoned structures in Anguilla's main town, The Valley. The island's English place names reflect its history as a British outpost.

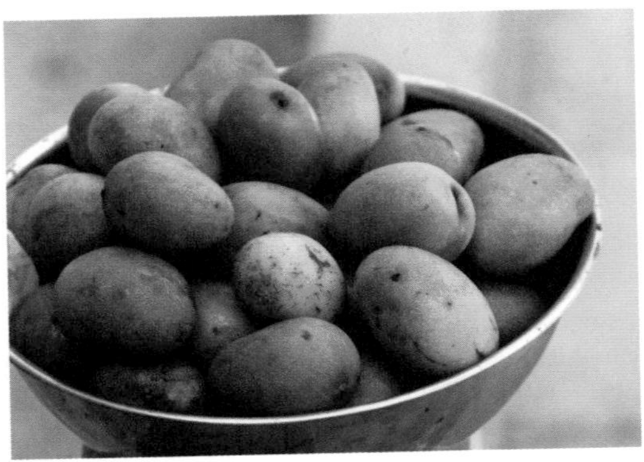

bankiebanx.net), a beach bar, restaurant, and music spot owned by the internationally known Reggae star Bankie Banx. (If Banx will be singing on the night you're there, you should have a reservation.) Built on waterfront land that has long been owned by Banx's family, Dune Preserve is so integrated with the beach that you almost feel it washed up from the ocean. In fact, parts of it did. The construction materials include driftwood and pieces of wrecked racing boats.

SATURDAY

5 *Sunning With the Stars* 9 a.m.

It's easy to while away time, especially over rum punches, debating the virtues of Anguilla's beaches. At Maundays Bay the sand sifts through the toes as fine as powder, as white as snow; at Shoal and Rendezvous Bays, it shines iridescent, with a slightly gritty sheen; at Little Bay and Sandy Ground, it turns from basic beige to pink at sunset. But in practice, setting out with a towel and beach bag, it's hard to say where one beach ends and the next begins. And as Anguilla's beaches blend into one another, its sun worshipers can cross the invisible lines, too. Thanks to local custom, all 33 beaches are open to all comers. That means you can plop down on the dazzling white sand at **Cap Juluca** (Maundays Bay), an elegant resort favored by A-listers. You can stay all day if you want to. Just be discreet as you scan the surroundings for movie stars, and don't expect the uniformed attendant to stop by your spot with one of Cap Juluca's fluffy towels.

6 *Everybody's Uncle* Noon

Shoal Bay East, a beautiful stretch of floury white sand toward the northern end of the island, is often said to be the island's best beach. It's more populated with sunbathers and snorkelers than Maundays Bay, and restaurants and other small beach businesses give it a more commercial feeling, but the bright cerulean water and offshore coral make this a necessary stop. While you're here, have lunch at **Uncle Ernie's** (1-264-497-3907; $), a classic beach shack where pretty much everyone eventually stops in. The ribs are succulent and the coleslaw is tasty, and if there are no celebrities in sight, no one seems to miss them.

7 *Art Tour* 3 p.m.

Anguilla has more cactuses than palm trees, and almost as many art galleries and resident artists as cactuses. In a brief driving tour, you can see a few. At the **Alak Art Gallery** (Shoal Bay East Road; 1-264-497-7270), Louise Brooks sells her bright acrylic paintings, with island-inspired subjects like wayward goats and bold hibiscus flowers; they're also reproduced on bags and T-shirts. Lynne Bernbaum, a former Texan, shows her colorful geometric interpretations of island scenes at **Lynne Bernbaum Art Studio** (Sandy Ground; 1-264-497-5211; lynnebernbaum.com). The **Devonish Art Gallery** (Albert Hughes Drive near West End Road; 1-264-497-2949) displays the carved-wood sculptures of Courtney Devonish and the work of other local artists. **Uhuru Art Gallery** (Bedneys Plaza, West End; 1-264-772-4100; uhuruartgallery.com) specializes in Afro-Caribbean art.

8 *Anguillan Tastes* 8 p.m.

Among the best known of Anguilla's chefs is Dale Carty, who worked at Malliouhana, one of the

RIGHT The bay shore at Island Harbor, a tiny town near the eastern end of the island.

island's most luxurious resorts, and then opened his own restaurant, **Tasty's** (South Hill; 1-264-497-2737; tastysrestaurant.com; $$$), in 1999. Tasty's is now an island institution. Carty's interpretations of traditional Anguilla cuisine have included Stewed Chicken Grandma's Style, with rice and peas or herb-roasted potatoes, and Nan's Conch Creole, with coconut dumplings.

SUNDAY

9 *Leave Some Hoofprints* 10 a.m.

The easiest way to get acquainted with the island's beaches is to hoof it — on horseback. Take a guided ride along the beach and into the shallows at serene Cove Bay with **Seaside Stables Anguilla** (Paradise Drive; 1-264-235-3667; seaside-stables-anguilla.com). Just inland from this narrow strip of sand is Cove Pond, one of several saltwater ponds on the island.

OPPOSITE ABOVE Mangoes, part of the island fruit bowl.

ABOVE The Valley, Anguilla's capital, is a town of brightly painted humble structures, low concrete houses, government buildings, and stone churches.

THE BASICS

Fly to Puerto Rico or another of the nearby islands and catch a small plane to Anguilla, or arrive by ferry from St. Martin. Several agencies offer rental cars.

Lloyd's Guest House
Crocus Hill, The Valley
1-264-497-2351
lloyds.ai
$
Canary-yellow hotel perched on the island's highest point, within walking distance of Crocus Bay. Bright, cheerful rooms; air conditioning; Wi-Fi.

Cap Juluca
Maundays Bay
1-264-497-6666
capjuluca.com
$$$$
Moorish-style villas tucked away on a secluded beach. A favorite of vacationing celebrities.

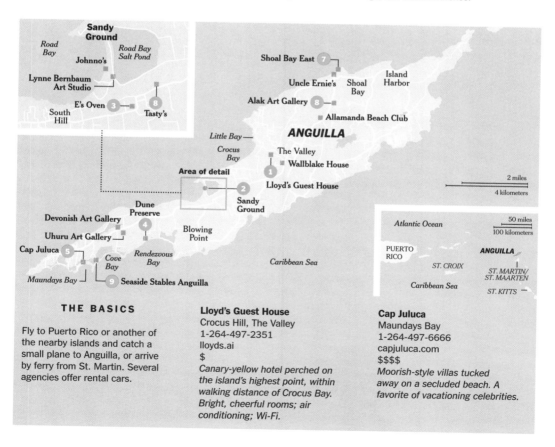

St. Martin St. Maarten

Among the accolades awarded to Caribbean islands (most beautiful beach, easiest on the budget, most relaxing), the award for most densely developed probably goes to St. Martin/St. Maarten, the half-French, half-Dutch island in the West Indies. That is not to say the island's natural beauty is ruined. It remains a stunningly picturesque place with some of the Caribbean's most arresting scenery (here it could win a prize, too). But all that development—boutique hotels, casinos, marinas, high-rise resorts—means visitors are never short on options. And thanks to a seemingly endless construction boom, those options keep multiplying. —BY JEREMY W. PETERS

FRIDAY

1 *For Wine Lovers* 5 p.m.

Conventional wisdom holds that the Dutch side of the island (St. Maarten) operates at a faster pace than the French side (St. Martin). In truth, both are bustling—the main difference being that the Dutch side has more branded full-service resorts, while the French side has more mom-and-pops. For a warm introduction to the island, head to the small French town of Grand Case and the bar at the **Love Hotel** (140 Boulevard de Grand Case; 590-690-660-765; love-sxm.com), which sits on stilts over the sand, offering an idyllic perch to watch the sun dip into the sea. Have a glass of wine and an appetizer.

2 *Andes on the Caribbean* 8 p.m.

You'll have plenty of time to sample the buttery-rich French cuisine. Opt instead for the unpredictable, eclectic menu at **Temptation** (106 Rhine Road, Cupecoy; 1-721-545-2254; rareandtemptation.com; $$$), a restaurant on the Dutch side that mixes and matches cuisines to generally good effect. One season's menu included veal osso bucco, chicken and shrimp pad thai, shortribs with paella, and a duck-breast-and-fried-rice combination called Quack Quack Chow Mein.

OPPOSITE Plane watching off Sunset Beach, at the end of the Princess Juliana Airport runway.

RIGHT A lineup of flavorings and island rum at the Love Hotel in Grand Case, on the French side of the island.

3 *Roll the Dice* 10 p.m.

Gambling is one of St. Maarten's biggest draws. And aside from the blare of a yacht horn or the squeak of a tree frog, the synthesized ping of the slot machine may be the island's most recognizable sound. Near the French border, the **Princess Casino at Port de Plaisance** (Cole Bay; 1-721-544-4311; princessportdeplaisance.com) feels removed from the ceaseless drumbeat. In addition to the usual blackjack, poker, and roulette tables, the casino is known for its colorful floor shows with dancers in feather headdresses and billowing gowns gliding across the stage.

SATURDAY

4 *Prime Beach* 10 a.m.

Few experiences are as uniquely St. Martin as a stroll down the beach at **Orient Bay**, known for its pulsing beach bars at one end and a naturist resort at the other. (You've been warned: this is a clothing-optional beach.) Get there early and rent a chair and umbrella from one of the dozen or so bars that line the beach. **Kakao Beach** (on Orient Bay; 590-590-874-326; kakaobeach.com) has one of the biggest spreads on the water and some of the nicest scenery, offering not only chairs in the sand but also thatch-canopied tables spread out in a small grove of palm trees.

5 *Seafood Riviera* Noon

Grand Case is the island's culinary center. Elegant French bistros line both sides of the main street, which hugs the beach. **Talk of the Town Too** (Boulevard de Grand Case; 590-590-296-389; $$) won't win awards for refinement. Its open-air dining area consists of little more than picnic tables, a grill, and a chalkboard menu. But there is a satisfying sea breeze, and you can haggle for your meal. Tell the servers what the competition is charging for a grilled lobster, and they might cut you a deal. Expect a decent-size lobster tail with homemade sides like rice and beans and corn on the cob. For dessert, just a minute on foot down the street is **La Crepe en Rose** (Boulevard de Grand Case), a pink-and-white food cart that serves crepes with a variety of fillings, including fruit jams and Nutella.

6 *Just a Little Farther* 2 p.m.

Some of the island's natural beauty is hidden behind artificial eyesores. Case in point: the hike through the nature preserve known as the **Wilderness** on the island's northernmost tip. To get there, you have to first walk past a landfill. But once you clear the trash-strewn first leg of the trail, you will be rewarded with sweeping vistas. The trail hugs a steep hill through fields of cactus and then deposits you on a rocky shore. Keep going, and you will shortly reach your reward—the sands of the pristine, secluded **Petites Cayes** beach.

7 *Jet Blast* 5 p.m.

The signs—they say "Danger" in bright red letters and depict a man getting blown off his feet by a landing jet—could not be clearer. Yet that doesn't seem to deter people from lining up on the beach at the foot of the runway at Princess Juliana International Airport to jump up as if they could touch the approaching aircraft with their fingertips. This spectacle poses several confounding questions: Don't they realize they can't jump high enough to reach the planes? And don't they realize what would happen to them if they did? Save your dignity and watch from a safe distance at nearby **Sunset Beach Bar and Grill** (Caravanserai Resort; 1-721-545-2084; sunsetsxm.com). The rumble from the approaching aircraft will still rattle your table as you savor a bottle of beer and snack on pizza.

8 *Quayside Dining* 8 p.m.

One of the most ambitious and pricey developments on St. Maarten is the **Porto Cupecoy** (portocupecoy.com), a marina, condo, retail, and restaurant complex built by Orient Express Hotels. Everything is immaculate, like the neatly arranged beach tables with umbrellas, and the carefully manicured landscaping. The same goes for the restaurants. At **Aux Quatre Vents** (590-690-774-340; $$$), an attractive French restaurant with views of the marina, look for dishes like seafood risotto, tuna steak, and sweetbreads wrapped in phyllo.

9 *Red Rum* 11 p.m.

Bars with traditional Caribbean flair—life preservers on the wall, an umbrella in your drink—are easy enough to find on the island. For something decidedly lacking in tropical flair, head to the **Red Piano** on the Dutch side (Simpson Bay Resort & Marina; 1-721-544-2503; simpsonbayresort.com). The piano is indeed red, as are the walls and tabletops. Live bands play many nights, and the action goes well into the early morning hours. Try the guavaberry rum, a local specialty, made from—you guessed it—guavaberry.

SUNDAY

10 *Pain au Chocolat* 9 a.m.

A decent, and decently priced, breakfast can be hard to come by on this island. But along the waterfront boulevard in Marigot, the capital of

the French side, are dueling bakeries that serve up affordable fresh croissants (chocolate and plain), tarts (with a variety of assorted fruits like strawberry and pineapple), and éclairs. Choose either rival: **La Sucrière** (Boulevard de France; 590-590-511-330) or **Sarafina's** (Boulevard de France; 590-590-297-369).

11 *French Dip* Noon

Some beaches are overdeveloped. Some are untouched. For something in the middle, head to **Baie Rouge** on the island's French side. The beach is a wide, gradually sloping crescent of pillowy, straw-colored sand. A natural jetty juts out at one end, offering views of the soaring cliffs that bookend the beach. Access is simple. The beach lies right off a main road and there is a parking lot a few steps from the sand, another sign that on this island they build wherever there is land.

OPPOSITE A spill on the sand at Orient Bay, which is known less for beach sports than for pulsing bars and a naturist resort (nudity encouraged) at one end.

ABOVE Beachside development, a familiar feature of St. Martin/St. Maarten. Though densely built up, the island remains stunningly picturesque.

THE BASICS

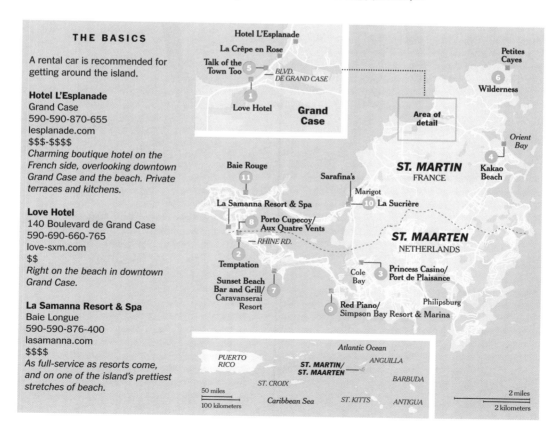

A rental car is recommended for getting around the island.

Hotel L'Esplanade
Grand Case
590-590-870-655
lesplanade.com
$$$-$$$$
Charming boutique hotel on the French side, overlooking downtown Grand Case and the beach. Private terraces and kitchens.

Love Hotel
140 Boulevard de Grand Case
590-690-660-765
love-sxm.com
$$
Right on the beach in downtown Grand Case.

La Samanna Resort & Spa
Baie Longue
590-590-876-400
lasamanna.com
$$$$
As full-service as resorts come, and on one of the island's prettiest stretches of beach.

St. Barts

Getting to St. Barts (the French island of Saint Barthélemy) isn't easy, not even with your own Gulfstream. On the final leg, you'll have to trade your million-dollar jet for a tiny puddle jumper, before threading between two jagged peaks and touching down on a teensy runway that, islanders like to joke, is as short as an aircraft carrier's. That might explain the island's exclusivity. Although Jay-Z, Beyoncé, and a rotating cast of celebrities have kept St. Barts in the tabloids, this tiny French island still exudes a chic, laid-back vibe unspoiled by gawkers and day-trippers. And despite a new wave of wine bars, chichi boutiques, and designer restaurants, the island's main attraction remains its luscious white-sand beaches, fringed by the pool-blue waters of the Caribbean.

— BY ANDRÉA R. VAUCHER

FRIDAY

1 *Samba to the Beach* 5 p.m.

For an introduction to the sexy international vibe of St. Barts, watch the sunset at **Dõ Brazil** (Shell Beach; 590-590-290-666; dobrazil.com), a bistro and bar owned by the former tennis star Yannick Noah, on Shell Beach, the strip of sand closest to the island's main harbor, Gustavia. Order the signature Saravah (fresh ginger, pineapple, and cachaça, the Brazilian liquor) or a shot of homemade caramel vodka, and let the reggae tunes get you in the groove. Need to stretch your legs? Dive into the warm water. With its calm surf, this is perhaps the island's best beach for serious swimming.

2 *King Creole* 8:30 p.m.

St. Barts cuisine is not just about foie gras and escargots. **Eddy's** (Rue du Centenaire, Gustavia; 590-590-275-417; $$), an island institution set in a tropical garden, offers Creole cuisine with an Asian accent. Traditional favorites like spicy stuffed crab may be served alongside fresh tuna spring rolls and tom ka kai, the Thai chicken soup. The crowd, like the décor, is unassuming yet not unstylish.

3 *Quay Serà* 10:30 p.m.

Stroll along the quay in Gustavia and ogle the gigantic yachts where Russian billionaires, East Coast rappers, and tycoons like Ron Perelman hold parties and Cohiba-puffing playboys entertain young women. Drop in at **Le Bête à Z'Ailes**, also known as the Baz Bar (Gustavia Harbor; 590-590-297-409; bazbar.com), a waterfront sushi bar, for live jazz, blues, and funky soul. It draws an eclectic and lively crowd; it's the kind of spot where you could run into anybody from Naomi Campbell to sexy French sailors slamming back sake-tinis.

SATURDAY

4 *French Deli* 10:30 a.m.

Follow the latte-drinking crowd to **Maya's-to-Go** (Les Galeries du Commerce, St. Jean; 590-590-298-370; st-barths.com/mayas-to-go; $$), an upscale deli with an inviting patio, across the road from the airport. It's a great spot to pack a beach picnic. Try the Nico sandwich—goat cheese, arugula, and prosciutto on ciabatta—or the Vietnamese beef salad. Forgot sunscreen? Next door is the **Pharmacie de l'Aéroport** (590-590-276-661), a friendly drugstore that sells fancy products at duty-free prices.

5 *Who Needs Shade?* 11:30 a.m.

Of the island's 17 beaches, only one is not accessible by car: **Colombier**, on the northwestern tip. To

OPPOSITE Le Sereno, a luxury resort with private villas and 600 feet of beach, makes a good exemplar of the pampered and exclusive ambience of St. Barts.

RIGHT Dõ Brazil, a bistro and beach bar near the harbor in Gustavia.

get there, drive along pristine Flamands Beach until the road ends, park, and follow the old goat path. The hike, which affords magnificent vistas, takes about 30 minutes and, though not difficult, can be a bit vertiginous in places. Unless you're extremely sure-footed, you'll probably want something sturdier than sandals on your feet. The crescent-shaped beach has sand as fine as baby powder and water as calm as a bathtub. The only thing missing along this timeless stretch of nearly deserted sand is a little shade.

6 *Bada Bling* 3 p.m.

Gustavia has all the luxury brands (Hermès, Prada, you name it), but the more interesting shopping is in St. Jean, on the island's north coast. At **Angels & Demons** (Villa Creole; 590-590-275-906), you can scoop up the season's favorite accessories. And for head-turning bikinis, go to **Pain de Sucre** (Centre Le Pelican; 590-590-293-079; painde sucre.com), which will give you an idea of what everyone will be wearing in St.-Tropez and Malibu next summer.

7 *Catch a Ray* 5:30 p.m.

Get a front-row seat in the orange afterglow at **Le Restaurant des Pêcheurs**, the beachfront restaurant and lounge at Le Sereno hotel (Grand Cul de Sac; 590-590-298-300; lesereno.com). Nurse a vodka mojito on the open-air patio while marveling at the daredevil windsurfers and kitesurfers flying across the horizon.

8 *Pizza in Paradise* 9 p.m.

For good, simple food served on oilcloth rather than fine linen, head for the **Hideaway** (St. Jean; 590-590-276-362; hideaway.tv; $$). The people-watching is great, and the pizza is terrific. Plus the prices are among the lowest on the island. Try a crispy thin-crust pizza with prosciutto and mushrooms and a bottle of Valpolicella. You'll really feel like you belong when Andy, the owner, brings a bottomless glass of vanilla rum to your table for dessert.

9 *Moulin Rouge* 11 p.m.

Le Ti St-Barth (Pointe Milou; 590-590-279-771; letistbarth.com)—or the Ti, as everyone calls it—is so old school that it looks almost new. The décor, heavy on red velvet and feathered chandeliers, looks like something you'd find on a cheesy Paris-by-night

ABOVE Floating palaces at anchor in Gustavia harbor. Yachts here are often the scene of parties given by Russian billionaires, rap stars, and business tycoons.

BELOW Le Carre d'Or, a shopping mall in Gustavia that is well stocked with designer boutiques. Another good shopping spot is St. Jean on the north coast.

OPPOSITE At Le Ti St-Barth, late-night action begins when showgirls in French fetish finery climb atop the tables and get the crowd jumping to a disco beat.

tour. Though this is a restaurant, the real action begins after dessert, when showgirls dressed in fetish finery climb atop the tables and get the crowd jumping to a D.J.'s Euro disco beat.

SUNDAY

10 *Sea and Be Scene* Noon

See how the other half does brunch at the **Sand Bar** ($$$$), an open-air restaurant at the Eden Rock Hotel (St. Jean; 590-590-297-999; edenrockhotel.com), the island's glitziest hotel. Situated on the water's edge, the Sand Bar draws a high-octane crowd of moguls, rock stars, and their weekend arm candy. It also serves fine food. When it's on the menu, the Dover sole is to die for. Finish off the meal with a lemon tart, and then grab a chaise longue on the sand. It will cost you a few euros, but you can suntan all afternoon amid the glitterati.

Atlantic Ocean
50 miles
100 kilometers
ANGUILLA
ST. MARTIN/ ST. MAARTEN
ST. BARTS
BARBUDA
ST. KITTS
ANTIGUA
Caribbean Sea

Hôtel Emeraude Plage
Sand Bar 10
Maya's-to-Go/ Pharmacie de l'Aèroport 4
St. Jean
Pain de Sucre
Angels & Demons 6
Hotel Le Village
2 Eddy's
Gustavia
3 Le Bête à Z'Ailes
1 Dõ Brazil
SHELL BEACH

5 Colombier
POINTE MILOU
Le Restaurant des Pêcheurs/ Le Sereno 7
Le Ti St-Barth 9
8 Hideaway
St. Jean
Area of detail
Gustavia
ST. BARTS (SAINT BARTHÉLEMY)
1 mile
2 kilometers

THE BASICS

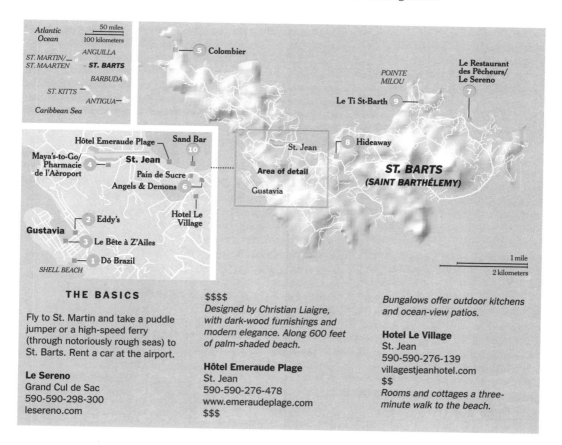

Fly to St. Martin and take a puddle jumper or a high-speed ferry (through notoriously rough seas) to St. Barts. Rent a car at the airport.

Le Sereno
Grand Cul de Sac
590-590-298-300
lesereno.com
$$$$
Designed by Christian Liaigre, with dark-wood furnishings and modern elegance. Along 600 feet of palm-shaded beach.

Hôtel Emeraude Plage
St. Jean
590-590-276-478
www.emeraudeplage.com
$$$
Bungalows offer outdoor kitchens and ocean-view patios.

Hotel Le Village
St. Jean
590-590-276-139
villagestjeanhotel.com
$$
Rooms and cottages a three-minute walk to the beach.

Antigua

Tiny Antigua, 14 miles long and 11 miles wide, is one of those famously paradisiacal islands that actually lives up to the hype. Pristine beaches (there are 365 of them, if you can believe the tourist brochures) fleck the coastline, and everywhere you look there is yet another exhilarating view of sea, cliff, or tropical landscape. An array of über-luxurious resorts have cashed in on the lush surroundings, and provide their well-heeled guests with so many hedonistic diversions that many never emerge to see what lies beyond the resort gates. Which is a shame, because if you drive from, say, English Harbour in the south to Dickenson Bay in the northwest, you'll find another, more intimate, Antigua: small towns bustling with activity, a cricket game in full swing, inland roads lined with "fig" (banana) trees, and everywhere, the stone remnants of windmills, a legacy of the island's colonial role as one of the Caribbean's most prolific sugar producers, when Antigua, a British outpost, was an island of slaves. — BY SUZANNE MACNEILLE

FRIDAY

1 *Escape the Dock* 4:30 p.m.

Nelson's Dockyard, in English Harbour, may claim to be the only remaining Georgian dockyard in the world, but before long its tourist shops, museums, and nautical buildings begin to feel Disneyesque. So find the path behind the Copper and Lumber Store Hotel that leads up to the ruins of 18th-century **Fort Berkeley**. A 15-minute hike will deliver a view of wide-open sea and precipitous coastline—a bracing introduction to the island's past and present. Below, in English Harbour, British trade ships once sought safety from storms; today, it's a favored pit stop for the Caribbean yachting community, which, during the much-anticipated spring Sailing Week, turns the town of English Harbour into party central.

2 *Join the Crowd* 7 p.m.

Sure, you could have a quiet dinner at the Copper and Lumber Store Hotel's restaurant, where the colonial/nautical atmosphere is laid on perhaps a bit too thick. But why resist the funky restaurants and bars on nearby Dockyard Drive, with their musical offerings—reggae, jazz, soca—pouring out into the street as tourists, locals, and crews from all those mega-yachts in the harbor prowl from one establishment to the next? A favorite spot is **Trappas Restaurant** (Dockyard Drive, 1-268-562-3534; $$), where the eclectic menus have included pumpkin soup and seared yellowfin tuna with wasabi and ginger.

3 *Custom Rum* 11 p.m.

End the night at the open-air **Abracadabra** (Dockyard Drive; 1-268-460-2701; theabracadabra.com), where local bands or D.J.'s provide the soundtrack and skilled bartenders concoct custom rum punches. When the scene gets too noisy, retreat to the chill-out garden in the back.

SATURDAY

4 *Lofty Views* 9 a.m.

More climbing, more stunning views, more military ruins—yes, you've done this already, but the hikes around **Shirley Heights**, just east of English Harbour, offer the island's most exhilarating and comprehensive panorama of the sheltered bays and

OPPOSITE A mill at Betty's Hope, a remnant from Antigua's days as a sugar producer powered by slaves and wind.

RIGHT The quiet beach at Half Moon Bay.

rocky coast of southern Antigua. Grab a snack at the **Shirley Heights Lookout** (1-268-728-0636; shirleyheightslookout.com), where a patio is high above the harbor.

5 *Testing the Waters* 11 a.m.

You'll be hard-pressed to find a more gorgeous combination of white sand and thrashing surf than **Half Moon Bay**, on the eastern edge of the island. The beach, more than half a mile long and curved around a blue bay, has been sublimely isolated since Hurricane Luis destroyed the sprawling Half Moon Bay Resort in 1995. These days, there's not a beach chair in sight, so you'll have to sprawl on the pillowy sand while you appreciate the wisdom of those who decided to turn this priceless piece of real estate into a national park.

6 *Worth the Drive* 1 p.m.

Navigate the challenging roads for an unhurried lunch on the breezy terrace of the extremely out-of-the-way **Harmony Hall** (Brown's Bay; 1-268-460-4120; harmonyhallantigua.com; $$), a lovely hotel and restaurant in a restored plantation house overlooking Nonsuch Bay. The fare runs to dishes like steamed lobster in court bouillon and pappardelle with lobster and cherry tomatoes. Afterward, peruse the gallery, where you can buy prints by local artists. Added bonus: Lunch guests may use the inn's motorboat to swim and snorkel at uninhabited Green Island.

7 *Betty's Hope* 3:30 p.m.

On a bare, windy hill in the center of the island, the ruins of the plantation known as **Betty's Hope** (about 10 miles east of St. John's, off Collins Road; 1-268-462-1469) are a reminder that Antigua was once, in effect, a huge colonial sugar mill, which ran on slave and wind power. The importance of sugar in the British colonial economy helps explain the existence of all those military ruins you were clambering over back in Shirley Heights. Today, Betty's Hope—named for a daughter of the owners—is a lonely place, strewn with tamarind and acacia trees, and the occasional herd of goats chewing grass near the restored windmill. A small but very good museum documents the brutal role of slavery on Antigua.

8 *Northwest Shore* 6 p.m.

Take a predinner stroll along the beach lining **Dickenson Bay**, where many of Antigua's resorts and restaurants are clustered. Grab a drink at a beachside bar and spend some time watching guests from the Sandals resort struggle with their windsurfing boards.

9 *Where Everyone Goes* 9 p.m.

The Caribbean laps so close to the open-air **Coconut Grove** restaurant on Dickenson Bay (1-268-462-1538; coconutgroveantigua.net; $$) that it's not unusual for the water to occasionally wash right into the dining room. Guests take it in stride. Tables are moved back. Candles are relit. Coconut Grove draws a loyal local crowd—as well as a steady

ABOVE Take a short hike from Nelson's Dockyard to Fort Berkeley, built in the 18th century, for a walk at the ramparts and a stunning view of rocky coastline.

BELOW A telephone booth becomes a whimsical bit of beach decór at Siboney Beach Club.

stream of guests from the Siboney Beach Club, which it is a part of — thanks to its easy, elegant vibe and the chef's amazing talents with traditional Caribbean ingredients. Favorites include seared red snapper in a saffron curry sauce and coconut shrimp in a thick, crisp batter served with a rich coconut sauce. After dinner, head to the bar, a favorite watering hole for the expat community; conversations continue well past midnight.

SUNDAY

10 *Yes You Can* Noon

Shortly after Barack Obama was first elected president of the United States, Prime Minister Baldwin Spencer of Antigua and Barbuda announced to the world that Antigua would rename its highest point, the 1,300-foot Boggy Peak, Mount Obama. The formal renaming took place a few months later. So end your visit on a historic note, and tackle the trails, which will earn you views of Montserrat and Guadeloupe.

ABOVE Paintings and nature's artwork, visible through the window, at the art gallery at Harmony Hall.

THE BASICS

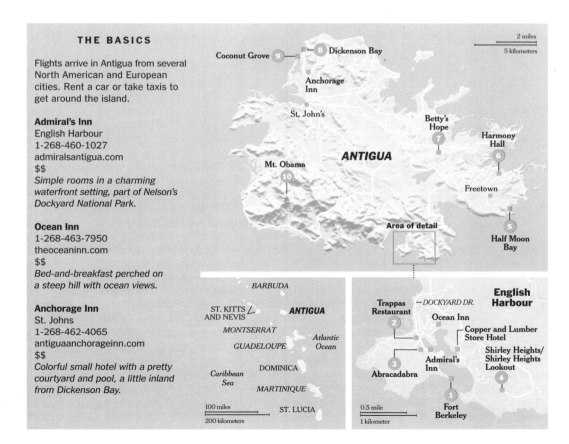

Flights arrive in Antigua from several North American and European cities. Rent a car or take taxis to get around the island.

Admiral's Inn
English Harbour
1-268-460-1027
admiralsantigua.com
$$
Simple rooms in a charming waterfront setting, part of Nelson's Dockyard National Park.

Ocean Inn
1-268-463-7950
theoceaninn.com
$$
Bed-and-breakfast perched on a steep hill with ocean views.

Anchorage Inn
St. Johns
1-268-462-4065
antiguaanchorageinn.com
$$
Colorful small hotel with a pretty courtyard and pool, a little inland from Dickenson Bay.

2 miles
5 kilometers
Coconut Grove 9
8 Dickenson Bay
Anchorage Inn
St. John's
Betty's Hope 7
Harmony Hall 6
ANTIGUA
Mt. Obama 10
Freetown
Area of detail
5 Half Moon Bay
BARBUDA
ST. KITTS AND NEVIS
ANTIGUA
MONTSERRAT
Atlantic Ocean
GUADELOUPE
DOMINICA
Caribbean Sea
MARTINIQUE
ST. LUCIA
100 miles
200 kilometers
English Harbour
Trappas Restaurant 2
DOCKYARD DR.
Ocean Inn
Copper and Lumber Store Hotel
Shirley Heights/ Shirley Heights Lookout 4
3 Abracadabra
Admiral's Inn
1 Fort Berkeley
0.5 mile
1 kilometer

St. Lucia

The lush Caribbean island of St. Lucia has long been associated with luxury, thanks to its exclusive hotels and celebrity guests, from Oprah Winfrey to Justin Bieber. But the island has always had an earthy streak, and even high-end hotels offer rooms without a fourth wall (but with plenty of mosquito netting). In the dramatic Piton mountain region on the south end of the island, near the town of Soufrière, some historic estates take the earthy concept a bit further — one combines tourism with farming, another has opened a spa in the jungle canopy — and restaurants offer field-to-fork menus. All are within easy reach of St. Lucia's abundant natural attractions, which include hot springs, rain forests, mountains, and, of course, the sea.
— BY ELAINE GLUSAC

FRIDAY

1 *Full Immersion* 3 p.m.

Plunge into the Caribbean at the island's picturesque Sugar Beach on Anse des Pitons on the southwest shore between the two Piton mountains. Both mountains — Gros Piton and the steeper Petit Piton — along with nearly 7,200 acres of land and sea surrounding them, make up a Unesco World Heritage Site. Swimmers can get to the public beach by taking the road to the **Sugar Beach Resort** (1-758-456-8000; viceroyhotelsandresorts.com; formerly known as the Jalousie Plantation). Park or have your taxi drop you at the gated entry, and walk downhill to the water (all beaches are public in St. Lucia, even if they are in front of hotels). Bring a snorkel and look for sinuous trumpetfish on the north end of the cove below Petit Piton.

2 *Nature Therapy* 4:30 p.m.

Bamboo might be more closely associated with Asia, but St. Lucians have made it their national plant, based on its use in everything from construction to musical instruments. Have your muscles unknotted with bamboo sticks used rolling-pin-style at the Sugar Beach Resort's **Rainforest Spa**, which is open to visitors as well as hotel guests. Its seven thatch-roofed massage bungalows rest on stilts in the forest where a natural stream provides a rushing-water soundtrack during treatments. Afterward, work up a sweat in the steam bath built into the ruins of an 18th-century aqueduct used by the original plantation's sugar mill.

3 *Dinner and Rum* 7:30 p.m.

Stick around for the evening at the resort — which is almost like a small, upscale town — and order a shot of 12-year-old Admiral Rodney Extra Old St. Lucia Rum at the **Cane Bar**, one of the few trendy bars on this stretch of the island. Then join other guests — mostly couples in resort-wear finery — and make a night of it dining in the neighboring **Great Room** ($$) on innovative Caribbean dishes like scallops on a puree of Jerusalem artichoke or mahi-mahi with green fig mash.

SATURDAY

4 *DIY Candy* 10 a.m.

Cacao farming on St. Lucia got a boost when the Britain-based chocolate maker **Hotel Chocolat** (1-758-457-1624; thehotelchocolat.com) opened a six-room hotel and restaurant, Boucan, on its 140-acre cacao-growing Rabot Estate in the highlands behind Petit Piton. A chocolate factory is on the premises, and you can take a tour that starts in the cacao orchards and includes a chef-led session in mashing and sweetening roasted beans by hand, and then

OPPOSITE Gros Piton and Petit Piton, the landmark peaks of St. Lucia, and the town of Soufrière.

RIGHT Enjoying sand and sea. St. Lucia's natural attractions also include hot springs and rain forests.

making your own chocolates. Each guest leaves with candy for the road, a souvenir too tempting to make it all the way home.

5 *Table at the Farm* 12:30 p.m.

Nearly everything on the plate at **Jardin Cacao** restaurant at **Fond Doux Holiday Plantation** (1-758-459-7545; fonddouxestate.com; $$) near Gros Piton is grown on the surrounding 135-acre estate. Ten guest cottages and two restaurants help support the farm. Harvest fare might feature pumpkin soup and snapper with lemongrass, seasonal carrots, and christophene, an island squash. Tour the grounds to sample a guava off the tree or witness the cacao-drying operation before the beans are shipped off to Hershey's.

6 *Art & Craft* 2:30 p.m.

T-shirts and trinkets dominate the few shops in Soufrière. But if you're in the market for more than rum or hot sauce, take a trip to the low-key **Hummingbird Beach Resort** (1-758-459-7985; istlucia.co.uk) on the north end of the town beach. Its Batik Gallery shows the work of the Hummingbird's owner, Joan Alexander-Stowe, and her son, David Simmonds, who design and print tropical flora and fauna motifs on colorful cotton runners, wraps, and wall hangings.

7 *Garden Walk* 3:30 p.m.

Stop and smell the ginger blossoms at **Diamond Falls Botanical Gardens** (1-758-459-7155; diamondstlucia.com), a few minutes by car west of the Soufrière waterfront. Once part of a sprawling 18th-century estate granted by King Louis XIV, the six-acre garden is devoted to ornamentals including heliconia, anthurium, and bougainvillea. A path through the foliage will lead you to 55-foot-high Diamond Falls.

TOP Cacao beans drying at the Fond Doux Holiday Plantation.

ABOVE A massage at the Rainforest Spa, in the Sugar Beach Resort.

8 *Mud Pack* 4:30 p.m.

Everyone from cruise-ship crowds to contestants on *The Bachelor* flocks to **Sulphur Springs Park** (1-758-459-5726; soufrierefoundation.org), a five- or 10-minute drive south of Soufrière, to bathe in the mineral-rich mud and warm waters found in the collapsed caldera of a dormant volcano. For maximum tranquillity, arrive after 4 p.m., when the crowds have left (at 5 p.m., the springs officially close but are not evacuated, and you are likely to be joined by locals). The boiling mud pots and steaming fumaroles are behind a fence just uphill from the stream-fed bathing area. Slather on the mud that collects behind a dammed pool and let it dry before rinsing off. (Save the white bikini for the beach. This process softens the skin but tends to stain light clothing.)

9 *Place Setting* 7 p.m.

The reputation of the bar and restaurant at **Ladera Resort** (1-758-459-6600; ladera.com; $$$) could rest on location alone, at 1,100 feet above shore, framing views of Petit Piton. But this was also the neighborhood's farm-to-table pioneer and still emphasizes food from local sources. Start your evening at sunset in the open-air **T'Cholit Bar** with a rum-and-lime ti' punch accompanied by snacks of spicy coconut chips and pickled christophene. After dark, take a table in the terrace dining room of **Dasheene Restaurant**, one story up, to sample such locally inspired dishes as pepper-marinated grilled shrimp and "rundown" rack of lamb spiced with cacao in coconut sauce.

SUNDAY

10 *Sunrise Summit* 7 a.m.

After days of gazing upon the Pitons, it's time to climb one. Beat the heat with an early start up **Gros Piton**, a three-to-four-hour round-trip hike topping

ABOVE The Ladera Resort is 1,100 feet above the shore.

RIGHT The Great Room restaurant at Sugar Beach. Local menus emphasize the island's fish in many preparations.

out at 2,619 feet with panoramic Atlantic-to-Caribbean views. Guides from the Gros Piton Tour Guides Association, in cooperation with the St. Lucia Forestry Department (1-758-286-0382; geocities.ws/sluforestrails/index) will lead you from the trailhead in Fond Gens Libre, a community on the south slope of the mountain, up a strenuous trail with rocky and slippery stretches, often using tree roots as steps. For those lacking the legs, nearby **Tet Paul Nature Trail** (1-758-720-1779; soufrierefoundation.org) follows a gentle rise between the two Pitons.

11 *Hidden Beach* Noon

Having earned your indolence, spend the afternoon at **Ti Kaye Village Resort and Spa**, about 40 minutes' drive north of Gros Piton along the east coast (1-758-456-8101; tikaye.com). It fronts Anse Cochon, one of the best bays for underwater sightings of elusive sea horses. The resort sells day passes to nonguests. Ocean views are front and center wherever you recline, from beach chaise to spa table.

ABOVE The 18th-century Fond Doux Holiday Plantation operates chocolate tours and serves hearty Creole lunches.

OPPOSITE The Sugar Beach Resort is nestled between the rock walls of the two Pitons.

THE BASICS

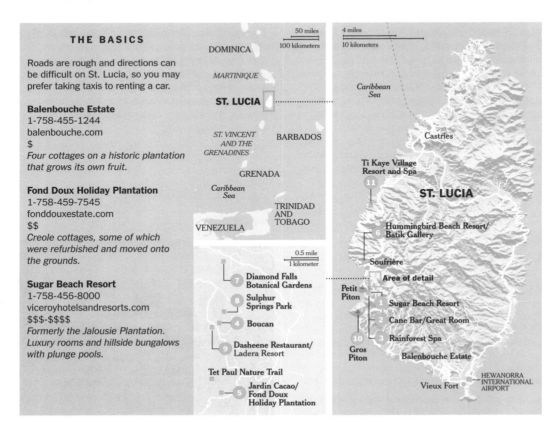

Roads are rough and directions can be difficult on St. Lucia, so you may prefer taking taxis to renting a car.

Balenbouche Estate
1-758-455-1244
balenbouche.com
$
Four cottages on a historic plantation that grows its own fruit.

Fond Doux Holiday Plantation
1-758-459-7545
fonddouxestate.com
$$
Creole cottages, some of which were refurbished and moved onto the grounds.

Sugar Beach Resort
1-758-456-8000
viceroyhotelsandresorts.com
$$$-$$$$
Formerly the Jalousie Plantation. Luxury rooms and hillside bungalows with plunge pools.

STORAGE
97/10/10
BRANDONS
STR.73
STORAGE
BRANDONS
1995/N
LITRES.
STR.69
L/ALC.
STORAGE
1998/NO
LITRES.
STR.73
L/ALC.
BRANDONS
STORAGE
BRANDONS
(21)
3398

Barbados

Tucked in the southern corner of the Lesser Antilles, Barbados is the easternmost island in the Caribbean. Its west coast is its famous side, known for its powdery beaches, water as clear as if it poured from a tap, manicured estates, really manicured resorts, and even more manicured golf courses. That part of the island is known as the Platinum Coast, so named for the color of its sparkling coastline and its preferred credit cards. The eastern coast, sequestered from the posh resorts by acres of sugar-cane fields and thick forests populated by wild monkeys, is rugged and wilder, with thundering surf rolling in off the Atlantic. The south, highly developed but more egalitarian, is welcoming and affordable. Whether your budget is regal or limited, you can enjoy Barbados and still have a few bucks left over for a bottle of rum.

— BY DANIELLE PERGAMENT AND ALICE DUBOIS

FRIDAY

1 *Get Your Feet Wet* 1 p.m.

All beaches in Barbados are free to the public, and a good place to start is on the south coast, not far from the airport, at **Miami Beach**, also known as Enterprise Beach. For lounging and swimming, it is easy and family-friendly, with soft white sand and a picnic area shaded by tall pines. A lifeguard is usually on duty, chairs and umbrellas are available for rent, and a food truck sells cheap refreshments.

2 *Rum at the Source* 3:30 p.m.

Rum was invented in Barbados and is available almost everywhere, even at gas stations. It's cheapest at the source, so visit the headquarters of **Mount Gay Rum** (Spring Garden Highway, Exmouth Gap, St. Michael; 1-246-425-8757; mountgayrum.com), the oldest rum brand in the world, dating back to 1703. Arrive early enough for a distillery tour, and then do your shopping. A one-liter bottle of top-shelf Extra Old won't break the bank, and enjoying it back home is a great way to savor your Barbados memories long after your sunburn fades.

3 *Eat Fish and Party* 7 p.m.

The southern fishing town of **Oistins** is home to an open-air fish fry where locals and tourists line up at dozens of food stalls for generous portions of fresh marlin, tuna, and snapper ($$). The fish fry is held every night, but Friday is the time to go, when the music is turned up and the market turns into a raucous street party. If the thumping bass has your teeth rattling, walk down the road to **Lexie's** (1-246-428-1405), a 24-hour beachside bar with a different kind of dance party. On weekends, the D.J. spins croony tunes from the 1950s and '60s, while dignified-looking couples twirl ballroom-style around the sweltering dance floor.

SATURDAY

4 *The Windblown East* 11 a.m.

Bathsheba, the main town on the east side of the island, is set amid a wild landscape of tide pools and hulking boulders. The wind barrels in relentlessly off the Atlantic here, sweeping the hillside and everything with it: the mountain face is hollowed by the warm blasts; palm trees arch leeward, their seaside fronds thinned from the gale; waves endlessly roll in from

OPPOSITE The Mount Gay Rum Distillery on Barbados. The name, dating back to 1703, is the world's oldest rum brand. After your tour here, shop for rum to take home.

BELOW Horse and rider near Surfer's Point, a popular surf break on the southern end of the island.

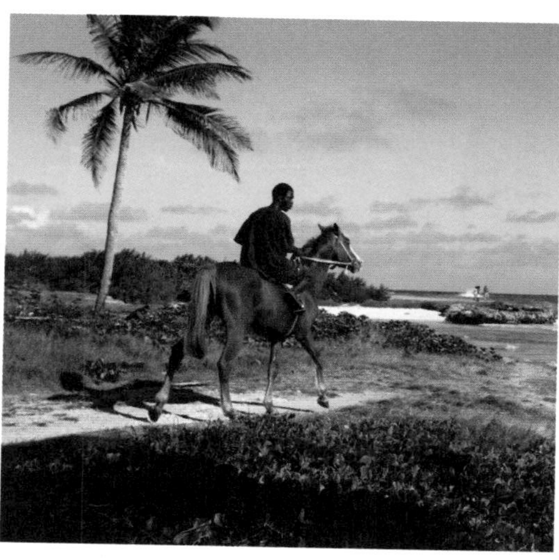

the vast ocean. The powerful breakers make the beaches here unsafe for swimming, but the natural tide pools formed by the boulders are deep enough so that you can spend some lazy time soaking in the warm, clear water.

5 *Magical Wave* Noon

Bathsheba's waves have attracted some surfing champions, but the real celebrity in town is **Soup Bowl**, the island's biggest wave. On a map, Barbados looks as if it were drifting out into the open Atlantic, which is exactly what makes Soup Bowl ideal. A wave can travel nearly 3,000 miles in the open ocean, undisturbed by sandbars, reefs, or land, before it breaks here. Surfers have to know what they're doing, and they're fun to watch. But so is the wave itself. "When Soup Bowl is good, it gives you goose bumps," said Melanie Pitcher, a surfing instructor and owner of Barbados Surf Trips. "When it's breaking clean, people come here after work and stand on the beach to watch. It's pure magic."

6 *Atlantic View* 1 p.m.

For lunch, find your way to the charmingly decrepit **Atlantis Hotel** (Tent Bay, Bathseheba; 1-246-433-9445; atlantishotelbarbados.com; $$$), an oceanfront fixture that is well into its second century. Ask for a table on the porch, which overlooks Bathsheba's rocks and surf and the colorful fishing boats in Tent Bay. Try the flying-fish sandwich or breadfruit salad, or if your appetite is up to it, the fixed-price three-course lunch.

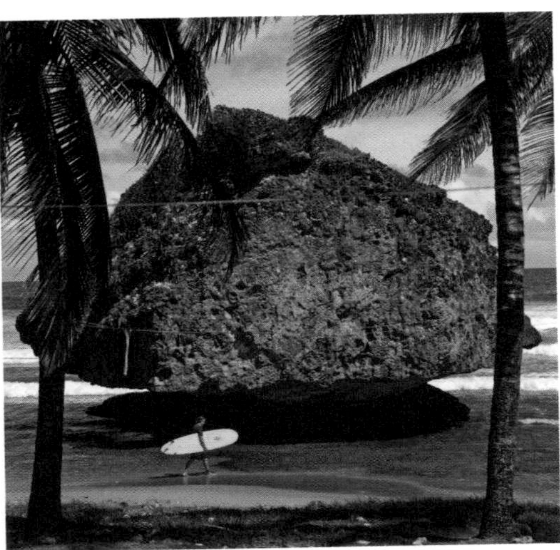

7 *Grab a Board* 3 p.m.

As the locals will remind you again and again, what makes Barbados unique is that there is a wave for everyone, not just for the champions who challenge Soup Bowl. Where the Atlantic meets the Caribbean on the island's southern tip, the coastline alternates between carved-out bays, sheltered from the wind and perfect for surfing, and the rougher points where the wind can lift a kitesurfer 30 feet off the water. "Our smaller waves are the most consistent," said Zed Layson, the owner of **Zed's Surfing Adventures** at Surfer's Point, a popular break. "You can close your eyes and point to the calendar—any day you hit, Barbados will have great beginner and intermediate waves." For lessons and board rentals, contact one of the three main surf schools in Barbados: Zed's (Surfer's Point, Inch Marlow, Christ Church; 1-246-428-7873; zedssurftravel.com), **Burkie's Surf School** (108 Plover Court, Long Beach, Christ Church; 1- 246-230-2456; surfbarbados.net), and **Barbados Surf Trips** (1-246-255-3509; surfbarbados.com). All of them teach all levels.

8 *Recuperation* 8 p.m.

Recover from your battle with the waves at **Aqua Restaurant & Lounge** (Hastings Main Road, Christ Church; 1-246-420-2995; aquabarbados.com; $$$$), a popular restaurant with sleek décor and beautiful waitresses. There are views of the water and lots of glass walls, and everything, from the entrance to the bar, is lighted from underneath. The menu is a collection of Asian-inspired seafood and local chicken and meat dishes, but Aqua's raison d'être is the bar. Try the Bajan Pride—after a couple of them, you'll be feeling duly patriotic.

SUNDAY

9 *Gospel Brunch* 9 a.m.

All-you-can-eat Sunday brunch buffets are popular in Barbados, and one of the best is at **L'Azure** (Crane Beach, off Highway 5; 1-246-423-6220;

thecrane.com; $$$), a restaurant in the high-end Crane Resort. The setting is picture perfect, overlooking Crane Bay in the island's southeast, and the food is good. But what really sets this brunch apart is live Caribbean gospel music. The menu includes brunch basics like pancakes and omelets as well as fish dishes, salads, and desserts. Make a reservation; there are two seatings.

10 *Off the Radar* 10:30 a.m.

Some of the most memorable beaches on Barbados are not on the tourist track. Tucked away a few miles north of the Crane Resort is the bite-size beach at **Bottom Bay**. Hemmed by high cliffs and backed by a grove of shady palm trees, it is rarely crowded. The surf may be too high for much swimming, but the beauty and peace of this beach are stunning. Heading northeast on Highway 5, drive past the turnoff for Sam Lord's Castle and look for a sign.

OPPOSITE Mushroom Rock, part of a wild landscape of tide pools and boulders in eastern Barbados. Swimming here is dangerous, but surfers challenge the waves.

ABOVE High spirits at a local surf shop.

THE BASICS

Most major car-rental companies will deliver a car to the airport upon your arrival.

Little Arches Hotel
Enterprise Beach Road, Christ Church
1-246-420-4689
littlearches.com
$$$
Boutique hotel near Miami Beach and the Friday fish fry at Oistins.

Sea-U! Guest House
Tent Bay, Bathsheba
1-246-433-9450
seaubarbados.com
$$
East-coast refuge with ocean-view verandas and four-poster beds.

Surfer's Point Guest House
Inch Marlow, Christ Church
1-246-428-7873
zedssurftravel.com
$
Kitchens, great views, and an in-house surf shop.

2 miles
5 kilometers
Caribbean Sea
BARBADOS
Soup Bowl 5
Bathsheba 4
6 Atlantis Hotel
Sea-U! Guest House
HIGHWAY 1B
HIGHWAY 2A
HIGHWAY 3
HIGHWAY 4
HIGHWAY 5
Bottom Bay 10
ST. MICHAEL
Mount Gay Rum 2
L'Azure 9
CHRIST CHURCH
Aqua Restaurant & Lounge 8
Oistins
Lexie's 3
Burkie's Surf School
Miami Beach 1
SURFER'S POINT
Little Arches Hotel
7 Zed's Surfing Adventures/ Surfer's Point Guest House
GUADELOUPE
LESSER ANTILLES
DOMINICA
MARTINIQUE
ST. LUCIA
BARBADOS
GRENADA
TRINIDAD AND TOBAGO
VENEZUELA

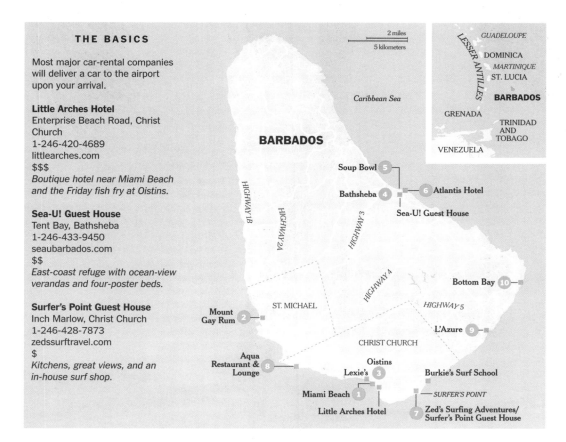

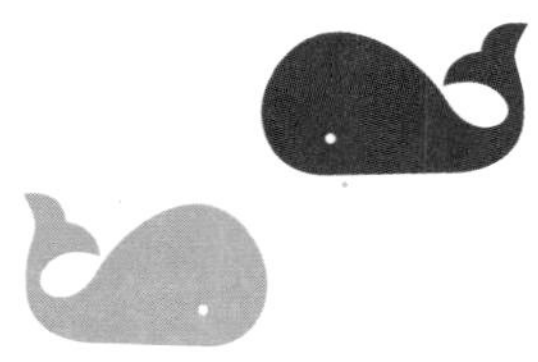

Bequia

The largest of the Grenadines — the necklace of 32 islands west of Barbados that unfurls south from St. Vincent — Bequia (pronounced BECK-way) covers only about seven square miles, around a third the size of Manhattan. It's not so tiny that you find yourself eating at the same restaurant every night, but it's manageable enough so that you can get just about anywhere you need to go in less than 15 minutes by taxi. Bequia has a variety of locally owned small hotels and inns, some high-end boutiques, and modest guesthouses. But no major chains, no super-saver deals popping up on the Web. The people are friendly and approachable, swimming at the same beaches the tourists use, drinking with them at the same bars at the end of the day. Dogs roam freely. Goats may be tethered to trees. — BY JEREMY W. PETERS

FRIDAY

1 *Port of Call* 3 p.m.

About 5,000 people live on Bequia full time, and **Port Elizabeth** is their hub of activity, where the bank, the government offices, and the main market square are located. Ferries in the harbor deposit and pick up passengers shuttling between St. Vincent and the other islands of the Grenadines. Go for a walk and soak in the atmosphere. Women amble down the main street, balancing large baskets of laundry on their heads with seemingly little effort. Local vendors sit at card tables in the shade, selling handmade baskets and jewelry. The town is nestled deep inside one of the Caribbean's most scenic natural harbors, the westward-facing Admiralty Bay, which looks as if it's been scooped out of the center of the island's verdant interior, leaving steep virgin hillsides that slope into the Caribbean. In the mornings and early afternoon, the sea appears cobalt with patches of teal; when the sun sets, it takes on a silver glaze. You could pass a day gazing at the view from various angles and feel that it was time well spent.

2 *Inn With the Yacht Crowd* 4 p.m.

The yachting set long ago found Bequia. If you're curious about their carefree world, get a glimpse of it by stopping for a drink or two at the beach bar in the **Frangipani Hotel** (Admiralty Bay; 1-784-458-3255; frangipanibequia.com). Owned by the same local family for more than a century, it's a favorite of sailors cruising the Grenadines.

3 *Try the Callaloo* 6 p.m.

Many of the restaurants and bars in Port Elizabeth are about a five-minute walk from the center of town along the same waterfront path where you found the Frangipani. Its name, the Belmont Walkway, suggests slightly more purpose and continuity that are evident. Follow it to the **Fig Tree** (Belmont Walkway; 1-784-457-3008; figtreebequia.com; $$), a harborside bistro known for its sunset view. The sociable owner, Cheryl Johnson, serves up dishes like conch souse, chicken in creole sauce, and callaloo, a green vegetable soup that is a staple of the Caribbean diet.

SATURDAY

4 *Sellers and Buyers* 9 a.m.

Port Elizabeth is a hive of activity from early morning through midafternoon. The **market,** a series of open-air stalls on the edge of the harbor, teems with Rastafarian farmers selling bananas, okra, and breadfruit. Even if you're not in need of fresh produce, it's worth a visit just to watch the eager growers swarm their prey: the sailors who have come in off their yachts looking to restock. If you jump in to make some purchases of your own, don't be surprised by what can appear to be a very flexible

OPPOSITE A water taxi in the Tobago Cays near Bequia.

BELOW Fresh-picked fruit at the Firefly Plantation.

exchange rate; it seems to fluctuate from one stall to the next. But it all evens out somehow in the end.

5 *The Water's Edge* 11 a.m.

The **Belmont Walkway** is an even better walk at midday, when the views are brightly lighted and you can take your time to meander. A concrete path shaded by palm and sea-grape trees, the walkway skirts the shore of Admiralty Bay. The sea laps gently up to and sometimes over the path; the waves gurgle and bubble as they wash in and out.

6 *Lobster Pie* 1 p.m.

Lunch on an outdoor terrace with views of Admiralty Bay is one of the better island traditions. At **Mac's Pizzeria** (Belmont Walkway; 1-784-458-3474; $$), a spot that has been around for decades, the lobster pizza is an island institution. If you're visiting in the wrong season for these particular crustaceans, choose from familiar lunch items like salads and conch fritters.

7 *By Land or by Sea* 3 p.m.

From Port Elizabeth, you can get to **Princess Margaret Beach** in one of two ways: by sea, in one of the dinghies whose owners operate them as water taxis, or by land, on a steep, narrow staircase that zigzags down from the main road. The beach, a long, wide stretch of soft sand bordered by a dense grove of palms, is just around a small, rocky peninsula from Admiralty Bay, but is not easy to reach by walking along the shore. It's a secluded, unspoiled spot, perfect for a lazy afternoon of swimming and sunning.

8 *Punch in Paradise* 6:30 p.m.

When it's time for a rum punch and a long, lazy dinner of fresh local fish, wash up at **Jack's** (Princess Margaret Bay; 1-784-458-3809; $$). Tucked away in one corner of Princess Margaret Beach, it exists in its own Eden. Besides serving good food in a glorious setting, it has live music some nights.

SUNDAY

9 *Whale Watchers* 9 a.m.

Cross to the other side of the island to **Friendship Bay**. There's no central square or commercial center over here, but there's a crescent-shaped beach where the water is calm and shallow enough that you can swim out a good distance from the shore and survey the surrounding hillsides. On the easternmost end of the bay, a grassy peninsula juts out into the cyan-colored water and then curls back in toward the shore

ABOVE A ferry docked in the harbor at Admiralty Bay.

OPPOSITE Fishermen heading into Friendship Bay. For a fee, some fishermen here will take travelers for boat rides.

like a comma. If you scan the hills all the way to the westernmost end, you'll see a small concrete bunker used as a whale lookout. But it's not as innocent as it sounds: locals use it to spot breaching humpbacks during whale-hunting season. (The tradition runs deep on Bequia, where many people take pride in the annual harpooning expeditions that are permitted in their waters under international regulations.) Some of the fishermen you may see along this beach will take you for a sightseeing ride in their boats for a modest and negotiable fee.

10 *Island Hopping* 10 a.m.

If you have time to linger in the Grenadines, you can hop a fast ferry to Mayreau or Mustique. Or any

number of tour operators will take you on a day trip to the **Tobago Cays**, a marine park about an hour by sea to the south (tobagocays.org). Among the cays to explore is **Petit Tabac**, essentially just a sand bar with grass and a few palm trees running along its spine. Another, **Baradal**, is a haven for sea turtles. (There's more turtle protection back on Bequia, at the **Old Hegg Turtle Sanctuary**; turtles.bequia.net.) Take snorkeling gear; the park is home to abundant coral and tropical fish.

4 Market
Port Elizabeth
Admiralty Bay
Belmont Walkway 5
Fig Tree 3
2 Frangipani Hotel
Gingerbread
6 Mac's Pizzeria
Caribbean Sea
1 mile
2 kilometers
Old Hegg Turtle Sanctuary
Spring Bay
Firefly Plantation Hotel
BEQUIA
Area of detail
1 Port Elizabeth
8 Jack's
Princess Margaret Beach 7
Bequia Beachfront Villas
9 Friendship Bay
10 miles
25 kilometers
ST. VINCENT
ST. VINCENT AND THE GRENADINES
BEQUIA
Caribbean Sea
MUSTIQUE
Tobago Cays
10
BARADAL
MAYREAU
PETIT TABAC

THE BASICS

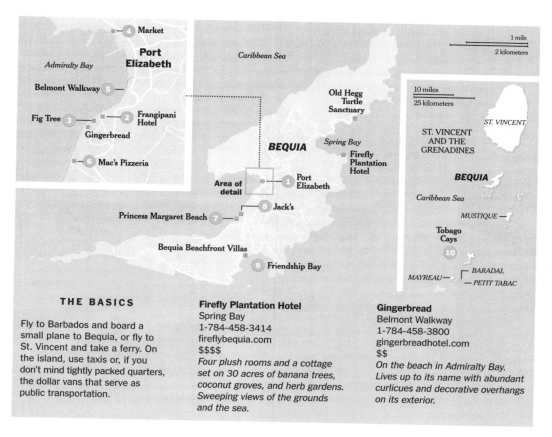

Fly to Barbados and board a small plane to Bequia, or fly to St. Vincent and take a ferry. On the island, use taxis or, if you don't mind tightly packed quarters, the dollar vans that serve as public transportation.

Firefly Plantation Hotel
Spring Bay
1-784-458-3414
fireflybequia.com
$$$$
Four plush rooms and a cottage set on 30 acres of banana trees, coconut groves, and herb gardens. Sweeping views of the grounds and the sea.

Gingerbread
Belmont Walkway
1-784-458-3800
gingerbreadhotel.com
$$
On the beach in Admiralty Bay. Lives up to its name with abundant curlicues and decorative overhangs on its exterior.

Curaçao

Curaçao, 44 miles off the coast of Venezuela, is a multicultural mélange of the Netherlands, the Caribbean, and South America. Although it is technically a new country, having became autonomous within the Kingdom of the Netherlands in 2010, it has a long history. As a Dutch colony, it was a salt producer and slave port; during the 17th century, Jews from Spain and Portugal took up residence; in the early 1900s, an oil refinery lured more foreigners. Today, about 150,000 people, representing some 50 nationalities, live in Curaçao, speaking four languages: Dutch, English, Spanish, and Papiamentu, which fuses the first three with Portuguese and African dialects. Joined by European and North and South American tourists drawn to the island's beaches and cerulean waters, they celebrate their cultural blend most exuberantly in their pre-Lenten carnival and in the hybrid music that keeps the airwaves humming by day and the dance clubs buzzing at night.

— BAZ DREISINGER AND SETH KUGEL

FRIDAY

1 *Local Color* 2 p.m.

Punda, the picture-perfect center of Willemstad, the capital city, is filled with 17th-century buildings resembling multihued gingerbread cookies. While beaches and diving are the big tourist draws on Curaçao, Willemstad is also a good stop for a traveler who knows that there are history and culture to explore. Visitors can stroll the cobblestone interior of **Fort Amsterdam**, which was erected in 1635, shortly after the Dutch had wrested control of Curaçao from the Spanish. (Peter Stuyvesant, later to be governor of the colony on Manhattan Island, was director of the new Dutch colony; it was during this period that he lost his leg in a battle with the Portuguese over the island of St. Martin.) The temple building of **Mikvé Israel-Emanuel** (599-9-4611067; snoa.com), founded in 1651 and the oldest continuously operating synagogue in the Western Hemisphere, is open for tour. And the **Kurá Hulanda Museum** (Klipstraat 9; 599-9-434-7765; kurahulanda.com/mission) documents Curaçao's horrific role in the slave trade.

2 *The Liqueur and More* 4 p.m.

Punda is shopping central, and aside from Curaçao liqueur — the snow globe of local souvenirs — you'll also find Dutch luxury goods. Look for embroidered linens and the easily recognizable blue-and-white Delft pottery. For Gouda cheese, walk along Breedestraat, Madurostraat, and Heerenstraat, which are lined with upscale Dutch shops and a few international chain stores.

3 *Dutch Palms* 8 p.m.

Zanzibar (Jan Thiel Beach; 599-9-747-0633; beach-restaurants.com; $$) is a beachfront complex of drinking dens and restaurants set beneath palm trees and crammed with Dutch tourists and expatriates. Dodge the omnipresent cigarette smoke, slide into a booth facing the sea, and order drinks and a casual dinner: pizza, pasta, or a heartier entree like ribs or fried fish.

4 *Musical Fusion* 10 p.m.

Check out Zanzibar's outdoor stage area to see if a local band is playing. The island's signature local music, born in the early 1980s, is called ritmo kombina

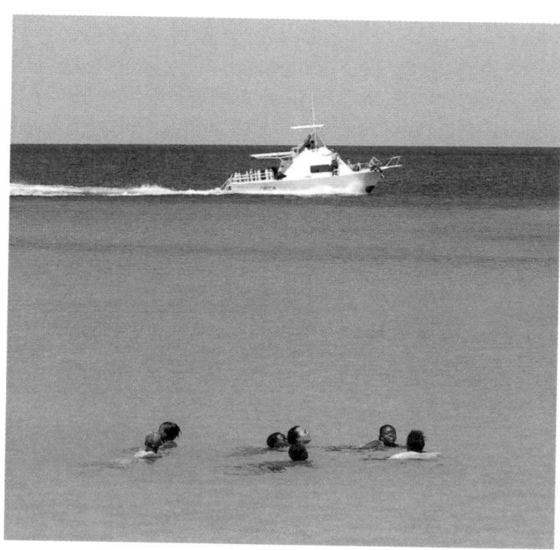

OPPOSITE Dutch-influenced buildings and Caribbean colors blend amiably on Curaçao. The island became autonomous within the Kingdom of the Netherlands in 2010.

RIGHT Swimmers at Abou, one of Curaçao's 35 beaches.

(literally, "combined rhythms" in Papiamentu). Ritmo mixes the updated sounds of the island's multicultural stew: merengue, salsa, soca, reggae, zouk, and more. Another local genre is tumba, a descendant of Curaçaoan slave music that resounds in parades and parties during carnival season. If you can't find local music at Zanzibar, check the schedules of some of the other clubs and stages around town. Willemstad after dark brims with possibilities. In neighborhoods and beachfront areas, modish nightclubs and outdoor live-music venues serve up sundry soundtracks.

SATURDAY

5 *Dodge the Divers* 10 a.m.

Curaçao's 35 beaches are diverse, with white, black, and gold sand. Some are clogged with cruise-ship passengers; others are deserted except for a few fishermen. A local favorite easily accessible from Willemstad is **Marie Pampoen Beach**, the antithesis of the resort right next to it—no waiters or beach chairs—but with the same lustrous sea, so clear you can make out the tiny silver fish darting by as you take a swim. Don't be surprised if someone goes by in full scuba gear: this is also a popular spot with snorkelers and divers, who wade in and head out to the coral reefs.

6 *High Point* 2 p.m.

Curacao is a dry island, 171 square miles of desertlike terrain surrounded by cerulean waters. On your way to the island's north end, you'll pass through country reminiscent of Georgia O'Keeffe's New Mexico paintings. Electric-yellow houses dot arid stretches, and cactuses along the dusty roads resemble grand pipe cleaners. Your destination is **Christoffel National Park** (599-9-864-0363; christoffelpark.org), which has 20 miles of trails, three former plantation houses, and **Mount Christoffel**, at 1,239 feet the island's highest point. The lookouts there offer striking, faintly ominous views: limestone cliffs, waves crashing furiously on black-sand beaches, hawks circling above.

7 *Shore Dinner* 8 p.m.

Dine alfresco, just off the beach, at **Belle Terrace** (130 Penstraat; 599-9-461-4377; avilahotel.com; $$$) in the Avila Hotel, an 18th-century Dutch colonial mansion turned chic hotel. The Avila is in the newly gentrified **Pietermaai** section of the city, where quaint colonial buildings have been transformed into trendy bars and restaurants and the cobblestone streets teem with Dutch students and locals. At

LEFT The Floating Market in Willemstad. Vendors bring in their produce on boats and tie up to sell it on the dock.

Belle Terrace, the tables are well dressed in white linen and the fare runs to dishes like mahi mahi with lemongrass and spring-onion risotto, or hazelnut-encrusted beef tenderloin.

8 *Woodsy Jazz* 9 p.m.

Blues, a bar and restaurant sprawled across a wooden pier at the Avila, is ground zero for Curaçao's jazz and blues scene. It has the cozy ambience of a tree house: planks for walls, unadorned wooden floors, a jam-packed bar. Waiters make the rounds, bearing heaping trays of food like Dutch bitterballen (savory meatballs) while patrons down Bacardi Gold. From a loft space hanging over the bar, jazz musicians play for a 35-and-up crowd.

OPPOSITE Punda, a waterfront shopping area, is a place to find Delft pottery, Dutch linens, and Curaçao liqueur.

SUNDAY

9 *Undersea Scenery* 9 a.m.

In a divine bit of justice, what Curaçao lacks in above-ground verdancy it makes up for in underwater abundance. Dive centers dot the coastline, offering plenty of opportunities to explore the natural and shipwreck-created reefs. Many good sites can be reached by swimming from shore; others are accessible by boat. **Ocean Encounters** (599-9-461-8131; oceanencounters.com) operates out of several of the island's resorts, including the Hilton, and offers instruction and several different options for diving and snorkeling. **Discover Diving** at Lagun Beach (599-9-864-1652; discoverdiving.nl) offers a picturesque setting and inexpensive gear rental. Living coral, colorful reef fish, sea turtles, lobsters, and anemones are all waiting for you to spot them in the clear, warm water.

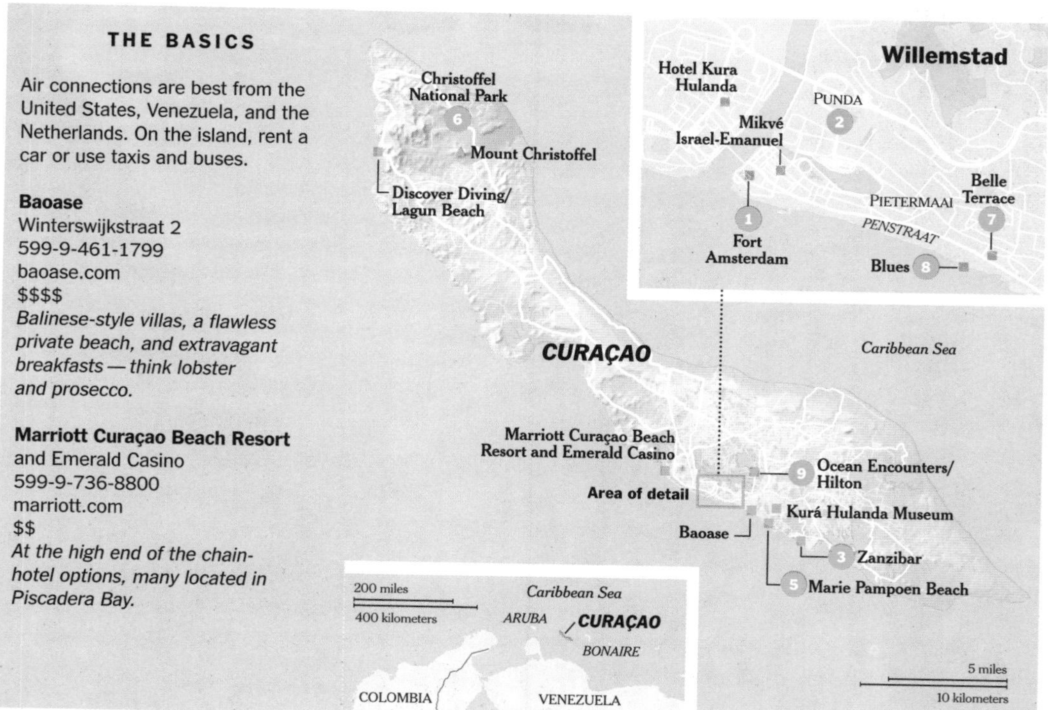

THE BASICS

Air connections are best from the United States, Venezuela, and the Netherlands. On the island, rent a car or use taxis and buses.

Baoase
Winterswijkstraat 2
599-9-461-1799
baoase.com
$$$$
Balinese-style villas, a flawless private beach, and extravagant breakfasts — think lobster and prosecco.

Marriott Curaçao Beach Resort and Emerald Casino
599-9-736-8800
marriott.com
$$
At the high end of the chain-hotel options, many located in Piscadera Bay.

Aruba

The world long ago discovered the stunning shores of Aruba, a constituent country of the Netherlands that lies just off the coast of Venezuela. Expensive resorts and flashy hotels line its renowned Eagle and Palm Beaches, sun-kissed visitors in baseball caps flock to shiny casinos, and cruise ships pull up to Oranjestad, the port city and capital. But Aruba is more than hotel rooms and slot machines. You needn't venture far to discover its more authentic side, and even within shouting distance of the crowds, you can find a quiet spot on a perfect beach: white sand edged on one side by Technicolor turquoise waters and on the other by palms and the native divi-divi trees, bent and pummeled into fantastic shapes by the wind.

— BY JONATHAN VIGLIOTTI AND BARBARA IRELAND

FRIDAY

1 *Down by the Divi-Divis* 3 p.m.

First stop: the beach. Aruba's are all public and free, even when they're hidden behind an imposing facade of high-rise hotels. Slather on extra sunblock (the island's trademark winds make it hard to tell when you're getting burned), find a path between the tourist palaces, and walk out to claim your place in the sun. **Palm Beach** offers a classic scene, with clear, calm water and soft sand. But it's packed with tourists. For a quieter, equally beautiful alternative, head south to nearby **Eagle Beach**, an idyllic place for reading, swimming, and shell collecting. Splash in style in front of the **Divi Aruba** resort (J. E. Irausquin Boulevard 41; 1-?297-525-5200; diviaruba.com). Just don't try to use the Divi's beach chairs.

2 *Aruban Feast* 7 p.m.

The tulip fields are missing, but this is the Netherlands, and the island cuisine often mixes Dutch staples with the typical Caribbean ingredients like okra, papaya, and the seafood from just offshore. **Gasparito** (Gasparito 3; 297-586-7044; gasparito.com; $$), off the beaten track but worth the ride, serves traditional Aruban food alongside more standard fare. Sit on the tiled terrace and try the keshi yena, a concoction of shredded meat or fish and Gouda cheese.

3 *Casino Country* 9 p.m.

Join surfers and scuba divers for a drink at the **Caribbean Store** (13-A Palm Beach; 297-586-5544). This shack is a Friday-night hot spot where you can get a recap of the day's surfing and diving with your cold beer. If you prefer casinos, you're home; every hotel seems to have one. The **Crystal Casino** (arubacrystalcasinos.com) in the Renaissance Aruba Resort (L.G. Smith Boulevard 82, Oranjestad; 297-583-6000; renaissancearuba.com), decorated with elaborate chandeliers, is a favorite, and if things go bad at the tables, you can pick up your mood with a fruity drink just down the street at **Iguana Joe's** (Royal Plaza Mall; 297-583-9373; iguanajoesaruba.com).

SATURDAY

4 *Gouda in the Morning* 9 a.m.

Skip the pricey breakfast buffets at hotels and have a Gouda-and-bacon omelet at **Salt and Pepper** (J. E. Irausquin Boulevard 368A; 297-586-3280; saltandpepperaruba.com; $$), where you can get a hearty and inexpensive jump-start to the morning.

5 *It's a Wreck* 10 a.m.

Aruba, with its clear, shallow water, is considered one of the best places in the Caribbean for shipwreck diving. The skeletal remains of half a dozen ships

OPPOSITE Aruba is better known for the serene aquamarine waters at its famous beaches, but on the eastern coast, rugged terrain meets thunderous waves.

RIGHT Snorkelers above an offshore shipwreck.

are submerged right off the island's coast, and to see some of the wreckage you don't even need scuba gear. **Red Sail Sports** (J. E. Irausquin Boulevard 348A; 297-586-1603; aruba-redsail.com) takes snorkelers on a catamaran to the wrecked *Antilla*, a German merchant ship scuttled by its crew during World War II, and two other spots. The four-hour trip includes a hot lunch and an open bar. Beware, the drinks are stronger than they taste.

6 *Aloe Island* 4 p.m.

Locals and tourists alike do their shopping in downtown Oranjestad, where you'll find island crafts, designer clothes, Delft china, T-shirts that change color in the sun, and toiletries made from locally grown aloe vera. Aloe was introduced here in the 19th century, immediately thrived in the hot, dry climate, and was soon the island's dominant cash crop. It's still a major export. Learn about Aruba's trade history at the **Aloe Museum** (Pitastraat 115; 297-588-3222; arubaaloe.com), and buy some after-sun lotion to soothe your burn. There's more shopping to the north at Palm Beach; if you're prospecting there, don't miss the shops on the beachfront side of the hotels, where you can get a new bikini while the sand is still damp on your flip-flops.

7 *Sun Dance* 6 p.m.

Thrill seekers should trek to the island's eastern coast, where rugged terrain meets thunderous waves at **Dos Playa**, a favorite with surfers. For an unforgettable sunset, drive past the **California Lighthouse** at the northwestern tip of the island to an area locals call the Arashi flats. In a dramatic performance every night, the fading sun dances on a jagged landscape of cactuses and divi-divi trees.

8 *Dinner on the Dock* 8 p.m.

Hovering over the ocean like a glowing lantern is **Pincho's Grill and Bar** (L. G. Smith Boulevard 7; 297-583-2666; arubasurfsidemarina.com; $$$$), set on a rustic pier at the Surfside Marina. This place oozes romance with its breathtaking sunsets, live music, and flickering candles. One night's grilled Aruban wahoo fillet was melt-in-the-mouth delicious.

9 *Bar Scene* 10 p.m.

Live up to the Caribbean cliché at the surprisingly down-to-earth **Moomba Beach** (J. E. Irausquin Boulevard 320; 297-586-5365; moombabeach.com). This tucked-away beachside hut has it all: good-looking bartenders, cheap drinks, and live music on weekends.

SUNDAY

10 *Sex Among the Insects* 10 a.m.

The spirit-lifting **Butterfly Farm** (J. E. Irausquin Boulevard; 297-586-3656; thebutterflyfarm.com) far outclasses the typical butterfly exhibit. As 35 species flutter around, often landing on the guests, a knowledgeable guide explains all the facts of their brief lives, including a butterfly sex act that lasts for 48 hours.

OPOSITE ABOVE Sunset at the Arashi flats.

OPOSITE BELOW A divi-divi tree, gnarled by many years of resisting the wind, clings to the shore.

ABOVE Cactuses frame the California Lighthouse.

THE BASICS

Rent a car at the airport.

Ocean 105
L. G. Smith Boulevard 105
297-592-0287
arubaoceanfront.com
$$
Small apartment hotel nestled on a coral ledge overlooking the Caribbean. Steps from Boca Catalina beach, known for snorkeling.

Aruba Marriott Resort
L. G. Smith Boulevard 101
297-586-9000
arubamarriott.com
$$$$
Every resort amenity from round-the-clock free snacks to paddleboard yoga.

Boardwalk Hotel Aruba
Bakval 20 North
297-586-6654
boardwalkaruba.com
$$$
Casitas within easy walking distance of Palm Beach.

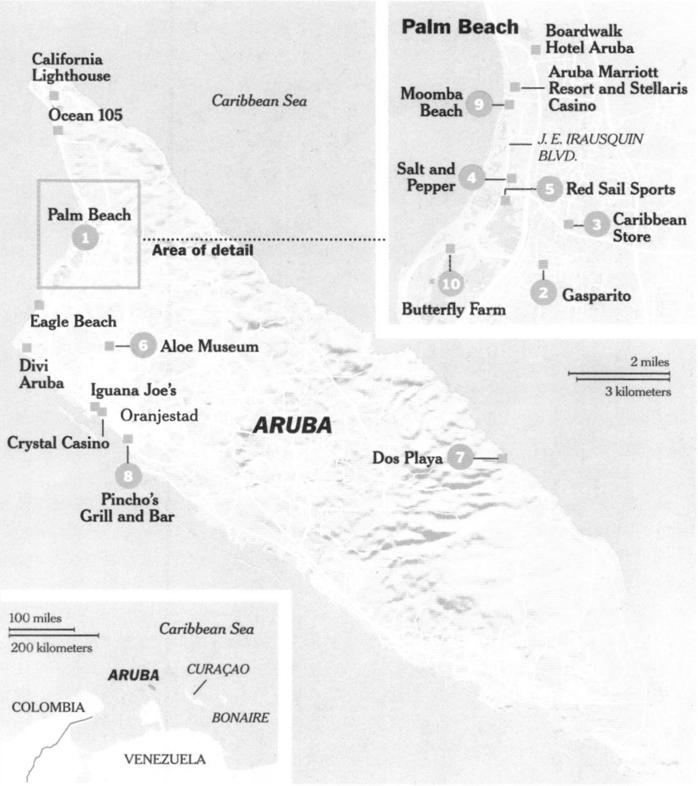

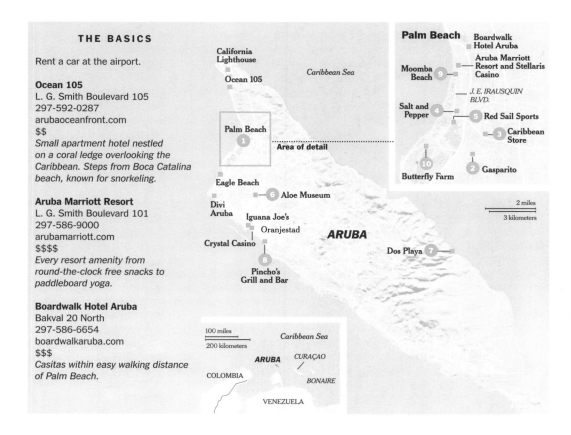

Trinidad

Trinidad, just seven miles off Venezuela, is not piña colada territory. That's part of its allure: Unlike virtually every other Caribbean island — including Tobago, its far smaller partner in the Republic of Trinidad and Tobago — Trinidad is not driven overwhelmingly by tourism. That means that in lieu of sunbathing hordes and "Yah, Mon" T-shirts, you'll find miles of unspoiled beaches and waterfalls visited and enjoyed by the local population; a Creole culture with roots in Africa, India, Europe, and China; and a bustling capital city enriched by oil wealth and offering some of the Caribbean's most electrifying night life. Partying, after all, is a national tradition in Trinidad, which is home to an annual pre-Lenten Carnival that is the Caribbean region's biggest. — BY BAZ DREISINGER

FRIDAY

1 *Urban Tropics* 3 p.m.

Caribbean islands aren't usually celebrated for their capital cities, but Port of Spain is worth some exploring on foot (safest in the daylight hours). Here you can shop for locally mixed reggae and soca CDs in busy **Independence Square**, gaze at the ornate Victorian-style buildings known as the Magnificent Seven alongside the **Queen's Park Savannah** — an urban park with corn-soup and coconut-water vendors — and stroll around the posh-yet-funky Woodbrook neighborhood. There, you can glimpse a burgeoning visual- and performance-art scene at **Alice Yard** (80 Roberts Street; aliceyard.blogspot.com), a historic house turned gallery and creative hub, and shop for Caribbean couture, including avant-garde carnival costumes, at **Satchel's House** (6 Carlos Street; 1-868-627-8640; meilinginc.com), a charming boutique owned by the local designer Meiling.

2 *Liming on the Avenue* 8 p.m.

"Liming" — hanging out, usually with alcohol — is a rigorous sport in Trinidad. Its hub is the night-life strip **Ariapita Avenue** in the Woodbrook section, known as the Avenue. Bars, lounges, and public bacchanal (as Trinidadians put it) abound. At the indoor-outdoor bar **Stumblin** (42 Ariapita Avenue; 1-868-223-5017; stumblintt.com), patrons tend to consume enough Johnny Walker and Angostura rum — 1919 is widely considered the best grade — to live up to the bar's name. For something more upscale, nearby **More Sushi** (23 O'Connor Street; 1-868-622-8466; morevino.com; $$) serves up scrumptious rolls with combinations like crab salad wrapped in salmon, plantain and pineapple salsa, and salmon and tuna with curried mayo.

SATURDAY

3 *Get Your Tourist On* 10 a.m.

Maracas Beach, a 45-minute drive north of Port of Spain, is as close as Trinidad gets to a commercial beach. Never mind the water, though; head straight to the humble food stalls and taste what folks flock for: bake-and-shark — a hunk of fried breaded shark tucked inside a doughnut-like bun and dripping with mouthwatering condiments. Then keep moving, 14 miles north to **Blanchisseuse**, where a stunning stretch of oft-deserted beach is calmer and quieter, and Marianne Bay offers respite from the heat. Still feeling outdoorsy? Take a 30-minute hike along the Marianne River, through lush greenery and dramatic bamboo forests, and cool down in beautiful **Avocat Falls.**

OPPOSITE Carnival time in Port of Spain.

RIGHT A class at the Academy for the Performing Arts.

4 *Brazil, Trini-Style* 6 p.m.

The romantic setting — a handsomely restored Creole house — is classically Trini, but the food is a continent away: **Ipanema** (12 Victoria Avenue; 1-868-625-0711; $$$$) offers churrasco-style dining, allowing carnivores to indulge in beef, pork, chicken, lamb, and sausage. There are seafood and vegetarian options, too, not to mention the vital ingredients that give the cuisine away as local: homemade pepper sauces and piquant chadon beni, a ubiquitous relish.

5 *Steel and Glass* 8 p.m.

Trinidad invented the steel pan, said to be one of the few musical instruments born in the 20th century, but the island is devoted to other kinds of music as well. Take in a concert at the gleaming **National Academy for the Performing Arts** (Frederick Street and Queen's Park East; 1-868-625-8519; Port of Spain), which has a 1,219-seat performance hall, steel-pan classrooms, and a diverse performance schedule.

6 *V.V.I.P.* 11 p.m.

Trini revelers love their V.I.P. sections — not to mention their V.V.I.P. and, yes, V.V.V.I.P. sections. See how high up Port of Spain's V.I.P. ladder you can climb by negotiating past those velvet ropes at the popular **51 Degrees** nightclub (51 Cipriani Boulevard; 1-868-627-0051; 51degrees.biz). Soca music and live performances by Caribbean stars keep patrons moving until dawn. During Carnival season, which runs roughly from just after Christmas into February, the place is crammed with revelers representing the Carnival bands they will parade with on the big day. Most popular of these all-inclusive bands — and responsible for plenty of all-you-can-drink extravaganzas during the season — are Island People (islandpeoplemas.com) and Tribe (carnivaltribe.com), whose costumes have been known to sell out within minutes of going on sale.

ABOVE The Archbishop's House, one of the ornate Magnificent Seven buildings in Port of Spain.

LEFT A shopping day in Port of Spain.

SUNDAY

7 *Doubles Feast* 7 a.m.

What could possibly justify such an early wake-up call? One word: doubles. It's a street-food breakfast staple made of fried Indian-style bread filled with curried chickpeas and spicy pepper sauce. Although it can be found all over the island, those who take their doubles seriously (that is, all Trinidadians) often head toward Curepe in central Trinidad. Devotees can go right to the little-known source: the **Doubles Factory** on El Socorro street, which supplies island vendors.

ABOVE The National Academy for the Performing Arts contains a 1,219-seat hall and classrooms for all kinds of performers, including steel-pan players.

BELOW Neon lights and a vigorous night life take over after dark in Port of Spain.

8 *Little India* 9 a.m.

Once you're in the central part of the island, you might start wondering what country you're in: the region is the historic hub of Trinidad's East Indian community, which has roots in the 19th century, when indentured servants were brought to the island from Asia. In **Chagaunas**, about 11 miles south of Port of Spain, shop for spices and silk flowers in cluttered shops and markets, and then pay homage to the Nobel laureate V. S. Naipaul at the trapezoid-shaped **Lion House**, immortalized in his 1961 novel *A House for Mr. Biswas*. Pose alongside a flamboyant 85-foot statue of the Hindu god Hanuman, rising above the humble village of **Carapichaima** like a surreal piece of Las Vegas in Trinidad. Nearby, the majestic

Temple by the Sea at Waterloo is sure to generate meditative moods. A postwar-era reconstruction of a Hindu temple, it was erected in water so as not to take up profitable sugar-cane land.

9 *Buffet, With Music* 2 p.m.

If you don't leave Trinidad with your belly bursting, you haven't really been to Trinidad. The Sunday brunch buffet at the **Chaud Creole** in the tony, suburban St. Ann's section of Port of Spain (6 Nook Avenue; 1-868-621-2002; chaudcreole.com; $$$$) can prevent such a tragedy. All the local favorites are on full display at this chic respite from the hustle and bustle, from souse (spicy pickled pig or chicken feet) to flour dumplings boiled in coconut milk, handmade rotis, and curries galore. Added attraction: live classical guitar entertainment.

ABOVE A steel-pan class at the Academy of Performing Arts. Trinidad invented the steel pan, said to be one of the few musical instruments born in the 20th century.

OPPOSITE Produce for sale in Port of Spain. The island's Creole culture and cuisine reflect its mixed population, with roots in Africa, India, Europe, and China.

THE BASICS

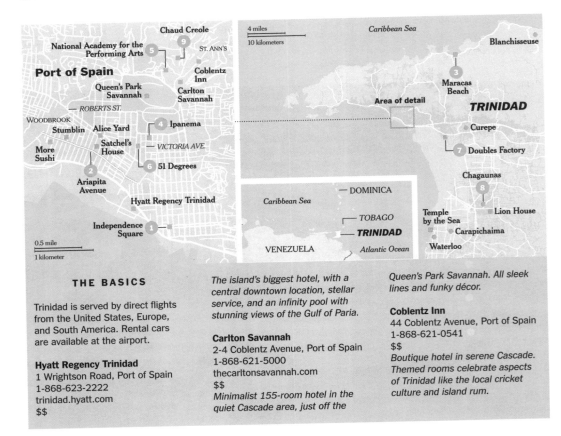

Trinidad is served by direct flights from the United States, Europe, and South America. Rental cars are available at the airport.

Hyatt Regency Trinidad
1 Wrightson Road, Port of Spain
1-868-623-2222
trinidad.hyatt.com
$$
The island's biggest hotel, with a central downtown location, stellar service, and an infinity pool with stunning views of the Gulf of Paria.

Carlton Savannah
2-4 Coblentz Avenue, Port of Spain
1-868-621-5000
thecarltonsavannah.com
$$
Minimalist 155-room hotel in the quiet Cascade area, just off the Queen's Park Savannah. All sleek lines and funky décor.

Coblentz Inn
44 Coblentz Avenue, Port of Spain
1-868-621-0541
$$
Boutique hotel in serene Cascade. Themed rooms celebrate aspects of Trinidad like the local cricket culture and island rum.

090100
PADS EA.
Stayfree
Maxi

Indexes

BY DESTINATION

BY COUNTRY/TERRITORY

AFTER DARK

THE OUTDOORS

SHOPPING

SPECIAL INTERESTS

ONE OF A KIND

Contributors

WRITERS

PHOTOGRAPHERS

ADDITIONAL PHOTO CREDITS

De los Monteros, Fernando Espinosa/ Flickr RM/Getty Images 12
Ferrer, Sigfrido López/Flickr RF/ Getty Images 158
Frederick, Rene/Getty Images 32
Freeman, Ed/Getty Images/ The Image Bank 68
Frink, Stephen/Getty Images/ The Image Bank 195
Fundación Municipal Turismo para Cuenca 118 (above)
Guiziou, Franck/Getty Images/ Hemis.fr RM 220
Hauser, Patrice/StockImage/ Getty Images 190
Hill, Robin/Digital Vision/ Getty Images 185
House, Steven R. 64
Hughes, Herv/Getty Images/ Hemis.fr 161 (below)
Image Source/Getty Images 163
Kazemi, Kaveh/Getty Images 104–105
Kennedy, Paul/Getty Images/ Lonely Planet Images 122
Kirilos, Pedro/Riotur 127 (below)
Lahti, Hannele/Getty Images/ National Geographic RF 280
Lawrence, Michael/Getty Images/ Lonely Planet Images 4, 196
Lemmens, Frans/Getty Images/ The Image Bank 106
Leue, Holger/Getty Images/ Lonely Planet Images 268
Lewis, Justin/Getty Images/ The Image Bank 210
Lezama, Diego/Getty Images/ Lonely Planet Images 130
Machado, Silvestre/ Photographer's Choice/ Getty Images 126
Marvil, Rebecca/Getty Images/ Photolibrary RM 100 (below)
Nacinovic, Marcelo/Flickr RF/ Getty Images 142
Pillitz Christopher/The Image Bank/ Getty Images 156
Pastorello, Angelo/Getty Images/ SambaPhoto 125
Plush Studios/Getty Images 254
Ponti, Viviane/Getty Images/ Lonely Planet Images 160
Santelices, Erika/AFP/Getty Images 221
Savage, McKay/Getty Images/ Flickr RF 121
Schlebusch, Preston/The Image Bank/Getty Images 28
St. Clair, Inti/Getty Images/ Photodisc 224
Sweeney, Jane/Getty Images 82, 100 (above)
Tepper, Natalie/Getty Images/ Robert Harding World Imagery 223
Touzon, Raul/Getty Images/ National Geographic Creative 222 (above)
Turek, Michael/The Image Bank/ Getty Images 174
Vallenari, Flavio/Getty Images/ E+ 262
Wheatley, Christian/E+/ Getty Images 245
Woodhouse, Jeremy/Getty Images/Photographer's Choice RF 98, 146
YinYang/Getty Images/ Vetta 120

Editor Barbara Ireland
Project management Alex Ward
Photo editor Phyllis Collazo
Itinerary maps Natasha Perkel
Illustrations Olimpia Zagnoli
Editorial coordination Eric Schwartau and Nina Wiener
Art direction Marco Zivny and Josh Baker
Design and layout Marco Zivny and David Knowles
Production Jennifer Patrick

To stay informed about upcoming TASCHEN titles, please request our magazine at www.taschen.com/magazine, find our app for iPad on iTunes, or write to TASCHEN America, 6671 Sunset Boulevard, Los Angeles, CA 90028, USA; contact-us@taschen.com; Fax: +1-323-463-4442. We will be happy to send you a free copy of our magazine, which is filled with information about all of our books.

Hohenzollernring 53, D–50672 Köln, www.taschen.com

ISBN 978-3-8365-4425-2 Printed in China

Acknowledgments

We would like to thank everyone at *The New York Times* and at TASCHEN who contributed to the creation of this book, starting with all of the writers and photographers, both *Times* staffers and freelancers, whose work appears in it.

For the book project itself, special recognition must go to Eric Schwartau and Nina Wiener at TASCHEN, the dedicated editors behind the scenes; to Natasha Perkel, the *Times* artist whose clear and elegantly crafted maps make the itineraries comprehensible; to Phyllis Collazo of the *Times* staff, whose photo editing gave the book its arresting images; and to Olimpia Zagnoli, whose illustrations enliven every article, the cover, and the regional maps.

Guiding the transformation of newspaper material to book form at TASCHEN were Marco Zivny, the book's designer; Josh Baker with Marco Zivny, art directors; David Knowles, layout designer; Jennifer Patrick and Jordan Romanoff, production manager and assistant; and Sean Monahan, who created the region maps. Anna V. Walker and Anna Skinner copy-edited the manuscript.

Fact-checking for the book was in the hands of Patrick Jude Wilson. At the *Times*, Heidi Giovine helped keep production on track at critical moments.

But the indebtedness goes much further back, and deeper into the *New York Times* staff. This book grew out of the work of all of the editors, writers, photographers, and others whose contributions and support for the weekly *36 Hours* column built a rich archive over many years.

For this legacy, credit must go first to Stuart Emmrich, who created the column in 2002 and then refined the concept over eight years, first as the *Times Escapes* editor and then as Travel editor. Without his vision, there would be no *36 Hours*. His successors in the role of Travel editor, Danielle Mattoon and then Monica Drake, have brought steady leadership to the column and support to the *36 Hours* books.

Suzanne MacNeille, the direct editor of *36 Hours* at *The Times*, and her predecessor Denny Lee have guided *36 Hours* superbly through the world by assigning and working with writers, choosing and assigning destinations, and assuring that the weekly column would entertain and inform readers while upholding *Times* journalistic standards.

The talented *Times* photo editors who have overseen images and directed the work of the column's photographers include Lonnie Schlein, Jessica De Witt, and Gina Privitere.

Among the many editors on the *Times* travel copy desk who have kept *36 Hours* at its best over the years, three who stand out are Florence Stickney, Steve Bailey, and Carl Sommers. Editors of the column on nytimes.com have been Alice Dubois, David Allan, Miki Meek, Allison Busacca, Danielle Belopotosky, and Samantha Storey, and Josh Robinson. *Times* fact-checkers who have helped keep the weekly column accurate over the years include Emily Brennan, Rachel Lee Harris, Rusha Haljuci, and Nick Kaye.

And a special acknowledgment goes to Benedikt Taschen, whose longtime readership and interest in the *36 Hours* column led to the partnership of our two companies to produce this book.

— BARBARA IRELAND AND ALEX WARD

HAVANA
MEXICO CITY
PANAMA CITY
MEXICO &
CENTRAL
AMERICA